GROWTH IN HOLINESS

OR

THE PROGRESS OF THE SPIRITUAL LIFE

BY

FREDERICK WILLIAM FABER, D.D.

Author of

"All for Jesus," "Spiritual Conferences," "Bethlehem,"
"The Foot of the Cross," "The Precious Blood," etc., etc.

"Occurramus omnes in unitatem fidei, et
agnitionis Filii Dei, in virum perfectum, in
mensuram, aetatis plenitudinis Christi . . .
"Veritatem facientes in charitate, crescamus in
illo per omnia, qui est caput, Christus."
—AD EPHESIOS 4:13, 15

TAN Books
Charlotte, North Carolina

WITH THE APPROBATION OF THE
MOST REV. ARCHBISHOP OF BALTIMORE

An edition of this book was first published in 1855.

This present edition was retypeset from the 15th American edition published by John Murphy & Co., 182 Baltimore Street, Baltimore, in approximately 1890.

The type in this book is the property of TAN Books and may not be reproduced, in whole or in part, without written permission of the publisher.

Library of Congress Catalog Card Number: 90-70233

ISBN: 978-0-89555-400-0

Printed and bound in the United States of America.

TAN Books
Charlotte, North Carolina
www.TANBooks.com
2012

TO

MY BLESSED PRINCE AND PATRON,

SAINT RAPHAEL,

ONE OF THE SEVEN WHO STAND ALWAYS BEFORE GOD,

GLORIOUS, BENIGNANT, BEAUTIFUL,

THE FIGURE OF HIS PROVIDENCE,

PHYSICIAN, GUIDE AND JOY OF SOULS,

COMPANION OF WAYFARING MORTALS,

AND ANGEL OF THEIR VICISSITUDES,

BY WHOM

THE TENDERNESS OF THE FATHER, THE HEALING OF THE SON,

AND THE GLADNESS OF THE HOLY GHOST

ARE MINISTERED TO WANDERING MEN

WITH THE EFFICACIOUS POWER OF AN ANGELIC SPIRIT

AND THE COMPASSIONATE, PATHETIC LOVE

OF A KINDLY HUMAN HEART.

THE ORATORY, LONDON,
FEAST OF ST. RAPHAEL
1855

CONTENTS

Prefatory Epistle

My dear Father Antony,

In a walk by the seashore at Lancing four years ago, I gave some reasons why I should not publish anything on the spiritual life until a given date. That date is past, and here is my book. I have little to say in the way of preface, and that little shall be in the shape of a letter to you, because it will be a memento of our mutual affection which will give both of us pleasure; for it will recall the eventful nine years which we have now spent together, and which it has pleased God should be equal to a long life for their various trials and almost romantic vicissitudes.

There are two objects for which books may be written, and which must materially affect their style. One is to produce a certain impression on the reader while he reads: the other, to put before him things to remember, and in such a way as he will best remember them. The present work is written for the latter object, and consequently with as much brevity as clearness would allow, and as much compression as the breadth of the subject and its peculiar liability to be misunderstood, would safely permit.

I dare not presume that there will not be many contradictions to so large a volume, in which every sentence, and frequently each clause of a sentence, is a judgment on matters about which all pious Catholics have a more or less formed opinion. But so generous a measure of indulgence has been dealt to me before, that I cannot persuade myself it will now be altogether withdrawn, especially as the book will not be found to contain one intentional word or unfavorable criticism either of men or things. This is my only boast. For the rest, I have done no more than try to harmonize the ancient and modern spirituality of the Church, with somewhat perhaps of a propension to the first, and to put it before English Catholics in an English shape, translated into native thought and feeling, as well as language.

Much of the material of the book has fully observed the Horatian precept of *Nonum prematur in annum,* and the rest has been nine years growing. But it is a very easy thing for a man to go wrong in spiritual theology, and to stray into the shadow of condemned propositions. It will not therefore be conceitedly making much of a little thing if I say that I retract beforehand in the amplest and most unqualified manner anything, whether of thought or of expression, which may be uncongenial, not only to the decisions of the Holy See, but also to the approved teaching of our religious orders and theological schools. May God be with my work where it speaks the mind of His Church without exaggeration and with sincerity!

Ever, my dear Father Antony,
Affectionately yours,
FRED. W. FABER

The Oratory, London
Feast of St. Hugh, 1854

"Quin etiam juniores, quanquam theologicis literis imbuti, talem debent reverentiam senioribus iis, quibus vita cum scientia concordat, ut vix propter aliquas novas suasiones quantumcumque apparentes pertinax unquam feratur cito contra determinationes eorundem assertio. Virtus quippe, qualem habebant genitam ex multis experientiis, longè certiùs arte judicat et operatur.

"Per paucam instructionem intellectûs, in scientiis praesertim divinis, causantur nonnunquam errores in eis, qui se totos devotioni tradiderunt, dum voluerunt plus sapere, quam sibi satis erat."   —GERSON

"Consultius nihil fieri a nobis potest quam ut nostras semper opiniones et voluntates, linguas pennasque aptemus ei disciplinae, que in universali viget Ecclesia eo aevo, quo nos summi providentia numinis collocavit." —THOMASSINUS

"Noli eos imitari, qui nullum legendi ordinem servant; sed quod forte occurrerit, quodque casu repererint, legere gaudent: quibus nihil sapit, nisi quod novum est, et inauditum. Consulta enim, et vetera omnia, quantum libet utilir, fastidiunt. Tanta instabilitas procul a te cit: ipsa enim non promovet, sed dispergit spiritum; et periculose laborat, qui hoc morbo vitiatus est." —DACRIANUS

GROWTH IN HOLINESS

Chapter I

TRUE SIGNS OF PROGRESS
IN THE SPIRITUAL LIFE

The spiritual life is made up of contradictions. This is only another way of saying that human nature is fallen. One of the greatest contradictions, and practically one of the most difficult to be managed, is that in spirituality it is very important we should know a great deal about ourselves, and at the same time equally important that we should think very little about ourselves; and it is not easy to reconcile these things. I mention this difficulty at the outset, inasmuch as we shall have in the course of this treatise to look very much into ourselves, and consequently we run the risk at the same time of thinking very much of ourselves; and this last might do us more harm than the first would do us good.

No knowledge in the world can be more interesting to us than to know how we stand with God. Everything depends upon it. It is the science of sciences to us, more than the knowledge of good and evil which tempted Adam and Eve so violently. If we are well with God, all is well with us, though the thickest darkness of adversity be round about. If we are not well with Him, nothing is well with us, though the best and brightest of earth be at our feet. It is natural that we should desire to know if we are making progress in the spiritual life; neither is there anything wrong, or even imperfect, in the desire, provided it be not inordinate. It would be an immense consolation to us if we should have reason to suppose we were advancing; and if, on the contrary, we had grounds for suspecting something was amiss, there would at least be a sense of safety and security in the feeling that at all events we were not going

1

on in the dark about the matter which concerns us more nearly and dearly than anything else. Love likes to know that it is accepted and reciprocated; and in the case of God especially, that it is not rejected as it deserves to be; and fear is equally anxious for the same knowledge because of the eternal interests which are concerned in it.

But however much we may desire it, we cannot have anything like an accurate knowledge of our progress in the spiritual life; and that for reasons on God's side as well as on our own. On His side, because it is His way to conceal His work; and on ours, because self-love exaggerates the little good we do. We do not even know for certain whether we are in a state of grace, or as Scripture expresses it, whether we deserve love or hatred. For we have each of us a cavern of secret sins about us; and as the Inspired Writer warns us, we must not be without fear even of forgiven sin.

There are wrong ways of trying to gain this knowledge which the impatient heart seeks so anxiously. All desires become inordinate in the long run, if they are not sharply schooled and tightly kept under; and it is when they become inordinate that they hit with such fatal ingenuity upon wrong ways of satisfying themselves. One of these wrong ways is pressing our directors to tell us their judgment about us, which they are naturally very reluctant to do, both because they shrink from apparent pretension to supernatural gifts, such as the discernment of spirits, and because they are aware that such knowledge is hardly ever good for us to have. Then, when this artifice proves unsuccessful, we take arbitrary and artificial marks of our own, as children run sticks into the sand to time the tide by; and, as might be expected, we select wrongly where we had no right to select at all; and having made a mistake, we are obstinate in it, and as is usual with men, the more obstinate in proportion as we are more mistaken; and so the end of it all is delusion. And even when we do not seek to know our own interior state by one of these wrong methods, we do what is equally wrong by disquieting ourselves constantly upon the subject, which is nothing less than a forfeiting of blessings and graces nearly every hour in the day.

But in truth, as it is with the hour of our death, so it is with our growth in grace. It is in every way not good for us that we should have any certain or exact knowledge about it. It is as much as ever we can do to keep ourselves humble, even when our faults are open and glaring, and any good there may be in us so little as to be almost invisible. What then would it be if we were truly growing in grace, and making rapid strides in the love of God? Surely the less we know, the easier it will be to keep humble. Moreover, the absence of such exact knowledge renders us more supple and obedient, both to the inspirations of the Holy Ghost within us and to the suggestions of our spiritual directors without us. Just as it is ignorance of their maladies which makes the sick so amenable to their physicians, so it is with our ignorance of our proficiency in the spiritual life. And how much of this proficiency depends on this twofold obedience to inspirations and direction! Furthermore, the very uncertainty is itself a perpetual stimulus to greater generosity toward God. For the worst of all excessive self-inspection is that the good grows and swells as we look at it, and because we look at it; and hence, a man whose eye is always turned inward on his own heart has, for the most part, a strangely exaggerated notion of the amount of what he is doing for God. Whereas it is the very disproportion between the greatness of what God has done for us and the spirit of Fatherly love in which He has done it, and the littleness of what we do for God and the spirit of niggardliness in which we do it, that makes us crave to love Him more, and to work for Him more self-denyingly. Hence I conclude that it would not be for our own best interests to know exactly, and for certain, how far we had got on the road to perfection.

Nevertheless, a certain amount of knowledge of our state is possible, desirable and even necessary, so long as it be desired moderately and sought for rightly. We need consolation in so difficult and doubtful a battle; and we are not yet sufficiently detached not to find an especial consolation in the knowledge of the operations of grace within our souls. We cannot be much given to prayer without obtaining more or less insight into God's dealings with us; and indeed, if we do not know the graces which God is giving us, we shall not know how to correspond to them. So that some amount of such knowledge is absolutely necessary to our carrying on the Christian warfare at all, and the lawful ways of acquiring it are prayer, examination of conscience and the spontaneous admonitions of our spiritual director.

This is enough to say about the knowledge of our own spiritual state. It is a very difficult and dangerous subject. The less of such knowledge we can do with the better, because it is so hard to seek it rightly or to use it moderately. Still it cannot be dispensed with altogether, though its importance varies with the spiritual condition of the individual.

Thus it is important for us to put before ourselves clearly the particular condition of the spiritual life which we are now concerned with. Persons are what is called converted: that is, they are turned to God and commence a new life. They do penance for their sins; they abjure certain false maxims which they held; they feel differently toward God and Jesus Christ; they commit themselves to certain practices of mortification; they pledge themselves to certain devotional observances; and they put themselves under the obedience of spiritual direction. Then they have their first fervors. They are helped by a supernatural promptitude in all that concerns the service of God: by sensible sweetness in prayer, by joy in the Sacraments, by a new taste for penance and humiliation and a facility in meditation, and often a cessation, partial or entire, of temptation. These first fervors may last weeks or months, or a year or two even; and then their work is done. We have corresponded to them more or less faithfully. They have had their own experiences, peculiarities, symptoms and difficulties. They have a particular genius of their own and need a direction which is suitable for them, and is not suitable for anything else. Now they have passed away, and are out of our reach. We shall meet them again at the judgment seat— and not before.

But where have they left us? At the commencement of a new stage in the spiritual life, a very trying and a very critical time. The mere passing away of fervors, which were never meant for anything more than a temporary dispensation, leaves us immersed in an uncomfortable feeling of lukewarmness. The characteristics of our present state are that we seem to be left more to ourselves than we were. Grace appears to do less for us. Old natural character comes up when the fervors that overlaid it are gone out and begins to tell again with amazing vivacity. We felt as if we were more thrown upon the manliness and honesty of our own purposes and wills, and were, at least less sensibly, buoyed up by the various apparatus of the supernatural life. Our prayers become drier. The ground we are digging is stiffer and stonier. The work seems less attractive in proportion as it grows more solid. Perfection does not feel so easy, and penance unbearable. Now is the time for courage, now is the trial of our real worth. We are beginning to travel the central regions of the spiritual life, and they are, on the whole, tracts of wilderness. Here it is that so many turn back and are thrown aside by God as frustrated saints and broken vocations. The soul I am addressing has come to this point and is toiling on, burnt by the sun and wind, ankle deep in the sand, filled with despair from the infrequency of the water-springs, querulous for the want of cool quiet shade, and greatly inclined to sit down and give the matter up as hopeless.

For the love of God, do not sit down! It is all over with you if you do. If I only knew, you say, that I was getting on, if I could really believe I was making any way at all, I would force my weary limbs to advance! Two are better than one, saith Scripture; so let us toil on together for awhile, and talk of our helps and hindrances. We are not saints, you know. Perhaps we are not aiming at saints' heights; and if we are not, then we must not take saints' liberties. The lessons we want must be sober, and safe, and low. Anyhow, we must neither turn back nor sit down.

Are we getting on? There is not a well or a palm to measure by; there is only sand and an horizon. Courage! Here are five signs. If we have one of them, it is well; if two, better; if three, better still; if four, capital; if all the five, glorious.

1) If we are discontented with our present state, whatever it may be, and want to be something better and higher, we have great reason to be thankful to God. For such discontent

is one of His best gifts, and a great sign that we are really
making progress in the spiritual life. But we must remember
that our dissatisfaction with ourselves must be of such a
nature as to increase our humility, and not such as to cause
disquietude of mind or uneasiness in our devotional exercises. It must be made up of a rather impatient desire to
advance in holiness, combined with gratitude for past graces,
confidence for future ones and a keen, indignant feeling of
how much more grace we have received than we have corresponded to.

2) Again, strange as it may sound, it is a sign of our growth
if we are always making new beginnings and fresh starts. The
great St. Anthony made perfection consist in it. Yet this is
often ignorantly made a motive of discouragement by persons
confounding fresh starts in the devout life with the incessant
risings and relapsings of habitual sinners. Neither must we
confound these continual fresh beginnings with the fickleness
which so often leads to dissipation and keeps us back in our
heavenward path. For these new starts seek something higher,
and therefore for the most part something arduous; whereas
fickleness is tired of the yoke, and seeks ease and change.
Neither again do these beginnings consist in changing our
spiritual books, or our penances, or our methods of prayer,
much less our directors. But they consist in two things chiefly:
first, a renewal of our intention for the glory of God; and
secondly, a revival of our fervor.

3) It is also a sign of progress in the spiritual life, when
we have some definite thing in view: for instance, if we are
trying to acquire the habit of some particular virtue, or to
conquer some besetting infirmity, or to accustom ourselves
to a certain penance. All this is a test of earnestness, and
also a token of the vigor of divine grace within us. Whereas
if we are attacking no particular part of the enemy's line,
it is hardly a battle; and if we are shooting without an aim,
what can come of it but smoke and noise? It is not likely
we are advancing if, as people speak, we are going on in
a general way, without distinctly selecting an end to reach
and actively forcing our way to the end we have thus consciously selected.

4) But it is a still greater sign that we are making progress if we have a strong feeling on our minds that God wants something particular from us. We are sometimes aware that the Holy Spirit is drawing us in one direction rather than in another, that He desires some fault to be removed, or some pious work to be undertaken. This is called by spiritual writers an attraction. Some have one persevering attraction all their lives long. With others, it is constantly changing. With many it is so indistinct that they only realize it now and then; and not a few seem to be without any such special drawing at all. (It was remarked by Mother de Blonay that those who are destined by God to spend the great part of their lives in religious superiorships are, for the most part, without any peculiar attraction, because it is a "universal spirit" which the Holy Ghost desires to form in such souls.). It implies of course an active self-knowledge, as well as a quiet inward eye of prayer; and it is a great gift, because of the immense facilities which it gives for the practice of perfection, for it almost resembles a special revelation. To feel then, with all sober reverence, this drawing of the Holy Ghost, is a sign that we are making progress. Yet it must be carefully remembered that no one should be disquieted because of the absence of such a feeling. It is neither universal nor indispensable.

5) I will venture also to add that an increased general desire of being more perfect is not altogether without its value as a sign of progress—and that, in spite of what I have said of the importance of having a definite object in view. I do not think we esteem this general desire of perfection sufficiently. Of course, we must not stop at it nor be satisfied with it. It is only given us to go on with. Still, when we consider how worldly most good Christians are and their amazing blindness to the interests of Jesus, and their almost incredible impenetrability by supernatural principles, we must see that this desire of holiness is from God—and a great gift—and that much which is of surpassing consequence is implied in it. God be praised for every soul in the world which is so fortunate as to possess it! It is almost inconsistent with lukewarmness; and this is no slight recommendation in itself: and although there is much beyond it and much above it, yet

it is indispensable both to what is beyond and what is above. Nevertheless, we must not be blind to its dangers. All supernatural desires, which we simply enjoy without practically corresponding to them, leave us in a worse state than they found us. In order to be safe we must proceed without delay to embody the desire in some act or other, prayer, penance, or zealous deed: yet not precipitately, or without counsel.

Here then are five fairly probable signs of progress, and none of them so far above our heads as to be unpractical to the lowest of us. I do not mean to say that the existence of these signs implies that all is as it ought to be in our spiritual life, but that it shows we are alive, advancing and in the way of grace; and the possession of any one of these signs is something unspeakably more precious than the best and highest gift earth can give. I repeat, if we have one of these signs it is well; if two, better; if three, better still; if four, capital; if all five, glorious. Now see! we have made a little way. We are further into the wilderness, and if as footsore as ever, at least a trifle less fainthearted.

Chapter II

PRESUMPTION AND DISCOURAGEMENT

You will see by the last chapter that I have made a sort of map of the spiritual life in my own mind. I have divided it into three regions of very unequal extent, and of very diversified interest. First there comes the region of beginnings—a wonderful time, so wonderful that nobody realizes how wonderful it is till they are out of it, and can look back on it. Then stretches a vast extent of wilderness, full of temptation, struggle and fatigue; a place of work and suffering, with angels, good and bad, winging their way in every direction; the roads hard to find and slippery underfoot; and Jesus with the Cross meeting us at every turn. This is four or five times the length of the first region. Then comes a region of beautiful, wooded, watered, yet rocky mountains, lovely yet savage too, liable to terrific tempests and to those sudden overcastings of bright nature which characterize mountainous districts. This last is the land of high prayer, of brave self-crucifixions, of mystical trials and of heights of superhuman detachment and abjection, whose rarefied atmosphere only chosen souls can breathe.

I have joined myself to a soul who is out of the region of beginnings and has just entered on the great central wilderness, whose long plains of weary sand join the verdant fields of the beginners with the woody mountains of the long-tried and well-mortified souls. God calls some to Himself in their first fervors; others mature in grace on the mountain heights. But more die in the wilderness, some at one point of the pilgrimage, some at another. Of course there is only one good time for each of us to die, and that is the exact hour at which

9

God wills that death should find us. But as the great body
of devout men die while they are crossing the central wilderness, it is this wilderness of which I wish to speak: the wilderness of long, patient perseverance in the humbling practices
of solid virtue.

Persons who are aiming ever so little at perfection are the
choice portion of God's creation, and are dear to Him as the
apple of His eye. Hence everything that concerns them is of
consequence. Thus it was important that they should have some
signs furnished them, by means of which they could estimate
with some probability the progress they are making in the
spiritual life. But they often mistake for signs of progress things
which, taken by themselves, do not tell either way; and thus
they fall into delusions which take them into bypaths, tire them
out and then bring them back again into the road miles behind
where they were, when they first wandered. These false signs
will form the subject of this chapter. The consideration of
them is of the more importance, inasmuch as it brings us
across a great many facts about the spiritual life which it exceedingly concerns us to know.

The soul, then, at this stage of its journey is beset by two
opposite temptations. Sometimes it is attacked by one, sometimes by another, according to different moods of mind and
diversities of character. These temptations are discouragement
and presumption; and our chief business at this point is to
be upon our guard against these two things.

Discouragement is an inclination to give up all attempts
after the devout life, in consequence of the difficulties by which
it is beset and our already numerous failures in it. We lose
heart; and partly in ill-temper, partly in real doubt of our
own ability to persevere, we first grow querulous and peevish
with God, and then relax in our efforts to mortify ourselves
and to please Him. It is like the sin of despair, although it
is not truly any sin at all. It is a sort of shadow of despair,
and it will lead us into numberless venial sins the first half-
hour we give way to it. What it shows is that we trusted too
much to our own strength and had a higher opinion of ourselves than we were at all warranted in having. If we had
been truly humble, we should have been surprised we did

not do worse, instead of being disappointed we did not do better. Many souls are called to perfection and fail, through the sole and single mischief of discouragement.

Meanwhile persons trying to be spiritual are peculiarly liable to discouragement, because of their great sensitiveness. Their attention is riveted to a degree in which it never was before on two things: minute duties and observances, and exterior motives; and both these things render them uncommonly sensitive. Conscience, acted upon by the Holy Ghost, becomes so fine and delicate that it feels the jar of little infirmities that never seemed infirmities before; and not only is its perception of sin quickened, but the sense of pain which sin inflicts is keener. The difficulty and the hiddenness of the work in which they are engaged augments still more this sensitiveness, especially as they are so far from receiving visible support from those around them, that they must rather make their account to be called enthusiastic and indiscreet, singular and affected, by those even who are good people, but have the incalculable ill-luck to be good in their own way, not in God's way. Moreover early piety is never wise. How should it be, since experience alone can make it wise? The world complains of the mistakes of beginners in religion, not seeing that they only make these mistakes because they are not yet quite so unworldly and anti-worldly, as please God they will be by and by. One of these mistakes is that they exaggerate their own faults, and this at once leads to discouragement. Besides that, they are working to high models, Jesus and the Saints; and when they have done their best, and what is for them really well, it must be so terribly below what they aimed at that they can hardly help being disappointed. What is more trying to spirits and temper than to be invariably playing a losing game? And what else can a man do who has made up his mind to be like his Crucifix?

But the upshot of all this discouragement is that it renders us languid and unjoyous—just the two worst things that could happen to us, because they make anything heroic simply impossible. If a man has tight hold of his adversary in a wrestling match and is suddenly seized with languor, all is over with him; for the victory depended on the play of his muscles and the firmness of his hold. A victorious army can beat a vanquished army of twice its numbers, because the joy of victory is such a moral power. Thus to be languid and unjoyous, and that so early in the day, is quite fatal to us; and it is in these two things that the bane of discouragement consists.

As to presumption, I believe it is much less common than discouragement. A man must be a fool to be presumptuous in religion. Nevertheless we can be very foolish when we least expect it. St. Theresa says humility is the first requisite for those who wish to lead an ordinarily good life; but that courage is the first requisite for those who aim at any degree of perfection. Now presumption is never very far from courage, and hence we must be upon our guard against it. We may fall into it in many different ways, and I will mention some of them. There is a proverb that the first blow is half the battle. I do not think it holds in spiritual matters; and the reason I do not think so is that such a number of persons are called to devotion and an interior life, who break down and abandon it. The fault was not in the first blow. It was vigorous enough, loving enough, humble enough. The fault was later on; it was either that they got tired of mortification, or that they fell into a common superstition about grace, and when it did not come true, they were disgusted. This superstition consists in imagining that grace is to work like a charm, almost without the concurrence of our own wills. A man will not get up at his proper time in the morning. He says he cannot; which is absurd, for there is no physical power holding him down in his bed. The fact is he will not; he does not choose to do it; the virtue of it or the obedience of it is not worth the pain of it. He pleads that over night he made a resolution to get up next morning, and asked the souls in Purgatory to get him up. The morning comes; the air is cold; meditation is uninteresting; sleep is pleasant. No souls have come from Purgatory to pull him out of bed, draw his curtains, light his fire, and the rest. It is not therefore his affair. He has done his part. He finished it all last night: but grace has not worked. What can he do? This is only a picture of a thousand other things. Multitudes who would have been nigh to saints remain nigh to sinners from this singular superstition about grace. What we want is not grace—it is will. We have already a thousand times more grace than we correspond to. God is never wanting on His side. It is the manly, persistent will which is wanting on ours.

But to return. The first blow is not half the battle in the devout life. But we think it is. We become impatient with the extreme and mysterious slowness of God's movements, and we think the work begun is as good as the work ended; and knowing what the Saints have done, when after long austerities they had consummated their union with God, so far as on earth may be, we presume, and imitate them in the letter, without discerning the spirit. Or again we mistake the vigor of Divine Grace for the fortitude of our own will; and so we turn against God some special accession of supernatural strength which He has compassionately vouchsafed to us. Experience has not yet shown us by how many defeats each spiritual victory is gained. We shall find that out presently; for it is a grand fountain of humility. Moreover, there is a peculiar pleasure and an exalting sense of power which for a long time sensibly accompanies cooperation with grace. We bring it with us out of our first fervors, and it does not go away all at once when they do. And we mistake this for acquired habits of solid virtue. Or we dwell on our own good works, and then a mist rises out of them and we see them double. Or injudicious friends praise us and remark how devout we have grown of late, and think they are doing us a kindness while they are thus overthrowing the work of God in our souls. All these causes lead us into presumption, and presumption into indiscreet excesses, and indiscreet excesses into self-trust, and self-trust into an inevitable reaction against the interior life altogether.

Neither must we forget to note, though it belongs rather to a treatise on the Beginnings of the Spiritual Life, that in the earlier stages of our course, and especially in the remains of our first fervors, there are some things which greatly resemble what we read of in advanced saints. The fact is, we are only just settling into our normal state. God has hitherto been doing far more than it is His will to do for a continuance. Our beginnings are sometimes almost as supernatural as our endings may be. We are not to expect that the long interval between the two will be so. We must part company now with a great deal of sensible sweetness, with many secret manifestations of God and fervent aspirations which have sometimes perhaps made us fancy that we should soon be saints. Now this likeness of our beginnings to certain features of more advanced states entices us occasionally into a secret presumption. We have no idea how heavy the mere pressure of time will be upon us hereafter, nor how long the road really is, though the mountains look so near. Without one additional duty, without one new temptation, nay I will put it more strongly still, with fewer duties and fewer temptations the mere continuance of going against our natural inclinations, which is implied in the service of God, is a drag upon us more fatiguing and more depressing than we could have conceived beforehand. Perseverance is the greatest of trials, the heaviest of burdens, the most crushing of crosses.

These two dangers of discouragement and presumption lead us into opposite mistakes with regard to our spiritual progress. Hence it is of consequence to be on our guard against certain symptoms which discouragement will take as proofs we are not advancing, and presumption as proofs we are greatly advancing; when in reality, taken by themselves, they tell neither way. I proceed to consider five of these uncertain signs of progress, and to look at each of them under the double aspect of presumption and discouragement.

1) After watching ourselves for a time, we perceive that we either do or do not conquer some besetting fault. We presume upon this. But let us consider. It may be no real proof of progress, for our temptations may from many causes happen to be weaker at that particular time. The devil by his natural subtilty may foresee that we shall thus examine ourselves, and thus rest upon the result of our examination; and wishing to inspire us with false confidence, which is always fine weather for his campaign, he may draw off his forces and leave us in temporary peace. Or again, our faults may be changing from some change in our exterior life, or from the force of years, or any other cause. That our faults do change is certain, and these changes give birth to some of

the most remarkable phenomena of the spiritual life. Or again, from some little infidelity to grace, the sensitiveness and delicacy of our conscience may be in punishment a little dulled; and hence we may be less conscious of our falls. Is there anyone who has not experienced this punishment? Hence there is no ground for presumption simply in our perceiving that we have fallen less often into some besetting fault. But then there is also no reason for discouragement because we happen of late to have fallen oftener. We must go on taking observations for a long time before we can safely begin to draw inferences from them. It may be, for many reasons, that we are more conscious of our falls just now than we were before. Or God may allow us to fall in order to keep us humble, or to conceal from us the progress we may be making in some other direction. Or it may be that our great enemy has made a dead set against us in that particular respect. We may be actually supporting a charge, not merely marching through a difficult country. We do not know enough about ourselves to be reasonably discouraged, then, by this first sign.

2) We presume or are disheartened in proportion as we have or have not sensible sweetness in our religious exercises. But presumption should remember that this sensible sweetness arises very often from physical causes, from good health, fine weather or high spirits, and even when it is an operation of grace it is sometimes a testimony of infirmity and a mark of spiritual infancy. It is the bait of God's condescension to tempt us on, when we have not sufficient solid virtue to distinguish between Him and His gifts, and to serve Him for His own sake, not for theirs. It is a bait to be eagerly seized, for it brings forth solid fruits. Yet it is God's gift, not our progress. At the same time it is very unreasonable to be discouraged by the absence of this sensible sweetness. For it is a gift, not a virtue; and God gives it to whom He wills, and when He wills, and in what measure He wills. Nay, His very withholding it is sometimes a favor; for it is meant to raise the soul to a higher state, to ennoble its love, and to increase its occasions of meriting. Even if it is a chastisement it may be a favor. People very often insist on giving way to low spirits because they are sure that such or such a symptom in their

spiritual life is a divine punishment. Truly, a spiritual man, when he is peevish, is the most unreasonable of all complainants. I cannot see anything disheartening in being punished by God. On the contrary, when He punishes He does not ignore us; and His ignoring us would be the really terrible thing. And when He punishes, it is a father's punishment, and the hardness of the blow and the number of the stripes are in truth but measures of the affectionateness of the punishment. Never let us wish God to put off His punishments. It is a wish He might easily grant, and for which we should pay dearly in the end. God is interested in us and full of merciful purposes when He condescends to chastise us. While one hand wields the rod, the other is filled with special graces, which we shall receive when nature has been sufficiently hurt and mortified.

3) Another experience which we are in the habit of making too much of is our finding or our not finding that mental prayer and meditation grow easier. For meditation is in itself ordinarily so difficult that anything like an increased facility in it presently awakens presumptuous feelings. But we should recollect that the habit of prayer is a different thing from the grace of prayer; and meditation is such a discursive method of prayer that it is quite easy to form a habit of it without its going at all deeply into us, or affecting our interior life. Instances of this come across us continually in the shape of men who never miss their morning meditation, yet seem to be none the better for it, do not lead more mortified lives or vanquish their dominant passion or govern their tongues, or become more recollected. Not but that the habit of prayer is an excellent thing; only it is not the gift of prayer, and we are apt to exaggerate its importance from confounding it with the gift. It may also happen at any particular time that the subjects of our meditations may be easier to us, as being more suitable to our genius. The different times of the ecclesiastical year may bring this about. It may be Christmas, or Lent, or Corpus Christi. For some can meditate easily on the Passion who cannot meditate at all on the Infancy; and some find rest and devotion in the Gospel narratives and parables who can make nothing of Our Lord's Mysteries. Or

our bodily health may be better, our sleep sounder, or our circumstances more cheerful, or the excitement of some great feast, coming or gone, may be still upon us and help us. All this is against our presuming simply because for the while meditation goes on more swimmingly and smoothly. At the same time we have no reason to be discouraged if meditation, so far from growing easier, seems to become impossible to us. It is a long work to gain facility in mental prayer, and it is acquired much more by mortification than it is by habit; and our progress in mortifications, while it must be steady and unsparing, must also be gradual and cautious, erring rather on the side of too little than too much, because of our wretched cowardice. Moreover, as I shall have to show in the sequel, dry meditations are often the most profitable, and of course it is just the dryness that makes the difficulty. And, to put it at the worst, there is not necessarily the least venial sin in want of readiness at prayer; and surely it is a great thing for us at this stage, and remembering old times, that God's grace keeps us from offending Him. It is not a sign of a low estate to be immensely joyful at the mere absence of sin. There are better things in store for us; but God grant that as we force our way we may never lose the simplicity of that satisfaction! I will not allow that we have always a right to be discouraged even by our sins, but I am sure we ought not to be discouraged by anything which is short of sin.

4) We are often apt to philosophize on the phenomena of our temptations, and to be elated or cast down by what we fancy we observe in that region. But even if the sky look cloudless and serene, we have no warrant to be elated. Our temptations may at any particular time be fewer in number, as I have observed before. They may also be of a less attractive character, in consequence of some change in our outward circumstances. Or our minds may be full of some interesting occupation which completely possesses them and so distracts them from the temptations, without there being anything meritorious or supernatural in it. It is sometimes true that the world helps us as well as hinders us by its multifarious distractions. They prevent much sin, though they spoil much recollection. It is this which makes solitude so dangerous except

to tried virtue. But suppose a very tempest of temptations is raging round us; discouragement would be as unreasonable in this case as presumption in the other. The very vehemence of the temptations is a sign of the devil's anger; and he is far too sensible to be angry for nothing. When the Bible speaks of his being angry, it is added that it is because his time is short. We must have provoked him by the way in which we have hung on to God, or by the marks of special love which God has made to shine upon us, and which Satan may be able to see more clearly than ourselves. If the temptations frighten us rather by their obstinacy and long continuance, as if they were determined not to leave us until they had got a fall out of us, we must be on our guard indeed, but with joy and thanksgiving. For the very continuance of the temptation is a proof that so far, at least, it has not been consented to. The dog goes on barking, says St. Francis de Sales, because he has not been let in. Furthermore, which may be the result of Satan's natural sagacity and foresight, an access of new and unusual temptations is often a sign that a season of peculiar grace is at hand. Therefore, with Jacob, we must wrestle till the dawn.

5) At different seasons we feel the effect of the Sacraments more or less decidedly. Certainly there are times when it almost seems as if the Sacraments were going to destroy faith, so palpably do we see and hear and taste and touch and handle and realize grace. This is especially true both of Confession and Communion. Nevertheless, there is no room for presumption here. The grace of the Sacraments is not our merit; and the sensible effect of them may often be apparent, and yet its being sensible arise actually from other causes, physical or mental. Or God may see that we are unusually weak, and so may give us an unusual grace, and make it more sensible in order to inspirit the lower part of our soul more effectually. Yet, if the Sacraments become insipid, losing what little sensible savor they had to our souls before, we must not be discouraged as if some evil were befalling us. It is no proof that we are not receiving in abundant measure the solid grace of the Sacraments. The Saints have experienced similar things, even after they had become saints. And, more-

over, though this perhaps is taking you a little too near the mountains, bare faith is by far the grandest of all spiritual exercises.

Perhaps you will say that this is an unsatisfactory chapter: all negatives. But have you not got far enough to see that inward peace is the great thing you want? And nothing so effectually secures that as the wise and skillful handling of these two temptations, presumption and discouragement. Besides, if it was a great thing to know what are signs of progress, it is far from a little thing to know what are not signs, especially when they pretend to be.

Chapter III

HOW TO MAKE THE MOST OF OUR SIGNS OF PROGRESS

I must now suppose the soul of my pilgrim to have some or all of the signs of progress enumerated in the first chapter. It cannot be content with merely contemplating them; it must set to work to cultivate them—and how is this to be done? This is the question to which the present chapter must furnish an answer. But a word of general advice at the outset. At this early stage of the devout life we must be careful not to take too much upon ourselves, not to fly too high, not to promise God great austerities, nor burden ourselves with numerous practices. We must not be cowardly and fainthearted; but we must be moderate and discreet. To be gentle with ourselves is not necessarily to be indulgent to ourselves. The punishment that is not too much for a man would kill or maim a child.

In the spiritual life there are generally particular aids of grace or means of grace appropriated to particular epochs; and just as this epoch has its own dangers, presumption and discouragement, so it has its two aids or means, recollection and fidelity; and its great work at present is to get used to these two things. In our beginnings, while our first fervors were burning in our hearts, we hardly felt the need or realized the importance of these things. They came of themselves. Impulses of grace did it all; and the generosity of young love supplied for a great deal of painful and dry self-discipline. Thus we were recollected without feeling it, and faithful without knowing it. But those days are passed away.

Many books have been written upon recollection, of more

paragraphs than I must use words. To put it quite shortly, recollection is a double attention which we pay first to God and secondly to ourselves; and without vehemence or straining, yet not without some painful effort, it must be as unintermitting as possible. The necessity of it is so great that nothing in the whole of the spiritual life, love excepted, is more necessary. We cannot otherwise acquire the habit of walking constantly in the presence of God; nor can we without it steer safely through the multitude of occasions of venial sin which surround us all day long. The whispered inspirations of the Holy Ghost pass away unheard and unheeded. Temptations surprise us and overthrow us; and prayer itself is nothing but a time of more than usual distractions because the time out of prayer is not spent in recollection. The very act by which we apply our attention to prayer does little more than empty our minds of our duties, so as to give more room for distractions than we had while hand and head and heart were in the occupations of daily life.

This habit of recollection is only to be acquired by degrees. There is no royal road to it. We must make the occasional practice of silence one of our mortifications, if we can do so without singularity or ostentation; and seeing that for the most part we all talk more in conversation than others would wish us to do, it would not be hard to mortify ourselves in this way. We should also watch jealously any eagerness to hear news, and to know what is going on in the great world around us. Until we feel the presence of God habitually and can revert to Him easily, it is astonishing with what readiness other subjects can preoccupy and engross us; and it is just this which we cannot afford to let them do. Newspapers keep not a few back from perfection. Visiting the Blessed Sacrament daily is another means of acquiring recollection. We feel the visit long after it is over. It makes a silence in our hearts and wraps an atmosphere around us, which rebuke the busy spirit of the world. The practice of retaining some spiritual flower, maxim or resolution from our morning's meditation, in order to supply us with matter for ejaculatory prayer during the day, is a great help to the same end. Bodily mortification is a still greater, especially the custody of the senses, when we can practice it unnoticed. But the greatest help of all is to act slowly. Eagerness, anxiety, indeliberation, precipitancy, these are all fatal to recollection. Let us do everything leisurely, measuredly and slowly, and we shall soon become recollected, and mortified as well. Nature likes to have much to do, and to run from one thing to another; and grace is just the opposite of this.

I do not know a better picture of recollection than Fenelon's description of grace, which he sent to a person who was just going into a convent. "God would have you wise, not with your own wisdom, but with His. He will make you wise, not by causing you to make many reflections, but on the contrary by destroying all the unquiet reflections of your false wisdom. When you shall no longer act from natural vivacity, you will be wise without your own wisdom. The movements of grace are simple, ingenuous, infantine. Impetuous nature thinks much and speaks much. Grace thinks little and says little, because it is simple, peaceable and inwardly recollected. It accommodates itself to different characters. It makes itself all to all. It has no form nor consistence of its own; for it is wedded to nothing; but takes all the shapes of the people it desires to edify. It measures itself, humbles itself, and is pliable. It does not speak to others according to its own fullness, but according to their present needs. It lets itself be rebuked and corrected. Above all things, it holds its tongue, and never says anything to its neighbor which he is not able to bear: whereas nature lets itself evaporate in the heat of inconsiderate zeal." (*Lettres*, tome v., p. 398.).

The peculiar rewards which recollection brings with it show how appropriate a grace it is to this particular epoch of the spiritual life. The difficulties of prayer are more easily surmounted, and some of its more dangerous delusions avoided. It seems also to prevail more with God when it is offered from a recollected heart, and the answers come quicker and more abundantly. Sweetness and sensible devotion once more revisit the soul along with the peace in which recollection plunges it; and liberty of spirit, arising from the detachment from all earthly things—which is gradually the consequence of recollection—enables us to fly, rather than walk, along the path of perfection.

Without recollection, this liberty of spirit becomes mere license and dissipation, and our spiritual life nothing but a presumptuous imitation of the freedoms which the Saints have purchased by years of heroic self-restraint and disinterested love. How many fall into this pitfall, whence they are drawn out only to go down into Egypt as bondsmen! For recollection is itself a holy captivity, to which we are unwilling to submit; but from which we only free ourselves to meet a worse and harder slavery. Vanity and cowardice are equally the sworn foes of recollection, for to vanity it is always unfolding pictures of self which are anything but flattering, and cowardice is perpetually annoyed by its loud calls to reform and mortification, which grow more irksome the longer they are delayed.

In a word, at this season of our pilgrimage, external things, though a necessary probation, are a trial almost above our grace to bear. They begin by engaging, possessing, preoccupying us; and no sooner are our minds completely filled by them than they beguile our hearts and entice us into a thousand human attachments which, however spiritual their pretexts may be, are nothing more than a veritable slavery. The mind and heart thus subdued, nothing is wanting but the third and last process of corrupting us, which is accomplished by dissipation, sensuality and the maxims of the world. We may be sure, then, that without recollection we shall make no progress.

Fidelity is the other great aid of this epoch of the spiritual life. What is meant by it is this. Even although we may not be living under a rule of life, still as a matter of fact the duties and devotions of one day very much resemble those of another. It is practically as if we promised God certain things, and a particular round of religious observances—so much so that conscience reproaches us whenever we causelessly intermit any of them. Thus these daily observances come to be a kind of condition of our perseverance. They acquire a sort of sanctity, and become the ordinary channels by which God pours His grace into our souls. The tempter sees all this, and estimates this daily perseverance at its just value. He puts forth all his strength to throw us out of it, and makes us fretful and irregular. He makes it feel heavy to us as a weight of lead. Or he represents it to us as a dangerous formality. Or he reminds us that we are not bound to it either by obedience or by vow. Or he contrives that we should read something that was meant for scrupulous persons, and mistakenly apply it to ourselves. Or he makes us fancy that such regularity is not good for our health. Any pretext will do, so long as he can allure us into unfaithfulness, either to the movements of grace, or to our routine of spiritual exercises. His anxiety to make us unfaithful is the token to us of the paramount importance of fidelity.

The legitimate decay of our first fervors, when their time was accomplished, has naturally thrown us more upon ourselves. This is an anxious thing, though it was always intended, and must have come sooner or later. But one consequence of it is that it has become more necessary than ever for us to wear a yoke of some kind, and to learn what ascetical writers call the spirit of captivity. This is of great value to us, as it makes all our conquests and acquisitions real, and preserves them for us. Moreover, we stand in need of cheerfulness to face the long outstretching desert that lies before us; and nothing keeps alive in us a holy joy more effectually than fidelity to grace and our appointed observances. The sense of wretchedness which follows frequent or habitual laxity drives us to seek consolation from creatures and to re-enter the world that we may have the pleasure of forgetting ourselves there awhile, and hiding ourselves from the merciful persecution of exciting grace. Besides which, the formation of virtuous habits is interrupted by our unfaithfulness, and this weakens our whole position, and makes our future harder, while actual ground also is lost by the intermission. In a word, fidelity is the raw material of perseverance; and to perceive this is to see that its importance cannot be exaggerated.

These, then, are for the present our two guardian angels, recollection or a constant peaceful attention to God and the issues of our own hearts, and fidelity, as well to the inspirations of grace as to the daily practices which counsel, obedience or our own choice have caused us gradually to bind upon ourselves. Bearing this in mind, I come to a direct answer to my question: What are we to do in order to cultivate the signs of progress which we perceive in ourselves? I will make five recommendations.

1) Let us at once do something more for God than we are doing at present. Let us examine what we actually do, and see what it amounts to, and how far it exacts any effort from us. Let us think whether we could not bear more, and yet not faint beneath the burden. Can we add anything, without much hardship? I put this last question, because I am sure that just now it is the safe course to pursue. We shall be all the more heroic for it in the end. There is no heroism like discretion. Watch the Church canonizing a saint, and you will see how this idea haunts her and pursues her. But whatever we add, however trifling it may be, should be something to be seriously persevered in. It must not be a novena, or a month's prayer, but something solid. And do not let us be hasty in deciding that we cannot afford to do more at present. Be cautious; but be generous, as well.

2) There is, however, something which we can infallibly do—and that is, put a more interior spirit into what we actu-·ally do. Some men are so shocked by the sight of any wanton waste in housekeeping that quite apart from all mercenary considerations, it makes them downright melancholy. We may well be sorrowful in the spiritual world to see the waste of good words and works for the mere want of an interior spirit and a supernatural intention. Men are sowing good seed on rocks all the day long. Alas that it should be so! For, with a little pain, how easy it seems to aim each of our actions to the greater glory of God, and inwardly to unite our will to His in all we plan or do or suffer. The difference between an action with this interior intention and without it may almost be called infinite; and the results of the practice to our souls in the way of holiness are immense. The results of prayer and mortification are not to be compared with those of an interior spirit. Of course, time is required to mature them. They do not manifest themselves in a day. Nothing is less revolutionary than the spiritual life. Its changes are constitutional, imperceptible and slow. We must not imagine we shall find ourselves saints when we have practiced this interior spirit

for a month. But we may be quite sure that if we persevere, something great will come of it.

3) Another way of cultivating the signs of progress which we perceive in ourselves is to pray for a greater desire of perfection. I repeat what I said before, that we do not value this mere desire at its proper price. If we did, we should make more use of it; for we always use what we esteem. It is in reality praying against worldliness, accustoming ourselves to unworldly standards and ideas, and destroying the old influence which the corrupt maxims of the world are still hiddenly exercising over our hearts. It conveys to us a much truer and more reverential appreciation of the majesty of God, of the lovingness of grace, and of the incomparable pre-eminence of all spiritual things. It is true that we seldom fulfill what we desire; for it is as of old—the spirit is willing, but the flesh is weak. Nevertheless, what we do accomplish bears some proportion to what we desire, and especially to the vehemence of our desire. These are great reasons for fostering this supernatural desire the most we can. Rodriguez' treatise on the value to be set on spiritual things is in my judgment the most excellent part of his most precious book.

4) It is of importance also not to allow ourselves to rest in any pursuit except the service of God. By resting, I mean feeling at home, reposing on what we do, forgetting it is a mere means even when we do not err so far as to mistake it for an end, being contented with what we are, not pushing on, nor being conscious that we are fighting a battle and climbing a hill. Nothing can excuse the neglect of the duties of the position in life which God has conferred upon us. All is delusive where these are not attended to and made much of. They are as it were private sacraments to each one of us. They are our chief, often our sole, way of becoming saints. But while we perform them with all the peaceful diligence which the presence of God inspires, we must jealously realize that they are means, not ends, subordinate and subservient to the great work of our souls. No amount of external work, not the unsleeping universal heroism of a St. Vincent de Paul, can make up for the want of attention to our own souls, such as resting in our external work would imply. Hence we should

be jealous of any great pleasure in our pursuits, even when they are works of Christian mercy and love. It is always a pleasure to do good; yet it must be watched, moderated and kept in check, or it will do us a mischief before we are aware. The thought of eternity is a good help to this. It brings down the pride of external work and takes the brightness and color out of our successes; and this is well, for such brightness and color are nothing more than the reflection of ourselves and our own activity.

5) There are also practices of humility peculiar to this stage of the devout life, which we must not omit to notice. We must not wish to forget our sins and give ourselves up to the exclusive consideration of the immensity of God's love. It is too soon for that yet. Indeed, in the sense in which we are often inclined to take it, the time for it will never come at all on this side of the grave. We should be filled continually with wondering thankfulness that we, of all men, should have been so visited by God, and so deluged with His choicest grace. It must almost try our faith that being what we are, God should have been to us what He has been. O blessed incredulity! O happy soul, that has to fight against this modest unbelief! We must not be anxious about the heights we are likely to reach in the spiritual life. It is a subject on which we ought never to exercise our thoughts at all. Whatever grace God may intend to give us, He has already given us far more than we have corresponded to. Let us live in this thought, and make a hermitage of it for ourselves. We may desire as much as we please, so long as we do not calculate or contemplate. Humility must give a character to our very pursuit of virtue. It must not be disquieting or inordinate. Virtue itself is a means, not an end; for virtue is not God, nor union with God. Do not think this admonition strange. It is one that was constantly in the mouth of St. Francis de Sales. We are so bad that we can make even our pursuit of virtue a hindrance to our love of God. To sit quietly among our own faults and meannesses, and to feel that there is our place, is no slight thing. When Job sat down upon the dunghill, he was to the eye of God a pleasant picture, because he was expressing the feelings and the humility of a creature in the presence and under the hand

of his Creator. Pursue virtue earnestly, but not eagerly. Do not waste time by continually going back to measure the ground you have traveled over. Do not be exacting to yourself; for that will infallibly lead first to hurry, and then to ill-temper, and then to a forgetfulness of your own badness, and then to a doubt of God's goodness. Be slow. I shall have to say this a hundred times; because there is not a difficulty or a danger of the spiritual life in which it is not necessary advice. Last of all, it belongs to our present humility on no account to desire any supernatural things to happen to us such as voices at prayer, visions and the like. A person who desires such things may become a prey to dreadful delusions at any moment; and even if God really vouchsafed such gifts, they would be accompanied with great danger to our unpracticed and not yet thoroughly mortified souls. We should probably wrest them to our own destruction. Yet it is not an uncommon temptation at this crisis. If St. Theresa thought it well to pray that God would lead her by the common way, how necessary must such common guidance be to us! Still, I would hardly advise that we should pray for it, lest the very prayer should fill our heads with perilous conceits. There is no weakness or folly which need even surprise us in self-love.

In these five ways we may correspond to the graces which God has already given us, and cultivate those fair fresh promises of growth in holiness which He has allowed us to exhibit in our souls. But I will not leave the subject of progress without putting before you an extract which Orlandini gives us from the papers of the Jesuit, Peter Faber, the companion of St. Ignatius. It is a common mistake, says Orlandini, for men aiming at perfection to pay more attention to their daily falls than to the further pursuit of virtue and progress in spirituality. Of this Faber used often to complain, saying that it seemed as if people took a greater pleasure in studying the art of mistaking and falling, than that of acquiring the beauty of virtue. He called this a *fraud* in the spiritual life. For although it is a virtue to avoid vice, yet to be always contemplating and deploring our sins, keeps the soul down from higher and better things, and retards its holy impetuosity whereby it attempts great works and rapidly climbs heights of virtue, which are of themselves fatal to the vices we less wisely try to diminish by this perpetual inspection and review of self.

Chapter IV

THE SPIRIT IN WHICH WE SERVE GOD

Theory is not much without practice; yet without a good theory practice for the most part is not itself worth much, for it is neither fruitful nor enduring. If this is true in most things, it is especially so in the spiritual life. Now God is to us very much what we are to Him. With the innocent Thou shalt be innocent, and with the perverse Thou shalt be perverted. Having then observed in ourselves certain signs of progress, been put upon our guard against certain pretended signs, and seen what we can do to cultivate the promise we have observed, it is desirable that we should clearly understand in what spirit it is that we commit ourselves to God, and pledge ourselves to serve Him. A clear idea is a great help to us, and consistency is no slight part of perseverance. Let us then thoroughly understand what we are about, what we are promising, what sort of a life it will lead to, and what God may reasonably expect of us after our own voluntary professions.

What I have to show, then, in this chapter is that without liberty of spirit we can never be perfect, that there is no true or safe liberty of spirit which does not follow as a consequence from the spirit in which we serve God, and hence that the only right spirit in which to serve Him is one of self-sacrifice and generosity. When we have mastered this chapter and turned it into practice, we are already miles beyond where we were before. People never go far enough, unless they start with a clear view of how far they ought to go.

I will begin with the spirit in which most men serve God. There are many difficulties in life. Some men have more, some less. But the most fearful of all no one can get rid of, namely, that of having to deal with God. To have to deal with God is a necessity as awful as it is indubitable and unavoidable. Contrast His reality with our untruth, His power with our weakness, His law with our disobedience. Enumerate His known perfections, remembering that there is no great or small with Him because of His immensity and completeness. Analyze His tremendous sanctity, and meditate separately on every element of it, its awful minuteness, its unbearable purity, its unspeakable sensitiveness, its terrific jealousy. On our side there is a multitudinous fertility, day and night, of thought, word, work, omission and intention: on His side, the noting of all this, the stern requisition of an invariably pure intention, the strict account, the severity of the punishment, the eternity of the doom, and the infallible inevitableness of it all.

His court in Heaven we could not see and live, because of its radiant purity. The strong angels tremble and are shaken; Our Lady is all abased; and the Sacred Heart of Our Lord Himself is flooded with reverential fear.

Along the line of Sacred History there gleam like lights the dreadful chastisements which God has inflicted on venial sins. Moses, and David, the man of God whom the lion slew and Oza who upheld the swaying Ark—these examples are overwhelming disclosures of the sanctity of God; and the notable thing is, that what seems to anger God in these faults is the want of wholeness of heart with Him. Let us look at our past lives by this light, and have we not cause to tremble; or even at our present practice, and have we a right to be without fear? What a thought for us that He knows at this moment how we are to stand to all eternity, what pains we are to endure, or what bliss we shall enjoy. It is enough to take away our breath to know that this is known, even though we still are free. Surely nothing can be conceived more awful than having to deal with God.

What then follows from this? Undoubtedly nothing less than these five simple truths.

1) That His service is our most important, if not our sole, work. This is so obvious that it requires only to be stated. Time and words would alike be wasted in the attempt to prove

it. Yet alas! even spiritual persons need to be reminded of this elementary truth. Let us subject ourselves to a brief examination upon it. Are we thoroughly convinced it is true? Has our past life shown proof of it? Is our present life modeled upon it? Are we taking pains that our future life shall be so? What is the result when we compare our worldly promptitude and industry with our preference of the service of God over all other things? Are we in any way on the lookout for His greater glory or our own greater union with Him? Is it plain at first sight that we have no object or pursuit so engrossing and so decidedly paramount as the service of God?

2) That the Spirit in which we serve Him should be entirely without reserve. Need I prove this? What is to be reserved? Can there be reserves with God? Can His sovereignty be limited, or our love of Him ever reach the measure of enough? But have we no reserve with Him now? Is there really no corner of our heart over which He is not absolute Lord? Does He ask of us freely what He wills, and do we do our best to give Him all He asks? Have we no implicit bargain or condition with Him that He is only to go so far with us and no further? Is our outward life utterly and unconditionally dependent on Him? And if it is, is the kingdom of our inward intentions reposing peaceably beneath His unquestioned sceptre?

3) That our ruling passion should be horror of sin, even venial sin, and unworthy imperfections. Now do we so much as know what this feeling means? When we read of it in spiritual books, does it not sound to us like an unreal exaggeration? Have we even heartily prayed for an increased hatred of sin? Are there not many evils which afflict us far more keenly? Are we attracted to Gethsemane, and to the mysterious vision of our Master crushed, like the grapes in a wine-press, beneath the mental horror of the world's sins? Until we know something of this horror of sin, supernatural principles can hardly be said to have taken possession of our minds.

4) That we should avoid, as if it were sacrilege, any slovenliness in our dealings with God. Surely the terror of His majesty, as well as the immensity of His love, should make this one of our fundamental axioms. There is a personal contempt

about slovenliness which makes it perfectly horrible to couple even the idea of it with God. It is far more truly a practical atheism, than many gross sins into which the vehemence of our guilty passions may betray us. Yet how do matters stand with our meditation, vocal prayer, Mass, Confession and Communion? And if it be so with our directly spiritual duties, what shall be said of those occupations of our calling out of which we are to work our salvation, and which can only be sanctified by extreme purity of intention?

5) That the only one fact of any especial importance to us is whether we are honestly serving God or not. Shall we be saved or not! The whole of life's solemnity and seriousness resolves itself into that one overwhelming doubt. We should have nothing so much at heart as this. Nay, rather we should have nothing at heart but this. How dead to self we should soon become under the shadow of this universal, life-long question! Yet how does the case really stand? A little wrong, a trifling injustice, an insulting word, a piquing of our self-love and personal vanity, stirs us more effectually and interests us more really than the chances of being lost or saved. And yet we are aiming at a devout life! And yet we dream that we are serving God!

It is plain, without speaking of high things or of fervent devotions, that merely to carry out in the service of God these five self-evident truths, we must serve Him in a spirit of generosity and self-sacrifice. But the spirit of generosity may be looked at in two ways; as it exists in our own hearts, and as it actually inspires our conduct. We are thinking of it just now in the first point of view. Its victory over our external actions is a work of time and combat. It will not only be long before it is achieved, but in point of fact it never will be achieved to the extent which we ourselves see to be possible. What I want to impress upon you is that even as a theory it is of immense utility. Unless we see clearly what it is to be generous with God, and have steadfastly determined to be so, there is no likelihood that the slightest degree of generosity will actuate our external conduct. What we want in our present position is that we shall not, consciously at least, have any reserves with God, that we shall set no definable bounds either to our love of Him or to our sacrifice for Him, that we shall not fix our eye on any imaginary point of future perfection and say that when we are arrived at that we shall be content, that as we read or hear of the states and stages of the spiritual life and the practices of courageous mortification, we shall never feel of any of them that it will never be a practical matter to us. You see I am putting it all in the negative. I am not saying you shall positively determine at some future time to do this or to suffer that. I should not wish it. I am only saying you must not exclude as impossible or impracticable any amount of perfection. You must have no reserve. You have nothing to do with the future. You have to follow the present grace, and then the grace which shall present itself next, and then the grace after that, and so on, till God draws you to a nearness to Himself which it would frighten you now even to picture to yourself. You must abandon yourself to grace and follow its lead. But unless you see the reasonableness of this, and make up your mind to it steadily beforehand, you are quite sure not to do it. This is what I mean by having a good theory of generosity. If you have not the theory now, you will never have the practice hereafter.

Undeniable as the common sense of this may be, corrupt nature will often plead eloquently against it. Consequently this theory must not be merely a loving instinct in the heart or an habitual resolution in the will. You must verify it as an intellectual conviction. You must have persuaded yourself of it. If not, when temptation comes, you will tremble from head to foot with indecision, and end by fainting. It is well, therefore, to make it a frequent subject of meditation. You must accustom yourself to true views about the Gospel. You must see that, all through, it is a religion of suffering, of mortification, of self-sacrifice, of consuming love, of self-forgetting zeal, of self-crucifying union, in a word, it is the religion of the Cross and the Crucified. You must get well into you the truth so unpalatable to nature that self-denial is of its essence, and that it must be daily self-denial, not only that we may be perfect, but even that we may be our dear Lord's disciples.

In truth, Jesus is our model, of whom the Holy Ghost bade

the Apostle say that He pleased not Himself. Fix your eyes
on this Divine Exemplar; familiarize yourself with the mysteries of His Sacred Humanity, until the spirit of them passes
into you. Learn the secret of His Infancy, of His eighteen
years' Hidden Life, of His three years' Ministry, of His week's
Passion, of His forty days of Risen Life. Where is there any
self? Is it not all sacrifice in detail? Is not all unreserved
generosity for the glory of His Father, and the perishing souls
of men? This unreservedness is the grand characteristic of
the Incarnation. Look at His Passion. Take His Divinity for
the first point of your meditation on it. How did He use it?
He restrained it from consoling Him; He let it strengthen Him
that He might suffer more, even beyond the ordinary limits
of human endurance; it was all the while actually giving physical strength and vigor to His executioners to torment Him
with, and its concurrence was the weight and the force of
the burning lash. Then look at His soul. In it He foresaw
His Passion all His life long, so that it was a fear and a suffering of three-and-thirty years. Gethsemane was, as it were,
the crucifixion of His Soul, as Calvary was of His Body;
and all through the Passion His Soul was pierced by woes
and humiliations which have never been surpassed or equalled
for continuity, variety and keenness. Then cast an eye upon
His Sacred Body. Nothing is held back. Head, Hands, Feet,
Eyes, Mouth, Back, Heart, all have their own torture, all contribute their own peculiar agony to the grand Redeeming Sacrifice. His Blood is shed quite wastefully, over the olive roots
of Gethsemane, on the pavement of Jerusalem, into the braided
thongs and the knotted lashes, all along the way of the Cross,
up Calvary, and on the holy wood of the Cross, and it is
shed until the emptied Heart has not another drop to give.
Now compare all this with our own mean reserve and half-
heartedness! Toward God what scanty prayers, what careless
examens, what heartless Confessions, what cold Communions, what human respect, what grievous sins! Toward our
neighbors, how selfish in action, how unkind in word, how
censorious in thought! Toward ourselves, how indulgent, how
conceited, what pampering of our body, what worship of our
will!

The great lesson of the Crucifix is wholeheartedness with
God, the spirit of joyous abandonment and generous sacrifice. We may get a clearer idea of it if we look at it from
another point of view. We are quite capable of conceiving
a man, a saint he could not be, exempt from all actual sin,
and observing to the full all the Commandments in the letter,
and yet without generosity to God. It is, of course, a theological impossibility; but we are capable of conceiving it. This
sinless man might, without breaking any Commandment, be
occasionally dull-hearted with God, grudging Him heroic service and counsels which did not oblige. He might be sometimes inclined to bargain with God, and to think he had now
done quite as much as was discreet. Now and then he might
give way to the feeling that his obedient life was irksome,
because of the unwearied and unremitting sacrifice which it
entailed. At intervals he might even have fits of lukewarmness, in matters plainly short of sin. He might look on Jesus
without any glow of enthusiasm, and his acts of love might
up to a certain point be remiss. All this is possibly and imag-
inably consistent with entire sinlessness. Yet what is the disposition of this unsinning monster, but the portrait of a devil,
or something very like it? And why, except for the absence
of all generosity with God? It is just this which stamps, not
the unchristian, but the anti-Christian character upon it.

Of a truth there has been a pure creature, who has been
exempt from every shade of sin; and yet, if we may say so,
sinlessness is not her highest prerogative, even independent
of the Divine Maternity. Cast an eye over her sixty-three years,
and you will see what is meant by generosity toward God
and unreservedness with Him. Her first act of love and use
of reason at the very moment of the Immaculate Conception
was an entire and joyous surrender of herself to God, and
it was never retracted for so much as an instant through all
those years. The thought never crossed her of being aught
else than all for God. So when she made her vow of virginity,
as the most perfect offering to the infinite sanctity of God,
she sacrificed apparently the one object which was nearest
and dearest to every Jewish maiden's heart, even the hope
of being the Mother of the Messias. Then again when she

consented, in obedience to those who had a right to command her consent, to espouse St. Joseph, what an utter abandonment of self it was! Even her consent to the Incarnation, and her acceptance of the dignity of Mother of God, were acts of generosity, not only because of the unequalled suffering they involved, but also because of the violence she was called upon to do to her deep humility. Her Presentation of Jesus in the Temple and her acceptance of Simeon's prophecy were equally examples of her self-forgetting generosity with God. Amidst all the trials of the Sacred Infancy she called for no miracles to alleviate her cares. In the Holy House of Nazareth her life was nothing else than a perpetual oblation of Jesus and of herself to God. Her poverty was perfect; neither did she seek for spiritual consolations, but was contented with the almost unbroken silence of her Divine Son, when she longed for Him to speak. She parted with Him unselfishly when He went upon His three years' ministry, which, even when she followed Him, at least broke up and rendered desultory her intercourse with Him. She consented to His Passion, and cooperated with Him in all its steps. She spent fifteen years of resigned desolation upon earth, when He had ascended, and like a magnet had almost drawn her Immaculate Heart up to Heaven with His own. She gave Him away to the Eternal Father in the Ascension, and without a murmur took John for Jesus. How wonderful must her detachment have been, who could detach herself even from the presence of our dearest Lord, and which had nothing, not even Himself, that it did not generously abandon to the will of God!

Such is the spirit in which, according to our measure and degree, we must resolve, by the help of His grace, to serve Almighty God; and among the many reasons why this should be so, I must notice one, because it belongs to our present reflections. We have heard much of liberty of spirit, and we have read that without it we can never reach perfection. Everyone agrees in saying great things about liberty of spirit, and in desiring it for himself. But few have any clear notion of what they themselves mean by liberty of spirit: and for the most part, when they suppose they are exercising that liberty, they are in reality only making free with God and their religious duties in a way which will be sharply visited on them at last. Liberty of spirit does not then consist in being free from a rule of life, and not having set duties for set times, nor in changeableness with devotions, pious books and the like, nor in the absence of self-accusation when we neglect any of our exercises, nor in not making a scruple of what other good people make a scruple, nor in being offhand and careless with the details of our actions on the ground that God looks at the heart, nor in addressing hot words to God, and courting His merciful caresses, when we are taking no sort of pains to mortify ourselves and keep our passions under. All this is slovenliness and impertinence, not Christian liberty of spirit. Yet how many do we see who by slightly and unconsciously degrading God in their own ideas, and then making themselves very much at home with His service, imagine that they are enjoying the breadth and room and invigorating air of liberty, when they are all the while debauching the very principles of reverence and religiousness in their own minds, and are drinking venial sin, as thirsty beasts drink water!

If, however, it is not easy always to recognize liberty of spirit, and to distinguish it from rudeness, irreverence, or an unscrupulous self-trust, the difficulty is very much narrowed by reflecting that in most cases we can tell what is not liberty of spirit. For no one can by any possibility have a true liberty of spirit, who is not serving God in a spirit of generosity. Now it is easy for us to know whether we are doing or trying to do this or not; and if the answer be in the negative, then we may be infallibly certain that anything about us which looks like liberty of spirit is in reality something else, and probably something highly undesirable. It is a help to us then to know so much as this, that if we have not generosity, we have not liberty. (I am not speaking of liberty in the theological or metaphysical sense; but of *liberty of spirit*, a characteristic of Christian piety.). The one answers to the other. Or at least without generosity there can be no liberty, though from interior trials there may at particular seasons be generosity without liberty.

The spirit of Jesus is a spirit of liberty. Scripture has passed it into a Christian proverb, that where the spirit of God is, there is liberty. When first it came into the world, it was a spirit of liberty from the bondage of fear and dark superstition which had reigned over the heathen, from the narrowness and doubt and grovelling appetites of the Greek and Roman unbelievers, and from the slavery of ceremonial and positive precept which had schooled the Jews for our Saviour's coming. It is a spirit of liberty because it is a law of love, not because it is love only, but because it is a law also, and a law of love. It is liberty because of the munificent superabundance of the Great Sacrifice, and, above all other reasons, because Jesus is God.

Hence we might naturally infer that the same liberty would penetrate into our most intimate relations with Our Lord, and give a character to every phase of the spiritual life. And such is, in truth, the case. For Christian liberty consists in freedom from sin, as degrading to our nature and destructive of self-respect, as in itself full of wretchedness, as the most grinding of tyrannies, and above all as an offense against an infinitely good God. It consists in freedom from the penalties of sin, such as God's anger, Hell and an evil death. But it is also freedom from worldliness, that is, from a heart set on the world, from a mind full of it, from low views, and from that series of successive disappointments which befall every man who finds comfort in the world. It is a freedom from slavery to other men; for it makes persecution nothing more to us than a means of meriting, and calumny a sweet likeness to Jesus, while it begins the work which is only to end with the last breath we draw, deliverance from human respect. But most of all, liberty of spirit is freedom from self; for how shall the freedman of Christ sink to be the slave of self? To be free from littleness, from self-love, from secret meanness, and from the haunting of our own shame, this is to be free indeed, and there is no other freedom which deserves the name.

In one word then, liberty of spirit consists not at all in being more free with God or less anxious in the discharge of our spiritual duties, but in this single thing, detachment from creatures. Liberty and detachment are one and the same thing. He is free who is detached, and he only. And it is plain that no one can be detached who is not generous, also;

for generosity consists in detaching ourselves, always at cost and with pain, from creatures for the sake of the Creator.

Oh that we were all made free with this heavenly freedom! For there is nothing to which the glory of a free soul can be compared but the worshipful magnificence of God Himself. The soul detached stands on a height and breathes the air of Heaven. Creation lies far below it, like a speck in space. Angels and saints are its court and purity its atmosphere. Jesus is its brother, its companion, and its likeness. Its will is always done, because it is always with the will of God; so that in this sense it is omnipotent as He is. Its wisdom is supernatural, and unintelligible to earthly minds. Its peace is endless, profound and above the reach of foes. Its joy is absolutely in the unspeakably joyous life of God, and in nothing short of it. Oh, how wonderful is the dignity of those who have been ransomed by the Precious Blood of Jesus, and so sweetly justified by His victorious Resurrection! The heavens are not so high as is their liberty, nor the sea so deep, nor the plains of earth so wide. Poverty cannot soil it, grief cannot sadden it, death cannot end it. Oh, beyond all words that an over-full heart can utter, blessed, thrice blessed be God, for the freedom wherewith Christ hath made us free!

Chapter V

WHAT HOLDS US BACK

It seems now as if we had got our course clearly laid down, and had received our instructions as to the spirit in which we should serve God. We are fairly out of harbor, but how is it that we are not making way? We see others around us in full course, but no breeze is filling our sails. Whether it is that we are still under the influence of the shore, or whether it be that something else is in fault, it is clear that we are not catching the wind. Such is the common complaint of many souls at this period. Something holds them back; and they do not all at once see what it is. Our business now is to discover these secret obstacles, and see how to deal with them.

Our first step must be to examine the symptoms which betray that all is not right with us. First of all we experience a want of power in resisting temptations, in going through with our penances and in being faithful to our devotional observances. Then we feel a want of elasticity in surprises which come upon us, in changes, in trials of temper, in the management of exterior duties, and the reconciliation of them with devotion and the interior life. Moreover we are conscious of a certain deficiency of inward light. Our examinations of conscience become hazy and dim. An inclination to scruple and littleness grows upon us, and we seem to lose the sight of God which we had before, and which, imperfect as it was, was a true illumination. There is a vagueness about our spiritual combat which we feel requires more definiteness, as well as more vigor. And added to all this, a sort of drowsy laziness is creeping over us like the oppression of a dream.

Something is wrong, it is clear; the question is, what? Here

41

are three wants—power, elasticity and inward light—to be accounted for. They arise from various causes. Partly they are the result of the attention we have been almost obliged to pay to ourselves and the interior experiences of our souls in these early stages of the spiritual life. Self-inspection is always dangerous, even when it is necessary; and consequently it is never to be practiced without its proper accompanying antidote. Self-knowledge is both a grace and a necessity and a blessing; yet none of these things prevent its being a danger also. The danger is in its leading us to unreality, sensitiveness, affectation, and that which is the most disgusting of vices in the spiritual life, sentimentality. It may be also that we have not exercised faith sufficiently, and this may account for the three wants in question. We have gone by feeling, or by sweetness, or by impulse, rather than by faith; and hence we have mistaken God's gifts for God, and have accustomed our eyes to so strong an artificial light that we cannot see in the soft twilight which belongs to the Christian life. Or we have not been sufficiently solicitous to keep ourselves in harmony with the spirit of the Church, neglecting certain devotions, or lightly esteeming them, such as confraternities, scapulars, indulgences and the like. Or we have not looked sufficiently out of ourselves to the objects of faith, but have rested on self-improvement too exclusively and too anxiously; and devotion never can neglect doctrine without paying dearly for it in the end. There is nothing Satan can clog our wheels with more effectually than an untheological devotion. Or again, our mistake may have arisen from our neglecting external works of mercy and edification, and our not being so scrupulously careful as we should be in our intercourse with others.

From all this we are led to conclude that our secret obstacles consist of three mistakes in our interior life, and two in our exterior. The present chapter shall consider the first three, and the next chapters the fourth and fifth of these mistakes.

1) It is not impossible that what is holding us back is defective devotion to our Blessed Lady. Without this devotion an interior life is impossible, for an interior life is one wholly conformed to the will of God; and our Blessed Lady is

especially His will. She is the solidity of devotion. Yet this
is not always sufficiently kept in mind. Beginners are often
so busy with the metaphysics of the spiritual life that they
do not attribute sufficient importance to this devotion. I will
mention some of the considerations which they do not seem
to lay to heart. Devotion to the Mother of Our Lord is not
an ornament of the Catholic system, a prettiness, a superfluity, or even a help, out of many, which we may or may
not use. It is an integral part of Christianity. A religion is
not, strictly speaking, Christian without it. It would be a different religion from the one God has revealed. Our Lady is a
distinct ordinance of God, and a special means of grace, the
importance of which is best tested by the intelligent wrath
of the evil one against it and the instinctive hatred which heresy
bears to it. She is the neck of the Mystical Body, uniting,
therefore, all the members with their Head, and thus being
the channel and dispensing instrument of all graces. The devotion to her is the true imitation of Jesus; for, next to the
glory of His Father, it was the devotion nearest and dearest
to His Sacred Heart. It is a peculiarly solid devotion, because
it is perpetually occupied with the hatred of sin and the acquisition of substantial virtues. To neglect it is to despise God,
for she is His ordinance, and to wound Jesus, because she
is His Mother. God Himself has placed her in the Church
as a distinct power, and hence she is operative, and a fountain
of miracles, and a part of our religion which we can in nowise
put in abeyance. Spirituality must be orthodox. This is self-
evident. Now doctrine could not be orthodox which pretermitted the office and prerogatives of the Mother of God; so
neither can spirituality be orthodox, if it be distinct or separable from a just devotion to her, and a devotion generous as
well as just. Indeed a mistake in doctrine is doubly dangerous
when it is worked up into the spiritual life. It poisons everything, and there is no mischief which may not be predicted
of the unfortunate soul which is the subject of it. If then you
have the symptoms of something wrong, something retarding
you, look first of all if your devotion to our Blessed Lady
is all it ought to be, in kind and degree, in faith and in trust,
in love and in loyalty. Perfection is under her peculiar patronage,

because it is one of her special prerogatives as Queen of the Saints.

2) It may be that you are wanting in devotion to the Sacred Humanity of Jesus and His mysteries. Even this is possible, and not so uncommon as we could wish to believe it. Yet who could doubt that the devotion which may not leave us on the highest heights of contemplation, is quite indispensable in the states of the spiritual life which we are considering? It must interpenetrate every part of the Christian life; and being a Christian means this, if it means anything. Christ is the Christian's way, the Christian's truth and the Christian's life. To lead a holy life is to be the Spouse of the Incarnate Word; and therefore the love of the Incarnate Word is the very heart of holiness. The love of the Sacred Humanity is of three kinds: one represents our interior affections toward Our Lord, another the proofs of the sincerity and solidity of those affections, and another the operations which Jesus Himself causes in the souls that are sufficiently well disposed. They are called, respectively: affective, effective, and passive love.

Affective love of our dear Lord consists in an intense desire of His glory, in a joyous complacency in the success of His interests, and in an affectionate, beautiful sorrow at the view of sin. It leads us to pour out our whole souls in confidence before Him, to complain of our coldness and imperfections, to put before Him our pains, wearinesses, disgusts and trials, and to abandon all to Him with a quiet and childlike indifference.

Effective love makes us the living images of Jesus, representing in our own lives His states, His mysteries and His virtues. We bear His image outwardly by continual mortification, by diminishing and narrowing our bodily comforts, by regulating our senses, by cutting down the extravagant requisitions of the world and society, by a jealous moderation of innocent affections and pleasures, and a perpetual repression of all vanity and conceit. Our interior life is conformed to Jesus by liberty of spirit, which means detachment from creatures and conformity to His will. Our external actions have His character stamped upon them when we act as His members, and all our actions are done in dependence upon Him, and according to His movement.

Passive love I speak of, rather that we may learn to thirst for what one day may be ours, than that it is, ordinarily speaking, to be looked for at this stage of the spiritual life. It is cheering to see how close, please God, we may one day be to Jesus even before we die. His first operation in this supernatural state is to wound our souls with love, so that we lose our taste for everything which is not Him or His. It is as if a new nature were given us, so little in harmony with the wretched world around us, that we languish and pine, as out of our proper element. Then He deepens the wound, and makes all our thoughts, affections, words and works to be imbued with His love, until we are unable to do anything but seek after Him, like the Spouse in the *Canticles*. Every love is renounced but His, every idea effaced from our minds but of Him, and everything which is out of relation of Him drops from our remembrance as though it had never been. So that He possesses our soul altogether, and it is not so much we who live as He who lives in us. Then He sets us all on fire with resistless love, and makes us break out into actions of heroic charity and supernatural union with Him, while all the time He so deepens in us the sense of our own vileness and nothingness that we do nothing but deplore the meanness of our service and the dullness of our hearts. And lastly He throws us into a state of purifying suffering, and fastens on our shoulders the perpetual Cross, when we seek for nothing but to suffer more, and shrink from nothing but to suffer less. So He strips us of ourselves, and makes us wholly His. But all this is a long way on. Look up and strain your eyes. I do not know that you will so much as see the mountaintops where all this will be found. But good cheer! It is something to know that those fair heights are really there.

It is inconceivable what advantages we derive from these exercises of love of the Incarnate Word. The heart detaches itself from creatures; self-love burns down and goes out; imperfections are corrected; the soul is filled with the spirit of Jesus, and advances with giant strides along the paths of perfection. See then, if you are catching no wind in your sails,

whether your love of Our Lord's adorable Person and Sacred
Humanity is all it ought to be, all He meant and all He asks,
or at least whether you are distinctly cultivating it, and doing
your best daily to make it grow.

3) The third deficiency, and I am inclined to suppose it
by far the most common, may be a want of filial feeling toward God. I wish I could be very clear, as well as very strong,
about this, because so very much depends upon it. If our
view of God is not uniformly and habitually that of a Father,
the very fountains of piety will be corrupted within us. We
shall incur the woe of which the Prophet speaks; our sweet
will be bitter, and our bitter sweet.

Our position toward God is that of creatures. See what is
involved in this. We belong absolutely to Him. We have no
rights but those which He compassionately chooses to secure
to us by covenant. Our life is at the mercy of providence,
and providence is not a mere course of external events, but
the significant will of Three Divine Persons, One God. Our
condition in the next life is known to Him already; and we
on our part know that more grace than He is obliged to give
is necessary for us, although we know of an infallible certainty that He will give it us, if we choose to correspond
to what we have. Yet this last consideration cannot wholly
allay the nervousness which the view of our position naturally
causes us. Reflection on the attributes of God, His omniscience,
omnipotence, immensity and ineffable holiness, is not calculated to diminish this feeling. Nevertheless the conviction that
the spirit of adoration, the temper of worship, the instinct
of religiousness, reside simply in our always feeling, speaking, and acting toward God as creatures, that is, as beings
who have no independent existence but have been called out
of nothing by Him, is in reality so far from projecting a gloomy
shadow over us, or exciting an internal disquietude, that the
more seriously these truths are received into the soul, and
the more unreservedly the sovereignty of God is acknowledged
by us, the more tranquilizing, supernaturally tranquilizing, will
their effect be found.

Yet this does not appear on the surface, nor until the mind
has become habituated to, and imbued with, religious thought.

We are tempted to look at God in almost any light rather than that of a Father, as well because of our own helplessness as His overpowering immensity and omnipotence. Yet our spiritual life depends entirely on the view we take of God. If we look at Him as our Master, then His service is our task, and the ideas of reward and punishment will pervade all we do. If we regard Him as our King, surely we must be crushed by the indubitable rights of His unquestionable despotism, and nothing more tender than an abstraction of dutiful loyalty may we dare to cherish in our hearts. If we look at Him as our Judge, the thunders of His vengeance deafen us, the awful minuteness of His indictment strikes us dumb, and the splendor of His intolerable sanctity blinds us. If we consider Him exclusively, in any one of these lights, or in all of them, it is plain our service of Him will take its character from our views. Hardness, dryness, untempered fear and a consciousness of our being unable to stand upon our rights will necessarily make us cowardly and mean, cringing and mercenary, querulous and as disrespectful as we dare to be.

But we may even look at Him as our Creator, and yet be wrong. For it is possible to consider a Creator to be an independent and eternally self-existing Being, who for His own good pleasure, as First Cause, has called creatures out of nothing, and cares as little for them as He is beholden to them. Yet it seems to me as if to be a Creator implies the being a Father too. The very will of Creation is surely a stupendous act of paternal tenderness. Thus God is not only our Father and our Creator also, but He is our Father because He is our Creator. A rational creature, to be a creature, must be a son also. We bring with us out of our primal nothingness the filial tie. Creation ranges itself rather under goodness than under power or wisdom. So that if I knew no more of God than that He was my Creator, I ought to feel that He was my Father also. *Qui plasmasti me miserere mei:* Thou who formedst me have mercy on me, was the lifelong prayer of the penitent of the desert. There was a sort of right, or a sound of right, in the very appellation, which endeared it to her lowliness and timidity.

However this may be, there is no truth more certain than

that God is our Father; and that all that is most tender and most gentle in all paternity on earth is but the merest shadow of the boundless sweetness and affectionateness of His paternity in Heaven. The beauty and consolation of this idea surpass words. It destroys the sense of loneliness in the world and puts a new color on chastisement and affliction. It calls consolation out of the very sense of weakness, enables us to trust God for the problems we cannot solve and binds us by a sense of most dear relationship to all our fellowmen. The idea enters into and becomes the master thought of even all our spiritual actions. In sin, we remember it; in aiming at perfection we lean upon it; in temptations we feed upon it; in suffering we enjoy it. He is our Father in the ordinary events of life, in protection from a thousand evils which He never lets us feel, in answers to prayer, in blessing those we love, and in forbearance with ourselves, forbearance with a degree of coldness and incorrigibleness which is almost incredible, even to ourselves.

He is our Father not nominally only, but really also. As I said, the tie comes out of creation. The Creator has a marvelous and mysterious sensible love for His creatures, with which no earthly affection can compare for indulgence or for tenderness. Moreover He has been pleased to make our interests identical with His, and He has so created us in His likeness and image as that we should reflect even His Divine Majesty. But He is our Father also by covenant; and as He ever effects what He promises, this new paternity is as real as the other. And beyond all ties of nature, grace and glory, by which He calls us children, He is our Father in a way we can never fully know, in that He is the Father of Our Lord Jesus Christ.

Out of this filial feeling toward our heavenly Father comes ease of conscience as to past sin. We can trust Him, in sweet confidence, even with the unutterable decision of our eternal doom. We enjoy liberty of spirit in indifferent actions, mingled with an intense desire to serve Him which our filial love inspires. Out of it come also a sweet forgetfulness of self, enjoyment in prayer, patience in doubts, calmness in difficulties, lightheartedness in trials and an uncomplaining contentment in desolation. We worship Him for His own blessed sake, because He is our dear Father. Happy sunshine of this thought! It falls upon our souls with triple beam, more trust in God, more freedom with God, more generosity with God!

I have dwelt upon this because it is of paramount importance that we should be thoroughly imbued with the true spirit of the Gospel; and the missing of it so frequently as men do, is partly owing to their not remembering every hour of the day that our Blessed Lord is God, and partly to their mixing some other idea of God with that of Father, and allowing the harsher element to preponderate. The spirit of the Gospel is tenderness; and these three wants I have been examining, of devotion to Our Lady, of devotion to the Sacred Humanity and of filial feelings toward God, are at once effects of want of tenderness and causes of the continued want. This is the great occult hindrance. With your chivalrous desire for perfection, your disgust with the world and your appreciation of high things, you expect to be making progress, and are disappointed. I have already asked you to examine yourselves and see whether you are not wanting in devotion to our Blessed Lady, to our dear Lord's Sacred Humanity and to the ever-blessed Paternity of God. Now let me put it in another shape. The want of these three things means in reality the want of tenderness, though it means other things as well. But the absence of tenderness in religion is often of itself enough to stay man's growth in holiness. It is worthwhile, therefore, to say something on this head. A man may be in a certain sense religious: he may fear God, hate sin, be strictly conscientious and honestly desire to save his soul. All these are most excellent things. But you cannot say that the Saints were men of this sort. They had about them a sweetness, a softness, a delicacy, a gentleness, an affectionateness— nay, I will dare to say, a poetry, which gave quite a different character to their devotion. They were living images of Jesus. This, in our far inferior measure and degree, we also must strive to be, if we would grow in holiness.

By tenderness is not meant a mere impressionableness, softheartedness or a facility of tears. These are as often marks of cowardice, laziness and a want of resolute will and

earnestness. True tenderness begins in various ways. Its progress is marked by a sorrow for sin, without thinking of its
punishment, by what I have elsewhere called a touchiness about
the interests of Jesus, by childlike docility to our superiors
and spiritual directors, by mortifying ourselves and not feeling it a yoke, by never thinking of stopping short at precepts
without going on to counsels, and by a very faint, incipient,
and as yet scarcely discernible, appetite for humiliations. According as it is formed in our souls, all the characteristics
of sanctity gather to it and group themselves round it. For
love is a greater safeguard against sin than fear, and tenderness renders our conversion to God more entire by making
it more easy. It especially attracts Jesus, whose Spirit it is,
and who will not be outdone in His own peculiar sweetness.
Without this tenderness there can be no growth; and while
it renders duty more easy, and consequently the performance
of duty more perfect, it instills into us the especially Christian-
like instincts such as love of suffering, silence under injustice,
a thirst for humiliations and the like. Moreover, it deepens
sorrow for sin into a contrition which is worth more to the
penitent soul than any gift that can be named. Look at the
phenomena of the Incarnation—what are they? Helplessness,
unnecessary and unobliged suffering, sacrifice, abasement, continual defeat, no assertion of rights, carelessness of success
and most pathetic wrongs. And what is our response to all
these things, but the temper which is expressed by that one
word, tenderness?

The Sacred Infancy teaches us tenderness; the Passion tenderness; the Blessed Sacrament tenderness; the Sacred Heart
tenderness. But look at the common life of Jesus among men,
and you will see more clearly what this tenderness is like.
There is first the tenderness of Our Lord's outward deportment. The narrative of Palm Sunday is an instance of it. Also
His way with His disciples, His way with sinners and His
way with those in affliction or grief who threw themselves
in His road. He quenched not the smoking flax nor broke
the bruised reed. This was a complete picture of Him. There
was tenderness in His very looks, as when He looked on the
rich young man and loved him; and St. Peter was converted

by a look. His whole conversation was imbued with tenderness. The tone of His parables, the absence of terrors in His sermons, and the abyss of forgiveness which His teaching opens out, all exemplify this. He is no less tender in His answer to questions, as when He was accused of being possessed, and when He was struck on the face. His very reprimands were steeped in tenderness; witness the woman taken in adultery, James and John, and the Samaritan, and Judas. Nor was His zeal less tender, as was evidenced when He rebuked the brothers who would fain have called down fire from Heaven upon the Samaritan villagers, and also by the sweet meekness of His divine indignation when He cleared the Temple.

Now if Our Lord is our model, and if His Spirit be ours, it is plain that a Christian-like tenderness must make a deep impression upon our spiritual life, and indeed give it its principal tone and character. Without tenderness we can never have that spirit of generosity in which we saw that we must serve God. It is as necessary to our interior life, or our relation with God, as it is to our exterior life or relation with others; and there is one gift of the Holy Ghost, namely piety, whose special office it is to confer this tenderness.

If then the secret obstacles of which you complain concern your interior life, and arise from defects in your devotional feelings and exercises, cultivate these three devotions: to our Blessed Lady, to the Sacred Humanity of Jesus and to the Paternity of God, and great results will follow. Put yourself right in these three things, and the sails will no longer idly flap against the mast.

Chapter VI

EXTERNAL CONDUCT

I hinted in the last chapter that one reason why we felt ourselves hindered by some secret obstacles was that we had neglected our external conduct, and had not been careful to apply the principles of the spiritual life to our intercourse with others. It is to be wished we could always remember the importance of this. But there is a more especial necessity for us to bear it scrupulously in mind in the earlier stages of the devout life. For a beginner has great temptations to esteem very lightly his external conduct. He has recently been learning for the first time the importance of pure intention, habitual recollection and the supremacy of an interior life. Moderation is difficult to human nature, and what is novel never gives fair play to what is old and familiar. Hence, though no one would dare to put it into words, a beginner filled with the true but to him fresh thought that the interior life is far superior to the exterior, thinks the latter positively worthless, or even regards it as a temptation. The esteem of the one unfortunately breeds in him a disesteem of the other, especially as a person who has only recently begun to be thoroughly religious is always very much troubled with an inclination to entertain contemptuous feelings about persons and things. Contempt is the most universal temptation of beginnings. To be a man of one idea is an easy thing, and there is a look of chivalry about it which helps the delusion. When a beginner preaches a crusade against anything, we may always suspect delusion. The spirit of a reformer is the contradictory of the ascetical spirit. A crusade against ourselves may be well enough, though better not even that, until we have learned

to subdue ourselves. But to attack other men's faults is to
do the devil's work for him; to do God's work is to attack
our own.

How different is the wisdom of St. Ignatius! When we practice particular examen of conscience, he would have us choose
for the first object of our holy persecution, not the fault which
troubles us most or seems of the greatest magnitude, but the
one which most annoys our neighbor and gives him disedification. This must be our model.

Now let us think how it is that beginners, for I may almost
say we are but beginners in spirituality—though what may
be technically called our beginnings are past—how it is for
the most part that they offend those around them and bring
devotion into discredit and disrepute. I would not be harsh,
as the world is, in speaking of these faults, for with what
difficulties are they not surrounded, what enormous allowances
are they not privileged to claim, and what an immense thing
it is that they should thus be working heart and soul for God
at all! Besides which, it is the old leaven of the world to
which they belonged, not their new principles, which are to
blame for what is ungraceful or amiss in their behavior.

They offend them by indiscretion, not observing the propri-
eties of time, place, age, person and circumstances; by inconsistency, because their conduct must appear such to those who
cannot discern in them the internal war which they are wag-
ing; by irritability, far less probably than what the most unkindly
critic would forgive if he saw the inward soreness and the
weariness of spirit which strife and temptation cause; by singularity, because it is not easy for a man at once to take up
with a new set of principles and always apply them correctly
and gracefully to the claims of conflicting duties; and finally
by what is in truth no fault of his, but scandal taken rather
than given, because the maxims of the Gospel are so rudely
uncongenial with the maxims of the world.

We must therefore persuade ourselves that it is very important to our spiritual progress and interior holiness that we
should take great pains in our intercourse with others, in order
that we may be to them the good odor of Christ. Negligence
on this point is the reason why many fail in their attempts

after perfection; and while they are looking within for the cause of their ill-success, the true reason of it is to be found all the while in their external conduct.

Now there is a wrong as well as a right in every spiritual question. There is a wrong way of trying to edify people, as well as a right one; and we will consider the wrong one first. We must never attempt to edify others by any sacrifice of principle, to show, for example, how free we are from bigotry, or how independent of forms and ceremonies, or what liberty of spirit we have regarding the observance of certain positive precepts. This is only saying that we must not do evil that good may come. Yet there is no slight temptation to a man, especially if he has a little fit of unusual discretion upon him, to show others at some expense of strict principle that our holy religion is not so harsh and cruel as it seems to be to the votaries of the world. The attempt moreover is always as unsuccessful as it is wrong.

We must never do anything in order to edify others, for the express purpose of edifying, which we should not have done except to edify them, and in the doing of which the motive of edification is supreme, if not solitary. Edification must never be our first thought. The evangelical rule is to *let* our light shine before men *that* they may see our good works, *and* glorify our Father who is in Heaven. We must take great pains not to disedify; but it would be very dangerous to take great pains to edify. The two things are very different, although they are often confounded; and you will not unfrequently meet with souls whom self-love has so gnawed and corrupted that their perfect restoration would be little less than a miracle, and the mischief of which is to be traced to a wrong theory of the duty of giving edification. Look out to God, love His glory, hate yourself and be simple, and you will shine, fortunately without knowing it or thinking of it, with a Christ-like splendor wherever you go and whatever you do.

We must not make unseasonable allusions to religion, or irritate by misplaced solemnity. An inward aspiration or momentary elevation of the soul to God will often do more, even for others, than the bearing of an open testimony, which principle does not require, and at which offense will almost inevitably be taken. There is a silence which edifies without angering; though I admit that the practice of it is far from easy. Probably we practice it most successfully when we realize it least, but act out of a heart which is in union with God. A man is annoyed with sacred things when they are unseasonably forced upon him; and thus even a well-meaning importunity may be a source of sin.

But if a wrong theory of edification not only causes us to make many false steps in our external conduct, but also injures and sometimes positively devastates our souls, what shall be said of a wrong theory of fraternal correction? Oh, how much scandal and disedification to others, how much overweening self-importance to themselves, has resulted from men holding a wrong theory about this most difficult of duties and most obscure of obligations! We must bear in mind that there are very few who, by standing or advancement, are in any way called upon to correct their brethren, fewer still who are competent to do it sweetly and wisely, and none whose holiness is not tried to the uttermost by its perfect discharge. While, on the other hand, those who have rashly assumed to themselves this delicate responsibility have not only sinned themselves by disobedience, disrespect, conceit, bitterness, assumption and exaggeration, but have caused sin in others, and made the things of God an offense to them, and a stumbling-block in their road. Hence, before we attempt fraternal correction, we should be quite sure that we have a vocation to it, and we should have made quite sure of it by the judgment of others as well as our own; and when we are clear of the vocation, we must still preface our correction with prayer and deliberation. It may be added that to correct our brother for the sake of edifying a third person is a practice which can hardly ever fail of producing unpleasant consequences, and it can only be said not to injure our humility, because it is rather a proof that we have no humility to injure. In the present stage of the spiritual life, then, little more need be said of the obligation of fraternal correction than that it exists. Further on, God will charge us with it, and we shall know how to use it. Should it by chance become a duty now,

only let us fear it and think twice, and He will help us to
the rest.

These, then, are ways in which we must beware of trying
to edify our neighbor. Let us now see how we ought to edify
him. This must be in two ways: by the mortification of Jesus,
and by the sweetness of Jesus. And first, by the mortification
of Jesus. Silence under unjust rebukes, abstinence from rash
and peremptory judgments, and not standing out in an ill-
natured and pedantic way for our rights, obliging others unselfishly and with pains and trouble to ourselves, and not exaggerating in an obstinate and foolish manner unessential points
where all men have a right to their liberty; these are the ways
by which we should practice the mortification of Jesus in our
intercourse with others; and independent of the edification
we shall give thereby, the amount of interior perfection which
we shall attain by these practices is beyond all calculation.
For there is hardly a corrupt inclination, a secret pride, or
a fold of self-love which they will not search and purify.

But we must also edify others by the sweetness of Jesus.
A soft answer turneth away wrath, saith Scripture. Kind and
gentle words, such as those of our dear Lord, are an apostolate in themselves. Whereas clever, sharp words, such as we
have often a strict right to use, are continually doing the devil's
work for him and damaging the souls of others, while they
are inflicting no slight wounds upon our own. Our manner,
too, must be full of unction, and be of itself a means to attract
men to us, and make them love the spirit which animates
us. Coldness, absence of interest, an assumption of superiority for some unexpressed reasons, or even an obviousness
of condescension, are not unfrequently to be found in pious
persons. They have not yet mastered the spirit that is in them
so as to use it gracefully, or they do not appreciate the delicacy
and universality of its tenderness. They have not a true picture
of Jesus in their minds; and thus they can hardly exhibit Him
at all in their outward conduct. Our very looks must be brought
into subjection to grace. The more earnestly we are striving
to form Jesus in our hearts, the more will His sweetness tran-
spire through our features without our knowing it. Except in
times of great physical pain, and that does not always prevent

it, the inward peace and harmony of the soul reflect themselves discernibly upon the countenance. It has been observed that in the Gospel of St. Mark, written at the dictation of St. Peter, there are frequent allusions to Our Lord's look and gestures; and the story of the young man who had not the heart to give up his money, and St. Peter's own conversion, show what the sweetness of our Saviour's look could do. This sweetness is also practiced when we praise all the good we can detect in others, even where it is mingled with what is not so. A man who praises freely, yet not extravagantly, is always influential in conversation, and can use his influence for the cause of God. A critical spirit, on the contrary, amuses by its smartness, or frightens by its malignity, but it neither softens, attracts, persuades, or rules. The practice of putting favorable interpretations upon dubious actions is another exercise of this Christ-like sweetness. They must not be forced or unnatural, much less must they excuse positive sin; but short of this, there is ample scope for this kindly practice; and you will never practice it without having done some missionary work for the glory of God, although you know it not. We must also beware of looks, manners, and especially of a certain silence, by which we make others feel that we are inwardly censuring them. Nothing is more irritating than this. When sin makes the Saints silent, there is a sorrowful sweetness in their silence, as if they were grieving for the offender's sake, and were striving to love him in spite of his sin. This censorious silence, so little like the sweetness of Jesus, causes others to bristle up and put themselves inwardly in an attitude of defense, and so it drives out the little grace that was actually in them, and hardens their hearts against the admission of more. Such a silence is in fact the most pointed fraternal correction, and no one has a right to exercise it who has not ascertained his right, according to the methods already stated, to correct his brother. And even then, it is the most dangerous way of discharging a most dangerous obligation.

It belongs also to the sweetness of Jesus that we should not allow our piety or devotion to be inconvenient to others. When St. Jane Frances de Chantal first put herself under the direction of St. Francis de Sales, her servants used to say

that Madame's old director made her pray once or twice a
day, and all the world was incommoded by it, but her new
director makes her pray all day long, and yet no one is incon-
venienced. A little management surely would be sufficient
to contrive that neither communions nor prayers should disturb the least family arrangement, or exact one tittle of self-
denial from others. Not that they should grudge it, unhappy
souls! but that it belongs to the sweetness of the spiritual life
that we should not ask it.

Thus it is that our intercourse with others should at once
sanctify ourselves and edify them by the double exercise of
the mortification and sweetness of Jesus. But it must have
occurred to us that at this stage of our career, our intercourse
with others resolves itself mainly into government of the tongue.
I do not know which of these two things is the most astonishing, the unexpected importance of the place assigned to this
duty in Holy Scripture, or the utter unconcern which even
good men often feel about it. Unless a man takes the
Concordance, and looks out in the Bible all the passages which
have reference to this subject, from *Proverbs* and *Ecclesiasticus*
to *St. James,* he will have no idea of the amount of teaching
which it contains on this head, nor the actual quantity of that
single volume which it engrosses. Still less will he realize
the strength of what inspiration teaches. It is not consistent
with the brevity at which I am aiming to enter at length into
the subject. It is enough to suggest to each one this single
question, "Is the amount of scrupulous attention which I am
paying to the government of my tongue at all proportioned
to that tremendous truth revealed through St. James, that if
I do not bridle my tongue, all my religion is in vain?" The
answer can hardly fail to be both frightening and humbling.

But how is this government of the tongue to be practiced?
The very detailing of the evils will, impliedly at least, suggest
the remedies. Listen to an hour of conversation in any Christian company. How much of it turns, almost of necessity as
it would seem, on the actions and characters of others! The
meaning of judging others appears to be this: the Judgment
seat of Our Divine Lord is as it were already set up on the
earth. But it is empty. It is waiting for Him. We, meanwhile,

unmannerly and unbidden, keep ascending the steps, enthroning ourselves upon His seat, and anticipating and mimicking His judgment of our brethren. To put it in this way brings home to us the wretchedness of what we are doing. It will also surely assist us in endeavoring to cleanse our conversation of so much unnecessary canvassing of the motives and actions of others. Yet for the most part we have gone far along our road in devotion and done ourselves many an irreparable mischief, before we bestow half the carefulness on the government of our tongue which it not only deserves, but imperiously requires.

The first effect of spirituality on our minds is to sharpen our critical turn. We have new measures to measure with and new light to see by, and the characters of our neighbors get the disadvantage of our fresh powers of observation. Make this the subject of your particular examen, and you will be surprised to find how numerous are your falls. Indeed it is difficult to exaggerate either the facility, the multitude, or the fatal effects of the sin which all this talking about others leads to, even with the best and kindliest of intentions. At the end of our examen, our resolutions on the subject must be very minute, and our falls must be visited, quietly but determinedly, with some voluntary punishment each time.

It would be impossible to speak of all the ways in which the attention of spiritual persons at this stage should be turned upon their external conduct. As I have said, self-introversion is full of dangers, and even the amount of inward attention to self which is necessary is full of dangers. Besides, a beginner cannot possibly, even if it were desirable, occupy himself wholly with the interior life, unless by an unusual attraction of the Holy Ghost. The very attempt would make him morbid, unreasonable and unhappy. In most cases, therefore, it were much to be desired that persons in the early stages of the spiritual life should have some external religious work to do, in order that they be at once busied for God and called off from such a self-inspection as might by its excess end in some spiritual disease, and perhaps bodily ailment as well.

All persons, for instance, can make much more of their worldly calling than they have done hitherto by putting a supernatural intention into it. They can join confraternities, provided they do not allow themselves to be overloaded with vocal prayers. Most men can give alms; but to turn their alms to the temporal necessities of others into alms to their own spiritual necessities as well, they must give till they feel the giving, till it touches, nips, hurts. Without this, where is the sacrifice? Many also can give time, talent and pains themselves to the works of mercy, which their pastors or others set on foot around them. Time and pains are worth as much as money to the objects of your charity; they are worth ten times as much considered as spiritual blessings to yourself. But, do not be in a hurry, and do not act without counsel; but allow yourself to be guided to some good work in which you can take an abiding interest, and which will suit your spirit, means and inclination.

It is surely an obvious mistake for persons to start on a spiritual course as if they were going to be hermits. It is to confound an interior with a solitary life. Their fight is to be in the world's common ways, and their business with its engrossing and multifarious interests, and their trials are to be in no slight measure from their fellowmen. They therefore must make allowance and arrangements for all this. It must enter into their calculations. It must influence their decisions. True it is that at the moment of conversion as in the state of contemplation, we realize nothing but God and our own soul. It is a blessed gift, this singleness of vision, blessed at its own time and in its own place. It is one of our beginnings which is so like our endings. But it is not to be our ordinary or normal state of things.

Yet how many there are who make this mistake! They are beginning a devout life. They are determined to be all for God, and they project a plan or system for their future spiritual life. They legislate for mental prayer, for examen of conscience, for Confession and Communion, for particular devotions and for mortifications. Everything is laid out with the greatest accuracy, the estimate accepted, the plans approved. Yet no mention of their intercourse with others, or their duties toward others, or mercy for others, finds a place! As if this were either not to be at all, or were to have no connection with the spiritual life, or were so easy and obvious to arrange as not to be worth forethought! This must surely be a mistake, and its influence cannot but be widely and enduringly felt in our future course. What is all very well for Camaldoli can hardly be the thing for Change or Piccadilly.

I would even venture to recommend something to give the mind a more decidedly external direction at this period of the spiritual life. For, to tell men so soon as this to throw themselves out of themselves upon God as the object of faith and love would not only be unpractical, because premature, but would lead probably to a want of proper self-government and so to delusions. I would recommend that our favorite devotion should be prayers for the conversion of sinners, with oblations, reparations, Communions, and the like, all turned in that direction. God is always working with unusual energy in some portion of the Church, and is waiting there ready with an uncommon profusion of graces, until we cooperate with Him by our intercessions. Devotion to the conversion of sinners, when and where God pleases, is full of the thought of God and falls in with all the fundamental ideas upon which our own interior life is organized. Hence, to take but a selfish view of the matter, its appropriateness at this period of the spiritual life.

Nevertheless, if a man feels no attraction to this devotion, he need not be cast down as if he lacked something indispensable to a spiritual life. Such a zeal is so desirable that men have been led into disheartening exaggerations about it. But I remember that Da Ponte in his *Spiritual Guide* says that, while in the highest states of perfection such a zeal is always found, nevertheless there are very good people whose memory of their own sins is so vivid, and their timid vigilance about their own souls so engrossing, that they are utterly without zeal for the souls of others. And Richard of St. Victor, in his *Preparation for Contemplation*, states that the case is not an infrequent one of souls poor in spirit, rejoicing in hope, fervent in charity, and eminent in works of sanctity, who yet are quite tepid and almost lazy *(valdè tepidae ac desides)* in their zeal for souls. This doctrine will serve for some of us as a weapon against discouragement, and for others as a caution against temerarious judgments. Both Richard of St. Victor and Da Ponte belong to the unexaggerating school of spiritual writers.

Chapter VII

THE RULING PASSION

We come now to the last of the five secret obstacles which we accused of hindering our progress and preventing our making way with the favorable breezes of the Holy Spirit. It may be said to belong to our interior as well as our exterior life; though it is chiefly in the exterior that we have to combat it. Everyone who is well read in old-fashioned spiritual books remembers the distinguished place which the remora always occupied in them. This was a certain mysterious and mischievous little fish, who by fastening itself to a huge ship in full sail could bring it to a dead standstill. Our belief in the laws of mechanics and of natural history are unfortunately fatal to the remora: would that anything might turn up which would be equally fatal to the ruling passion, of which this hidden and almost omnipotent little fish was the figure! But alas! while we may safely expunge the remora from our catalogue of fishes, the ruling passion still remains a subject for continual and weary legislation and police on the part of those who desire to grow in holiness.

It seems an exaggeration to say that every man in the world has a decidedly ruling passion; and the best writers do not go so far. It is however undeniably true that almost all men have such a passion; and the fact of its being hidden from them is no proof to the contrary; for it is its nature to conceal itself. While it exists in the soul, dominant and unattacked, its influence may be called universal. It forms the motive for apparently contradicting actions and gives a tone and color to the whole life. It is the cause of at least two-thirds of a man's sins. The other passions are obliged to acknowledge

its empire; and as domination, not mere sin, is the object
of its ambition, it will actually help us in combating our other
passions; by so doing, it extends its tyranny, and moreover
creates a diversion in favor of itself. Other passions blind us
to our sins. But the ruling passion is not content with this.
It goes so far as to make our vices look like virtues. Hence
it is a direct road to final impenitence. It is this which gives
the fearful character to the ruling passion. It is with our souls,
as it is with a ship, when the current is stronger than the
wind. She keeps setting upon the rocks, and if she cannot
get her anchors to hold, she is lost. Nay, it is worse with
the soul, whose means of safety are less; for there is no such
thing as an anchorage in the spiritual life.

Now if this be true, few subjects can be more interesting
to an earnest man than this of the ruling passion; for no obstacle to progress is more common, or more secret, and therefore none more dangerous. But let us understand at the outset
that it would be untrue to say that there could be no progress
in the spiritual life until the ruling passion is vanquished. Perfection will hardly attain this entire victory after years of manly
perseverance. But it is true that there can be no progress until
an active war is being waged against it. Hence this war is
a duty which brooks no delay.

Here then is one of the most important businesses of our
lives, to discover what is our ruling passion; and it is as difficult as it is important, because of the secrecy in which that
artful passion invariably wraps itself. There are, however, two
methods, either of which pursued honestly and for a sufficiently long time, will probably bring us to the knowledge
we desire.

The daily practice of self-examination soon furnishes us with
very numerous observations regarding ourselves. It is not however safe to draw any practical inferences from them, until
time and vigilance have verified them under different circumstances and perhaps even opposite temptations. We shall then
come at last to perceive that there is one passion within us
more conformable than any other to our whole natural temperament, one which, taken by itself, expresses far more of
our entire character than any other. We shall find that such

a passion as this is further characterized by our feeling a peculiar repugnance to combat it, and when accused of it by others, we shall probably answer that while we acknowledge we have many faults, yet certainly we cannot charge ourselves with this. Moreover this passion is found to have an extraordinary power of instantaneously kindling our other passions, and of strangely making its appearance in almost all our thoughts and plans, as self-love perceptibly does with at least half mankind. While it makes a livelier impression upon our interior life than any other passion, it also causes the greater number of the disorders which disgrace our external conduct. The majority of our falls, and all our greatest falls, are attributable to it, while it habitually exposes us to the greatest dangers and the most frequent occasions of sin, and thus has more lasting and troublesome consequences than any other of our passions, bad and ruinous as they may be. It takes some time to find out all this. But we may be sure that any passion, of which all or the greater number of these things are true, is in reality our ruling passion, a principle of spiritual death within our souls.

The other method of discovering our ruling passion necessarily resembles the first in many respects, and fixes its attention upon the same symptoms; but it is easier because it does not imply so universal or so incessant a watchfulness. Perhaps because it is easier, it is less successful, or is longer at least in attaining success. Some writers of ascetical theology recommend the one, and some the other. This second method then consists of waiting for any unusual joy or sadness which stirs our soul without an obvious reason, and to inquire whence either of these emotions arises. Even if there should be an apparent cause, the joy or the sadness may be so disproportioned to it as to lead us to suspect some additional hidden cause; and the probability is that it lies in some satisfaction or displeasure of our ruling passion. We must be strangely unobservant of ourselves if we have not experienced these vicissitudes of high and low spirits, for which there was not sufficient on the surface of our lives to account; and whatever be the result of our examination of them, we may be quite sure such phenomena are never without an important bearing on our spiritual life.

Then, again, we go to confession more or less frequently; and certain venial sins and faulty imperfections form the matter of our self-accusations. Particular faults are perpetually recurring. It is even a subject of annoyance to us that the matter of our confessions does not vary more than it does. They are always turning on three or four faults. Now when we have satisfied ourselves deliberately what these three or four things are, we are naturally in proportion to our earnestness led to examine them, to see from what roots they spring and what circumstances develop them. Almost always it will be found that they come from one common root; and the discovery of this common root will be the discovery of our ruling passion. A fault which is both an abundant and a persisting source of venial sins can hardly be anything less than our ruling passion.

Again, there is a kind of low spirits which differ from the sadness spoken of before. There are times when everything seems to come to an end. We are tired of strictness. Prayer weighs upon us as intolerably heavy. Spiritual reading inspires disgust. We feel reckless about temptation, and even the habitual fear of sin has so completely ceased to be sensible, that it appears as if we could fall at any moment. The thought of God does not arouse us as it has been wont to do. Care for souls and loyal zeal for the Church are sentiments so passed from us that we have almost forgotten what they are like, just as men in winter cannot clothe the landscape in verdure and foliage, and imagine it as it was in summer, so as to satisfy themselves. We yearn for the sights and sounds of worldliness as if they would be a relief; and our heart leaps up at any consolation which has not to do with spiritual things. Our very associations have faded out from us, and anything like a habit of godliness to all appearance has dropped away as though it had never been. An intense weariness comes over us, and a nausea for spirituality, which makes us ill-tempered with God, rather than afraid of offending Him. The misery of these fits of low spirits can hardly be exaggerated. Can the danger of them be exaggerated either? For they are accompanied, not so much with sadness, which is more or less softening, as with irritability, which is no home for grace, but rather a proximate preparation for all kinds of venial sin. It is of God's sheer mercy if the evil is stayed even there. Miserably unhinged and unfitted for the task as we are, then, we must even in our wretchedness attempt some kind of self-examination, and question ourselves as to the cause of this dismal oppression. It has none of the marks of a divine subtraction of sensible sweetness. Its features are not like those of a passive purgation of spirit, as mystical theologians call them. It is an operation, possibly diabolical, but most probably entirely human. If we can arrive at the cause, the probability is that we have discovered our ruling passion. It is too fundamental a mischief to come from anything short of it. Persons of soft and effeminate character, sensitive and sentimental, loving bodily comforts, not practicing any regular mortifications, and careful of their eating, drinking and sleeping, are peculiarly liable to these spiritual visitations of waking nightmare. In other words, to be attacked by them is a symptom, though not an infallible one, that our ruling passion is sensuality, which almost rivals self-love both for its universality and its successful artifices to disguise itself and appear other than it is. How many are there whose apparent enjoyment in religion, together with their mild views of moral theology, their familiarity with God, their comfortable intimacy with our Blessed Lady, their aspirations of disinterested love, their depreciation of mere dry precept and hard conscientiousness, their facility in making saints' words and feelings their own—all come, though they little think it, from the luxurious refinements of modern ease, and a secret ruling passion of sensuality!

Thus this second method of discovering our ruling passion is not so much a continuous examination of our whole conduct, as a waiting for, and seizing upon, certain salient points of it, as those which are likely beforehand to be developments of this dominant inclination. But hidden as its presence and influence are, there are certain things of almost daily occurrence in which this serpent, in spite of itself, discloses its operations. It mixes with all our sins, no matter against what virtue or Commandment. It is the feature which all our sins will be found to have in common. Self-love in one man, sensuality in another, vanity in a third, ambition in a fourth, or in a fifth that most unconquerable of monsters, simple indolence. So, too, we often resist temptations, without supernatural motives, and as it would seem, without calling grace to our aid. Or, to speak more accurately, suggestions of evil that in some moods would be temptations to us, in other moods have no such magnetic character, and hence they fall off from us harmlessly, like spent arrows off a shield. It is often our ruling passion which is our shield. It distracts from the pleasures offered to us, or it turns them aside as interfering with some deeper scheme of its own. We are preoccupied men, who do not see and hear. We do not notice these temptations, so that strictly they never become temptations at all.

There are some persons who are so strongly persuaded that everything about them is as it ought to be, that they are prepared to defend themselves on all points, and as a matter of fact do so. These are few in number, because the blindness of self-love, though universal, is seldom total. Still, such specimens are to be met with and studied; for there is much in them, which, doing no good to themselves, is a capital warning to others. To these, what I am now going to say will not apply. But men, who are satisfied that their conduct is not uniformly and on all points defensible, will find that there are certain points on which they invariably defend themselves, certain points on which they are morbidly sensitive. The soreness discloses the ruling passion. This is almost an infallible method of detection. Separate the circumstances, the conversation, the excitement, whatever it may be, see on what subject you defend yourself in all manner of circumstances, hot or cool, taken by surprise or with deliberation, and you may be sure that the subject indicates the ruling passion: though, of course, a good many symptoms must be observed, as the same symptom may point to vanity or to self-love, to sensuality or to indolence.

While we are conducting these all-important investigations, we must remember likewise to take our director into our council. We are very blind in matters which concern ourselves, even when we have to do with mere external interests. Still more are we blind in things pertaining to self-correction. And when we consider the peculiar characteristic of the ruling passion that it passes vice off for virtue, we have additional reasons for distrusting our own solitary judgment in the matter. Hence it is that a director frequently discovers a penitent's ruling passion, before the penitent has discovered it himself. But under any circumstances we must consult him. He must help us in the search. He must approve the discovery. He must guide us in the warfare which we must forthwith wage against our domestic enemy.

It does not come within the scope or brevity of this treatise to urge persuasive motives for a scrupulous and almost frightened attention to this subject of the ruling passion. My object is, as you know, merely to describe symptoms and to suggest means. But so much must be said. They who have not a ruling passion are very few in number; and they who have can have no more important or pressing affair than the discovery of it and the warfare against it. Saul was ruined, and Solomon fell for the want of this. The lost vocation of Judas was the work of his ruling passion, which had coexisted, remember, with all the immense graces implied in his having had a true vocation to that unequalled apostolic office; and that his vocation was true is, by some theologians, considered to be of faith, because of Our Lord's words, I have elected you. The punishment of not seeing the Promised Land, under which Moses ended his days, was the work of his ruling passion, which he had come so near to utterly vanquishing, that whereas by nature he was the hastiest of men, by grace he became what the Holy Spirit calls him, the meekest of men. Other portions then of the spiritual life may have superior attractions to this, others may seem to urge us more swiftly along our road, or give at once a more supernatural turn to our character. But none can compete in urgency and importance with this duty of overcoming our ruling passion. You must stop at this. You can never think of leaving such a fortress untaken in your rear. God will go no further. His current of graces will cease flowing upon you. It will be by nature and by temperament that you are advancing, not by grace. With you or without you, He will sit down before that citadel, and when He has waited long enough for you to see the error and to come back and to cast up your entrenchments against it, and you do not come, He will in the awful language of Scripture give you over to your own desires, and leave the field, and you will wander on, in your own strength, and along your own road, till you fall fainting and die by the way, and they that come after shall see you and say, "Lo! another frustrated saint, another broken instrument, another lost vocation!"

The dryness then of this duty must not repel us, nor its difficulties discourage us. We must consider them well, but our hearts must not sink at the consideration. The greatest difficulty is that of discovering this ruling passion. To a brave man that should be half the battle; and we have already considered the methods by which that knowledge may in ordinary cases be attained. The blindness this passion causes both as to itself and other sins is an outwork as strong as the fort itself; and its pretense of virtuous indignation against the other passions is but the dust it raises and flings into our eyes, as we advance to the attack. The treachery of our own hearts, willing to acknowledge any passion to be our ruling passion rather than the one which really is so, is a domestic enemy that must be strictly watched, lest in the very heat of the assault it play us false. But I have seen many overcome these difficulties with a little manly effort. They have got so far without a check, and without a wound. The difficulty I fear still remains to be considered, the difficulty which has been so fatal to many, and continues to be fatal to numbers of souls daily.

It is the cowardice and pusillanimity which lead us to believe that we never shall really overcome our ruling passion. At first men try to persuade themselves that there is a great deal of unreality and exaggeration in what is said on this subject, and that far too much stress is laid upon its importance and success. Now be it observed I lay no stress upon the success of our warfare, but only on the importance of our being really at war. Not that success is not to be looked for at last, and that it is an immense gain. But I lay the stress on the warfare, not on the victory. Presently a series of defects and a complete check of their spiritual progress lead men to see that the matter was not exaggerated; indeed they feel that the difficulties of the work have been estimated too cheaply. They are then inclined to despair of the whole matter, and to abandon the task as useless. They fall into low spirits from being continually beaten, until they are as pusillanimous as cowed children. Every defeat is a loss of moral power and so leads to defeat again. The very means which we are urged to adopt look fearful to us, and we have not the heart to adopt them and use them with that unshrinking firmness which is necessary. But, are we prepared to abandon the spiritual life altogether, and not to aim at perfection? If not, we must be up and doing. Delay is making matters less hopeful every hour. What is hard now, may soon become impossible.

The means which we must adopt are certainly of a painful kind. We could hardly expect it to be otherwise in expelling such an enemy. Cutting, burning and lying wakeful, what else can do us any good? The first means is to repress instantaneously the very first movements of what we have now discovered to be our ruling passion. We must not wait till they gain strength, or bring delectation with them and so become downright temptations. But we must cut them down at once; and this work is endless and continual. There is no resting over it or sleeping at it. Secondly, we must take great pains to foresee and avoid the occasions of this ruling passion. We must legislate for this, spend time upon it, and shape our daily life accordingly, so far as the relative duties of our station will permit us to do so. Thirdly, our strictness with ourselves on this subject must be persevering and intermitting. An interval will let all go at once, and we shall almost have to begin over again. And fourthly, as I have said before, we must penance ourselves for each willful carelessness and guilty fall, and our penances must be such as will make us feel them and fear them. They must go to the quick, if it be but an instant.

All this is not very encouraging, it must be admitted. But nothing is insurmountable to him who loves God. Beware of the delusion into which Satan will try to lead you. It is that of believing all this pain about our ruling passion a work fit only for saints, and belonging to the higher stages of the

spiritual life. This is one of the devil's choice axioms in almost everything. A wise man will distrust it whenever he
hears it. So far is it from being true in the present case, that
it would be more true to say that until this work has advanced
a good way towards its completion, the soul never can enter
the higher stages of the spiritual life at all. It is an indispensable work. It must be done; and moreover it must be done
now. It is true that some of the hardest work of the spiritual
life comes early on. This is an instance of it. Let nothing
mislead you. Prayer is tempting, and liberty of spirit is inviting. There is a dignity about austerity, which allures even
while it appals. The love of humiliations is attractive to the
enthusiastic heart, and a first taste of calumny makes us thirst
for more, as one savor of bitterness gives us an appetite, while
much of it clogs us with sickliness. But let nothing draw you
off either to the right hand or the left. There is your ruling
passion. That is the work; there is your vocation; there is
your grace, and at present not elsewhere. Visions and raptures, miracles and mortifications, and the bright lights of
contemplation, will not succeed in moving us one step on-
wards, unless we are the while keeping up a tedious running
fight with our ruling passion. I have seen many men who
have brought their ruling passion into very tolerable subjection: I never saw one yet whose ruling passion was indolence,
and who had made any satisfactory progress in bringing the
incorrigible unresisting rebel beneath the sway of grace. Yet
I do not say that even that enemy is invincible.

Chapter VIII

OUR NORMAL STATE

Everything in the world seems to have a peculiar beginning and a peculiar ending, with a normal state between them; and it is always this normal state which gives the truest character of a thing; for it expresses its nature and ruling idea. Yet the phenomena of the spiritual life appear to be of a different kind. It seems at first sight as if the spiritual life could have no normal state, except the being a perpetual dissatisfied progress, whose highest mark would always be a disappointment, as falling so far below even reasonable and legitimate expectation.

The greater part of its time and attention is taken up with mere preliminaries. What with means, vigilances, reparations, commandments, prohibitions and warnings, almost the whole of a spiritual book is occupied with studying the chart, rather than starting us on our voyage. The last chapter of many books gets no further than a fall launch. Then it seems as if we never did get into a fixed state, such as we could call normal or habitual. What follows no rule can give no rule; how then can it be normal? Fallen nature cannot go to God either in a groove or down an inclined plane, any more than men can march through an embarrassed country or fight a battle on mathematical lines.

Moreover, the experiences of the Saints are nothing more than a continually shifting scene of vicissitudes, and alternations of bright and dark, which baffle all induction, so various, perplexing, unruly and contradicting are they. Even as a panorama gradually unfolded, the spiritual life has no apparent unity, completeness or dramatic completion. As a jour-

ney it is up-hill; and its paths, therefore, like all mountain-
tracks, devious, winding and seemingly capricious. Hence there
is no feeling of working up to a table-land, where we may
hope to try other sinews and enjoy the level.

Yet for all this the spiritual life has a kind of normal state;
and we shall find the knowledge of it a help to us. It consists
in a perpetual interchange of three dispositions, sometimes
succeeding each other and reigning in turns, sometimes two
of them occupying the throne at once, and sometimes all three
at the same time exercising their influence conjoined. These
three dispositions are struggle, fatigue and rest; and each of
them requires an attendant satellite to give them light in the
night-time of their revolutions. Struggle requires patience. Fatigue must be proof against human respect. Rest must lean
upon mortification, for nowhere else can she safely sleep.
So I have now in this chapter to describe these three dispositions which make up our normal state; and in the three following chapters to consider patience, human respect and
mortification.

1) I must speak first of struggle. There seems theoretically
to be no difficulty in this idea; yet practically it is not an
easy one to realize. If the tradition of the Universal Church
is harmonious and conclusive on any one point concerning
the spiritual life, it is that it is a struggle, strife, combat, battle, warfare, whichever word you may choose. No one doubts
it. A man would be out of his senses who should doubt it.
Reason proves it, authority proves it, experience proves it.
Yet see what an awkward practical question for each one of
us rises out of this universal admission. At any moment we
may turn round upon ourselves and say, Is my religious life
a struggle? Do I feel it to be so? What am I struggling against?
Do I see my enemy? Do I feel the weight of his opposition?
If my life is not sensibly a fight, can it be a spiritual life
at all? Or rather am I not in one of the common delusions
of easy devotion and immortified effeminacy? If I am not fighting, I am conquered; and surely I can hardly be fighting,
and not know it. These are very serious questions to ask ourselves, and we ought to be frightened if at any time we cannot
obtain satisfactory answers to them. A good frightening! what

an excellent thing it is now and then in the spiritual life! Yet
in these times it seems as if we were all to be invalids in
holiness; for spiritual direction expends its efforts in producing a composing silence round about our sickbeds, as if the
great thing was not to awake us; and the little table near has
a tiny homeopathic opiate for each devout scruple as it rises,
to lay it to sleep again, as if it were not true that these scruples are often, like the irritability of a patient, signs of returning strength. Is simple convalescence from mortal sin to be
the model holiness of the nineteenth century, at least for luck-
less souls living in the world?

Oh, how one comes to love this great huge London, when
God has thrown us into it as our vineyard! The monster! It
looks so unmanageable, and it is positively so awfully wicked,
so hopelessly magnificent, so heretically wise and proud after
its own fashion. Yet after a fashion it is good also. Such a
multitudinous remnant who have never bowed the knee to Baal,
such numbers seeking their way to the light, such hearts grace-
touched, so much secret holiness, such supernatural lives, such
loyalty, mercy, sacrifice, sweetness, greatness! St. Vincent Ferrer
preached in its streets, and Father Colombière in its mews.
Do not keep down what is good in it, only because it is trying
to be higher. Help people to be saints. Not all who ask for
help really wish it, when it comes to be painful. But some
do. Raise ten souls to detachment from creatures, and to close
union with God, and what will happen to this monster city?
Who can tell? Monster as it is, it is not altogether unamiable.
It means well often, even when it is cruel. Well-meaning persons are unavoidably cruel. Yet it is often as helpless and
as deserving of compassion as it is of wrath and malediction.
Poor Babylon! would she might have a blessing from her unknown God, and that grace might find its way even into her
Areopagus!

But what does our struggle consist of? Mostly of five things;
and if there were time for it, we might write a chapter on
each of them. First, there is positive fighting. You see I am
letting you off easily, for some would say that the Christian
life is always a fight, even an actual battle; and that doctrine,
sought to be verified in your practice, might often be very

discouraging. I call it a struggle, and I make positive fighting
only one part of it. Secondly, there is taking pains, such as
pitching tents, cleaning arms, gathering fuel, cooking rations,
reconnoitering. Thirdly, there are forced marches. If I ask
you whether you are fighting, and you answer, No, but I am
footsore, I shall be quite content, and will not tease you any
more. I do not even object to an occasional bivouac; it all
comes into my large and generous sense of the word warfare.
Fourthly, there is a definite enemy. By this I do not mean
that you must always know your enemy when you see him.
A vice may come and play the spy in the clothes of a dead
virtue. But you must have an enemy in view, and know what
you are about with him. To invade the world, and then look
round for an enemy, is not the businesslike thing I understand
by the spiritual combat. Fifthly, there must be an almost continual sensible strain upon you, whichever of your military
duties you may be performing. If you feel no differently on
your battlefield from what you used to feel in the hay field,
you will not come up to my mark. These are the five things
of which our struggle consists.

But you will ask, what are the enemies against whom I
have to struggle? Seven; and the natural history of each of
them might occupy a little treatise by itself. We must now
dispatch them with a few words. First, we have to fight against
sin, not only with actual temptations in times when they press
us hard, but at all times with the habits which old sins have
wound so tightly and so fearfully around us, and with the
weakness which is a consequence of our past defeats. The
reason why men are so often surprised into grave sins is not
always to be found in the vehemence of the temptation, and
their want of attention to it at the time; but in their want
of attention to the general moral weakness which past and
even forgiven sin has left behind it.

Secondly, we must struggle with temptations, and we must
struggle with them with amazing courage, not as foes whose
lines we have to break, and then the country will be clear
before us, but as foes who will thicken as we advance. The
weakest come first, at least if we except those which tried
to hinder our giving ourselves up to God at the first. The

stronger come next. The robustness of our temptations seems to be in proportion to our growth in grace. The choicest are kept to the last. We shall one day have to give battle to the pretorians, to the devil's bodyguard; and probably it will be when we are lying, white and weak, on a deathbed. We must bear this in mind about temptations, else we shall make too much of our victories, and be disheartened by the smallness of their results. No victory that we gain is worth anything to the victories we have yet to gain. Still, a victory is always a victory.

Our third enemies are our trials; and our trials, like our temptations, grow as we advance. We are forcing our way into a more difficult country. We see evil where we did not see it before. Thus we have more things to avoid than formerly. We are attempting greater things, and climbing higher hills. All this has its encouraging side. But then in proportion to the greatness and the height, so is the difficulty. Then holiness has a whole brood of trials and troubles of its own, the like to which do not exist in the free-living, easy-mannered, fair-spoken world. Its interior trials are enough of themselves to keep a stout saint occupied all his life long. Scaramelli wrote an entire treatise on them. Some men have more, some less. What is necessary to remember is that we have not faced our worst yet. We must not cry victory when the battle is in truth but just begun.

Fourthly, we have to struggle against the changes of our own faults. After all, there is something very comfortable in a habit, when once the labor of acquiring it has been surmounted. We have got into a particular way, and it is a trouble to be put out of it. Improvements in tools only make them more awkward at first to old workmen. David felt so little at ease in Saul's armor, that he went back to his shepherd's dress and his favorite old sling. So it is with ourselves. We get into a certain way with ourselves, a certain hatred of ourselves, and a certain severity with ourselves. It was hard to get used to it; but we did so at last, and now do pretty well. Then by age or outward circumstances, or through some interior crisis, our faults change, and we have a new warfare to learn. Moreover, these changes of our faults are often imperceptible at the time. We are not conscious of what is going on. And as our characters sometimes turn right around, we may go on neglecting something which we ought to observe, and observing something we may now safely neglect; nay, we may even be playing the game of some new passion, while we think we are mortifying old ones. This is a perplexity. It annoys and distracts us in our struggle, even if it does nothing more. We must be prepared for it.

Teasing imperfections are our fifth enemy. The warfare against them is neither dangerous nor dignified—but wearing, harassing and annoying. Certain infirmities seem at times to be endowed with a supernatural vitality, and will not be put down even by our most earnest and persevering efforts. Habits of carelessness in saying office or Rosary, slight immortifications at meals, the use of particular expressions, matters connected with external composure and recollection, are all instances of this at times. It seems vexatious that we should be in bondage to such very little things, and it is a trial both of faith and temper. But God sometimes allows that we should entirely miss our aim when striking at them, in order that our devotion may be hidden from the eyes of others, who might wither it by praise, or that we ourselves should bear about a thorn in the flesh, as the Apostle did, to keep us humble and make us truly despise ourselves. Perhaps grace is often saved under the shadow of an imperfection; and there are many imperfections which are more obvious and humiliating than really guilty or unworthy in the sight of God. Under any circumstances, the tiresome struggle with our imperfections will not end, even with Extreme Unction. It will cease only with our breath, only when we are actually laid to rest in the bosom of our indulgent and heavenly Father.

The sixth object with which we have to struggle is the subtraction of divine light and sensible aid, whether it come upon us as a purifying trial or as a chastisement for unfaithfulness. This is like Jacob's struggle when he wrestled with God; or rather it is a wrestling with God, self, and the evil one, all at once. For no sooner does God withdraw His sensible assistance from us than the devil attacks us with renewed violence, and we ourselves give way to wounded self-love and to despondency. It is with us as with the Israelites in Egypt: we have more bricks to make, and the straw not found us as of old. At least it seems so. Yet God is with us when we know it not. We could not so much as hold on, if He were not so. But it is hard to realize this with a sheer and simple faith, when sensation and sentiment are quite the other way. Mercifully this struggle is not perpetual. It comes and goes; and if we could get ourselves to look on it beforehand as a significant visitation of mysterious love, we should be able to bear up against it more gently and more manfully than we do. Ordinarily we weary ourselves too much of violent effort, and then lie helpless and supine in a kind of petulant despair. Losing our temper with God is a more common thing in the spiritual life than many men suppose. It dashes back to earth many a rising prayer, and vitiates many a brave mortification. Happy they who can wrestle with God in uncomplaining prayer, in self-collected reverence, and yet by His grace with the vigorous will to have the better of Him.

This brings me to the seventh enemy with whom we have to struggle. It is familiarity; and familiarity especially with three things: prayer, Sacraments and temptations. As I have said before, to have relations with God is a very fearful thing. To love God is a bold and arduous thing. It was of His compassion that He made that to be of precept which was in itself so unspeakable a privilege. Yet it is hard to love warmly and tenderly, and to love reverently as well. Hence it is that, with so many, familiarity fastens upon love, and blights it. Familiarity in prayer consists of meditating without preparing, of using words without weighing them, of slouching postures, of indeliberate epithets, of peevish complaint, and of lightly making the petitions of saints our own. All this is an intolerable familiarity with the great majesty of God. It grows upon us. Use brings slovenliness, and slovenliness makes us profane. Familiarity with the Sacraments consists in going to Confession with a very cursory examination, and a mere flying act of contrition, making no thanksgiving afterwards and setting no store by our penance; as if we were privileged people, and were entitled to take liberties with the Precious Blood. With the Blessed Eucharist it consists of frequent Communion without leave, or forcing leave, or making no preparation, or careless thanksgiving, as if forsooth our whole life were to be considered adequate preparation and adequate thanksgiving, and that it shows liberty of spirit to be on such free and easy terms with the Adorable Sacrament. Familiarity with temptations is to lose our horror of their defiling character, to be remiss and dilatory in repelling them, to feel our loathing of them diminish, not to be sufficiently afraid of them, and to take for granted that we are so established in any particular virtue that our falling is out of all question. These familiarities grow upon us like the insidious approaches of sleep. We feel an increasing reluctance to throw them off and shake them from us. It will not be so much the thoughts of Hell and Purgatory, wholesome as they are, which will keep us right, as frequent meditation on the adorable attributes of God. Oh, if our flesh were but always pierced with the arrows of holy fear, how much more angelic would our lives become!

2) Such is our struggle, and such the seven principal enemies with whom we have to contend. The second disposition in which I make our normal state to reside is fatigue. This is something more than the pleasant feeling of being tired. Indeed if there is pleasure in it sometime, it is far more often a weary and oppressive pain. For the fatigue of which I speak is caused by the struggle which we have just been considering. It consists first of faintness, which the mere continuity of the combat superinduces; secondly, of disgust, a loathing for all sacred things; thirdly, of irritability, not only from frequent defeat, but from the harassing nature of the warfare; fourthly, of low spirits, especially when the arm of grace is less sensibly upholding us; and fifthly, of a feeling of the impossibility of persevering, which is not despair, because we do not cease our efforts, only we make them with the mere force of the grace-assisted will, not with the hope and energy of the heart. This fatigue may obviously be felt during a battle as well as after it: and as we may both offend God, and also do very foolish things injurious to our own interests, under the heavy hand of this fatigue, it is important for us to get a clear idea of it, and to investigate its causes.

These causes are seven in number, and each of them is

accompanied by its own peculiar trials, dangers and temptations. The first cause is the constant opposition to nature which the spiritual life implies. I am not speaking so much of voluntary mortification, though that also must be taken into the account. But everything we do in the spiritual life is contrary to the will and propensions of our corrupt nature. There is no pleasure to which we dare yield an unlimited assent. There is no spiritual enjoyment which is not more or less suffering to poor nature. What a joy is prayer; yet to nature mortification even is less irksome than prayer. Our tastes, wishes, inclinations, instincts, what we seek and what we shun, are all more or less thwarted by the effort to be holy. When nature offers us any assistance, we doubt her and suspect her intentions, and when we use the force she supplies, we do it in a harsh, ungraceful manner toward her. Her very activity, which is the making of so many of us, we regard almost as an enemy, hurrying us as it does out of the calm presence of God, and into endless indiscretions. The custody of the senses, even such an amount of it as is an absolute duty, is a bondage which nature is ill able to bear. In a word, in proportion as grace takes possession of us, we grow out of sympathy with our own very nature, and in some respects with the outward creation generally. This becomes visible to the eye when it reaches the point which it does often attain in saints and ecstatic persons. Their illnesses, sufferings and apparently unnatural valetudinarian states are simply the result of the supernatural and mystical character of their lives. As mystical theologians teach, the nutritive, nervous and cerebral systems are all deranged by the entire possession which grace has taken of the soul, especially in those whose lives are contemplative and interior. But this begins in a slight measure, as soon as we commence the spiritual life in good earnest, and it must obviously produce fatigue. The mere rowing against the stream perpetually must make us stiff and tired. And not only can there be no peace with nature, but, except in an ecstasy, no truce either; and from what the Saints tell us, it appears that nature takes a terrific vengeance on them for their ecstasies, when they are passed.

Another cause of fatigue is in the uncertainty in which temptation so often leaves us, as to whether we have consented or not. To walk blindfolded or to find our way in the dark is in itself a tiring thing. Clear light mitigates fatigue. But when we are uncertain whether we have offended God or not, whether such or such an action was against our vows or resolutions, we lose our elasticity. If we have really conquered, we have no sense of victory to buoy us up; and if we were vanquished, we should be better able to face the disaster manfully, if there was no doubt about it. But as a mile's walk with the sun in our faces or the dust in our eyes is longer than ten without such annoyances, so is it with this uncertainty which temptation casts over us in spite, as it goes away. It tires and unnerves us.

A third cause of fatigue is to be found in the daily monotonous renewal of the combat. Sameness is wearisome in itself. This is in great measure the wretchedness of imprisonment, however comfortable and roomy our dungeon may be. The sun shines in at our window, the morning breeze comes there, and the little birds sing without; and for a moment our waking thoughts do not realize where we are or what we have to encounter. But when we are fully aware that we have another day before us of uncheckered monotonous confinement, the soul sinks within us, forlorn and weary, even after long hours of refreshing sleep. So it is in the spiritual life. Is it to be always combat? Is the pressure never to be taken off? Is the strain never to be relaxed? Is the hold never to be let go? And when we are obliged to answer ourselves with the simple "Never," this hourly renewal of the old, old strife becomes almost insupportable. Take any one besetting infirmity, for instance want of government of the tongue, or unworthy pleasure in eating and drinking, how jaded and disgusted we become long before we have made any sensible impression upon the strength of the evil habit!

A fourth case of fatigue is in the little progress we make in a long time. Success hinders fatigue. The excitement carries us on, and supplies fresh forces to nature, enabling her to draw on the secret funds of her constitution, which, otherwise, nothing but the death-struggle would have brought out. On the contrary, defeat is akin to lassitude. Besides this, slow walking is more tiring than fast. Men hurry up and down a short quarterdeck, because a funeral pace makes them low-spirited and footsore. These are all types of what the spirit feels. Our small progress deprives us of all natural encouragement. For our minds must be thoroughly saturated with supernatural principles, always to realize that one evil thought repelled, one angry humor smartly chastised, one base envy well warred down, one thorough *Deo gratias* in a piece of ill luck, may be really hundreds of leagues of progress; and each of them worth more than the whole world to us, as something which pleases God, and which God alone has enabled us to do. Unfortunately we usually realize our supernatural principles most when we feel fatigue least; and it is for this reason that our slow progress is so wearisome. A calm at sea is fatiguing, even though no physical effort is called for on our part. To scale Parnassus in the face of a blustering wind and a drenching rain is less tiring than to rock idly and helplessly for a day in the Gulf of Corinth, with beauty enough in sight to feed mind and eye for weeks.

The universality of the vigilance which is required in the spiritual life is a fifth source of fatigue. We have not only to be always on the alert, but our watchfulness has such a wide extent of ground to cover. Everything else in the spiritual life we can concentrate, except our vigilance; and that we cannot concentrate. The nearest approach to it is the practice of particular examen of conscience, quite one of the most helpful and operative practices of the spiritual life. But that is not in reality so much a concentration of our vigilance, as that the fixing our attention very earnestly on one fault helps to keep us awake, and makes our eyes quick to see anything stir and our ears sharp for the slightest sound. And who will say that particular examen is not fatiguing in itself? He is a happy man who keeps to it without missing, for as much as one single moon. Truly vigilance is a tiring thing in itself: what then must it be, when we add to it universality and uninterruptedness? Yet such is the vigilance the world, the flesh and the devil exact from us continually. Liberty of spirit is a mighty boon. It dispenses with many things. But woe be to him who dreams that it dispenses him from watchfulness!

A sixth cause of fatigue is in the mere wear and tear of
duration. A light work will tire, if it is sufficiently prolonged;
and the work of the spiritual life is simply unending, and
the pressure of it continuous. It is true that this fatigue is
easier to bear than some of the others, because there is something consoling in the thought that we have persevered so far.
Nevertheless it forms one of the difficulties of perseverance.
For while we feel fatigued at the present moment, the future
presents us with no other prospect. A lifelong vista of work
stretches before us: long or short as it may please God; still
always work. There is no retiring on a pension or half-pay
from the military service of the spiritual life.

Seventhly, fatigue is generated by fatigue itself. We get tired
of being tired. And this produces a sort of torpor most dangerous to the soul. We become indifferent to things. We grow
callous to the feeling of our own unworthiness, to the horror
of sin, to the glorious desirableness of God and of union with
Him. We are like a broken musical instrument. We give no
sound when we are fingered. There is something in this state
analogous to the swept and garnished heart of which our Saviour
speaks, into which seven devils might easily enter, worse than
the first who had been ejected from it. The only safety in
this kind of fatigue is more occupation. We must burden still
more the already overburdened spirit. This remedy requires
faith. Nothing but snow itself will draw the frost out of the
bitten limbs of the sealer of the Antarctic. It is a cruel cure,
but a specific. So it is with this tiring of being tired. If you
do not load it more, even to making it restless, angry, rebellious, if you will—in a short time you will be on the brink
of seriously throwing up the service of God altogether.

These are our seven fatigues; and I am almost afraid of
what I have written. I fear lest it should discourage you. Alas!
it is not the truest kindness to throw a false rose-colored light
over the harsh and rocky portions of the spiritual landscape.
Man must not represent as wholly ease, what God has made
in part most difficult. But you must remember, this is only
one side of the picture, and the dark side. I have had to dwell
upon it here, because this was the place for it; and I have
put it at the worst, for I have assumed throughout that God

uniformly subtracted sensible sweetness and interior consolation from you all the while. Yet this is hardly ever so, perhaps never, and certainly never with any souls to whom He has not first given immense gifts of courage, fortitude and endurance, or a peculiar attraction to walk by faith only. When I come to the chapter on Spiritual Idleness, I shall show you how to avoid the dangers with which this fatigue is fraught. Meanwhile I will say no more than this, first, that the spiritual joys of holiness far more than counterbalance its fatigue, and secondly, that whatever you do, I counsel you not to rush from the momentary and apparent dullness and uninterestingness of the things of God to seek refuge and consolation in creatures. The consequences of such a step are dreadful. I had almost said irremediable. But I have seen things which show that it is not quite irremediable. I hope no mistake of any kind in the spiritual life is irremediable. The case of a tepid religious has been quoted as such. But we know that even such cases are curable, because they have been cured. And what can be incurable if they are not?

3) The third disposition which makes up our normal state is *rest,* seemingly the very opposite of the fatigue of which I have just spoken. But we must not imagine this rest to consist either in a cessation from struggle, or a deliverance from fatigue. This is contrary to the idea of the spiritual life. The rest of which I speak is a truer rest, a higher rest, a rest of altogether a different kind. It has these five characteristics. First, it is supernatural. Tired nature cannot supply it. It were no rest at all if it came from any fountain short of Heaven. If it comes from any human heart, it can only be from the Sacred Heart of God made Man. Secondly, it lasts but for a little while at a time. It comes and goes like an angel's visitation. Yet, thirdly, brief as its visit is, its effects are lasting. It refreshes and animates us in a way which no earthly consolation can even imitate, much less rival. It is food in the strength of which we can go all the way to the mountain of God. Fourthly, it is very peaceful. It produces no excitement. It moves away none of our existing devotions or spiritual exercises. It is no disturbing force to our vocation, no overruling impulse to our discretion. And last of all, it unites us

to God: and what is that union but a participation of His eternal tranquility, a foretaste of the Sabbath in His paternal lap forevermore?

In trying to draw out for you the varieties of this welcome and beautiful rest, I must caution you not to be cast down if I make it consist in things which seem far above your present attainments. The fact is that these high things are begun in you. It may still be with them their day of small beginnings. Nevertheless they are begun; and with them comes the gift of rest, to increase as they increase, but to be from the very first a substantial gift of our compassionate Father who is in Heaven.

This divine rest consists first in detachment from creatures. As we grow in holiness our attachments to creatures weaken, and those that remain riveted are riveted in God. It is not that sanctity lies in unfeelingness. Look at St. Francis de Sales stretched on the floor of the room where his mother had just died, and sobbing as if his heart was broken. Strong angels look at the prostrate saint without upbraiding; for his grief is a human holiness rather than a human weakness. Not for a moment, said he, in all that tempest of grief was his will removed one line's breadth from the sweet sovereign will of God. All that is irregular, earthly and inordinate in our attachment fades out. Nay, we are sensibly conscious to ourselves of an actual decay of all strong feelings, of whatever kind, in our hearts. And the absence of these is rest; for strong earthly feelings are a tyranny.

Secondly, we have now no worldly end in view; and thus there is nothing proximate to disquiet us. What success can we have to look forward to? Is it a point in riches we would fain reach? Or a summit on which an ambitious imagination has often placed us in our daydreams? Or a scheme that we are burning to realize? Such things belong not to the spiritual. They know nothing of them; except that they have been burned by them in former times. They have scathed them, and passed on. Not even works of mercy now can be ends of themselves, ends in which to rest. They are but stepping-stones we lay down for God's glory and His angels to pass over the earth and bless its misery. There may be rest in straining to a supernatural end, or the very strain may be more welcome than the most luxurious rest. But there can be no rest for those who are straining after a worldly end, blameless even if perchance it be.

Thirdly, holiness brings us rest, because it delivers us even from spiritual ambition, in any of its various forms. As I have already said, the inordinate pursuit of virtue is itself a vice, and the anxious desire to be speedily rid of all our imperfections is a delusion of self-love. To desire supernatural favors is almost a sin; to ask for supernatural tokens is nearly always an indiscretion. Present grace is not only the field of our labor; it is also the haven of our rest. We must trust God and be childlike with Him even in our spiritual progress. We must make a bed of our vileness and a pillow of our imperfections; and nothing can soil us while humility is our rest. Ambition is not the less wrong, nor greediness the less repulsive, because they are spiritual. When God feeds us with His hand, is that a time for eagerness? When spiritual ambition is mortified, not into indifference, but into patience, prayer and calm hope, then there is rest.

One consequence of all these dispositions is a readiness to die; and this is in itself a fourth source of rest. What is there to keep us? Why should we linger on? Dare we pray with St. Martin to stay and work if we are necessary to God's people? Are we so foolish as to dream we have a mission, which is to delay us like Mary after the Ascension, or the Evangelist St. John till the first century was run out? When we are going on a journey, and are not ready, we are all bustle and heat. Preparations have to be made, our last orders given, and our farewells said. But when all is done, and it is not time yet, we sit down and rest. The rooms do not look like home, because we are going, and our attachments are packed up, like the works, merits and forgiven sins of a dying man. If we have any feeling besides that of rest, it is rather impatience. But in a spiritual man impatience to die would be no trifling immortification. Consequently the readiness to die, without impatience, is rest. The contented animal that stretches itself in the shade of the noonday field does not rest with greater sensible enjoyment than the immortal soul that is bravely detached from mortal things.

It belongs to our nature to incline to rest in ends, and not in means. This opens out to us a fifth source of rest. For everything is an end, no matter how transient, if only it be referred to God. Indeed it is an end in a sense in which no merely earthly thing can be so; for it participates in the end of all ends and ultimate rest of all things, God Himself. Hence our very struggle is rest, our very fatigue rest; for they are both made up of countless things each of which is in itself a resting place and an end. Has not everyone felt at times, only too rarely, the joy steal over him that he has no wish or will before him? Nothing is unfulfilled, because God is everywhere. He feels for God and has found Him; and so he has nothing to seek, nothing to desire. Possible evils are allowed to present themselves to his imagination, only that he may realize more utterly the gladness of his complete in- difference to them. He is at rest. Earth has hold of none of his heartstrings. The whole world is full of ends to him. He can lie down anywhere; for everything is a bed, because he refers all things to God. If this kind of rest would sometimes last a little longer—but God knows best. Even the wish would break the deliciousness of that heavenly rest.

Humility furnishes us with a sixth source of rest. And this in two ways. First of all, it makes us contented, contented with our infirmities, though not contented with ourselves. God forbid this last should ever be! Thus it makes us unanxious, ungrasping, childlike and calm; and there is rest in the very sound of all those words. Secondly, it brings us rest in an- other way. For it not only subdues us by keeping us down in the sense of our own nothingness, but it exhilarates us by pouring the pure light of grace around us and making us feel how entirely we owe everything to God. Did anyone ever see a humble man with an unquiet heart? Except when some storm of grief or loss swept over him, never! Humility is rest, sweet rest and safe, and which leaves no reproaches or misgivings behind, and it is a rest within the reach of the lowest of us.

There is a seventh source of rest, of which it is hard to speak, because words cannot tell it. They only stand for signs, which give some idea of it. It is the rest which comes from the bare thought of God, or rather which is itself the bare thought of God. Sometimes, in a beautiful climate, we come upon a scene, which by its surpassing beauty so satisfies mind, heart and senses, that we sit entranced, taking it in without understanding it, and resting in the simple enjoyment of the sight. Thus for a while a man may sit amid the folds of Etna, beneath a shady tree, on the marvelous mountain shelf of Taormina, and look out upon the scene. Everything that wood and water, rock and mountain, dazzling sky and translucent air can do, with the grand spirit of old history brooding over all, is there. It cannot be analyzed or explained. We are taken in the nets of a beauty which masters us; and the sheer thought of it is a joy without thought for hours. This is a poor way of typifying the rest which is in the glorious, overshadowing thought of God. It is a self-sufficing rest, not only because He is almighty, all-holy and all-wise, nor because He is our own near and fatherly God, but simply and sheerly because He is God. Words will make it no clearer. God gives it to us sometimes and we know it; and seen through it, brighter than Sicilian air, more limpid than Arethusa's fountain, our struggle and fatigue look fair and delectable in that heavenly medium. But in whatever measure God visits us with this sort of light, true it is that such is the normal state of our spiritual life—struggle and fatigue and not only after these but also during these, there remaineth a sabbath for the people of God: for they rest in the languors of love here, till their rest deepens into His eternal bosom hereafter.

Chapter IX

PATIENCE

The three dispositions which compose the normal state of the spiritual life, struggle, fatigue and rest, are each of them beset with a darkness and difficulty of their own, requiring attendant virtues to enlighten them. Struggle obviously requires patience; fatigue is only safely endured when singleness of purpose secures us from human respect; and rest is in need of courageous mortification. In this chapter, therefore, we must speak of patience.

Is it not true that we do not ordinarily appreciate the importance of this virtue in the spiritual life? We readily admit the importance of prayer, examen, mortification and spiritual reading, as means of holy living and as forming a necessary portion of the ascetical exercises of each day; but it is to be doubted whether we allow its proper place to the exercise of patience. I am speaking especially to persons living in the world; and whose holiness consequently is of a more hidden character than that of religious, external circumstances concentrating it within, and not providing it with the almost hourly beautiful developments in which it would display itself with graceful freedom in conventional life. I say that the holiness of a holy person in the world is of a more hidden character than that of a religious; and it would seem at first sight as if this gave the secular the advantage. God forbid! If external circumstances make holiness in the world more hidden, and so form it into an interior spirit, the religious enjoys the inestimable privilege of obedience, which is a continual supernatural pressure upon the soul, training it in the most delicate interior spirit, and for the absence of which nothing else can compensate, and which is unlike any obedience a secular can pay to his director. But I make much of the fact, which both experience and the published lives of holy persons attest, that the holiness of a person in the world is more hidden; because it has sometimes been the fashion to write spiritual books in a strain of hyperbole and exaggeration, quite alien to the calm discretion and sober moderation which is needful in handling such matters, and the upshot of which is to represent all holiness to be in the cloister, and all the world beside a reprobate mass. Besides being unsound doctrine, the exaggeration is foolish in every way, and leads infallibly to a low standard of monastic perfection; just as in the days of Tronson, worldly priests tried to put the whole burden of sacerdotal perfection upon religious, in order that their own lives might be more easy and more free.

There is hardly any subject in the spiritual life more unfairly dealt with than this; yet if we refer to older writers, especially the three great Jesuit ascetics, Platus, Alvarez de Paz and Da Ponte, there is no portion of spiritual theology in which the principles are more clearly laid down than here. Monastic perfection is something far higher than any which can be aimed at in the world. Yet if we were to tell a nun that certain practices of perfection, which as a matter of fact are practiced by seculars, were only fit for the convent, we should at once lower her standard of her own obligations; and it would be much if nature did not get the better of grace, and cause her to settle down in a level of life no higher than that of holy seculars in society. So, if we represent the perfection attainable by a secular priest as the property of a religious, we injure at once both the religious and the secular, by lowering their standards. The religious recognizes in the portrait of a perfect secular the picture of a perfect monk, and the secular does not recognize himself at all. And, as Tronson shrewdly remarks, all this is the more mischievous because spiritual writers have often observed that, while it is a sign of a relaxed religious order to run down perfection in the world and among the secular clergy, because of the obvious consequences to the order itself of allowing this doctrine, the secular clergy, "far from testifying," I am using

Tronson's words, "this esteem of their own vocation, are often the first to combat it. If you do not believe me, make the experiment yourselves. Put forward an ecclesiastical maxim which tends to establish you [he is speaking to secular priests] in perfection, whether it concerns detachment from the world, or the flight from worldliness, or the condemnation of the world's maxims, to which ecclesiastics are more particularly and more strictly obliged, and you will see that ecclesiastics themselves will be the first to oppose you; so that they who ought to defend these truths, and who are engaged by their state to maintain them with the utmost vigor, are those who will contest them with the greatest heat and vehemence. See what we are come to!"[1] The same principles are laid down by Alvarez de Paz,[2] by Da Ponte[3] and by Placus.[4] This last writer says that the Church is made up of three orders, laymen, religious and clerics; and he says of this last, that "it has all the disadvantages, without the advantages of the other two states. For clerics have the same obligation of attaining perfection which religious have, and without doubt even a greater one, because of the excellence of their ministry, the divinity of the Sacraments and the government of souls. Yet they have not the helps which religious have, nor the influx of a richer grace." All these writers, with the exception of Tronson, were Jesuits: I quote one more, also a Jesuit, as spiritual theology has been one of their many excellences, and their writers are generally the most clear and defined, uniting science with their unction. It is F. Surin.[5] He says of the condition of a secular priest that his "state demands all the purity of life of religious and of solitaries; and the priest would delude himself extremely, who, to excuse the

---

1. *Entretiens,* tome ii., p. 11.
2. *De Vita Spirituali,* 1. ii., *Pars v. de Statu Clericali.*
3. *De Perfectione Ecclesiasticorum,* being the first of the seven tracts of the fourth vol. *de Perfectione.*
4. *De Bono Status Religiosi,* lib. i., cap. xxxvii. *Comparatio status religiosi cum ordine clericorum simplicium.* See also Walter Hilton, the *English Carthusians's Treatise to a Devout Man of Secular Estate,* teaching him how to lead a spiritual life therein. *London, 1659, near the little north door of St. Paul's.*
5. *Lettres Spirituelles.* Lett. xiv.

little care he takes to aim at the highest quality *(la plus haute saintété)*, when anyone speaks to him of a point of perfection, such as recollection, prayer, mortification, and zeal for the glory of God, should say that that is good for a Carthusian, a Capuchin, or a Jesuit, but that for himself he does not aim so high."

But in truth these great Jesuit ascetics were not in any way departing from the spiritual tradition of the more ancient Doctors. They have not got beyond the grand light of the Church, St. Thomas, the angel of the schools; and he professes to give us the tradition of Ambrose, Chrysostom and the older Fathers. He who defended the religious state and its perfection in his wonderful tract on Perfection says, "If then a religious is unordained, as in the case with lay brothers, it is manifest that the pre-eminence of order excels as to dignity. For by Holy Orders a man is deputed to the most dignified ministries, to serve Christ in the Sacrament of the Altar. *For this a greater sanctity is required than even the religious state demands;* for as Dionysius says,[1] the monastic order ought to follow the sacerdotal orders, and after their imitation ascend to divine things. Hence, other things being equal, a cleric in Holy Orders, when he does anything contrary to sanctity, sins more gravely than a religious who is not in Holy Orders, although the lay religious is bound to regular observances, and the clerk is not."[2]

I have dwelt upon this because unless we have our first principles clear on the subject of perfection in and out of the religious state, nearly everything that is said is capable of being taken the wrong way; and it has much to do with the subject of patience. For what I want to say is that while obedience, community life, exact observance of primitive rule, fidelity to the original spirit of the canonized founder and above all the practice of evangelical poverty, put the perfection

---

1. *In cap vi. Eccles. Hierarch.*
2. *Ad quod* (the priesthood, diaconate and subdiaconate) *requiritur major sanctitas interior quam requirat etiam religionis status. Quia, sicut Dionysius dicit, Monasticus ordo debet sequi sacerdotales ordines, et ad eorum imitationem ad divina ascendere. (Secunda Secundae. Quaest.* clxxxiv. *Art.* viii. in which he undertakes to show that a religious is more perfect than an archdeacon.)

of religious far above the reach of seculars *in kind,* there can be no question or comparison between them at all as *to degree.* A person may have a higher *degree* of a lower *kind* of perfection than another. Theologians say that probably some saints on earth have loved God more than some angels in Heaven. This illustrates my meaning; for no one will say that an angel in Heaven is not higher in kind than a saint upon earth. Thus a man in the world may attain a higher degree of perfection in his kind than a certain religious may have attained in the cloister in *his* kind; and so have corresponded more faithfully to grace, and be more acceptable to God. To deny this seems to be a simple confusion of principles. Men who dispute about it must be using words in two different senses. The thing itself is surely self-evident. Is there anyone who would rather be a very ordinary religious than a very holy secular?[1]

Furthermore, what obedience is to religious (not all that it is, but the functions it performs), that patience is to seculars. Independently of its directly supernatural virtue, obedience sanctifies the religious for four reasons principally: because it comes from without, because the religious has no control over its requirements, because he must be ready at all moments, and because it involves the giving up of his own will and way. Now all these four offices patience discharges in its measure to the secular. The circumstances which exact its exercise come upon us from without; we have no control over them; they may come upon us at all moments; and they

---

1. St. Thomas may be said to have exhausted the subject of comparative states of perfection in the last seven questions of the *Secunda Secundae.* Spiritual books are mostly written by religious, and for the use of religious. Hence it is that St. Thomas' doctrine on the perfection of the Secular Clergy is so often, not misrepresented, but simply pretermitted; although the non-recognition of it, injurious as it is to the best interests of the clergy, is almost equally so to the religious as lowering their standards of monastic perfection. A religious who is a priest has an obligation to a double perfection; yet loosely written books sometimes refer what belongs to his sacerdotal perfection to the obligations of his monastic state. The practice of evangelical poverty is a height unapproachable by seculars, to say coining of the sanctification of vowed obedience. The superiority of the religious state over the secular is immeasurable; but, I repeat, the difference is one of *kind,* not of *degree.*

always involve the sacrifice or the mortification of our own will and way. I do not say that patience equals religious obedience; but that it is itself the obedience of seculars. It is necessary to their perfection. What obedience is to the higher and different perfection of monks and nuns, that patience is to the indubitably lower, yet genuine perfection of men in the world.

A few words must be said of all the four exercises of patience, patience with others, patience with self, patience with our director and patience with God.

We may say that, partly from our own badness and partly from theirs, all mankind, far and near, kindred and strangers, are a trial to our patience in some way or other. If those who are above us exercise our patience, our natural inclination is immediately to revolt, and we are quite as much kept in subordination by human respect, by fear and the consequence to our own interests, as by the real grace of patience. Even when we obey we take the bloom off our obedience by a sulky manner, or by a sullen word, or a downcast look, or a complaint to others, or a general reproachful sadness of demeanor by which we manage to make superiors unhappy and disquieted, and to show them what an exercise of authority they are putting forward when they constrain us to what we do not like. The sanctifying power of half our life is lost by this single ungracefulness. If the trial of our patience comes from those below us, we sometimes proudly exhibit our sense of their inferiority. We crush them by a reprimand, or wither them by a look, or sting them with coldness. If the trial comes from our equals, how often do we offend by rudeness, abruptness, unkindliness and a want of mutual respect! When we are engaged with others in any kind of work, or are constantly in society with others, our patience is often exercised. We encounter stupid, passionate or importunate people; and we do not look at each of these meetings as a gift from God, who is going to watch how we behave and visit us accordingly. Almost every circumstance in life has a manner, time, place and degree, by which it tries our patience; and it is not too much to say, especially in the earlier stages of the devout life, that this exercise does more for us than fast or discipline; and that when we can go through with it for love of the sweetness of Jesus, we are not far from interior holiness.

The blessings which result from this practice in the interior life are manifold. The English spirit of always standing up for our rights is fatal to perfection. It is the opposite of that charity of which the Apostle says that it seeks not its own. Now this spirit is admirably mortified by the exercise of patience. It involves also a continual practice of the presence of God; for we may be come upon at any moment for an almost heroic display of good temper. And it is a short road to unselfishness; for nothing is left to self. All that seems to belong most intimately to self, to be self's private property, such as time, home and rest, are invaded by these continual trials of patience. The family is full of such opportunities, and the sanctity of marriage abounds with them. It may be added, for it is no slight thing, that there is not a spiritual exercise less open to delusion than is this, though the subtle, disheartening Guilloré fills three whole chapters with them.

In truth there are certain admonitions which are necessary concerning this exercise of patience with others. It is a practice which requires a long apprenticeship, so that it is in itself an exercise of patience. To be impatient because they are not patient is no uncommon exhibition in spiritual persons. Progress in the acquirement of this virtue is not easily perceived, as in the substantial self-denial there is often much inward trouble and heat. Hence we must take comfort and go on making efforts. It is a matter in which every effort is in reality an advance. There are also particular times when we must be very cautious not to be irritable and impatient. After long prayer, great sweetness in meditation, or an unusually fervent Communion, or, indeed, any spiritual effort, we are extremely liable to lose our temper, partly through a law of our physical constitution, and party because the devil wants to repair the losses we have just made him suffer. We must be content, therefore, at first with material patience, irritable patience. We must not be vexed or cast down about it. Something better will come of it presently. It is well to accuse ourselves of the slightest fault against patience at confession, to make frequent acts of contrition about it during the day, and to cast many a loving look at our Crucifix, that touching emblem of the patience of God. Strange to say, *notwithstanding God is impassible,* there is something peculiarly Godlike in the virtue of patience. If it is true of any one grace, besides charity, it is true of patience, that it is the beauty of holiness.

But if it is a hard thing to be patient with others, how much harder is it to be patient with ourselves! Indeed, so much is this branch of the virtue neglected that we seem almost to think its opposite a merit, as if impatience with self were a heroism or a meritorious mortification. There is a vast difference between hatred of self and impatience with self. The more of the first we have the better, and the less of the last. Once let us surmount the difficulty of being patient with ourselves and the road to perfection lies clear and unobstructed before us.

But what do we mean by impatience with self? Fretting under temptations, and mistaking their real nature, and their real value also. In actual sin, being more vexed at the lowering of our own self-esteem than being grieved at God's dishonor. In being surprised and irritated at our own want of self-control because of our subjection to unworthy habits. Being depressed because we experience lively movements of anger or give way to fits of sadness, even where, as is possible, there is no sin, either in the one or the other. Being annoyed with our own want of sensible devotion, as if it was at all in our own power, and as if patience in dryness was not just the very way to earn sweetness and spiritual consolation. Being disquieted because we do not find the remedies we have applied to our faults act as we expected, forgetting that they need time, and that we often put secret obstacles in the way. To these symptoms we may add a sort of querulousness about the want of spiritual progress, as if we were to be saints in a month.

All these dangerous symptoms of impatience with self come from one or other of four causes, and it is there we must seek them, and kill them in the nest, before they are able to fly. Verily they are birds of prey to our spiritual life. The first cause is self-love, which is unable to brook the disappointment of not seeing ourselves in times of trial come out beautiful, erect and admirable. The second is want of humility, which causes us not to appreciate our own real meanness, or to comprehend the incapacitating effects of our past sins. The third is the absence of a true estimate of the huge difficulties of the spiritual life, and therefore of the necessity of an utter divorce with the world and a formal abjuration of its maxims, before we can really give ourselves to God. The fourth is an obstinate disinclination to walk by faith. We fret under it. We want, nature wants, self-love wants, everything in short, except faith itself, wants—to see, to know, to be sure, to reason, to ascertain that success is inevitable.

To be patient with self is an almost incalculable blessing, and the shortest road to improvement, as well as the quickest means by which an interior spirit can be formed within us, short of that immediate touch of God which makes some souls interior all at once. It breeds considerateness and softness of manner toward others. It disinclines us to censoriousness, because of the abiding sense of our own imperfections. It quickens our perception of utterest dependence on God and grace, and produces at the same time evenness of temper and equality of spirits, because it is at once an effort, and yet a quiet sustained effort. It is a constant source of acts of the most genuine humility. In a word, by it we act upon self from without, as if we were not self, but self's master, or self's guardian angel. And when this is done in the exterior life as well as the interior, what remains in order to perfection?

There are various means by which we may cultivate this patience with ourselves. Frequent meditation on our own nothingness is a great help to it; and an especial dwelling upon any meanness and vileness and deceit of our past lives, the reconsideration of which can be attended with no danger because of the intrinsic disgust and cutting shame which the details of such meanness awake within us. When we hear of some great crime, we may consider that we might have done it ourselves, or perhaps worse, were it not for grace. We must be careful also at confession, and in preparing for it, not to mistake self-vexation for real contrition: and then we may persevere in asking for patience in a special way after Communion. We must try, it is very hard, but time wins its way through hard things, to rejoice in all encounters which show us our need of grace, and the possibility of dreadful sins which we always carry about with us. Neither must we be in a hurry to forget past sin and to force our way into the sunshine. If God gives us quite a depressing sense of sin, let us cherish it and stagger on beneath the burden. Blessed is any weight, however overwhelming, which God has been so good as fasten with His own hand upon our shoulders. In a word, patience with self is almost a condition of spiritual progress; and St. Catherine of Genoa is its patron saint.

From patience with self we must pass to patience with our director. Patience with superiors is of the essence of religious obedience; and a director is something like a superior without the overawing insignia of authority; but our obedience to him is and ought to be limited, and we may transfer it elsewhere any day without sin, if not without indiscretion.

Now we have first of all to subject our understanding to our director, and this in many ways and under many different circumstances. He often differs from us in our own view of ourselves, and puts a low price upon what we think rare and precious. He keeps us back when we are for bounding forward, and he spurs us on when we wish to sit down and rest, and admire the view which we have now climbed high enough to see. He persists that something we make much of is a delusion, and he will not agree with us as to what is really our ruling passion. He changes our line, and we think he is making a serious mistake with us, and while we are detailing to him some supposed inspiration, he looks cold and distracted, and as if he wished we would go away. There is surely ample room for the understanding to practice patience here.

The subjection of our will is not less trying. He thwarts our desires and gives us no reason but his own will, so that there are many things we repent we ever asked him. He refuses us austerities and extra-Communions, neither will he confer with us as often as we wish, or for as long time as our own self-love deems reasonable for persons of such importance to the Church as we are. He will not let us read the books we like to read, and he is provokingly slow in making up his mind on questions we have laid before him. When self-will has patiently gone through this, will it be far from being tamed into Christian docility?

We must be patient also with him when he is evidently mortifying us. This is not so hard, because it is more direct. He mortifies us by refusing us consolations, by giving us absolution without a word, when we have expected a conference, and are full of words which we want to pour out, and yet to let it seem as if he drew them out. He mortifies us by sending us to Communion without absolution, and otherwise ridiculing our scruples, by speaking harshly to us with manifest exaggeration, and by keeping us under monotonous mortifications which have long ceased to be mortifications, till we are almost wearied out, in other words, till they have become mortifications again, and of a better and more killing kind.

But it is a harder task to be patient with him when we are in doubt, half suspecting he is mortifying us, and yet not being quite sure whether it is not laziness or indifference. This takes place when he seems, almost studiously, to take no interest in us, and treats us as an annoyance to him, or when he contradicts, interrupts, or appears purposely to misunderstand us. At other times he says he quite forgets our case, and bids us repeat it, and looks as if he were making no effort to listen even then. Another while he contradicts himself, counter-orders things and gives opposite advice different weeks. Then he hints he would have us leave him, and when we refuse, submits to keep us with a languid and inattentive air.

But he may try our patience harder still. He may be, and often is, plainly in fault. Impatience, discourtesy and irritability are always faults, whatever amount of extenuation may be pleaded in their behalf. He may be guilty of occasional acts of substantial unkindness, and at times he may be destitute of the grace to bear with our weaknesses and to sympathize with our sorrows. Opportunities may offer when it becomes a duty on his part to make exertions and to take trouble for us, and he refuses to do so. Or he may visit us hastily with the fatal punishment of leaving us to direct ourselves, because we have been surprised into taking ourselves in hand, when we thought him listless and forgetful, and all the while he was praying and saying Mass for us. In all this he is clearly wrong, and yet we must have patience with him. And if direction were altogether a supernatural thing, patience would be easier, because it would be dignified. But with the great bulk both of penitents and directors, direction is, and ought to be, and ought never to pretend not to be, almost as much natural as supernatural.

We have still to speak of patience with God. The very word sounds strange. Let it not breed familiar or irreverent thoughts. It is a very serious question, and must be approached with the profoundest respect, remembering of what an infinite majesty and unfathomable condescension it is of which with all abasement we are venturing to speak. Again and again I have said, it is an awful thing to have dealings with Almighty God. His favors are our fears. And yet let us think of this with the intensest filial and confiding love. Oh, that we could always speak reverently of Him whom we do far more than either fear or love, whom we worship as our God!

God condescends to try our patience, who are dust and ashes, in various ways; and some of them are peculiar, or belong chiefly, to the spiritual life. His ordinary providence, therefore, the ways of His justice, and the darkness of His decrees, do not now concern us: His majesty is adorable, His glory inscrutable in them all. In the spiritual life He vouchsafes to try our patience first of all by His slowness. Slowness is the grand characteristic of the Creator as seen by the side of His creatures. Were it not for His slowness, where should we have been long since? We forget this, when His slowness makes us impatient. He is slow; we are swift and precipitate. It is because we are but for a time, and He has been from eternity. Thus grace for the most part acts slowly, and mortification is as long as levelling a mountain, and prayer as the growth of an old oak. He works by little and by little, and sweetly and strongly He compasses His ends, but with a slowness which tries our faith, because it is so great a mystery. We must fasten upon this attribute of God in our growth in holiness. It must be at once our worship and our exemplar. There is something greatly overawing in the extreme slowness of God. Let it overshadow our souls, but let it not disquiet them.

He tries us also by His hiddenness and by the impenetrable obscurity in which He shrouds almost all His supernatural processes, both in the Sacraments and out of them. As the Bible says, He is a God who conceals Himself. If we could see Him, so we say, Oh, then cheerfully would we follow Him! Oh, were we but sure it was He! But we cannot see Him. Often He could not show Himself to us, if He would. That is, His mercy could not, for the sight would slay us. Darkness is good for us when light would blind us. But look over the exercises, the trials, the temptations, and the vicissitudes of the spiritual life, and what a gain it seems as if it would be to us, could we only see Him! It is not so. It is best as it is. The enigma is our life. We must be patient with it. Sometimes He condescends to look mutable and fickle. He lets the moon amid the driving clouds of night be His emblem. He entices us into a road, and then leaves us just where it branches into two. He shows His face and then He hides it. We see it for a moment, and it is gone before we have caught the expression of it. Or the light so pleased us, we did not look at the dark objects it was meant to enlighten. Why does He interweave His bright and dark with us so perpetually? Sometimes He puzzles us as to His will. He lets half words fall into our hearts. He sends us what look like leadings, and are not so. He feigns, as Our Lord did when He made as if He would pass the boat that stormy night on the water. He lets us think that He has contradicted Himself, He who is eternal truth, unchangeable simplicity. He looks as though He were entrapping us, getting us to commit ourselves to Him, and then reproaching us, and going away as if we had offended Him, or changing His mien and throwing us into prison and making slaves of us, as if in contempt of our generosity, as if our best were an insult to Him, as it would be but for the infiniteness of His amazing compassion. One while He is the most indulgent of fathers, another while the least forebearing of masters: now the most patient of teachers, and again the sharpest of critics: here the most gracious of sovereigns, there the most exacting of despots: now almost a plaintiff to our human hearts, and again the most vindictive of persecutors. Look as Thou wilt, most gracious

Lord! nothing of Thee will we believe but that Thou art an infinitely good God, in Thy wrath remembering mercy, and as unchangeably a Father as Thou art eternally a God!

His chastisements also try our patience. Not only because they are never really light; for He never punishes in vain; but because they are unexpected, and seem inconsistent with what we have heard, and look disproportionate to such little failings. For if He caressed us when we greatly sinned, and forgave us even when we longed to be chastised, why for a trifling infidelity or an almost natural defect does the slow, heavy, regular lash endure so long? Does He forget we are creatures made of clay, and that if He does not mind, He will break us? Any chastisement which seems out of keeping with His usual dispensations tries our patience and is specially hard to bear. In the matter of answers to prayer we are equally bewildered. If He does not answer, faith faints. If He does, the answer is like Himself, it is slow and obscure and a riddle. Sometimes it is as if He answered in anger and took us at our word in a strange way for a Father. At last He abandons us. At all events there would be no bewilderment here, were we not told that this is precisely the hour of His especial and sustaining grace. Strange! for it is like a mountain falling on our hearts. It wrung a cry even from the silence-loving Heart of our ever-blessed Saviour on the Cross.

Shall I say then, be patient with God? Better say, Let us worship as heretofore; for is He not still God?

There are various ways in which we offend against this sublime exercise of patience. The first is by petulance in prayer, bold works of complaint, as if God had injured us, or as if He liked them, and that it was for everyone to dare to be with Him as Job was of old, and to pour out his heart in those bitter burning words, whereby God mysteriously acknowledged that he had justified himself. Or our impatience may show itself in an indiscreet and inordinate pursuit of virtue, a greediness for graces, and a wounded vanity from venial imperfections. It makes us capricious and fickle. We give up prayer, because the answer lingers. We weary of Sacraments because of their monotony. We shift our spiritual exercises, because they have not wrought miracles. We abandon medicines because health has not followed instantaneously. All infidelity is impatience with God. Thus we mar our mortifications by it. We begin them on impulse; we practice them without sobriety; and we leave them off because we are grown tepid and do not like the pain. So in the same manner a good work suggests itself: we cast up to Heaven one ejaculation, far more full of self-will than of pure zeal; and we begin the work forthwith without prayer or counsel or deliberation. What wonder we leave it half done? Is not the land round about us all full of these follies of impulse, impatience and conceit, which we ourselves have set up amid the mute wonder of pitying angels? We give ourselves vocations, and then charge them again. We confer missions on ourselves, tyrannize over ourselves by multiplying our responsibilities, and send ourselves on embassies to the very end of the earth. We can hardly relieve sorrow or allay distress, but there is some impatience in it. We pray God daily not to lead us into temptation, yet we are daily placing ourselves in dangerous occasions which we have reached almost out of breath, leaving Him far behind, who will not be hastened on His way.

But what are the remedies for this? We must study God. We must drink of the spirit of His ways. We must love God, ardently, intensely, to the death. But we must fear Him also, with a fear unutterable, abasing, perpetual. Fear must beat in our blood, and quiver in our limbs, and many a time tonguetie us and throw us down. Oh, how we shall love God, when we fear Him thus! Magnificent fear! thou art a gift of the Holy Ghost! We must wait for God, long, meekly, in the wind and wet, in the thunder and the lightning, in the cold and the dark. Wait, and He will come. He never comes to those who do not wait. He does not go their road. When He comes, go with Him, but go slowly, fall a little behind; when He quickens His pace, be sure of it, before you quicken yours. But when He slackens, slacken at once. And do not be slow only, but silent, very silent, for He is God.

Chapter X

HUMAN RESPECT

To give ourselves up to the spiritual life is to put ourselves out of harmony with the world around us. We make a discord even with much that is amiable and affectionate, and with which, as natural virtue, we cannot be altogether without sympathy. We live in a different world, have different interests and speak a different language, and the two worlds will not mingle. Grace holds us in one world, nature draws us down again into the other. This is the secret of the immense power which human respect has over us; and of the three dispositions which compose the normal state of the spiritual life, fatigue is the one which lays us most open to its attacks. We are weary of interior things and weakened by long combat, and a vigorous charge from an enemy who gets close to us under friendly colors is more than for the most part we can withstand. The good spirit, then, which should be the faithful satellite of our fatigue, is the presence of God, or singleness of purpose, or simplicity, but which I prefer to designate merely the absence of human respect, because no word seems so exactly to describe this spirit as the negative appellation in question.

There is much to be said of human respect. It is a fault most keenly felt by spiritual persons, and comparatively little felt by others. It is more like an atmosphere than anything else, and can hardly be caught and punished in distinct acts. Yet it is a thing of which there can be no doubt. We have an infallible consciousness of it. It gives undeniable evidences of its own existence. It destroys all liberty, and becomes the positive tyrant of a man's life. Yet if we look well into it, nothing can be more stupid than our submission to it. For we set little or no value on the separate opinions of individuals; and when the judgment is in our favor, it can do us no good, neither, unless true, can it afford us any rational pleasure. Indeed, its power is altogether in the prospect, and not in the present possession. Yet it is a most universal, and must be dealt with as one of the most inconvenient facts of the spiritual life. Look at a person who is completely under its domination. Watch him in society and public life, or in the bosom of his family, or in the intimacies of friendship, or at confession and in conference with his director, or even with God in prayer, or in utter solitude. It is as if the omnipresence of God was spunged out all round him, and that some other powerful eye was fixed upon him, ruling him with a power like that of the solar light, and causing in him at all times an almost preternatural uneasiness.

It is not difficult to see the evils of this miserable world-presence, this spirit which gathers all mankind up into an eye, and throws its portentous fascination upon our souls. It causes men to be false and insincere in their mutual relations, and to act inconsiderately with others. It destroys all generous enthusiasm either for charity or penance. It puts a man under the despotism of ridicule, which becomes a kind of false god to him. It is the contradictory of perfection, and while it is in force, renders it impossible; for it is always drawing us off from God to creatures. A brood of sins of omission follow it wherever it goes, sprung from shame and the fear of ridicule, and another brood of sins of commission, from the desire to please. In process of time, and the process is not slow, it establishes itself as an habitual distraction in prayer and meditation; and as to examination of conscience, it almost seems to supply food to the voracity of human respect.

It is as miserable as it is evil. The bondage of Carthusian austerity would be easier to bear. No slavery is more degraded and unhappy. What a misery to be ashamed of our duties and our principles! What a misery that every action should have a flaw in it, and a blight upon it! What a misery to lose at last, as we must inevitably do, the very thing for which all our sacrifices have been made, the respect of others! Misery of miseries, thus to lose even respect for self! Religion, which ought to be our peace, becomes our torment. The very Sacraments have a feeling of incompleteness about them, as if we did not, as we do not, use them rightly; and our communication with our director, which should be medicinal, is poisoned by this spirit. Surely we must try to get to the bottom of the matter, and to study the various phases of this disease of pious souls. A general wish to please, a laying ourselves out in particular subject matters in order to please, building castles in the air and imagining heroic acts, reflecting on the praise bestowed upon us, and giving way to low spirits when dispraised—these are all manifestations of this horrible human respect.

Human respect, however, is not so much a particular fault, as a whole world of faults. It is the death of all religion. We shall never have an adequate horror of it until we admit that these hard words are no exaggeration. Let us therefore look at the place which it occupies in the grand struggle between good and evil. First of all, let us trace its rise; for this is a difficult problem, considering how in detail we all disbelieve in each other. The especial task of Christians is the realization of the invisible world. They have different standards of right and wrong from the votaries of the earth. They live inextricably mixed up with the children of the world, as men using the same language with different meanings, and the confusion and apparent deceit grow worse every day, and the world, the owner of the territory or its lessee, more and more angry, and inclined, in spite of its theory of haughty toleration, to persecute those who thus willfully put themselves at variance with the public peace. Men feel that religious people are right, and on that very account they will not look the fact in the face, and realize it. They feel it, because they feel that they are not irresponsible. Yet they chafe at the judgments of God, and His incessant interference; at the quiet way in which He gives His judgments, and takes His own time to execute His verdicts. So, not being able to do without the judicial power, they consolidate God from Three Divine Persons into a function, a cause, a pantheistic fluid, or a mechanical force, and transfer the judicial power to man-

kind in a body. This seems to be the account of human respect in the mind. Men in all generations fret under God's
judicial power. It seems as if, because of this fretfulness, it
were one of the most unutterable of His compassions that
He should have confided his ultimate judicial rights to Our
Lord as Man, and that in virtue of the Sacred Humanity He
should be our judge. Looked at in a human point of view,
men's transfer of the judicial power to themselves may be said
to have worked admirably. Social comfort, a standard of en-
durable morals, and generally what may be called for the moment *live-ableness,* have come of it. It causes a certain amount
of individual unhappiness, because its police is harsh and rough,
and the procedures of its court unkindly and of the Draconian
school. But men have a compensation for this in its giving
over to them, utterly unquestioned, the whole region of thought.
Under the administration of God, thoughts were acts, and were
tried and found guilty as such. They furnished the most abundant materials for its tribunals, and were just what caused
His jurisdiction to press so heavily upon the soul. Now all
this is free. Calumny, detraction, rash judgments, spiteful
criticism—they make us wince as they visit our outward acts;
but we may be as base as we please in thought, and yet walk
through human courts with proud eye, and head erect.

No wonder that when once human respect had taken its
place among the powers of the world, it should cause especial
desolation in the religious mind, and become a worse evil
and a greater misery there than elsewhere. For it is itself a
sort of spurious counterfeit religion. For what is religiousness
but the sensible presence of God, and religion the worship
of Him? In religion, the presence of God is our atmosphere.
Sacraments, and prayer, and mortification, and all the exercises of the spiritual life are so many appointments, not only
for realizing it, but for substantially introducing it both into
body and soul. The respiration of our soul depends upon it.
It produces a certain kind of character, a type of its own sort
and easily recognized, a supernatural character which inspires
other men with awe, love, hatred or contempt, according to
the different points of view from which they look at it. To
the pure-minded, it is the greatest possible amount of happiness

on earth; for it infuses into us a certain marvelous unreasoning instinct for another world, as being faith's sight of Him who is invisible. Yet it is hardly conscious what it is it sees. Now is not human respect, in its own way, a simple copy and caricature of all this? A something which undertakes to perform for the world every function which the presence of God performs for the enlightened soul? It is in fact a mental paganism.

It is this similarity to a false religion which makes human respect so peculiarly dangerous. It does not alarm us by any grossness. On the contrary it forces sin into concealment. Not that this is any real boon to the best interests of men, for certain of the deadliest sins thrive best under cover. It confuses the boundaries between public opinion and itself, and pretends an alliance with prudence and discretion. This is a stratagem to be guarded against. For public opinion is within limits a legitimate power; and the man who because he was devout, should lay it down as a principle that he would never respect public opinion or be swayed by it, would be paving the way for the triumphs of delusion. Nothing can be more alien to the moderation of the Church. There is a vast difference between what my fellow citizens expect of me and show beforehand that they expect and give reasons for expecting, and the criticism they may pass upon my actions and my doing them rather with reference to that criticism than to the wish of God. Moreover, human respect unsupernaturalizes actions which are good in substance. It kills the nerve of the intention; but it gives us no such smart warning as the nerve of a tooth does in dying. It is like a worm in a nut; it eats away the kernel of our motive, and lets the fruit hang as fairly from the tree as ever. Religion is so much a matter of motives that this amounts to destroying it altogether, and as human respect introduces a directly wrong motive in lieu of the right one, it destroys spirituality in the most fatal way. Thus it is one of the completest instruments, which corrupt nature puts into the devil's hands and at his disposal for the destruction of souls. What can be more hateful than this, and what more odious in the sight of God? A caricature is always odious, and it is odious in proportion to the beauty and dignity of what it caricatures; and as we have seen, human respect is a caricature of the presence and judicial power of God.

Few are aware until they honestly turn to God, how completely they are the slaves of this vice. Then they wake up to a sense of it, and see how it is in their blood, as if it were their life and their identity, an inexplicable unconquerable vital thing. Its rise is a mystery, for which we can only invent a theory. No one can tell for sure how it rose, or when, or why; it has been like an exhalation from corrupt humanity, the spreading of a silent pestilence that has no external symptoms. There is not a class of society which it has not mastered, no corner of private life that it has not invaded, no convent cell but its air is freighted with the poisonous influence. It rivals what theologians call the pluri-presence of Satan. Its strength is so great that it can get the better of God's Commandments and of the precepts of His Church, nay, of a man's own will, which last conquest even grace and penance find it difficult to achieve. It appears to increase with civilization, and with the extension of all means of locomotion and publicity. In modern society men systematize it, acknowledge it as a power, uphold its claims and punish those who refuse submission. God is an ex-king amongst us, legitimate perhaps but deposed. It is much if we build Him in His own kingdom a house made with hands that He may dwell therein, and keep Himself within-doors. Surely if the evil one has not preternaturally helped human respect, he has at least concentrated his energies on its spread and success. He is never more a prince than when he stoops to be the missionary of human respect.

Look into your own soul, and see how far this power has brought you into subjection. Is there a nook in your whole being, wherein you can sit down unmolested and breathe fresh air? Is there any exercise however spiritual, any occupation however sacred, any duty however solemn, over which the attractive influence of human respect is not being exercised? Have you any sanctuary, the inside of which it has never seen? When you have thought it conquered, how often has it risen up again, as if defeat refreshed it like sleep? Does it not follow you as your shadow, as a perpetual black spot in the sweet sunshine? Yet how long is it since you turned to God, and became spiritual? How many Lents and Months of Mary have you passed, how many Sacraments received, how many indulgences gained? And yet this human respect so active, so robust, so unwearied, so ubiquitous? Can there be any question nearer your heart than what concerns the remedies for this evil?

The Church provides remedies for us in two ways: in her general system, and in her dealing with individual souls. She begins by boldly pronouncing a sentence of excommunication against the world, ignores its judgments in her own subject-matter of religion and proclaims its friendship nothing less than a declaration of war against God. She gives her children different standards of right and wrong from the world, and an opposite rule of conduct. All her positive precepts and her obligations of outward profession of faith are so many protests against human respect, and she canonizes just those men who have been heroes in their contempt for it. The world feels and understands the significance of these things, and shows it by anger, exhibiting all the quick jealousy of a conscious usurper.

But of far greater efficacy are the remedies which she administers to single souls in the confessional and in spiritual direction. The world dreads the secret power of that benign, cogent and unreported tribunal. First of all, the practice of the Presence of God is pitted against this universal human respect. We are taught how to act slowly, and to unite all our actions to God by a pure intention. We are bidden to take this fault as the subject of our particular examination of conscience, to pray earnestly against it, and to be full about our falls when we accuse ourselves in Confession. Even in indifferent things we are recommended to adopt that line of conduct which tells most against human respect, were it only for the sake of mortification. This is often the rationale of the seemingly absurd and childish mortifications imposed in religious houses. For human respect is but a veiled worship of self, which we seem to transfer to the world, because self is even to us so small an object. And whatever kills this worship of self, as such mortifications do, is a blow to human respect. In casting out devils, the Saints have often delighted

to use puerile means; so also may we cast this devil out of
ourselves. Once let our souls be possessed by a timid, childlike devotion to the Eye of God, eternal and unsleeping, and
human respect will die away and disappear, as the autumnal
leaves waste in the rain, and enrich the soil for the coming
spring.

But the great thing is to understand our real position in
the world and relation to it. This knowledge is a perfect fortress against human respect, which is one of the chief causes
of failure in aiming at perfection. Let us then try to ascertain
how pious people stand to the world, and the world to them.

When we give ourselves up to God, we deliberately commit
ourselves to live a supernatural life. Now what does a supernatural life mean? It means giving up this life altogether, as
seeing we cannot have both worlds. Altogether! I hear you
say. Yes! altogether. For how would you have me qualify it?
Not that we shall not be a thousand times happier and sunnier
even in this life; but it is from out the other life that the
sunshine and happiness will come. This life must go, and
altogether. There is no smoothing the word down. A supernatural life means that we do not make sin in the limit of
our freedom, but that we draw the line much nearer home,
by the evangelical counsels. It means mortification, and mortification is the inflicting of voluntary punishment on ourselves, as if passing sentence on ourselves and executing it
before the Day of Wrath. We put other interests, other loves,
other enjoyments, in the place of those of the world. A conviction of our own weakness is the groundwork of all our
actions, and we lean our whole weight on supernatural aids
and sacramental assistances, as depending solely upon them.
To a certain extent we even become unsocial by silence, or
solitude, or penance, or seeming eccentricity, or vocation.
In a word, we deliberately become members of a minority,
knowing we shall suffer for it.

Now, realizing this significancy of the spiritual life, what
is the view the world will naturally take of us and how will
it feel toward us? The world, half unconsciously, believes in
its own infallibility. Hence it is first of all surprised and then
irritated with our venturing to act on different principles

from itself. Such a line of action denies the world's supremacy, and contradicts its narrow code of prudence and discretion. Our conduct is therefore a reflection on the world, as if God had outlawed it, which He has. Its fashions, its sects, its pursuits, its struggles, its tyranny and its conceits are to us no better than a self-important, grandiloquent puerility. Meanwhile, though we ignore the world, the world cannot ignore us, for we are a fact, intruding on its domain and interfering with its hypothesis. We ignore the world, and ignoring is the policy of the extremes of weakness and strength. In our case it is of both, natural weakness, supernatural strength.

What sort of treatment then must we expect at the world's hands? It will have its phases and varieties according to circumstances. But on the whole we must expect as follows. If we succeed in what we undertake for God, or have influence, or convert persons, or take any high line, or reproach others by our examples, we must make our account to be hated. We shall be feared, and with an angry fear, when men see we have a view and go on a principle, which they do not; and they fear it because they prognosticate our success. Men will fear us also, when they think we are working for God in secret, and they cannot find out how, and this they call Jesuitism, a holy and a good word to ears wise and true! They will moreover suspect us of all manner of strange misdemeanors. They can hardly help it; for the disproportion of means to ends in supernatural conduct is ever a teasing, baffling problem to the carnal mind. They will blame us; for blame is easy; and we swerve from men's usual standard of praise. Moreover, condemnation of us is safe; for even so-called moderate men on our own side throw us overboard. With them indiscretion means provoking the world, and not being friends with that whose friendship the Holy Ghost tells us is enmity with God. We shall be misunderstood, because even those who would naturally take a good-natured view of us cannot see what we see. They have no grasp of our principles, and so they often think they have got logical proof of our inconsistency. Besides which, we cannot even give a good account of ourselves. We must expect also, hard as we must strive to hinder it, to be more or less at variance with flesh and blood. Vocations, devotions and penances have a sad though inculpable liability to disturb family peace. Parents are slow to give in to God, even long after children are come to years of ripe discretion. For instance, if a son marries, he will have liberty, because the world bids it; if he enters orders or religion, he will not, because only the Church bids it then. Yet they are good people, and religious in their way; why should not we be like them? So they think, and others say. We cannot see things in their light, and they cannot see things in ours.

Now to something of this kind, more or less, we committed ourselves when we took up the spiritual life in earnest. We knew what we were about. From that hour we parted company with the world, nevermore to do aught but fly from it as a plague, or face it as a foe. Human respect, therefore, must henceforth be for us either an impossibility, or an inconsistency, or a sin. What have we to do with giving or taking the world's respect, which we have bound ourselves eternally to disrespect? Enough for us that we have taken ourselves out of the world's hands, and out of our own, and put ourselves into the Hands of God, and we have felt those hands, O happy we! gently but firmly close over us, and hold us fast.

Chapter XI

MORTIFICATION—OUR TRUE PERSEVERANCE

The true idea of mortification is that it is the love of Jesus, urged into that shape partly in imitation of Him, partly to express its own vehemence, and partly to secure, by an instinct of self-preservation, its own perseverance. There can be no true or enduring love without it, for a certain amount of it is requisite in order to avoid sin and to keep the Commandments. Neither without it is there any respectable perseverance in the spiritual life. The rest which forms part of the normal state of the spiritual life is not safe without it, because of the propension of nature to seek repose in natural ways when supernatural are no longer open to it. Mortification is both interior and exterior; and of course the superior excellence of the interior is beyond question. But if there is one doctrine more important than another on this subject, it is that there can be no interior mortification without exterior; and this last must come first. In a word, to be spiritual, bodily mortification is indispensable.

Some have spoken as if bodily mortification were less necessary in modern times than it was before, and consequently that the recommendations of spiritual writers under this head are to be taken with considerable abatement. If this means that a less degree of exterior mortification is necessary for holiness now than was necessary for past ages of the Church, nothing can be more untrue, and it comes up to the verge of condemned propositions. If it means that increased valetudinarianism and the universality of nervous diseases, combined with other causes, discreetly point to a change in the kind of mortifications, the proposition may be assented to,

with jealousy, however, and wary limitations. The Lenten In-
dults of the Church may be taken as an illustration.

But this false doctrine is so deep in the minds of many
that it is necessary to combat it before we proceed further.
The degree of mortification and its idea must remain the same
in all ages of the Church: for penance is an abiding mark
of the Church. To do penance because the Kingdom of Heaven
is at hand is the especial work of a justified soul. To get
grace, to keep it and to multiply it, penance is necessary at
every step. And when we say that holiness is a note of the
Catholic Church, we show forth the necessity of mortification; for the one implies the other, the first includes the last.
The heroic exercise of penance must be proved to the satisfaction of the Church before she will proceed to the canonization
of a saint; and the quite recent beatification of Paul of the
Cross and Marianna of Gesù show how completely unaltered
the mind of the Church remains on this point. Marianna's
life is nothing but one unbroken series of the most startling
austerities, which make us shudder from the inventive cruelty
which they display. The life of St. Rose of Lima, by the side
of this other American virgin, looks soft and comfortable and
easy. It seems as if Paul were raised up to alarm the stagnant
eighteenth century, and to renew before the eyes of men the
austerities of St. Benedict, St. Bruno, St. Romuald, or St.
Peter Damian. He reanimated the old severe monastic spirit,
in contempt of all modern usages and mitigations, and for
a hundred years his children have trodden in their father's
steps with undecaying fervor. The existence and primitive vigor
of the austere Passionists is one of the greatest consolations
of the Church in these effeminate days.

We must remember also that, according to the teaching of
Scripture, it is quite a mistake to regard, as some unthink-
ingly do, the practice of mortification as a counsel of perfection, and a work of supererogation.

When carried to a certain degree, or when expressed in
certain ways, it is doubtless so. But mortification in itself,
and to a certain degree and under given circumstances, is of
precept and necessary to salvation. This is not only true of
the self-inflicted pains which are sometimes of obligation in

order to overcome vehement temptations, or of those various mortifications which are needful in order to avoid sin. But a definite amount of fasting and abstinence, irrespective of the temptations or circumstances of individuals, is imposed by the Church on all her children under pain of eternal damnation. This expresses the idea of penance for its own sake, and the necessity of it as one of the functions of the Church, as a soul-saving institute. When, therefore, men say that they do not practice mortification, but leave it to those who wish to be saints, they may on being questioned show that they are sound in doctrine, and do not mean the error which their words, strictly taken, imply; but we may be sure that the very use of such loose language is a proof that a real error about mortification is deeply imbedded in their minds.

Indeed, modern luxury and effeminacy, which are often pleaded as arguments for an abatement of mortification, may just as well be called forward to maintain the opposite view. For if it be a special office of the Church to bear witness against the world, her witness must especially be borne against the reigning vices of the world; and therefore in these days, against effeminacy, the worship of comfort and the extravagances of luxury. I believe, if this unhappy land is ever to be converted, of which there are many hopes and no signs, it will be by some religious order or orders who shall exhibit to a degraded and vicious people the vision of evangelical poverty in its sternest perfection. The land that has forsaken Christ must gather to the Baptist first, and be attracted to the Jordan by the simplicity of supernatural strictness, and antique austerity. Other things can do much, intellect, learning, eloquence, the beauties of Catholic charity, the sweet influences of a purified literature, the studiousness of a simple and apostolic preaching. But the great work, if the great work is in the counsels of God, I much think is a triumph in this land reserved only for evangelical poverty. Not poverty in the grotesque attire of medieval practice, once hallowed, but which would repel men now and invite contempt, because of certain developments separable from its real self, and at present unseasonable; but the beautiful poverty of the Apostles and first ages of the Church, with the common garb and bright clean face and hands of evangelical austerity. (*Matt.* 6:16).

If the Church has to witness always against the reigning vices of the world, each soul has likewise, if not to witness, at least to defend itself, against them. And how shall it defend itself against the worship of bodily comforts, except by depriving itself of them? Changeable as the world is, it is unchanging too. The world, the flesh and the devil, are practically the same in all ages: and so, practically, mortification has the same offices to perform. Whether we consider the soul in the struggles of its conversion, in the progress of its illumination, or in its variously perfect degrees of union with God, we shall find that bodily mortifications have their own place, and their proper work to do, and are literally indispensable.

But let us look for a moment at the various objections urged against this. First we are told that the health of the world is not what it is, and that if there is an equal, or even greater longevity, the normal state of health is more uniformly valetudinarian, and that if inflammatory attacks are less frequent, nervous complaints on the other hand are more prevalent, and that the relaxation of Church discipline on the subject shows her appreciation of these facts. All this is true, and doubtless many most important deductions are to be drawn from it. Still I maintain, it is more concerned with the kind of mortification than the degree. The conduct of the Church in the mitigation of fasting is as wise as the conduct of Leo XII was marked with the usual practical sagacity of the Holy See, when he caused the possibilities of the old observance of Lent to be medically investigated. Moreover the plea of health, while it is always to be listened to, is to be listened to with suspicion. We must always be jealous of the side on which nature and self are serving as volunteers. Great then as we must admit the consequences of a state of valetudinarianism to be on the spiritual life, a general and plenary dispensation from corporal austerities is not one of them; and we must remember also that our forefathers, who troubled their heads little enough about their nerves, and had no tea to drink, were accustomed to hear from Fr. Baker, who only gave utterance to the old mystical tradition, that a state of robust health was positively a disqualification for the higher stages of the spiritual life.

A second objection, and one sometimes urged in behalf of priests and religious, is that modern hard work is a substitute for ancient penance. The fewness of the clergy and the multitude of souls have certainly brought upon the ecclesiastics of this generation an overwhelming pressure of work; and it is true of them, as it always has been of religious orders engaged in the apostolate, that the measure of bodily austerity to be exacted of them is very different from that which we expect from contemplatives and solitaries. I do not say therefore that this objection expresses no truth, but only that it will not bear all the weight men put upon it. Certain kinds of penance are incompatible with hard work; while at the same time the excessive exterior propensities which hard work gives us are so perilous to the soul that certain other kinds of penance are all the more necessary to correct this disturbing force. All great missionaries, Segneri and Pinamonti, Leonard of Port Maurice and Paul of the Cross, have worn instruments of penance. The penalties of life, as Da Ponte calls them, are doubtless an excellent penance when endured with an interior spirit, and worth far more than a hundred self-inflicted pains. Yet he who maintains that the endurance of the former is a dispensation from the infliction of the latter, will find himself out of harmony with the whole stream of approved spiritual teaching in the Church; and the brevity of his perseverance in the interior life will soon show both himself and others the completeness of his delusion. Without bodily penance, zealous apostolic work hardens the heart far more than it sanctifies it.

A third class of objectors tells us to be content with the trials God sends us, which are neither few nor light. If they told us that the gay suffering and graceful welcome of these dispensations were of infinitely greater price than the sting of the discipline or the twinge of the catenella, most true and most important would the lesson be, and to many a hot-hearted spiritual suckling quite indispensable. Youth, when it is strong and well and is full of fervor and bathing in devotional sweetness, finds almost a physical pleasure in tormenting its flesh and pinching its redundant health. There is little merit in this, as there is little difficulty and less discretion. And at all times

one blow from God is worth a million from ourselves. But
the objectors fall into that mistake of exaggeration which runs
through so many spiritual books. Because A is more important than B, they jump to the conclusion that B is of no importance at all. Because the mortifications which God sends us
are more efficacious and less delusive, if rightly taken, than
the mortifications we inflict upon ourselves, it does not follow but that these last are, not only an important, but even
an indispensable element in the spiritual life. We may answer
them briefly as follows. Yes! the best of all penances is to
take in the spirit of interior compunction the mortifications
which the wise and affectionate course of God's fatherly providence brings upon us; but unless we have practiced ourselves
in the generous habit of voluntary penances, the chances are
very much indeed against our forming this interior spirit of
penance, and therefore of getting the full profit out of the
involuntary trials God sends us.

Besides these objections there is another one latent in many
minds, which should be noticed. Our present habits of life
and thought lead to an obvious want of sympathy with contemplation. It has no public results on which we can look
complacently, or which we can parade boastfully. Everything
seems waste which is not visible; and all is disappointment
which is not plain success. It is supernatural principles especially which are at a discount in modern days. Now it is easy
to see how this want of sympathy with contemplation leads
to a misappreciation of austerity. They are connected with
each other, and both enter deeply into the region of supernatural operations. To think lightly of either is to be out of harmony with the mind of the Church, and to injure our own
soul, whatever may be its vocation, by narrowing the range
of its supernatural vision.

From all these considerations it may warrantably be concluded that there is nothing in modern times to dispense us
either from the obligation or the counsel of bodily mortification, that on the contrary there is much in modern habits
to enforce the obligation and to urge the counsel, and that
all the modifications, to which the actual circumstances of
modern life point, concern themselves wholly with the kind

of mortification and not at all with the degree.

Something remains to be said on the uses of mortification. These are ten in number and all of them deserving a serious consideration. Its first use is to tame the body and bring its rebellious passions under the control of grace and of our superior will. Full half the obstacles to a spiritual life are from the body, and the treacherous succor which its senses give to our baser passions. These must be, I do not say altogether removed, but effectually crippled, before we can hope to make much progress. We never find in anyone a real earnestness of mind or seriousness of spirit, where honest attempts are not being made to keep the body in subjection. The reason why men are religious under sorrow and not at other times is that they do not practice bodily mortification, whereas sorrow afflicts and rebukes the flesh, and so for the time performs the functions of mortification. Sorrow acts on the soul through the body as much as through the mind.

The second use is to increase the range of our spiritual vision. Sensitiveness of conscience is one of the greatest gifts which God gives us in order to a spiritual life. The things of God, says the Apostle, can only be spiritually discerned. The process of our purification by grace depends on our increasing clearness of vision as to what is faulty and imperfect. From the discernment of mortal sin we come to that of venial sin, from venial sin to imperfections, from imperfections to less perfect ways of doing perfect things, and from that to a delicate perception of the almost invisible infidelities which grieve the Holy Spirit within us. And if bodily mortification is not the sole means by which this sensitiveness of conscience is obtained, it is one of the chief, as well from its own intrinsic method of operation, as from its power to impetrate the gift from God.

This brings me to the third use of mortifications of all kinds, which is to obtain power with God. Suffering easily becomes power in the things of God. The price He sets upon it is shown by the fact that the world was redeemed by suffering, and that suffering gives their palm to the martyrs and their crown to the confessors. The gift of miracles follows hard upon austerity. When we complain that we have no power with God, that our prayers remain unanswered, that our efforts to root out some besetting sin are unavailing, and that we give way to temptations and to surprises of temper or loquacity, it is for the most part because we are not leading mortified lives. It is in this that mortification so amply repays us for the pain it gives. For not only is it an immense gain to have power with God, but the obvious connection between the mortification and the power enables us not so much to believe in supernatural things as to handle them with our very hands and feel their weight. Indeed even a temptation may come from this. If, then, for the sake of our spiritual growth and the interest we feel in the glory of God, the triumph of the Faith, and the salvation of souls near and dear to us, we desire to obtain power with God, we must habitually and consistently practice mortification.

Its fourth use is to intensify our love. It is of the nature of love to thrive on no food so well as on the evidence of its own vigor; and nothing testifies to us so securely our love of God, as the infliction of voluntary austerities upon ourselves: and while it manifests our love, it augments it also. Pain, too, of itself prepares the heart for the emotions of love by softening it and making it childlike. And where the object loved and contemplated is one of sorrow and suffering, as Jesus is, love impels us more or less vehemently to imitation. Do we complain that our love of our dear Lord is slackening? Forthwith let us mortify ourselves in something, and the smoldering embers will break into a bright flame. As sure as power follows mortification, so also does love.

Its fifth use is to make us unworldly, and to inundate us with spiritual joy. Nothing is in itself so unworldly as mortification, because it is the killing of everything the world most prizes and cherishes. It breaks off all the inordinate attachments to creatures which we may have formed, and it hinders us from embarrassing ourselves with new ties; for mortification is found by experience to be so difficult that we dread to increase the breadth of the region over which we are compelled to extend it. And what is each new attachment but a fresh horde of savages to be brought painfully beneath control? As to spiritual joy, it flows like a tide into some empty place. In proportion, therefore, as our hearts are void of earthly attachments, and an attachment may be defined to be an affection which is not a duty, in the same proportion are they capable of enjoying the sweetness of God. Hence it is that mortified persons, when discreet, are always mirthful. The heart is lightened, because the burden of the body is taken off it. Nothing can make us unworldly but mortification. Have we never seen persons clouded round with sorrow so deep and dark, that we approached it reverently as we would a sanctuary, and yet it had not made the sufferer unworldly? That blessed office is the monopoly of mortification.

Its sixth use is to hinder our making a great mistake, which is the leaving the *Via Purgativa* too soon. This is perhaps the chiefest danger in the whole of the spiritual life. Many try to go so fast when they first begin, that they lose their breath, and give up the race altogether; and even if they do not, they cannot leave behind what they wish to leave, before the appointed time. They are like men running wildly to outstrip their own shadow. It cannot be. Nature wants to be out of her novitiate. Meditation would fain be thrust up into Affective Prayer, and the captivity of little things longs to expatiate in liberty of spirit. The bruised flesh asks to be let alone, and interior mortification requests to be allowed its primitive vagueness and to remain undefined. Weekly Communion gravitates to daily, and the soul a little tired of looking after itself, inclines to convert the world. If there is difficult navigation anywhere in the spiritual life, it is here. See! the reefs are strewn with wrecks, and the waves wash up at every tide the bodies of half-made saints, of broken heroes and frustrated vocations. No harm comes of keeping long in the lower parts of the spiritual life. All possible evil may come of mounting too quickly. An evil when it is mortified first looks dead. It feigns death, as beetles do. If it succeeds in deceiving us, and we pass on, we shall rue it bitterly. It is only the old story: look well to your foundations, dig them deep and build broad, and plan your building magnificently large, as if you were a prince. Mortification, of all things, helps us to do this. Its difficulty brings out our weakness. One while clumsy, another while cowardly, we are content to be kept down, when daily failures are telling us what would happen on the giddy heights above us. But how long shall the *Via Purgativa* last? Who can tell? It depends upon fervor. Anyhow, we must count it by years, not by months.

The seventh use of mortification is to be found in its connection with prayer. How many complaints are we daily hearing of the difficulties of mental prayer! Yet how few are seeking the gift of prayer by the single means which can succeed, namely, mortification! If we do not mortify ourselves, why complain? Listen to this vision, which Da Ponte relates as having happened to a person whom he knew. He gives it at length in the third tract of his *Spiritual Guide*. God showed this person the state of a tepid and idle soul, which is given to prayer without mortification. She saw in the middle of a wide plain a very deep and strong foundation, white as ivory, about which a fair, ruddy youth of admirable beauty was walking. He called her to him and said, "I am the son of a powerful king, and I have laid this foundation that I might build a palace for you to dwell in, and to receive me whenever I come to visit you, which I shall do frequently, provided you always have a room ready for me, and open as soon as I knock. In time, however, I shall come and live entirely with you, and you will be delighted to have me for a daily guest. Judge, however, from the magnitude of this foundation what the edifice is to be. Meanwhile I will build, and you must bring me all the materials." The lady began to be sore amazed and afflicted, for she deemed it impossible that she should of herself bring all the requisite materials. The young man, however, said, "Do not be afraid; you will be quite able to do it. Begin to bring something at once, and I will help you." So she began to look about for something, but presently stopped and fixed her eyes on the young man, whose beauty delighted and refreshed her. Yet she took no pains to please him. She feared him very much, when she saw that he was watching her. Nevertheless she did not blush at her disobedience. While she was thus loitering, she saw that the foundation was being gradually covered with dust and straws by the wind, and sometimes such whirlwinds of dust arose that she could not see the foundation at all. Sometimes floods of rain covered the whole with mud, which gradually spread over them, and caused a rank vegetation of weeds to sprout up. At last, nothing of the foundation remained but the spot which the young man's feet covered, and at last a sudden whirlwind covered him, and the foundation disappeared from her sight beneath a heap of filth. The lady was very much afflicted to find herself alone, especially as she was soon surrounded by ruinous heaps of lime, sand and stone. She bewailed her tepidity and idleness, but believing that the young man was still hidden in some of the cavities of the foundation, she cried out in a loud voice, "Sir! I am coming: I am bringing materials: I pray you come forth to the building; for I am deeply penitent for my sloth and delay." While she was in these dispositions, the vision was thus interpreted to her. The foundation signifies faith and the habits of other virtues which Christ infuses into the soul at Baptism, desiring to build upon them a fair edifice of lofty perfection, provided the soul cooperates with Him by bringing the necessary materials, observance of the divine precepts and counsels, which by the aid of the same Lord, it can do. But the soul is often so delighted with meditating on the mysteries of Christ that it becomes tepid and idle in the imitation and obedience of Him, and through this inattention and slovenliness, the habits of virtue are gradually obscured by venial sins, and the eyes of the soul so dimmed that they cannot see Our Lord. In punishment of this sloth He sometimes allows the soul to fall into a mortal sin, which stains and destroys everything. Then by the mercy of God it repents, finds the stones of contrition, the lime of confession and the sands of satisfaction all around it, and calls on Jesus with a loud voice to pardon the sin and to begin the building, for the second time.

The eighth use of mortification is to give depth and strength to our sanctity, just as gymnastic exercises give us muscle and play of strength. This is connected with what was said a while ago of not trying to get out of the *Via Purgativa* too quickly. When Simeon Stylites first began to stand upon his column, so Theodoret tells us, he heard a voice in his sleep which said to him, "Arise and dig!" He seemed to dig for a time, and then ceased, when the voice said to him, "Dig deeper!" Four times he dug, four times he rested, and four times the voice cried, "Dig deeper!" After that it said, "Now build without toil!" There can surely be no doubt but that the digging was the humbling toil of mortification. There is such a thing as a thin, meager piety, a religious sentimentality, which cannot go beyond the beauty of taste or the pathos of a ceremonial, a devotion for the sunshine but not for the storm; and the fault of the lank, crazy edifice that is raised by it is the absence of mortification in its original construction.

The ninth use of mortification concerns bodily austerities. Without exterior mortification it is idle to expect that we shall ever attain the higher grace of interior mortification. It is the greatest of delusions to suppose we can mortify judgment and will, if we do not mortify our body also. Interior mortification is certainly the higher; yet in some sense exterior is harder. It is harder because it comes first, and has to be exercised when we have as yet scarcely any empire over ourselves. It is harder because it is more sensible. It is harder because our victories are at best mean to look at, and our defeats palpable and discouraging. It is harder because habit helps us less. If our bodily penances are rare, each one has all the difficulties of a new beginning. If they are frequent, they fall on unhealed wounds. Whereas with interior mortification the victories always look dignified, and the defeats are surrounded by such a host of extenuating circumstances as veils their disgrace. We must remember that throughout our spiritual life we have our body for our companion, and none but a very few privileged saints have ever quite subdued it. Moreover, body has to be saved as well as soul, and so it is not true that, in devotion, exterior things are only a means to interior. They have, beside that instrumental character, an import and significancy of their own. There have always been two classes of heresies with regard to spiritual theology; and I cannot think of one heresy which has not come either from a disunion of the interior and the exterior, or a dwelling on one of them to the neglect and depression of the other. I tremble when people speak much of interior mortification, it sounds so like a confession that they are leading comfortable lives. On the other hand, when men exaggerate the importance of bodily austerities, the chances are either that they do not practice them at all, or that, practicing them, they rest in them with complacency and so are fakirs, not Christians, having no spiritual life which can deserve the name.

The tenth and last use of mortification is that it is a most excellent school for the queenly virtue of discretion. The truly mortified man will as little think of not listening to discretion as he would think of listening to cowardice. Discretion is a habit of hitting a mark, and there must be a supernatural truth in the eye, and a supernatural steadiness in the hand in order to attain this. Mortification is the grand subject matter of these trials of discretion: and the virtue will show itself in obedience, humility, self-distrust, perseverance and detachment from the penances themselves. This was the trial to which the bishops put Simeon Stylites. They sent a messenger to bid him come down from his pillar. If he hesitated, they should know that his extraordinary vocation was not from God. But the words were hardly out of the messenger's mouth, than he put one foot down from his column. In his docility they recognized the call of God, and bade him stay.

The details of mortification belong rather to the direction of particular souls. Each one requires a legislation for himself. There seems however to be a consent among spiritual writers that while pleasures, passions and pains are the three great fields of mortification, a certain order ought to be observed in our application to them. Pleasures should be mortified first, passions next and pains be undertaken last. They do not mean by this that there are three distinct and successive classes of penances, and that we must practice one till we are out of the other, any more than writers when they divide mental prayer into twelve or fifteen states mean that we go out of one into another, as if they were separate rooms. All that is meant is that upon the whole, a certain order is to be observed, and upon the whole one object to be sought at a certain time rather than another one.

Mortifications are divided into exterior and interior. Of the exterior there are five principal classes. First afflictive penances, such as fasting, discipline, hair shirt, catenella, cold and wakefulness. Of these the one which most requires jealousy is that which concerns loss of sleep, and next to it the bearing of cold. For the results of these to the health may be and often are permanent. And generally of all these penances, two things may be observed: first, that no one should ever take them out of his own head, without counsel and obedience; and secondly, that perseverance in them is of far greater moment than either quantity or quality. It has often been noticed that when a person becomes spiritual, one of the very last infirmities which leaves him is an immortified pleasure in eating and drinking. There is something wonderfully humbling in this: and we must pay particular attention to it, trying to mortify ourselves in something at every meal, and not to eat between mealtimes. It ought to be a mortification in itself to read what Brillat-Savarin has cleverly said, as Descuret quotes him in his *Medicine des Passions,* that there are four classes of men given to gluttony: the financiers, the physicians, the literary and the devout; the financiers for the sake of ostentation, the physicians by seduction, the literary by way of distraction and the devout by way of compensation!

The second class of exterior mortifications consists in the custody of the senses, in order to rebuke levity and curiosity, and in these singularity and affectation should be guarded against. Under the third class falls the patient bearing of illness and pain, and especially the acceptation of death in the spirit of penance. Under the fourth class come fatiguing and self-denying works for the good of our neighbor, or the relief of the poor, or the exaltation of the Faith; and under the fifth, all that is penal in the common tasks and daily vicissitudes of life, the obligation of work, the inconveniences of poverty, the weather, and like things, all which may become meritorious by being endured in an interior spirit of penance, and united to Our Lord's endurance of them in His thirty-three years.

Under the head of interior mortifications comes, first of all, the mortification of our own judgment, or rationale, as St. Philip called it. Can there be a harder task in the whole of the spiritual life? If you ask me how it is to be done, I answer—the words are easy; not so the practice—Distrust your own opinion, and acquire the habit of surrendering it in doubtful things. In matters about which you are clear, speak modestly and then be silent. Try never to have an opinion contrary to that of your natural and immediate superiors. Let their presence be the death of your own views. With your equals try to agree in matters of no moment, and above all, have no wish to be listened to. Judge favorably of all things, and be ingenuous in giving them a kindly turn. Condemn nothing either in the general or the particular; but make all things over to the judgment of God. When reason and virtue oblige you to speak, do so with such gentleness and want of emphasis that you may seem rather to despise than value your own opinion.

Mortifications of the will form another class. The tongues of others fill a third to overflowing. Spiritual desolations are a fourth, and horrible temptations, specially allowed by God, a fifth. All these have their own symptoms and require their own method of treatment which it would be out of place here to investigate. There is little left for the work of sanctification to do when our will is conformed to the will of God, and endures humbly and sweetly the adverse wills of others. The strife of tongues is a mortification from which few can hope to escape, especially if they are either endeavoring to do good to others or aiming at a high sanctity for themselves. It was one of the ingredients in our Saviour's chalice, and was considered by the Psalmist as so afflictive that he prayed God to hide him from it beneath the shadow of His wings. Spiritual desolations, so hard to bear, give both courage and humility to our relations with God, while unusual and obstinate temptations purify the soul, as in a very crucible, from all remains of earthly dross.

But if mortification has its difficulties, it has its dangers also. Many mortifications are preceded by vainglory, who blows the trumpet before them. Other mortifications she accompanies; and some even receive from her all their life, animation and perseverance. It is as if this evil spirit had a standing commission from her master, "Whenever a soul is about to practice a mortification there be thou also!" The remedy for this is to put all our mortifications under obedience. It is difficult then for either vainglory, ostentation, singularity, affectation, willfulness, or indiscretion to fasten upon our

penances and corrode their precious inward life. And they
are the six chief dangers of mortification. Neither must we
forget to be on our guard against a superstitious idea of the
value of pain growing up in our minds alongside of our austerities. Many mortifications remain mortifications when the pain
of them has passed away; and the value of them depends upon
the intensity of the supernatural intention that was in them,
not on the amount of physical pain or bodily discomfort. Mortification is a putting something to death, and the passion
that is dead already is more mortified than one that is only
dying, and yet the last feels pain, while the first is past all
feeling. It is astonishing how many are unconsciously deceived
by this superstitious notion of the value of the mere pain;
not that it is without value; but it is not the gem—it is only
the setting of it. It is this error which has given so much
vogue outside the Church, and sometimes also to unwary persons in it, to the delusion of thinking that perfection consists
in always doing what we dislike, which implies that our affections and passions will never be brought to like the things
of God or be in harmony with grace. Thus you hear of persons having a scruple whether they ought to be kind to others
because they have so much sensible pleasure in it, or visiting
the poor for the same reason, or following a peculiar bent
of devotion. Some even impose it as a rule upon the souls
they guide, in almost every instance with as much absurdity
as indiscretion. In the only sense in which sound mysticism
would allow such a maxim, it would require a special and
clearly marked vocation, and it would be as rare as the call
to make St. Theresa's and St. Andrew Avellino's vows, always
to do what was most perfect. Yet the Church stopped at those
vows when she was called upon to canonize the Saints, and
would not proceed till evidence was given her of a special
operation of the Holy Ghost. No one ever became a saint,
or anything like one, by ceasing to cultivate the sweeter parts
of his character or his natural virtues, because the doing so
was so great a pleasure. Yet Jansenism thought that the secret
of perfection lay in this single charm. It is a most odious
and uncatholic idea of asceticism.

  To the difficulties and dangers of mortification we must

add a word on its delusions. It is a fertile subject. Guilloré, who has treated of the subject at length and with his usual severity, sums it all up by describing the four classes of persons who are most subject to these delusions. The first class embraces those who have always led an innocent life, and on that account easily dispense themselves from austerities; and not being drawn to them themselves, they make no attempt to draw others that way. They do not see why they should maltreat a body which is so little rebellious, and inflict on it such constant pain when it teases them with but an occasional disturbance. The second class contains those who, though their lives have been far from innocent, are nevertheless, from softness of temperament, disinclined to austerities. They can hardly believe that anything which is so far above their cowardice, as this persecution of self, can be necessary and indispensable. Useful they are willing to admit it to be, but surely not necessary; for in that case where should they be? And are their intellectual views of perfection, or their sentimental aspirations after it, to end in smoke? The third class comprises those who have greatly offended God, and therefore think they must set no bounds to their austerities. Hence they go beyond the limits of sage reason on the one side, and the inspirations of grace on the other. The fourth class numbers men of fiery zeal and hot-tempered enthusiasm, whose peace is in war and their rest in struggle, and who satisfy nature by the chastisement of their bodies. But when the blood runs or the face grows pale, they are miserably deceived if they consider that to be a true spiritual mortification which has only been the rude satisfaction of a natural and impulsive passion.

Chapter XII

THE HUMAN SPIRIT

The three normal dispositions of the spiritual life require patience, mortification and the absence of human respect, in order rightly to perform the functions allotted them, and to avoid the dangers which beset them. But there are also three evil spirits which haunt the dispositions in question. Not that each disposition has exactly its one bad angel, and is not troubled by the other two; but on the whole, the disposition of struggle is liable to the attacks of what may be called the human spirit, fatigue to spiritual idleness, and rest to the neglect of prayer, or the unpraying spirit. We have, therefore, now to consider these three things: the human spirit, spiritual idleness and prayer.

The kingdom of darkness, the power and wiliness of Satan, the multitude of his subordinate ministers, the ceaselessness of their open or hidden warfare against the servants of God, cannot be too often the subject of our most grave meditations, as well as the object of our humblest fears and most prayerful vigilance. Still, it were to be wished that men's views of this agency of Satan were always kept within the due limits of sane theology. They not unfrequently run into something like Manicheism, and at least give us an idea of Almighty God which has drifted widely from that which Scripture teaches. We forget that the devil is only one of three enemies against whom at Baptism we vowed to do battle, and thus we transfer to him all the phenomena which belong rather to the flesh and the world. The same secret vanity which leads us to a superstitious view of grace, as a talisman which is to act without the cooperation of our own resolute will, is the source of these erroneous views of the devil's agency. It breaks the shame of our falls to believe that in every instance we have wrestled and been thrown by an evil angel of tremendous power, and not that through cowardice, effeminacy and self-love we have simply given in to the suggestions of our own irresolute will. Nay, in certain temptations men will allow themselves to be almost passive, from this horrible doctrine about the devil. Were they logical, they would soon come to believe the blasphemy of the necessity of sin. What their view really amounts to is this, that man is a certain organized reasonable instrument, who is possessed by the devil, and that God comes and tries to establish a counter-possession by means of faith, grace and Sacraments, and that man has little to do with the matter except to consent to be the battlefield of the two spiritual powers. Everyone shudders when it is put into these words. But follow a soul who has got this wrong idea into the whole region of temptations and scruples, and you will see what mistakes it makes and what misfortunes it encounters, and how at last, to use St. Bernard's figure, it needs no devil to tempt it, because it is a devil to itself.[1]

It is necessary, therefore, at this point, that I should ask my readers to remember what theology teaches them, that there is such a thing as a definite human spirit, the spirit of man, and of fallen man, and that it has ways and operations of its own which exercise a very material influence over the

---

1. The same doctrine is also taught very strongly by Father de Condren, General of the French Oratory. See his life by F. Amelote, p. 177, xiv. Of course this side of the question must not be exaggerated any more than the other. The doctrine of the personality and influence of the devil is peculiarly needed just now in order to meet the Sadduceism of the day, as has been remarked by Dr. Brownson in his *Spirit-Rapper.* Even Bayle in his *Dictionnaire* (Art. Plotinus) says to Christians, "Prove to your adversaries the existence of evil spirits, and you will soon see them forced to grant you all your dogmas." *("Mais prouvez-leur l'existence des mauvais esprits, et vous les verrez bientot forcés de vous accorder tous vos dogmas.")* The blasphemy of Voltaire on the subject is too well-known to need repeating here. Frederick Schlegel well said that history was nothing more than "an incessant struggle of nations and individuals against invisible powers." Fr. Ravignan remarked justly and pithily of the devils of the nineteenth century, "Their masterpiece has been to get themselves denied by the age." *(Leur chef d'oeuvre, Messieurs, c'est de siêtre fait nier par ce siécle.)*

whole of our spiritual life. What is usually taught about it
may be briefly stated as follows: There are three spirits with
which men have to do, the Divine, the diabolical and the
human. This last is a definite and distinct spirit of itself; and
consists of the inclinations of our fallen nature when not al-
lied to either of the other spirits. So that the mischief which
it causes in the spiritual life is chiefly of negative character,
inasmuch as it leads us to act from purely natural motives
and in a purely natural way, apart from grace. It is known
by its always gravitating, independent of any satanical impulsion, to peace, comfort, ease, liberty and making ample pro-
vision for the body. In a word, it is to good persons what
the spirits of the world and the devil are to bad people, incessantly acting upon them even when gross temptations would
have no effect. It vitiates what they do, without making it
wholly evil.

The various ways in which this human spirit develops itself
in the spiritual life are deserving of especial study. It often
causes hot feelings to be mistaken for visitations of the Holy
Ghost. Hence it is that determinations taken in moments of
exaltation and excitement are so little to be depended on. The
words of God in the soul effect what they say. The Divine
Voice may have uttered but a single sound, one little word,
but the work is done. It is safe to build upon it the edifice
of years. Judge then what awful consequences follow when
the mere effervescence of the human spirit is mistaken for
the fire of divine inspiration! We commit ourselves to a line
of action, or to a grave step in life, or even to a vow from
which we cannot easily be dispensed, on the strength of a
mere natural excitement. We may have put ourselves into a
condition in which unusual aids of grace are requisite in order
to avoid sin, and what we dream was God's covenant to give
us those graces, was nothing more than a palpitation of the
heart and a bounding of the blood. Many are the great beginnings which are undertaken in the human spirit, and as many
and as great the ruins which remain.

But it is not only in our commencements that the agency
of the human spirit is to be remarked. In the shape of self-
love it creeps into works well begun, and destroys their purity

and saps their strength. Or it comes upon good and single-minded intentions, and warps them from their first direction, and makes them useless for any supernatural purpose. Then when we find that something has gone wrong, the same human spirit makes us eager and anxious to set matters right and to renew our fervor in its own way. Consequently, as a means to this end, we undertake austerities on a mere physical impulse, and out of a humor of natural self-revenge. A tendency to talk about ourselves and to speak of our spiritual state and to let others know what we are feeling and experiencing is another operation of the human spirit which does the devil's work for him without his having the trouble of interfering.

But the human spirit can do more than give us an impulse toward good, it can furnish a certain amount of facility in doing it. Elihu thought the Holy Ghost moved him to reprove Job, and his spirit gave him no little depth and eloquence in his reproofs. Cardinal Bona says that when a spiritual man finds himself filled with great light, he must not be too quick in concluding that it is the work of grace.[1] It may come, he says, just as well from the natural vivacity of his disposition, or from the mere habit of meditating on the truths of religion, and the habit of meditation is a very different thing from the grace and gift of it, or it may come from a simple intellectual speculation on natural and divine things. Hence it is that often in the midst of such light our will remains dry and cold, and destitute of all the unction of the Holy Ghost. We do not judge a tree by its branches and flowers, but by its fruits; so we judge of these interior lights by the good works which they produce. If we examine these lights narrowly we shall often find some one little dark streak in them, something,

---

1. The criteria of Cardinal Bona, by which he distinguishes the human spirit from the diabolical, have attracted the notice of M. de Mirville in his first *Mémoire on Pneumatologie,* and he has promised to consider them at length, and in connection with Catholic theology, in his second *Mémoire. Nous étudierons aussi la veritable nature de cet ennemi domestique appelé la chair, ennemi que le cardinal Bona ne craint pas de ranger dans la classe des Esprits. Nous tâcherons tout à la fois de bien définir le vrai rôle de ces agents psychologiques et physiologiques, dans les phénomènes magnitiques, et de voir s'ils peuvent jamais y remplacer l'assistance d'un Esprit Etranger.* Prem. Mem. p. 81. 3me Edition.

it may be, contrary to prudence or alien to the principles of
Christian perfection. A dash of levity is an illustration of this:
for levity is an especial sign of the human spirit. Richard
of St. Victor says that when we are impelled to do any good
work easily and with a certain feeling of levity, that levity
ought to make us fear that our impulsion is rather from the
flesh than from the Spirit, especially if it is accompanied by
anything agreeable to nature. In like manner the joy with which
we are attracted to anything ought to be suspected, if it be
mingled with warmth or impatience; for the Holy Spirit is
moderate, patient, tranquil, and the movements He excites are
conformable to what He is in Himself.

Another mark of the human spirit is to be found in the
self-annoyance or disgust which arises in us at the view of
our own faults, which we shall have especially to consider
hereafter. It casts us down also because of the defects of our
good works or the ill success of earnest efforts. We wish all
to be square and neat; and there are some dispositions which
are more tried by the absence of finish and completeness in
their works than by an actual sin. There is an obstinate attachment to devotional practices, because we fancy they have done
us good, which looks like supernatural perseverance, and yet
is in truth nothing but the pertinacity of the human spirit.
If sometimes our inward life is inundated with a gushing variety of good thoughts and zealous projects, it is for the most
part to be attributed to the human spirit. The Holy Spirit inundates us slowly, noiselessly and with simplicity, like the
flooding of low-lying grounds by an oozing river. One thing
at a time, and all things in order, such are the characteristics
for the most part of divine operations. Unevenness and fluctu-
ation of spirits is another human operation, which need never
be mistaken for divine. The same also may be said of a delusion which leads us to fancy that self-respect requires such
or such a course of action in us. I am not saying that where
there is such a motive there is always sin, but that the action
is purely human, and must be content to take its chance as
such. It must not be disappointed if no blessing goes along
with it, and it is not allowed to enjoy the rights and immuni-
ties of evangelical prudence. Nothing is so completely left

to itself and to its own unassisted efforts by providence as human prudence, and the reason is obvious. It is, as far as it goes, an attempt on man's part to do without God, and to walk alone in his own wisdom. Yet how the world admires this human prudence, and the gravity of look and the solemnity of manner and the measuredness of words which are mostly its attendant gifts. O man! you are not truly prudent, because you are pompous, because you do not commit yourself to good people, or because your eye is grave, and your demeanor decorous, and your words flow as if they were worth a silver crown apiece; but you are prudent because your eye is calmly fixed on God, and your heart whole with Him, and your gait slow lest you should leave Him behind. Human prudence will earn you human respect. Will that bread satisfy you? You did not come into the world in order that you might go to your grave an unoffending and unproductive man! God wants something more of you than that you should be unoffending; and alas! to be unproductive is a capital offense against Him and souls. Yet with how many Christians is this unoffending nonproduction their very *summum bonum.* "To be ever safe is to be ever feeble"; if ever the spirit of evangelical prudence spoke plainly, it spoke in that golden apophthegm.

The spirit of unnecessary recreations, the spirit of mixed intentions, the spirit of dispensations, the spirit of little immortifications practiced under the pretext that we do not mean them to be habitual, the spirit which makes us speak lightly and with a false prudence about the enthusiasm of our first fervors in religion, all these are developments of the human spirit. And those peculiar developments, which show themselves most in each one of us, are those which fit themselves most readily to our natural temperament and disposition. It is to this quarter, therefore, that we must look most steadily, and prepare most carefully; for it is there that this "ignoble" spirit, as Scaramelli calls it, will invade us.

But the worst artifice of the human spirit is when it comes upon us in the disguise of virtue. We have a natural aptitude for some particular virtue, and we mistake that facility for grace, and so become deluded. The worst, says Scaramelli, is when this injurious spirit travesties some virtue, and makes us seem in our own eyes different from what we really are. For, as Richard of St. Victor says, the nature of man contains within itself a natural disposition to certain virtues, in the pursuit of which it meets with fewer impediments than in the pursuit of others; and on the other hand, every man has in himself a peculiar inaptitude and repugnance to the practice of particular virtues. Hence it comes to pass, very often, that a certain promptitude in doing good looks like devotion, and is not really so, but arises from natural inclination. From this doctrine, that great mystic infers that the thoughts, words, works and affections of imperfect persons ordinarily proceed from this low natural principle, and are consequently to be attributed to the human spirit.

Scaramelli proceeds to give cases in illustration of this doctrine. Beginners in devotion, and other imperfect persons, are often to be found who will run here and there all day long in works of mercy, who are all ingenuity in devising plans, and all hands in carrying them into execution. You would believe them to be very portraits of charity and zeal. Yet if you could penetrate into their hearts, you would find that all these anxieties and promptitudes are operations of nature, not of grace, arising in great measure, if not altogether, from an ardent and unquiet temper, which could not live if it were not always embarrassed with a thousand occupations. Another person you will find who is quiet and peaceable, and does not even resent an injury. It is as if he did not know how to be angry. You would believe him to be a very model of meekness. Yet if you diligently scrutinized his apparent imperturbability, you would see that it was not grace which moderated and refrained his natural character, but that he was of a cold, heavy and phlegmatic disposition. Again, you will meet with persons who are full of tenderness in prayer, and continually bursting into tears. You would suppose the manna of Heaven was being rained upon them by angelic hands. But put these tears into the balance of the sanctuary, and it will soon be evident that grace has the least share in them. They are legitimately claimed by a sanguine, tender and affectionate nature, whose imagination is vividly acted upon by any lovely or pitiful object. So others are to be met with who are so attentive at prayer, that they can pass entire hours in it without distraction. Your first thought is that they have arrived at a profound and habitual recollection, and perhaps a high degree of contemplation. But you will be mistaken. This attention may not only come from a heavenly light which fixes the mind on a divine object, but also from a strong imagination, or a profoundly melancholy temperament, and a certain fixedness which nails the mind to the objects on which it is meditating.

But let us look at ourselves. On some days we feel an extraordinary fervor, and a great deal of spiritual consolation; and so we believe ourselves to be full of God. But, alas! our poor soul deceives itself: this great consolation is but a work of nature. Some good fortune has befallen us, or some piece of happy news arrived, by which our sensitive appetite is dilated, and filled with cheerfulness and natural delectation. With this a slight amount of devotion is combined, which gives a tinge of spirituality to the whole mind. So that the fervor is nothing better than natural high spirits colored with devotion. We can soon test the truth of this. Let something happen to displease us, and the consolation is gone like lightning, the fervor cooled in an instant and our mind hard to be lifted to God. Alas, that it should be so easy to confound the impulses that come from God with those that nature gives, and to take the human spirit for the divine! Poor we! how shall we blush at the tribunal of God, when we find our actions which we believed to be the pure silver of supernatural virtues, to be only the worthless scoria of natural actions, or a drossy compound of nature and grace, where two-thirds are nature, to one-third grace. So says Isaias, *Argentum tuum versum est in scoriam, vinum tuum mixtum est aqua. (Is.* 1:22). All these sweetnesses which spring from natural cheerfulness, or quickness of perception, or mere habits of meditation, explain why it is that people can feel so much, advance so little, and fall back so often.

The corrosive power of this human spirit is shown by the way in which it causes natural temperament to mingle with and mar our good. Thus the zeal of a choleric man becomes bitter—a melancholy man ungraceful in his charity, and a cheerful man unrecollected in his prayers. But let us listen to Scaramelli commenting on that sweetest and most persuasive of mystics, Richard of St. Victor, if St. Bernard will not be angry at my calling him so. It is to be remembered that the human spirit mixes itself with the works of the most devout people, who are in the habit of regulating their actions with no slight perfection. Although this ignoble spirit has not the power utterly to spoil them, it nevertheless corrupts them to a certain extent, and lowers their perfection. Thus if a spiritual man is of an irritable disposition, he experiences in his zeal a certain bitterness and natural perturbation. If he is phlegmatic, he is remiss in correcting. If he is melancholy, his charity wants benignity. If he is high-spirited, his virtues are diluted by dissipation. In a word, as the liquor from the bottle of skin tastes of the skin, so the virtues taste of the natural disposition of the man in whom they dwell. Let every man, therefore, beware of the spirit that sleeps in his own bosom.

First of all, this human spirit is a most malignant spirit; for under the pretense of serving God, it is always seeking itself and its own natural satisfactions. And in the next place it is a most subtle spirit, which is always gliding like smooth oil into all our actions. Huge mortification is required to fight it well, and to beat it. On this matter, St. Bernard quotes the saying of the Wise Man, that he who overcomes himself is more to be esteemed than he who takes a city; for nature can take a city, but grace alone can take self. Let every one reflect, adds our author, that the greatest enemy of persons advanced in spirituality is neither the devil, nor the world, nor the flesh; for these three adversaries have either been already overcome, or are actually being combated. Their greatest enemy is the human spirit, which is the ally of self-love; and it cannot be overcome except by an incessant mortification of the will.

To this authority I would add that of Cardinal Bona; and I will paraphrase the passage in which he speaks of the human spirit, and compares it with the devil. Man has no more pernicius enemy than his own spirit; for it is full of deceits, artifices and disguises. It is inconstant. It takes different shapes.

It is curious, unquiet, the enemy of its own repose and a lover of novelty. The imagination produces nothing deformed or monstrous with which it will not occupy itself. There is nothing unruly, vain and ridiculous which it is not capable of embracing. Sometimes it appears altogether subject to the Spirit of God, sometimes enslaved to the spirit of Satan; and it never abides long in one stay. As it is full of artifices, it assumes different forms with a most surprising industry and a marvelous subtilty, so as to hide its own convenience and interests under the pretexts of the glory of God and of perfection. Under these captious appearances it is nevertheless very far indeed from seeking the glory of God or loving perfection. For it seeks itself in everything and loves itself excessively. It positively adores itself, and turning aside from their true end things the most holy, by a horrible sacrilege it refers them to itself. It is on this account that a man must far more distrust himself, and stand on his guard against himself, than against Satan. For no power external to ourselves is able to hurt us, unless we give him the hand at first, furnish him with arms when he begins the attack, and inwardly acquiesce in his designs and enterprises. Of a truth, many enemies push us to our ruin. The world pushes us thither: Satan pushes us: other men push us; but no one pushes us so violently and so dangerously as we push ourselves.

St. Bernard, in his eighty-fifth sermon on the Canticles, writes as follows: Everyone is his own enemy. Man urges and precipitates himself into evil in such a way that if he would only keep his own hands from suicide, he need fear the violence of no one else. Who can harm you, says St. Peter, if you have no desire except to do good? Your own consent to evil is the only hand which can wound and kill you. If when the devil suggests evil to you, or the world invites you to it, you withhold your consent, no misfortune can befall you. The devil may push you, but he cannot throw you down, if you refuse him your consent. How plain it is, then, that man is his own principal and most dangerous enemy!

I still dwell on this all-important subject, and at the risk of some little repetition, I will ask you to examine with me the marks by which Cardinal Bona distinguishes the human spirit, as we have already done those of Scaramelli and Richard of St. Victor.

First of all, he says, there are persons so touched with the remembrance of their sins, and the meditation of the sufferings of Christ, that they shed an abundance of tears, and are suddenly filled with a profound sentiment of compunction. This disposition leads them to chastise themselves with rude disciplines and macerations of the flesh. Others are touched in a lively way by the consideration of the joys of Heaven, and they all at once go into an ecstasy. Yet specious as these effects are, they do not come from the Spirit of God, but from the love of self, from the liveliness and application with which the soul has apprehended its objects, and from the natural change which a sudden and extraordinary emotion causes. This is easily seen when the impetuosity and ardor of this emotion is arrested; for then such persons not only relapse into a state of coldness and dryness, but even fall back into their old passions and vices. On the contrary, the true movements and impressions of the Spirit of God have nothing vain or unprofitable for the conversion of souls, but at once effect great things. Hence we must conclude that the discernment of spirits in these matters is very difficult. For we often attribute to the Spirit of God, and often also the spirit of the devil, that which really comes only from the dispositions and impressions of nature. Everyone, therefore, ought carefully to examine his heart, so that he may not be deceived by his own spirit, which St. Gregory calls a spirit of pride. Now no one can examine and discuss what passes in himself, unless he prepares for God a dwelling in his soul by chasing away every kind of presumption, and keeping himself down in distrust of self, and a sincere humility. For, as the holy Pope excellently says, no one can become the abode of God's Spirit, who has not first emptied himself of his own; for the Spirit of God rests only in humble minds, in quiet consciences and in hearts which tremble at His words.

Secondly, it sometimes happens that we begin a work truly for God and for His glory. But inasmuch as nature is always secretly seeking itself, insensibly and without our perceiving it, we forget the good pleasure of God in the progress of the work which we have begun, and instead of regarding attentively His glory and His will, we let ourselves go about seeking our own convenience and satisfaction. We find this out in the following way. If God arrests the success or completion of our work by any illness or accident, at once we are troubled and disquieted; and such a sadness and perturbation of our interior peace take possession of us, that it is as much as ever we can do to acquiesce in the Divine Will. There are few persons who are thoroughly aware of the malignity of that natural inclination which is at the bottom of all self-seeking, because it is so subtle and hidden. The very fact that good is in a certain sense conformable to our natural desires, causes us easily to lean toward ourselves. So that even in the intentions which seem to us the most pure and the most according to the will of God, we often seek ourselves, drawing rather to what suits our own inclination than what is precisely the most for the glory of God.

A similar defect may be observed in our love of mortification, especially when it is too ardent. For many mortify their senses, restrain their affections, punish their bodies and abstain from pleasures, with an appearance of virtue and zeal, who do all this in reality to be seen of men, or to give their own minds a satisfaction in which self-love seeks itself with all the address and artifice of which it is capable. For he who is impelled only by the instinct of grace always desires to be hidden. Nature as invariably seeks to display itself. Yet even those who are really full of supernatural and divine lights are not exempt from this fault, in consequence of their frequent insensible returns upon self and the views of self which are continually opening upon them, like landscapes seen through sudden openings in a wood, just at times when they ought to be most exclusively occupied with God.

Thirdly, it is very certain that we have need of the grace of God to pray do good works as we ought. But it is certain also that we can do virtuous actions from a human motive, from self-love, or from servile fear. We have moreover so little light in ourselves that we cannot clearly distinguish on what principle we act, whether it be divine or human. In truth we wish to raise our heart to God, and to disengage it from these returns upon self which are so full of imperfections. But sometimes this desire arises from a subtle and secret interest which we do not perceive. For we may desire to be stripped of our self-love by another self-love. We can desire and love humility through pride. Without question there is in our actions and interior dispositions a perpetual circle and incessant return of ourselves upon ourselves, which is almost imperceptible. There always remains in our heart a root of self-love which is extremely fine, subtle and volatile, and which is unknown to us. So that we are sometimes very far from guiding ourselves by reasons altogether divine and motives purely disinterested, at the very moment when we think we are doing so the most completely. Job's comforters are examples of this. Pure and true love of God, disengaged from all consideration of self, is extremely rare and exceedingly difficult. If men could hide themselves from the eyes of God and from the eyes of the world, there are very few indeed who would do good, and very few who would abstain from evil.

Fourthly, when we tease and worry ourselves, and are as it were in despair about our spiritual progress after we have fallen, all these dispositions come only from a secret self-confidence and pride. For he who is truly humble is never astonished at his falls. He knows that man is so feeble he can do nothing without the assistance of God. So that he asks the Divine aid, detesting his sin with a heart at once tranquil and contrite; and rising from his fall with courage and diligence, he renews his course with fresh fervor.

It is also a mark of the human spirit to attach itself to its exercises and functions, however good and holy, to such a degree that when superiors withdraw us from them and apply us to others, we indulge in murmurs and complaints, and imagine that we can never reach the perfection befitting our state, as if not to allow us always to do what we like were depriving us of the necessary means to attain perfection. For the pain which we feel under these circumstances does not come really from the fact that the things we have been forced to abandon were more suitable and efficacious for our perfection, but because we rested in them and leaned upon them with a vicious affection, and were complacently enjoying therein our own interest and satisfaction rather than the glory of God. Nature loves what is beautiful, what is good, what is perfect, and seeks to be pleasing and attractive to itself in these things. Hence it comes to pass that it hates everything that is defective in its enterprises and designs, and even in its most spiritual works: insomuch that these defects, as had been said before, torment and disquiet it, which is a sign that the love of the good and the perfect, however specious it seemed, was only the product of nature.

Fifthly, the human spirit instigates men who are learned and desirous of becoming more so, to learn the science of divine and supernatural things, partly to give them consideration from others, and partly to satisfy their curiosity. From this eagerness to appear learned in high matters proceed many rare, magnificent and subtle discourses whose only fruit is to tickle the ears, not to save the souls, of others. Hence also those writings of philosophers who treat of virtue in a pompous style, without spirit and without life, filling the soul with distractions, and dissipating it in an infinity of speculations and ideas, and without the least gift of inflaming it with love of God. Works which emanate from the natural capacity of the mind, and in the production of which grace has had no share, may doubtless contain an abundance of good things, but the fruit of them is very small. They are like the Apostle's sounding brass and tinkling cymbal. Whereas the words which are animated by the Spirit of God, although they have nothing lofty or elevated in themselves, nay on the contrary are far from anything of the sort, bring forth in their simplicity abundant fruit. The human spirit on the other hand is accustomed to distribute itself readily among external things, and to plume itself on the multitude and variety of its fine thoughts, and this causes it to swerve from the unity which is so desirable and so necessary.

Sixthly, in matters relating to virtue the prudence of the flesh is the inseparable companion of the human spirit. This is the reason why so many content themselves with mediocrity in the spiritual life, without aspiring to a perfect state. They measure everything by themselves and by their own weakness, and not by the power and efficacy of the grace of God.

They fear suffering and contempt, and ardently love riches, honors and bodily comforts, and to these things they refer all they do, or say or think. They wish to make an enjoyment of themselves, as if they were their own ultimate end; and forming an idol of themselves, they pay it the worship which is due to God. They let their soul be charmed by the enchantments of the world, and sell it as a slave to the goods of this present life.

As charity never seeks its own interests, so blind self-love seeks no interests but its own. And the power of this pernicious love over the soul is at once so malignant and so penetrating, that it not only mingles with temporal and earthly things, but even with heavenly and spiritual things, infecting with its venom the love of prayer, the usage of the Sacraments and the exercise of virtues. Even in these things men seek for praise and the reputation of sanctity, or secretly hope to obtain from God certain lights and spiritual luxuries and joys of soul, which only make them soft and vain. This venom of self-love taints even our works of penance; for frequently after a fall a sinner is touched with extreme sorrow, and chastises his body fiercely, not because of the offense against God, but because of the note of infamy which he has himself incurred, or through the fear of losing his reputation amongst men, or at least because he wishes to seem innocent in his own eyes. Yet as no solid peace is to be found among the perishable things of this life, there is so much inconstancy in a man's love of himself that he is incessantly changing his affections and pleasures, and knows neither what he wishes nor what he is doing. Sometimes he lets himself be rashly buoyed up by hope; sometimes he falls into despair; sometimes he breaks out into a vain joy; sometimes he is out of his depth in sadness. There is neither moderation nor measure in his conduct, and instead of being in a mean, he is always in extremes. He resembles a vessel, tossed hither and thither uncertainly on the waves, and at last striking on a rock, and becoming a miserable wreck. For as our Saviour has taught us, he that loves his own soul shall lose it. Now all that is said of the human spirit must be referred to this pernicious self-love; for it is the exciting cause of all the merely natural movements of the soul.

It is plain that Scaramelli and Bona drew from a single source, that that source was Richard of St. Victor, and that he spoke the spiritual tradition of his day, on a subject about which, more than almost any other in the spiritual life, it is needful to have clear and decided views.

You may ask how we are to test this human spirit, and how we are to rectify it. I answer briefly that we may test it in two ways and rectify it in two ways. Our first test must be whether we will or will not allow ourselves to be despoiled of our habits and practices by obedience. The second is whether a virtue is accompanied in us by its congruous virtues, which in the order of the Holy Spirit it would be, and is not an isolated and exceptional thing. The first means of rectifying it is to redirect our intention to the glory of God, even when in act we are obliged to abstain from what we desire; and the second means is to strive to put grace by degrees in the place of all other principles of action. But more of this in the next chapter.

We must remember that to be in a state of grace and to act from a principle of grace are two very different things. To act from a principle of grace is to make the pleasure of God the sole motive of our actions, to the exclusion of all mere natural motives; and to learn to know God more and more is the means toward the accomplishment of this magnificent end. In such a work as this there can be no rapidity, no vehemence, nothing sudden, nothing revolutionary. Grace must occupy as fast as it destroys; it must fill the void as it creates it. The aborigines must waste in the presence of the white man; but it must be a waste, not an extermination, else the wild beasts will be down upon the settlements. Some men turn away from this slow supernatural life because they weary of the yoke which is never off their necks, and some because they are persuaded such a life is impossible to man. Yet the Saints and the saintlike lived it, and were at large and at ease in it. Why not we? The state of grace seeks God and all other things in Him; the principle of grace seeks God and nothing else but Him. The state of grace is satisfied with clearness from sin; the principle of grace is ever forcing its

way upwards to divine union. The state of grace has calm
and storm alternately; the principle of grace, if it oscillates
at all, oscillates like the needle, in fidelity to its center. In
the beginning it is hard, yet with many consolations. Its progress is like the dawning of day. Its end is the eternal sunrise.
Why are there so few that live it? Because so few have faith.
"Thy truths, O Lord, are diminished from among the children
of men."

Chapter XIII

THE HUMAN SPIRIT DEFEATED

If we are willing to take the authority of St. Bernard and Richard of St. Victor, of Cardinal Bona and Scaramelli, we must suppose that the devil is guiltless of by far the greater part of the sins of good people, and that even temptation is far less exclusively his domain than we are often in the habit of considering it. We must not, however, push this doctrine too far, nor extend it beyond the limits, surely wide enough, within which approved writers confine it. Nevertheless, admitted even so far, we shall find if we have hitherto neglected it, that it is a doctrine full of practical results to us in the spiritual life. It gives us quite a different idea of our warfare. It throws a new light on scruples. It makes us change our tactics against temptation; and above all, it facilitates the practices of humility and self-distrust. When we refer everything to the devil, and he is in our thoughts and on our lips at every moment, we may be sure that we are as yet but on the threshold of the spiritual life, and have but a shallow knowledge either of it or of ourselves. There is hardly any point of spirituality which has suffered more from the customary exaggerations of men than this one of the devil's share in our temptations and our falls. Verily, he may truly claim the lion's share with most of men, and his office with holy people is both constant and arduous; so that he may well allow to his ally, the human spirit, its own unfortunate and independent prerogatives.

But we have not done with the human spirit yet. In this chapter I wish to speak of one of its most common developments, and then of the means by which the human spirit generally may be brought into subjection.

The development of which I am about to speak is touchiness about our reputation, a disease most fatal to the spiritual life, and yet one to which spiritual men are subject to a strange and unexpected degree. It is a perfect cankerworm to an interior spirit, and one of the most prolific causes of lukewarmness. Earth may be an unhappy place; but it is not the pressure of God's providence which causes most of the unhappiness, nor the roarings of the devil going about seeking whom he may devour. It is the human spirit operating in quarrels, coldness, conceit, rivalry, envy, strife, jealousies, misunderstandings and an exaggerated idea of little slights and wrongs. Now the suffering of all these things, and it is very acute, comes from fretfulness about our reputation. The excessive care of our reputation is naturally a besetting sin of times whose spirit of publicity does really make a Christian duty of the preservation of our good name.

But let us consider what this fretfulness brings in its train. It is obviously quite inconsistent with interior peace, which is the soul of the spiritual life. For how can we be at peace if we make ourselves responsible for what is not in our own power, but escapes from us on all sides? It breeds an exaggerated idea of our own importance, and so destroys humility. It causes suspiciousness, and so kills simplicity. It is a daily source of irritability, and so ruins charity. It is the crowned king of distractions, and so draws off our attention from God and eternal things. Yet see what folly it is! For if we get what we wish, what does it amount to in nine cases out of ten, but being better thought of than we deserve, looking differently to man's eye and to God's eye? And surely in reality we are what we are in the judgment of God, and we are nothing more. Thus, of all unreal satisfactions the preservation for the moment of our reputation is at once the most unfruitful, the most anxious and the most precarious. The only decent pretense for such a jealousy is that we may not lose the means of serving God; and to act with a single eye to His good pleasure would be a safer and more successful rule of conduct than to put our reputation out to nurse with the thousand tongues of men. Hence it was that saints, who were silent under all other calumnies, would not for the most part rest quiet under the imputation of heresy.

Everything which is corrective of the human spirit in general is a remedy for this touchiness about our reputation. But there are some remedies for it as a peculiar disease of itself. Special prayer for that end is obvious; and the same may be said of making it the subject of our particular examen, to find out how much we really offend in this matter. But the principal remedy of all is to keep our eye steadily fixed on the beautiful and potent example of our Blessed Lord in this very respect. As to His reputation as a teacher of doctrine, He was called a fool (*John* 10), and the questions of Caiaphas express the public opinion about Him. As to His morals, He was called seditious, drunkard and glutton. (*Luke* 7). As to His truth, He was esteemed a heretic and a Samaritan (*John* 8), and was openly accused of witchcraft (*Mark* 3); and when condemned to death He made no defense. The lives of the Saints hardly seem wonderful when we have well studied the excessive humiliations of Jesus with regard to His reputation. Even to those who are far from saints it may be given by God to know the sweetness of calumny, when we feel ourselves sinking out of man's sight into the divine depths of our Saviour's dear and awful Passion.

We must now proceed to examine the ways in which we are to combat the human spirit. And here it is of importance that we should put clearly before ourselves once more the position which we occupy in the spiritual life, inasmuch as the human spirit, though the enemy of every man born into the world, is especially the plague of the spiritual man. Who and where are we, then?

There are many Christians who seem to go no further than a hatred of mortal sin. We are not supposed to belong to them. There are others who strive conscientiously to avoid venial sin. We are not contented even with this. We are drawn to love, to love God and to love perfection, and to have no reserves with God. As to whether we shall be saints or not, our mind never rests on the subject. We should fling the thought off from us as a miserable temptation. All we see clearly before us is the resolution to have no reserves with God, and then

to leave all else to Him. This attraction grew upon us, and
now we have little doubt it is from God. For a time we had
little or no sensible fear of God, because sensible love was
so strong, but the fear is returning, without disquietude. We
seldom thought of Hell, and the thought of it hardly affects
us now. We sometimes caught ourselves making acts of love
when we intended to make acts of contrition. We were curi-
ously attracted toward the Sacraments, as if they were magnets, and we found it a great trial to leave prayer for our
daily duties. Indeed, we are only beginning to find out now
that the relative duties of our station in life are almost an
eighth Sacrament. We began to care very little for man's judgment of us, and we saw it was wise to be really obedient
to our directors.

It was plain that, however much of this was natural, much
also was supernatural. These dispositions amounted to a vocation, and this vocation was a gift which we might compare
with creation or with Baptism, without doing them dishonor.
To correspond to it was plainly a primary duty; but we made
up our minds that it would cost us something to do this. Paradise was not meant for cowards. And so we began.

And what were our beginnings like? All day long we had
a sensible heat of Divine Love in our hearts. We desired to
do great things, very great things, foolishly great things, for
God. We believed we should never grow tired of spiritual exercises. We were impatient to be saints, and we undervalued
the grace of perseverance. We were continually wondering
at the beauty of Jesus, and wanted to stand still and look at
it, while we were wearied and fatigued by our ordinary actions and relative duties. O happy days! Days of power, that
passed, but left their fruits behind them!

Sometimes we were tempted to undervalue them. But we
soon saw how stupid it was to esteem lightly any of God's
gifts, because someday they would hand us on to others. We
knew that these first fervors were a spiritual childhood, but
nevertheless that God meant something by them. We felt that
they were burning, felling and clearing a great deal of the
past, ploughing the present and sowing for the future. We
knew they would never return, that the Saints had had them,

and that they were a shelter from the world, just when its hot suns would have withered our souls and stricken them with barrenness. We were not, however, blind to the dangers of these fervors. We knew it would be dangerous to fall too much in love with sensible sweetness. We might become censorious. We might neglect the duties of our state. We might trust too much to self, and not be sufficiently dependent upon grace. We might take rash vows, or choose a state of life, or make some great change, in a heat. We knew also that someday there would be a reaction, and we could not tell what shape it might take. Hence we made some effort, but not so much as we might have done, to mortify self-love, to be cheerful when we fell, to be frightened of ourselves, to be open with our director, not to read high books or to attempt out-of-the-way methods of prayer, to avoid singularity, not to argue about religion or to talk of spirituality, and to have a special devotion to the silence of Jesus.

So at last we left the nurse's arms and tottered about the floor, often asking to be taken back again, not seldom with our little heads broken against hard tables and inconvenient chairs. Our strong good will for perfection remained, though the foresight of its difficulties was much less confused. We began to discern the difference between courage and presumption, and we saw that courage was always accompanied with a clear view and a keen sense of our own nothingness. We began to acquire some solidity in devotion, by sticking for a year or more to the acquisition of a single virtue, or the extirpation of a single fault. We became more recollected, without knowing it, and without seeming so. We grew modestly timid of adopting too many practices and committing ourselves to too many vocal prayers, scapulars, confraternities and the like. We saw the importance of gentleness, because the practice of so many other virtues is involved in it, because it is by far the most powerful interior motive-power, and because Our Lord proposes it to us in a special way. Yet in practicing this gentleness, we studiously mortified natural tendernesses, perceiving that they wound the jealousy of God and make the heart effeminate and incapable of grace. There was a day, it was a day of revolution, when we ceased making

general resolutions, and only made particular ones. We culti-
vated the spirit of faith, for it dawned upon us that it was
a gift capable of increase by culture. We learned prayer, as
boys learn a lesson, and never minded its being for the time
actually a hotbed of new imperfections. We were careful not
to make a show of being spiritual. We began to dislike our
ruling passion and instinctively to strike blows at it whenever
we had the opportunity. We were tolerably patient with the
slowness of our own progress, and attended to our present
grace. We became more and more reverently devoted to the
Sacred Humanity; and while somehow caring less about lights,
flowers and epithets, we were conscious of a wonderfully grave
and businesslike confidence in our dearest Lady.

Through all this we felt great sensible sweetness almost con-
tinuously, were unconscious of much progress, were dread-
fully tempted to self-trust and were periodically liable to
spiritual panics. Still the work was all right as far as it went.
All it had to do now was to *wear*. This is the one question
in all spiritual things: How will it wear? Alas! the world and
cloister! How choked up they both are with wornout and shabby
spiritualities, and never a Jew to go round to buy them!

But did all this go smoothly? Did we make no mistakes
after all? Oh, far from smoothly, and plenty of mistakes! Oh,
so many heartaches, doubts, panics, wearinesses and wayward-
nesses! First of all we did not, though we meant it, give ourselves up unreservedly to God. We kept back some attachments
that were not sinful, some things which we thought our circumstances admitted of. We struck a balance between prudence and principle, and forgot that concession and dispensation
are for the later, not the earlier stages, of the spiritual life.
We adopted fresh practices and strictnesses, egged on by self-
love, not the simple view of God's will, and we did not remember that we ought to consult and investigate our purity of intention as much in adopting a strictness, as in asking a
dispensation. We permitted ourselves in little laxities, with
regard to the custody of the senses, dress, talking, bodily fatigue, health and such matters. We gave way to discouragements, because of our faults, our increased self-knowledge,
our multiplied temptations, our inability to keep our own

resolutions and the subtraction of spiritual sweetness. Then, losing our hearts in this discouragement, we presently lost our heads, and fell into all manner of scruples from not distinguishing between temptation and consent, from secret tenacity of our own opinions, from an excessive fear of God's justice and a want of confidence in His mercy, from a morbid desire of avoiding semblances of sin and from an indiscreet austerity, solitude and sacrifice of recreation. Heart and head gone, spirits went next. We gave way to an inexplicable sadness, and were solely tempted to change our lives, to discontinue our strictnesses, to talk of our sorrows and to seek worldly consolations. Had we done any one of these four things, we might have been lost. The sadness did us a great mischief as it was; it drove us into self-introversion. We lost sight of the grand objects of faith, and went into an excess with our examinations of conscience; and then to extricate ourselves from this, we plunged into too many designs, and had too many irons in the fire and were inordinately disappointed when our good works did not succeed. There was altogether a want of childlike abandonment, both of our exterior plans, and of our interior conduct, into the hands of Providence. We wished to attempt to convert others before we had a right to distract ourselves from ourselves. Even perfection in the world must have a novitiate of looking after itself, as well as perfection in monasteries. However, we determined to set all right by talking very disparagingly of ourselves, and so made the worst mistake of all, and lost the few ounces of humility which we had so painfully scraped together. For it turned out in the end to be conceit which made us abuse ourselves. The upshot of it all was that we allowed ourselves to be too much engrossed with the metaphysics of the spiritual life and its exclusively interior things, so as to be drawn off from a loving attention to the Sacraments, to Jesus and to God. However, mistakes, like other things, have their day; and we can afford now not only to glean wisdom from our blunders, but amusement also.

But we have not done yet. The ugliest part is still to be confessed. These mistakes only concerned ourselves. There were others which concerned our neighbors. Oh, what disedification, both given and taken! There were scandals given to others aiming at perfection, scandals taken from others aiming at it and scandals taken by the world. How unlovely did we make the work of God appear! We talked about religion, and so illustrated by our words the inconsistency of our practice; and doubtless, as beginners always do, we talked above our state, and from books rather than experience. We adopted uncommon devotions, which looked still less inviting when exhibited together with our unhumble, unmortified, unobliging manners. We were impatient of contradiction, weary with prayer, irritable with penance, as persons accustomed to have it all their own way with their favorite spiritual books. We envied the spiritual advancement of others, took up with self-willed austerities which interfered with domestic arrangements, unnecessarily provoked the opposition of relatives and disturbed the comfort of others. The duties of our station were performed in a precipitate, perfunctory and ungraceful manner. We did not praise others with simplicity, because we were dissatisfied with them, and did not realize that God's leadings are numberless, and that others may not have our light. There was a bitterness in our zeal which was shown both in words and manner, and we were often inclined to threaten men with the judgments of God. We were censorious, and given to preach and moralize; and if we tried to avoid this fault we fell into an opposite one, and gave way too easily, when others for their own convenience wished us to suspend our strictnesses.

The world treated us unjustly, certainly. Yet we did the same in our turn to other spiritual persons. We misunderstood them, when we were complaining of being misunderstood ourselves. We did not remember in their case how many faults may consist with the beginnings of real piety. We ought to have known from our own experience that they were in all probability fighting a good fight with those very faults which were offending us, or that God was leaving them without aid in those particular respects for their humiliation and trial; and when all this ought to have been in our own minds, we sat by and allowed worldly people ill-naturedly to exaggerate these faults.

In our own case the harsh judgments of the world had much truth in them. They ought to have taught us lessons of humility.

They were probably far less true when they were doing injustice to others. They should have been, moreover, warnings to us when we were unconsciously becoming lukewarm. We might have accepted them as chastisements to us for our judgments of others. And at the worst we should have remembered Jesus, and been sweet-mannered. At all events here we are, having learned thus much from it all, that there are two spirits which effectually hinder all advance in the spiritual life: One is the spirit of taking scandal, and the other is the fidgety desire to give edification. For they both of them deny the five essential principles of the spiritual life, the law of charity which believes all things, the attention to self, the temper of concealment, the carelessness of men's judgments and the practice of the presence of God. In these five ways they destroy the interior life by a daily noxious infusion of mixed pusillanimity and pride.

And with all these miseries and mistakes we are not shipwrecked? No! that could hardly be to those who love Mary. And now with all this experience, and at this particular point of our growth in holiness, we are face to face with this enemy, the human spirit, seeking about for weapons wherewith to combat it.

The first one must be what spiritual writers often call the spirit of captivity. Grace is the opposite of nature; nature everywhere cries liberty, grace cries captivity; and without a resolute good will to take ourselves captive, we shall never beat down the human spirit. The spirit of captivity consists, as an eminent mystical writer tells us, sometimes in submission to a written rule, parcelling out our daily actions so far as our state of life will allow, sometimes in subjection to our director, even against our own judgment and without feints or wiles, sometimes in conformity to the law of Providence, especially where it thwarts and mortifies our natural liveliness and inclinations, and sometimes also in submission to that attraction of the Holy Spirit which is to many of us like a special revelation. There is also a captivity to frequently recurring, though not daily or obligatory, practices of devotion, a captivity to interior recollection with all its difficulties, trials and repressions of natural activity; and all mortification is itself but a shape of captivity.

The genuine spirit of captivity may be known by the following characteristics. It must be universal, extending its jurisdiction even where there is no question of sin. It must jealously include little things as well as great ones. It must be persevering, and not irregular, vehement or intermitting. It must act even when it has no sensible sweetness to sustain it. In these cases, nature will often get angry and gnash her teeth; but this is no real offense of our superior nature against the spirit of captivity. Love of God must be its motive and principle, even though it will not always be sensibly perceived.

This spirit of captivity is very needful, and commits blessed ravage on the human spirit. Yet it is not without its dangers. Indeed, if it had no dangers it would be good for nothing. We must be cautious, therefore, of making things obligatory upon ourselves, and so giving rise to scruples; and still more must we be careful not to take every busy, ingenious suggestion of further mortification which the human spirit will incessantly be whispering, as a divine inspiration. Captivity does not mean that we are always to do what we dislike. That for the most part is Jansenist perfection, the perfection of the *Theologia Sanctorum*,[1] a perfection which is on the Index. I have spoken of it before. In order to provide against excesses we must let our director legislate for us on the matter. If he allows us in numerous daily petty mortifications, he must fix the number, and give us an obedience always to interpret the doubts in our own favor. When this captivity discourages us or forms a distraction at prayer, it is best to neglect it totally for a while, in those particular matters in which it most troubles us. We shall find that a sort of habit of discernment will gradually grow up in us about it. We must pray for that gift of the Holy Ghost which is termed fortitude, St. Teresa's favorite gift of the seven. Liberty of spirit consists in exemption from cares, from remorse and from attachments; and captivity is the only road to this royal liberty.

The second weapon against the human spirit is the repose

---

1. This famous book in three folio volumes was written by Henry of St. Ignatius, a Carmelite, published at Liege in 1709 and condemned at Rome in 1714.

of the soul in its present grace and state. Our present grace does not mean unconquered infirmities in which we are to acquiesce. But it consists of the inevitable circumstances which surround us, considered as the ordinance and dispensation of God. It is the exact and infallible will of God with regard to us. In the present grace God gives us so much, and He gives us no more; He leads us so far, and no further; He means this, and He does not mean that.

Now to repose on our present grace is to look at it, and think of it, and measure ourselves by it. It is quite strange how little men think of the present as compared with the past and the future. Is is the genius of the human spirit, and it subserves its interests. It dies in this repose and acquiescence in the present; it expires when it is allowed to take no thought for the morrow; and in spiritual things especially it abhors this mystical death. The life of God Himself consists in an unbroken complacence in the present; and we must faintly imitate this adorable life in our souls. Moreover to acquiesce in it is to make it our occupation, no matter with what baying wolves of temptation we are beleaguered, or in what crucible of interior pains we are being tormented, or in what furnace of external persecutions we are being annealed. Indeed in this apparent standing still, all manner of progress is involved. For the spirit of faith is fed by it, the habits of patience with God and ourselves are formed and strengthened, our ordinary actions are done in the most perfect way, heroic humility is admirably practiced, and there is in our souls an incessant quiet multiplication of the degrees of Sanctifying Grace.

If we examine attentively our spiritual troubles, we shall find that almost all of them arise from the want of this acquiescence in our present grace. "Take no thought for the morrow" is a heavenly maxim quite as applicable to our interior conduct as to our exterior. Peace of heart is gained by it; for it is the most perfect remedy for all those things which disturb interior peace, which are chiefly precipitation, agitation and outward disasters. It checks precipitation, calms agitation and often prevents or mitigates the outward disasters.

The opposite line of conduct is the very masterpiece of the human spirit. It involves habitual opposition to the divine will.

It destroys interior peace. It causes discontent with God, with others, with our directors and with ourselves. It is a fertile source of spiritual envy of others. Under its influence all things are done ill, because they are done greedily, unquietly and hurriedly, as if the end of everything was nothing more than to get to the next thing; so that always being an intention ahead of our actions, all life is spoiled. It envelopes us in a fog of languor and sadness, which take all the nerve out of our mortifications; and its last stroke is to fill us with a gradually increasing nausea of the Sacraments, as over-praised recipes. The acquiescence in our present grace, on the contrary, seems to me to have been the grand gift of the great quiet-hearted St. Philip; and compared with the heavenly treasure of its solidity, what were his visions, ecstasies and night-long colloquies with his dear Madonna?

It may seem almost like a play upon words to say that hatred of self is a remedy for self-love, which always lies at the bottom of the human spirit. So it may be put in another shape. As I have said before, we are always in haste to get out of the Purgative Way in religion, and to enter the Illuminative, just as novices wish to be out of their novitiate, and long for the graver responsibilities of profession, because of its greater liberty. We are especially anxious to abandon the humbling subjects of meditation, which belong to that state, and especially meditations on the Four Last Things. Now, a long continuance of these very meditations, or at least a frequent recurrence to them, is a great means of combating the human spirit. St. Francis Borgia used to meditate as much as two hours daily on his own nothingness. Hence his characteristic virtue was humility. He was probably refreshed by supernatural lights, which enabled him to spend so long a time profitably on that subject. With him, it was most likely contemplation rather than meditation. Still, it is an example to us. A mind well exercised in the consideration of its own nothingness will be proof against many an arrow shot against it by the human spirit. It is not easy to hate ourselves; but until we come to do so with a good hearty hatred, we shall never consent to mortify ourselves, and so never be capable of union with God. This hatred is, by the grace of God, the inevitable product of deep reflection on our own nothingness.

The thoughts among which we should live familiarly are such as these: What are we in the order of nature? Simply created out of nothing, and so with no rights, but such as come from God's gratuitous covenant. To the degradation of our nothingness, we have added the guilt of rebellion. We are inferior to the angels, and akin to the beasts; mutable, and almost without self-control; subject to sufferings and indignities; helpless in childhood, and dishonorable in old age; our bodies tending to corruption, and our souls gravitating heavily to sin. What are we in the order of grace? Without it we are outcasts and exiles. Sanctifying Grace is altogether foreign to us, and from God; and actual grace must be superadded to habitual, and even then our will can destroy its efficacy. And in our best estate, self mingles with and mars our holiest actions. We have senses, but it is as much as we can do to keep custody over them; they are sources of temptation and sin, which often tyrannically overbear the soul. Our understanding is blind and stupid, imprudent, conceited and in a great measure dependent on our bodily health. Our affections are insubordinate and wild, and their tastes ignoble, continually fastening on low objects. If we could only come to judge ourselves by the same standard accounting to which we judge others, how royally should we hate ourselves! Ah! if we only demanded, and as severely exacted from ourselves what we exact from others, the same unselfishness all day and night, the same promptitude in generous deeds, the same high principles, the same pure motives! Alas! if we could only look upon ourselves from without, and at the same time have the knowledge of ourselves which we possess from within, we should soon be saints!

If we compare ourselves with a beast, the latter is no spot in God's creation. It is more patient than we are, and apparently has more self-control in pain. It corresponds better to the end of its creation than we do to ours. If we look at ourselves by the side of a fallen angel, he fell but once, and had no room given him for repentance. Many classes of sins are unknown to him, such as gluttony and drunkenness, because of the spirituality of his nature. He pines after God, even in his rebellion. He is without hope, and so has more show of right to be wicked. God does not love him, and the hapless creature knows that He never will love him.

But by God's grace we are kept from great wickedness, and these comparisons do not move us. Then let us measure ourselves by the side of holy men, by their innocence or heroic penance, by their generous zeal and arduous labors for God and souls, by their self-sacrifice and perseverance. Or let us take the angels, and think of their strength, their beauty, their understanding, their power, the wonderfulness and purity of their spiritual nature and its gifts. Cast an eye on our Blessed Lady, who is a mere creature, and sum up her dignity, her sanctity, her prerogatives, her sinlessness, her present empire. Kneel before the Sacred Humanity of Jesus, and scrutinize its definite grace, its merits, its beauty, its elevation, its Body, its Soul, its Union with the Word, and how it is the apex of the universe, the culminating point of all creation. Or go walk by the shore of that unresounding sea, the Immense and Incomprehensible God, cast a bewildered glance over the awful infinite abyss of His Perfections, known and named, or unknown and unnamed. And then, poor heart! think of what thou hast been, from youth upward, in thought, feeling and act, think of what thou art at this moment to the eye of God, even as thou knowest thyself (and how little dost thou know!), and think of what at best thou art likely to be!

We could wrestle better with the human spirit if we could keep ourselves down more. We sun ourselves in the brightness of high things, and this tells upon us like the enervating climate of southern latitudes upon the children of the north.

Chapter XIV

SPIRITUAL IDLENESS

If, of all graces, that of perseverance is the most precious, because it is the one which makes all the others of lasting value, certainly among the vices which beset the devout life, spiritual idleness is one of the chief; for it is the contradictory of perseverance. Yet I doubt whether, practically, we regard it with the fear which it deserves. All the three dispositions of our normal state, fatigue especially, are desolated by it. Struggle is tempted to give way to laziness, and to take recreation away from Christ. Fatigue is sorely drawn in its aching lassitude to fall off from dry interior faith, and to seek consolation in creatures, a step almost as fatal as going to sleep in the snow. And rest murmurs when the trumpet sounds to renew the fight, and would fain prolong itself by natural means when supernatural means have ceased.

I suppose it may be said that every man is an idle man. Did anyone ever see a man who did not naturally gravitate to idleness, unless perchance he had a heart complaint? Nay, so natural is it, that very idle men plead its very naturalness as a proof that it is almost irresistible. No man does hard work naturally. He must be driven to it, no matter whether it be by the love of money, or the fear of Hell. Idleness of its own nature is sweet, sweeter than the brightest gift the gay world can give. But spiritual men have a special inclination to be idle, which they do not always sufficiently consider. Nothing is more rare in the Church than a true contemplative vocation. Consequently, it is almost impossible for the generality of devout persons to spend their whole time in direct acts of the virtue of religion, and the cultivation of interior

163

motives and dispositions. Then, on the other hand, they conceive, not always judiciously, that their former habits of recreation, and their old amusements, are to be altogether eschewed. So that their piety creates a sort of void in them, and gives them nothing to fill it up with. This is one great reason why those who have no regular profession, or adequate domestic occupation, should engage themselves in some external work of zeal and mercy. However, if this theory to explain the phenomenon be not true, the fact is undeniable, and the world has long ill-naturedly pointed to it, that religious people, as a class, are uncommonly idle.

As this idleness is an effectual bar to progress, it is important that we should examine the matter narrowly; and if we do so, we shall find that there are seven developments of this spiritual idleness, about each of which something shall be said.

The first of them is what is usually called dissipation. It is easy to describe, but not easy to define. It is a sin without a body. It can make a body of anything and animate it. It works quietly, and hardly allows itself to be felt. Indeed one of its most dangerous characteristics is that a person is rarely aware, at the time, that he is guilty of dissipation. Its effects upon our devotion are quite disproportioned to the insignificance of its appearance. It can destroy in a few hours the hard-earned graces of months, or the fruit of a whole retreat; and the time immediately following a retreat is one of its favorite and chosen seasons. Let us see in what it consists. Everyone knows after he has been dissipated that such has been the case; but he does not always see in what his dissipation has consisted. The desolation of his soul is a proof to him that something has been wrong; but he cannot always give the wrong its name.

Dissipation consists, first of all, in putting things off beyond their proper times. So that one duty treads upon the heels of another, and all duties are felt as irksome obligations, a yoke beneath which we fret and lose our peace. In most cases the consequence of this is that we have no time to do the work as it ought to be done. It is therefore done precipitately, with natural eagerness, with a greater desire to get it simply done than to do it well, and with very little thought of God throughout. The French statesman's maxim, never do today what you can put off till tomorrow, admirable as it is for the prudent discharge of worldly duties, can seldom be safely practiced in the spiritual life. Neither would anything but confusion come of Lord Nelson's opposite rule, that a man should always be a quarter of an hour before his time. The great thing is to do each duty as it comes, quietly, perseveringly and with our eyes fixed on God. Without our having any set rule to observe, daily life has a tendency to settle itself into a groove, and thus each duty has a time which may be called its right time; and by observing this we shall avoid, on the one hand, being pressed by an accumulation of duties in arrear, and on the other being dissipated by having gaps of time not filled up. An unoccupied man can neither be a happy man nor a spiritual man.

Another symptom of dissipation consists in overtalking and prolonging immoderately visits of civility. By this is not meant that there is any point at which a person is bound to stop, or where anything positively wrong begins; but that there is such a thing as moderation in those matters, which is guided in each case by circumstances. Again, indulging in idle and indolent postures of body when we are alone tends to dissipate the mind and weakens the hold which the presence of God ought to have upon us. We must also be upon our guard against a habit, which is far from uncommon, of being always about to begin some occupation, and yet not beginning it. This wears and wastes our moral strength, and causes us to fritter our lives away in sections, being idle today because we have something in view tomorrow, which cannot be begun until tomorrow. The same dissipating result will be produced if we burden ourselves with too many vocal prayers and external observances of devotion. We shall always be in a hurry and under a sense of pressure, which will soon lead to disgust and low spirits.

A want of jealousy of ourselves at times and places of recreation is another source of dissipation. Recreation is itself a dangerous thing; because in one sense it ought to distract and dissipate us, if it is to do us any good; and of such consequence is this distraction, that recreation well-managed is one of the greatest powers of the spiritual life, a fountain of excellent cheerfulness, and a powerful enemy of sins of thought. But I must speak of this hereafter. All that need be said here is that a want of jealousy over ourselves at recreation is a cause of dissipation. The same may be said of building castles in the air and of that lax spirit which is always desiring dispensations from little obligations and self-imposed rules. I say self-imposed rules, for why impose them if they are not to be kept, and how can they be kept unless we be more jealous of seeking a dispensation when we ourselves are the dispensing power than when it must be sought from someone else?

The consequences of this dissipation are unfortunately too well-known to all of us to require any long description. First comes self-dissatisfaction, which is the cankerworm of all devotion. Then captiousness and self-defense, after which we feel that the power to pray is gone from us, as our strength goes from us in an illness. These are followed by positive ill-temper, in an hour of which we lose weeks of struggle and progress. With this is coupled a morbid inclination to judge and criticize others. Or if we have grace to keep down these more gross evils, our dissipation shows its power in multiplying our distractions at prayer, in making us peevish after Communion, or reserved with our director, or in drawing us into an effeminate way of performing our duties, and giving us a great distaste for penance.

The second development of spiritual idleness is sadness and low-spirits. It is no uncommon thing for spiritual persons to speak of sadness as if it were some dignified interior trial, or as if it were something to call out pure sympathy, kindness and commiseration—whereas in by far the greater number of instances it is true to say that no state of the spiritual life represents so much venial sin and unworthy imperfection as this very sadness. It is not humility, for it makes us querulous rather than patient. It is not repentance, for it is rather vexation with self than sorrow for the offense against God. The soul of sadness is self-love. We are sad because we are weary of well-doing and of strict living. The great secret of our cheerfulness was our anxiety and diligence to avoid venial sins, and our ingenious industry to root them out. We have now become negligent on that very point, and therefore we are sad. If indeed we still try, as much as we did before, to avoid actual venial sins, we have lost the courage to keep ourselves away from many pleasant times and places which we know to be to us occasions of venial sin. We content ourselves with an indistinct self-confidence that we shall not fall; and at once the light of God's countenance becomes indistinct also, and the fountain of inward joy ceases to flow. We desire to be praised, and are unhappy if no notice is taken of what we do. We seek publicity as something which will console, rest and satisfy us. We want those we love to know what we are feeling and suffering, or what we are doing and planning. The world is our sunbeam and we come out to bask in it. What wonder we are sad?

How many are there whose real end in the spiritual life is self-improvement rather than God, and how little they suspect it! Now perhaps it is true to say that we never attain in the way of self-improvement a point which seems to us quite easy of attainment. We are always below the mark we aimed at. Here again is another source of sadness. But whatever way we look at this miserable disposition we shall find that the secret fountain of all its phases is the want of mortification, and more especially of external mortification. In a word, who ever found any spiritual sadness in men trying to be good which did not come either from a want of humility or from habitually acting without distinct reference to God?

But the consequences of sadness are of the most fearful description. Nothing gives the devil so much power over us. Mortal sin itself very often gives him less purchase over our souls. It blunts the Sacraments and destroys their influence upon us. It turns all sweet things bitter and makes even the remedies of the spiritual life act as if they were poisons. Under its morbid action we become so tender that we are unable to bear pain, and tremble at the very idea of bodily mortification. The courage which is so necessary for growth in holiness oozes out of us, and we become timid and passive where we ought to be bold and venturesome. The vision of God is clouded in our soul, and every day the fit of sadness lasts it is carrying us further and further out of our depth, and beyond the reach of rational consolation. It seems a strong thing to say, but it is in reality no exaggeration that spiritual sadness is a tendency toward the state of Cain and Judas. The impenitence of both took root in a sadness which came out of a want of humility, and that want was itself the fruit of acting with a view to self, rather than a view to God.

Above all things we must be careful not to let sadness force us away from our regular Communions, or from any of the strictnesses we may practice. We must be all the more faithful to them because we are sad; and we must beware of adopting any change while the cloud is on us. Exactness in little duties is a wonderful source of cheerfulness; and set mortifications, few and not severe, but quietly persevered in, will cast out the evil spirit. We must look out for opportunities of giving way to others; for that brings with it softness of heart and a spirit of prayer. We must make the use of our time a subject of particular examination of conscience, and always have on hand some standing book or occupation with which to fill up gaps of vacant time. We must never omit our devotions to our Blessed Lady, whom the Church so sweetly calls "the cause of our joy"; and we must consider that day lost on which we have not thus done homage to her. Finally, we must regard, not the act only which we do, but the time which obedience has fixed for doing it, whether it be the obedience of self, rule, family or director; for the marvelous virtue of obedience resides often more in the time and manner of an act than in the act itself, just as the spiritual life itself consists not so much in an assemblage of certain actions, as in the way in which we do all our actions.

To these two idlenesses, dissipation and sadness, we must add a third; it is a kind of sloth, or general languor, which it is very hard to describe, but the main features of which everyone will recognize. Some time has passed since we had a clear view of ourselves. We have got out of sight of ourselves, and are journeying on like men driving in the dark. Then something occurs which wakes us up to a consciousness of our position. We find that we are continually making resolutions, and as continually breaking them. They form, as usual, part of our morning prayer, and in an hour or two they have passed from our minds as though we had never made them. Even if we reflect upon them and make some little effort to put them into execution, we find that they are utterly nerveless, and without power or animation. We do not exactly turn a deaf ear to the inspirations which we are receiving at all hours, but we are dilatory in carrying them out, and so the time for them passes by and another duty comes in the way, and it is too late. So that on the whole we hardly correspond to any of our inspirations.

All this is bad enough. But there is added to it a physical feeling of incapacity to make any exertion. It seems to us as if any effort was out of the question; and what is in truth merely a moral malady puts on all the semblance and feeling of a bodily indisposition, and soon causes one. We then begin to make light of serious twinges of conscience, and we are peevish and impatient of any warning or admonition, or of any attempt to bring spiritual matters before us. Everything that everybody does seems inopportune and out of good taste. Without rhyme or reason we have an almost universal nausea of men and things, and we give in to "the spirit of causeless irritation" which characterizes the paralytic, as Sir Walter Scott tells us of Chrystal Croftangry. It is as if life were worn out and we had got to the end of things, as if we had worked our way through the upper coats of existence down to what Bossuet calls "the inexorable ennui which forms the basis of human life." In this state we are not only distracted at prayer, but slovenly also; and even the Sacraments we treat with a kind of lazy irreverence and formal familiarity, which it is frightening to think of. In fact our state is a kind of passive possession of the spirit of disgust and sloth; it is as if we had lost the power of being serious, and were numb, or in a trance, so far as spiritual things are concerned. It is this state to which dissipation is always tending; and if we are so unfortunate as not to have checked it in its earlier stages, but find ourselves actually under this oppression, we must rouse ourselves and act with as much vigor as if we had fallen into mortal sin.

A fourth kind of spiritual idleness may be called useless

industry, which is a great temptation to active-minded men; for, as I said before, idleness is natural and pleasant to all temperaments, but has different phases for different characters. There is nothing in recreation which hinders our uniting ourselves to God; but there are a variety of unmeritorious occupations in which we can fritter away our time, and in which it is almost impossible for us to have any deliberate or distinct intention to glorify God. It is difficult to specify, but everyone knows that recreating and idling are very different things, and that idling much more often consists in doing useless or childish things, than in doing nothing at all. There are many kinds of reading, which are not wrong in themselves, but which for some reasons in our own particular case will dissipate us, or prepare distractions for our meditation, or will feed future temptations, and supply them with images ready at hand, or will be dangerous to us because they will inordinately engross us; and in which, in spite of our intellectual conviction that they are not wrong, we have an interior reproach, which, if we were in a right state of mind, would act as a prohibition. So in these days of cheap and rapid postage we ought to be more jealous of our correspondence than we are. Is it too much to say that every letter we write is more or less a drain upon our spirituality? And if this be so, ought we not to make a rule to ourselves against unnecessary letter writing, against the writing of any letter which either business or social propriety or affection does not render practically unavoidable? Time is precious, and we have little of it, and how much is spent in writing letters, and how many pretend that all their letter writing is safe because it is, they say, a veritable mortification! Attachments are multiplied and strengthened by correspondence, while it increases our objects of anxiety, magnifies our reasons for being nervous and restless, and caters for that idolatry of family ties which nowadays wages such a vigorous warfare against the manliness of Christian sanctity.

Letter writing tends also to increase the natural exaggeration of our character. We express ourselves in an exaggerated manner, and our style at last transfers its exaggeration to our feelings. We thus form a false estimate of things and are greatly troubled about small events, or highly excited about low expectations. What is the family circle generally, but ineffable trifles seen through a hugely magnifying medium? It reminds us at every turn of Wordsworth's real sufferer in the workhouse, when she says,

> I heard my neighbours in their beds complain
> Of many things which never troubled me!

Unreality is another obvious effect of excessive correspondence; for to make much of little things is to be unreal. Sacraments and prayer cease to have their natural and legitimate proportions, when we are so eager, and decisive, and communicative about children, residences, visits, summer plans and winter projects. We make a romance of ourselves in our letters, and paint life with an artificial rouge because its native complexion is for the most part unhealthy and dull. If our letters turn on religious subjects, so much the worse; for then they are full of detraction, levity and spiritual gossip.

Building castles in the air is another branch of this useless industry, and by far the least innocent. Did anyone ever catch himself building a castle in the air, which did not in some way redound to his own honor and praise? Can religious men spend an hour in giving magnificent mental alms, or bearing crosses heroically, or undergoing martyrdom, or evangelizing continents, or ruling churches, or founding hospitals, or entering austere orders, or arranging edifying deathbeds, or working miracles at their own tombs, without their being essentially lower and grosser, vainer and sillier men, than they were when the hour began? They acquire a habit of admiring fine things without practicing them. It is worse than novel reading, for here men write as well as read them. They become intoxicated with conceit and sentimentality. It gives a tincture of puerility to all they do, and lowers them in thought, feeling and purpose. Do not be startled at the strong words, but this castle-building literally desolates and debauches the soul. It passes over it like a ruinous eruption, leaving nothing fresh, green, or fruit-bearing behind it, but a general languor, peevishness and weariness with God.

The not managing our recreations well is of sufficient

importance to form a fifth kind of spiritual idleness. I have already said that recreation is a matter of immense importance in the spiritual life. The whole tradition of the Church is in favor of it; and I doubt if ever there was a religious house which persevered in strict observance for any length of time, without the recreations which are traditional in each order. For an order without traditions is an order without life, at least without the full life of maturity. It is either dead, or still an infant. It sounds strange to a man in the world that recreation should be compulsory in religious houses; yet that it is so, is part of the universal heavenly wisdom common to all monastic legislators. But in the world recreation is an affair of much greater difficulty, because so few rules can be given about it. All we can say is that one very important question concerns the kind of recreation in which we shall indulge. It must be suited to our state of life, and no less so to the particular point of advancement which we have reached in the spiritual life. It must be conformed to our natural character, and it must not throw us with companions who will do our souls an injury. The degree of it is another problem. God's glory must be kept in view, and we must never emancipate ourselves from a moderate fear of dissipation; and above all things it must be seasonable. For an inopportune recreation is always a loss of grace.

It is difficult to exaggerate the results of well-managed recreations. The spirit cannot always be on the stretch. The bow must be unstrung sometimes, or it will spoil. Now a well-managed recreation does three things; it preserves all the grace already acquired without suffering one fraction of it to be lost, or one degree of fervor to evaporate. The love of God runs on from the work into the recreation, and thus the habit of recollection remains unbroken, and we are keeping to the side of our heavenly Father in our amusements as closely as in our work or in our trials. Secondly, it not only keeps together the past, and preserves its spirit, but it gains us strength and freshness, bravery and promptitude, for the future. Old grace is consolidated, and the appetite for new is quickened. Children are said to grow more while they are sleeping than while they are awake. So it is with us in recreation. This is its third function. We grow on it. It is not standing still. It is not only a blessing for the past, and a blessing for the future; it is a present blessing, because it is present growth. It increases our cheerfulness; and whatever makes us cheerful in devotion gives us more power. It would be a great thing if recreation merely kept us from sin, by filling up and occupying vacant hours when the infirmity of human nature compels us to intermit our direct attention to religious things. We should owe to it our preservation from a thousand sins of thought, and dissipating inutilities both of mind and heart. But this is far below its real work. Its function is not less important in the spiritual life than is that of sleep in the natural life; and like sleep it has need of a wise, considerate and firm legislation.

I shall conclude the subject of recreation with the advice of Scaramelli. If our spirit ask of us imperfect things, such as diversions, conversation and superfluous alleviations, which are not called for either by our health or the discharge of our relative duties, the laws of perfection require us to mortify ourselves. I know that these recreations are the very food of those who are weak in spirit; as the Apostle says, He that is weak, let him eat herbs: for being deprived of the consolations which grace brings to pure souls, they feed their hunger and weariness with these earthly consolations. Richard of St. Victor says that a man finds food in his own nature, the food of sweetness, and food in accidental causes, such as prosperity and success. But this is not the spiritual food wherewith Christ refreshed Himself. Nevertheless it is the food of the imperfect, the potherbs of the weak: and is often useful food: for it partly heals and soothes the disease of sloth, which the mind suffers because of the penury of grace. But persons who are seriously bent on the attainment of perfection must deprive themselves to receive from God a greater abundance of grace and heavenly benedictions. If our spirit asks of us anything concerning food, sleep, clothing and diversion, which is necessary to the maintenance of life or the preservation of health or the right performance of our duties, or anything which obedience, fittingness and right reason also require, we must condescend to its requests and indulge ourselves in the necessary recreations. But in these cases a spiritual man must be careful to purify his intention, and to protest to himself that he only condescends to these things in order to do God's holy will, not to satisfy his own natural inclination, to please Him, not to please himself. So that his condescension may be rather to the instincts of nature than to its affections; and even in his condescension he may contrive to contradict his own satisfaction, and seek only the will and pleasure of God. In this manner the human spirit may have its appetite satisfied, without its satisfaction being any impediment to spiritual progress. I am aware that these things are difficult to put in practice, but St. Bernard says that we have but to lean confidently on God, and all will be accomplished, according to that Word, I can do all things in Him who strengtheneth me.[1]

A general indifference about the use of our time is a sixth manifestation of spiritual idleness. The use of time is a large subject; and it is one of far greater consequence than many suppose, in those who are aiming at perfection. Bellecius in his work on *Solid Virtue* gives a whole book to the one act of early rising, which is but a single instance of our use of time. We have to remember that time is the stuff out of which eternity is made, that it is at once precious and irrevocable, and that we shall have to give the strictest account of it at the last. Very few faults are irreparable, but the loss of time is one of those few; and when we consider how easy a fault it is, how frequent, how silent, how alluring, we shall discern something of its real danger. Idleness moreover, when it has fastened upon us, is a perfect tyranny, a slavery whose shackles are felt whatever limb we move, or even when we are lying still. It is a captivating bondage also, whose very sweetness renders it more perilous. But the worst feature about it is its deceitfulness. No idle man believes himself to be idle, except in the lucid intervals of grace. No one will credit how strong the habit of losing time will rapidly become. To break away from it requires a vehemence and a continuity of effort to which few are equal. Meanwhile the debatable land which lies between it and lukewarmness is swiftly traversed. The

---

1. *Discernimento degli spirit.* sect. 272, 273.

hourly accumulation of minute carelessnesses is clogging and hampering the soul, while it is also running us fearfully into debt to the temporal justice of God. It makes our life the very opposite of His. His minute notice of us stands in dreadful contrast with our half-intentional and half-unintentional oblivion and disregard of Him. I doubt if a jealous and conscientious use of time can ever, as many spiritual excellencies can, become a habit. I suspect time is a thing which has to be watched all through life. It is a running stream every ripple of which is freighted with some tell-tale evidence which it hastens to depose with unerring fidelity in that sea which circles the throne of God. It makes us tremble to think of St. Alphonsus just after he had made his solemn vow never to waste a moment of time. We feel that a man who with his humility and discretion dared to commit himself to such a life, could only end by being raised upon the altars of the Church.

The seventh and last development of spiritual idleness is loquacity. Thomas á Kempis says that he never returned to his cell after a conversation without entering it a worse man than he had left it; and another holy person said that he never in his life had repented of holding his tongue, whereas he had rarely ever spoken without being sorry for it afterward. What an insight this gives us into the very core of a saint's life! In spirituality when the tired soul seeks some undue vent or recreation, there is no relief, except castlebuilding, more dangerous than loquacity; and it is one of the commonest of temptations. Some are tempted to be loquacious with everybody who will be a listener; others only with certain people, who are sympathetic, and with whom to exchange sentiments is to rest their minds. Others are only tempted to talk at wrong times and on wrong subjects; and this is sometimes from the devil, and sometimes from the human spirit. As a general maxim it may be laid down that in a spiritual person all effusion of heart is undesirable, except to God, and that it is equally undesirable whether it be about God or about some indifferent subject. There is nothing to choose between them. The evil is in the effusion. We fancy it relieves us in temptation. But there never was a greater mistake. With the exception of certain temptations, solitude braces us up, where effusion weakens and enervates us. Pious people, before they begin to be saint-like, are notably loquacious; and it is often loquacity which retards the hour when the likeness of the Saints will pass upon them, or frustrates the process altogether. It is plain that every one of these seven idlenesses might be made the subject of a little treatise; but I have said enough for my purpose. Perfection in the world is a difficult affair, and many things are fatal to it. Idleness perhaps slaughters more growths in holiness than anything else; because it is so very hard for persons in the world not to be idle. Everything around us is pusillanimous and exaggerated. The ideas which pass current are little and low. The air we breathe is languor. The types we behold are pompous follies. Of spiritual romance there is enough, of spiritual foppery more than enough, but of healthy mortification and sincere manly devotion less than would seem possible, if the fact were not certain. Thus everything draws us to idleness and to inutility. It is a common observation that religious, of both sexes, are strikingly cheerful. This is owing in no slight degree to the preservation from idleness which rule and community life ensure. We have none of those helps, and therefore we have more to dread from this particular enemy. In fact the danger and the fatal character of idleness may be reckoned among the prominent characteristics of the attempt to attain perfection in the world. We have already found that for perfection in the world a peculiar exercise of patience is necessary in order to supply the place of a religious rule. So now we must give a more than common attention to the industrious use of time and the discreet management of recreations, in order to meet dangers which religious are beautifully defended from by community life, and a community life invented by a saintly founder. Idleness must be a very prominent object in our warfare, else we shall never attain to the perfection which the Saints tell us is open to people in the world.

Chapter XV

PRAYER

The spiritual life is quite a cognizably distinct thing from the worldly life; and the difference comes from prayer. When grace lovingly drives a man to give himself up to prayer, he gets into the power of prayer, and prayer makes a new man of him; and so completely does he find that his life is prayer, that at last he prays always. His life itself becomes one unbroken prayer. Unbroken, because it does not altogether nor so much reside in methods of mental or forms of vocal prayer; but it is an attitude of heart by which all his actions and sufferings become living prayers.

The life of prayer, therefore, which is the badge of the supernatural man, is the praying always. But what is it to pray always? What did Our Lord mean by it? To pray always is always to feel the sweet urgency of prayer, and to hunger after it. Grace is palpably felt and touched in prayer; hence it strengthens our faith and inflames our love. The peculiar trial of hard work is that it keeps us so much from prayer, and takes away the flower of our strength before we have time for prayer, and physical strength is very needful for praying well. In consequence of this attraction we acquire habits of prayer by having set times for it, whether mental or vocal. Not that a mere habit of praying will make anyone a man of prayer. But God will not send His fire, if we do not first lay the sacrifice in order. We must also practice ejaculatory prayer, and have certain fixed ejaculations, as well as make frequent spontaneous aspirations to Heaven during the day, at will, and out of the fervid abundance of our hearts. Besides this, there is a certain gravitation of the mind to God in a prayerful way, which comes from love and from the practice of the divine presence, and which ranges from intercession to thanksgiving, and from thanksgiving to praise, and from praise to petition, according as the moods of our mind change, and with hardly any trouble or any conscious process. To pray always is, furthermore, to renew frequently our acts of pure intention for the glory of God, and thus to animate with the life of prayer our actions, conversations, studies and sufferings.

This is to pray always: and see what comes of it! Into what a supernatural state it throws a man! He lives in a different world from other men. Different dwellers are round about him, and are his familiars, God, Jesus, Mary, Angels and Saints. They are the undercurrent of his mind, and often preside over the very expression of his thoughts. He has not the same interests, hopes and aims as other men. When he wishes to do anything, he goes to work in a different way from others, and he tests his success differently. Indeed, in nothing is he so remote from men of the world as in his tests of success, which are wholly supernatural and full of the unearthly spirit of the Incarnation. His views of the world are strange, although they are definite and clear, because somehow he sees the world confusedly through the vision of the Church; and he judges of the relations and distances of things according as they group around the central Faith. His affections become shifted, so that he is regarded even by those near him as an impassible man, and by those further off as a cold heart that is destitute of natural affections and the keen sympathies of kindred. Moreover the temper of repose which prayer breeds is unfavorable to success and advancement in a worldly sense, because it is unfavorable to the eager desire and restless pursuit of them.

This influence of prayer comes out in a man's opinions and judgments of men, measures and things. It is heard in his language. It is seen in his tranquility. It is recognized in his dealings with others, and is the ruling principle of his occasional apparent want of sympathy with others. Such is a man whose faculties, affections, and in some degree even his senses, have been mastered by the spirit of prayer. We should expect it would win men by its gracefulness, like an angel's presence. But it is not so, because its beauty requires a spiritual discernment. To the eyes of the world such a man has all the strangeness and awkwardness of a foreigner, which in sober truth he is. Yet such a man is striking to others in afterthought, as the Blessed Sacrament so often is to Protestants, when they have come unawares into His Presence and gone again. It is the way of God, and of the things of God, to be striking in afterthought.

The most serious business of the interior life is mental prayer, of which I will speak first. Spiritual writers, and even saints, have sometimes spoken as if meditation were almost necessary to salvation; and there are senses and cases in which this may be true. It is, however, quite certain that mental prayer is necessary to perfection, and that there can be nothing like a spiritual life without it. For mental prayer means the occupation of our faculties upon God, not in the way of thinking or speculating about Him, but stirring up the will to conform itself to Him and the affections to love Him. The subjects on which it is engaged are all the works of God, as well as His own perfections—but above all, the Sacred Humanity of Our Blessed Lord. The length of time to be spent in it will vary with individual cases; and there are a variety of methods out of which a man may choose. But it is most important he should keep to his method when he has chosen it. Of this, however, something shall be said hereafter.

Mental prayer, in itself difficult, is rendered still more so by the temptations which beset it. It is irksome, quite beyond all explanation as well as expectation; and its irksomeness tempts us to abandon it. Very often when we try to meditate, a sheer inability to think at all comes over us in a most unaccountable manner. Whatever may be the bodily posture which we are recommended to assume at prayer, its sameness becomes wearisome; and if we keep changing, anything worthy of the name of prayer is out of the question. Distractions torment us at every turn, and their name is legion. Sensible devotion is our only hope, and it is continually being withdrawn, without apparent fault of ours. Temptations to intermit our meditation seem specious, when temptations to abandon it altogether would be rejected. At other times we are tempted to think its importance has been exaggerated. And if we dare disturb nothing else about it, we satisfy our restlessness by varying our times for it, and even for this slight concession we often pay dearly.

Now the remedy for all these temptations consists in our considering our meditation as the great feature of our day, in our spending all the time we can in spiritual reading, in being full, open and obedient to our director in all questions concerning it, in weaning ourselves by degrees from sensible consolations, and in estimating at their proper value the fruits of a dry, or, as we often perversely call it, a bad meditation. We must throw our whole strength into this matter; for the practice of the presence of God, our strength against evil angels and evil habits, our habitual cheerfulness, our ability to carry crosses and all that we can do ourselves toward final perseverance, depend on prayer.

If we attentively examine the various methods of prayer which approved writers have given us, we shall see that they may be resolved into two, the Ignatian and the Sulpician, if we may call them by those names. The advantages of the Ignatian method are that it is more adapted to modern habits of mind, that it suits the greater number of persons, that it can be taught as an art and that most meditation books are framed upon it. The advantages of the Sulpician method are that it is a more faithful transcript of the tradition of the old Fathers and the Saints of the desert, that it supplies a want for those who on the other hand can make no way with the Ignatian method, and on the other have no aptitude for what is called Affective Prayer, and that it is in some respects more suitable for those who are often interrupted at meditation, inasmuch as it is a perfect work wherever it is broken off, whereas the power of the Ignatian method is in its conclusion. These are the characteristics of the two methods. No comparison can be instituted between them because they both are holy, both have schooled saints and the use of them is a matter either of choice or of vocation.

I will speak briefly of both these methods, and first of the Ignatian, which is by far the most widely spread. Meditation is a gift for which we must make special prayer; and with this prayer we must join an ardent desire for perfection in general. We must make a diligent use of the means recommended, and we must regard spiritual reading as being to meditation what oil is to the lamp. There are, therefore, two preparations to meditation; one is remote, the other proximate. Remote preparation consists partly in removing obstacles, and partly in obtaining the aids requisite. The obstacles to be removed are: a good opinion of ourselves and a want of concealment of our austerities and devotions, all affections to habitual infirmities, even though the infirmities themselves for the present remain habitual, dissipation of mind, negligent custody of the senses, and an offhand way of performing our ordinary actions. The aids which we require are the lower degrees of humility, simplicity and purity of intention in a general way, sufficient custody of the senses to insure tranquility of mind and a certain inconsiderable degree of mortification. Proximate preparation consists in reading, hearing or getting ready our meditation overnight, and especially in noting what fruit naturally comes of it, or is most suited to our present spiritual needs; before we compose ourselves to sleep we are to think briefly over it, and make some suitable ejaculation; when we awake we are instantly to recall the subject of meditation; while we are dressing, to think of it or nourish sentiments akin to it, to quiet our minds by making an act of the presence of God or of the Sacred Humanity for about the space of an *Ave Maria,* and this should be done before we kneel down, and to observe a strict silence from the time we have prepared our meditation till the next morning, so as to exclude dissipating thoughts and images. They who have submitted to the bondage of these regulations have found a blessing in them. Many minds cannot brook them. Without a knowledge of the individual case, no one can see how far, or from what particulars, persons may without prejudice be dispensed. There are not many to whom the whole array of the Ignatian method is necessary for any long time, but there are many who can never make good meditations now, but who would have done so if they would have constrained themselves and borne the yoke for a little while at first. These two preparations are followed by an act of adoration and a preparatory prayer.

After the preparations come the preludes, of which there are always two, and sometimes three. The first prelude consists in sketching to ourselves a rapid picture of the subject of our meditation. This helps to keep off distractions, just as looking hard at a thing makes us think of it. If we are distracted during the course of our meditation, then we revert to our picture, just as we look back to anything we are copying when a noise has made us look up. Some writers tell us always to put ourselves into these pictures, and to take care that the pictures are congenial with the special fruit we look for in that meditation. The second prelude is a direct petition for that fruit, which it is well to ask through the Saint whom the Church honors that day. In histories, there is a third prelude, which consists in very briefly going through the story. All the preludes together should not occupy above five minutes.

The preludes are followed by the body of the meditation, which consists of three things, the use of the memory, the use of the understanding and the use of the will. The use of the memory seems much the same thing as the first prelude, but it differs from it in length, in accuracy and in particularity. It consists, to put it as briefly as possible, in asking seven questions: Who? What? Where? With what means? Why? How? When? And this is applicable either to texts or mysteries. We need not take very long in this first part of the meditation, else it will pass off into a mere diversion of the imagination. Nevertheless, we must go through it very accurately, and with scrupulous exactness. For we shall find hereafter that the root of our affections and resolutions is here. A careless and perfunctory use of our memory will bring barrenness of reflections, dry formality in affections, and a want of compunction and nerve in resolutions. We must not be disturbed when we find memory trenching on the province of understanding. One is meant to glide off into the other; and there will be always left for the understanding the particular application of the general truth to ourselves and our present spiritual necessities.

For, by the understanding, which is the second part of the meditation, we do these five things. We apply the subject of our meditation to ourselves, we draw conclusions, we weigh

motives, we examine past and present conduct and we anticipate future dispositions. The main thing in the use of our
understanding is to be exceedingly simple. Like the use of
the memory, it also consists in asking seven questions. First,
What am I to think about this? Secondly, What practical lesson am I to draw from it? And the lesson must be particular,
not general, and it must be adapted to our employment, character and condition. Thirdly, What motives persuade me to this
practice? And they must be such as these, convenience, by
which I mean fittingness, utility, at least on supernatural
grounds, satisfaction, easiness, or necessity. Fourthly, How
have I acted up to this hitherto? And here we must be disinclined to let conscience answer satisfactorily, and only give
way to irresistible evidence when it is favorable. We must
insist on our own confusion. We must descend to particulars,
and we must jealously sift our present dispositions. Fifthly,
How must I act for the future? Here we must put imaginary
cases, not wild, unlikely, or farfetched, but such as may easily happen that same day. Sixthly, What impediments must
I remove? Here we must use the self-knowledge which our
daily examination of conscience gives us. On the whole our
impediments are mostly three: conceit, sensuality and dissipation. Seventhly, What means am I to choose? Here we must
be careful to be particular, not general and vague; and above
all, we must be discreet, and not load ourselves with too much.
Many are found in the evening without any cross at all because the one they fastened on their shoulders in their morning meditation was heavier than they could bear; so they threw
it down and were Our Lord's disciples only half that day.

The third part of the meditation is the use of the will. Without this, meditation is not mental prayer, but either a speculation or an incomplete examination of conscience. The use of
the will is twofold—the production of affections, and the production of resolutions. In reality affections may find their place
all over the meditation, in the application of the memory, and
even in the preludes. They can hardly ever be out of place wherever they come. It is a good thing to have texts or sayings of
the Saints in our minds for the more ready expression of holy
affections; but we must have collected them for ourselves, or

they will not have half the unction. We should never break off
an affection which has to do with humility, so long as there
is any sweetness in it. The whole hour would be excellently
spent in it, even to the neglect of the rest of the meditation.
The same, however, cannot be said of joy and triumph, which
are open to snares and delusions, and should be kept within
bounds. Even compunction cannot have the reins given up to
it, desirable as are its affections; for they tend to be immoderate and easily coalesce with self-love. If affections are slow
in coming, we must not lose our peace of mind and begin to
be restless, but quietly excite them by acts of faith.

But precious as are the affections of prayer, the resolutions
are still more valuable. Their place should not be only in
each point of our meditation, but at the close of each practical
doctrine in each point. They must be practical, and must not
consist in promising certain devotions and prayers, but in resolving to avoid this or to mortify that. They must be particular,
and not general. They must have to do with our present state
and with immediate action. To resolve to do so and so when
you arrive at such a point, or when such a time comes, is
castle-building, not resolving. If possible, our resolutions should
have to do with the probable events of the very day, so that
our particular examen may entwine itself with our meditation.
They must be founded on solid motives, and have been often
meditated, not rash, or offhand, or above our courage when
we cool down out of prayer. If anything, they should be below
what we might reasonably hope to do, and very humble. For
things seem easy in meditation, so that we do not distrust
ourselves sufficiently; and God rarely strengthens an over-
confident soul, and so we fail. How many of the downcast
tales which people tell about their not advancing should go
to the account of reckless resolutions in the half-natural, half-
supernatural heat of prayer!

We have now come to the conclusion of the meditation.
This is important, and must be gone through calmly and fervently. If done in haste, so as to be within the hour, or for
any other reason, it often spoils the whole meditation. We
must first collect all our resolutions together, and renew them.
This will often quicken with fervor the end of the hour that

was perhaps flagging through dryness and languor. The colloquies with God, Our Lady, or the Saints, follow next. In them we must be particular to ask for the special and predetermined fruit of the meditation; and with this we may couple any petition we have much at heart, and also a humble oblation of the resolutions we have made. A *Pater, Ave,* and the *Anima Christi* are next prescribed in most of the meditation books written on this system. We then leave off conversing directly with God; but we do not leave His presence. On the contrary, we are more than usually careful at that moment, lest the spirit of dissipation should come upon us, and there should be too sudden a reaction from the recollectedness of prayer.

If St. Ignatius could have his will, the meditation would not end here. He would have us sit down or walk about, and make what he calls the consideration of our meditation. The want of this he looks upon as the reason of continued bad meditations. If we reflected on them, and found out they were bad at the time, we should probably find out what it was that made them bad, and so avoid it for the future. Indeed, of such importance is this consideration deemed, that we are recommended to make it later on in the day, if we have omitted it in the morning. The consideration is divided into two parts, the examen and the recapitulation. In the examen we briefly review our overnight preparation, our first thoughts on rising, our beginnings, preparatory prayer, preludes, choice of fruit, the progress of the meditation, how we dealt with distractions in all the three parts, whether our colloquies were fervent and humble, whether we have listened to hear if God would speak in our hearts, and whether we have been free from irreverence of body, or rashness of speech, or precipitation of mind. If all this has been done fairly well, we thank Almightly God for the grace in the strength of which alone we have been successful. If it has been done ill, we make an act of contrition and a modest resolution for the future, without giving way to sadness or disquietude. We must always bear in mind that the time of prayer is God's punishment time. It is then that venial sins, little infidelities, inordinate friendships and worldly attachments will rise up and complain of us, and we shall be chastised for them.

The recapitulation resolves the lessons we have learned, the resolutions we have made and the fruit we hoped to obtain; and it implores once more the grace to keep our resolutions. We are then to take an ejaculation for the day, or some thought which shall be a spiritual nosegay to refresh us in the dust and turmoil of the world. Finally we are to write down the lights we have received and the resolutions we have made, so as to rekindle our fervor when it flags, by the perusal of them. This last practice, however, requires great discretion, and is not suitable for all. This consideration, St. Ignatius says, should occupy "about" a quarter of an hour.

The first perusal of the Ignatian plan is like a cleric's first look into a breviary. It seems as if we should never find our way about in it. But the processes are in reality so natural that they soon become easy to us, and follow each other in legitimate succession almost without effort or reflection. It is much more easy than it seems. The method of St. Francis de Sales is substantially the same, with some of the peculiarities of his own character thrown into it. The same may be said of the method of St. Alphonsus, which is that of St. Ignatius with somewhat more freedom, such as we should expect from the character of that glorious saint, who, to his many other titles to the gratitude of the modern Church, might add that of the Apostle of Prayer. Beginners are always inclined to dispense themselves from the mechanical parts of the system. But it is well worth our while to be patient for a few weeks. We shall never be sorry for it, whereas we shall regret the contrary line of conduct as long as we live. We must beware also of kneeling vacantly and doing nothing, which adds the fault of irreverence to that of idleness. We must not look out for interior voices, or marked experiences, or decided impressions of the divine will upon our minds, nor give in to the temptation of leaving the plain road of painstaking meditation in order to reach God by some shorter way. At first it is not well to read many books about prayer; but keep to the few oral advices of our director. We must always be trying, yet in a quiet way, to be shorter with our considerations and longer with our affections; and if all our meditation should be unmanageably dry, we must make some particular resolution before we leave our Crucifix, and so the time will not have been without fruit.

One word on what we call bad meditations. They are generally the most fruitful. The mere persevering at our priedieu the full time is an excellent and meritorious act of obedience. The mystery, which seems to lay no hold of us, is in reality soaking into our minds, and keeping us throughout the day more in the presence of God than we otherwise should have been. We ask something of God, and that is in itself a great action. We make a resolution of some kind, and we meet with an occasion of humiliation. God often thus sends us back, as a master turns back a boy, to re-examine our course and to discover little forgotten infidelities for which we have never done penance. Whenever we have made a bad meditation, and cannot see that it is our own fault, we may be sure God means something by it, and it is our own business to find out what. It is no little thing to be able to endure ourselves and our own imperfections. On the contrary, it is a fine act of humility, and draws us on toward perfection. In good truth we may make our bad meditations pay us a usurious interest, if we choose.

It is obvious that much of what has been said of the Ignatian method is applicable to all methods, in the way of direction and guidance. In speaking of the Sulpician method, therefore, I shall confine myself to those things which distinguish it from the other. M. Olier divides prayer into three parts: the preparation, the body of the prayer and the conclusion; and he generally uses the word prayer instead of meditation; and filled with the spirit of the old tradition, he and his interpreters recur to St. Ambrose, St. John Climacus, St. Nilus, Cassian and similar writers for rules and methods. They make three preparations, the more remote, the less remote and the proximate. The first is occupied in removing obstacles, the second in preparing what is necessary for praying well and the third is as it were the entrance into prayer. The more remote preparation may be said to extend over the whole of life, and is principally occupied with three obstacles: sin, the passions and the thought of creatures. No soul in a state

of sin can converse familiarly with God. The unquiet movements of human passions prevent inward peace which is a
necessary condition of mental prayer; and the thought of creatures is the foundation of all dissipation and distraction. Thus
the abandonment of sin, the mortification of the passions, and
the custody of the senses, form the more remote preparation
for prayer. The less remote preparation is concerned with three
times: the time when the subject of prayer is given overnight,
the time which elapses between then and the waking in the
morning, and the third is from our waking to our beginning
our prayer. The first requires attention; the second a review
of the subject and a strict silence; and the third the affections
of love and joy wherewith we should approach prayer. The
proximate preparation is almost a part of the prayer itself.
It comprises three acts: first, the putting of ourselves in the
presence of God; secondly, acknowledging ourselves unworthy to appear in His presence; and thirdly, confessing ourselves incapable of praying as we ought without the aid of
divine grace. For each of these three preparations very minute
rules are given, which are all taken from ancient sources,
particularly St. Gregory, St. Chrysostom, St. Bonaventure,
St. Nilus, St. Bernard and St. Benedict.

But it is in the body of the prayer that its chief characteristics are to be found. It consists, as the Ignatian does, of three
points; the first is called adoration, the second communion,
and the third cooperation. In the first we adore, praise, love
and thank God. In the second we try to transfer to our own
hearts what we have been praising and loving in God, and
to participate in its virtue according to our measure. In the
third we cooperate with the grace we are receiving by fervent
colloquies and generous resolutions. The ancient Fathers have
handed down to us this method of prayer as in itself a perfect
compendium of Christian perfection. They call it having Jesus
before their eyes, which is the adoration; Jesus in their hearts,
which is the communion; and Jesus in their hands, which
is the cooperation: and in these three things all the Christian
life consists. After their accustomed fashion, they deduce it
from the precept of God to the children of Israel, that the
words of the law were to be before their eyes, in their hearts,

and bound upon their hands. Thus St. Ambrose calls these three points the three seals. The adoration he calls *signaculum in fronte ut semper confiteamur;* the communion, *signaculum in corde ut semper diligamus;* and the cooperation, *signaculum in brachio, ut semper operemur.* Others again declare that this method of prayer is according to the model which Our Lord has given us. Thus the adoration answers to *Hallowed be Thy Name,* the communion to *Thy kingdom come,* and the cooperation to *Thy will be done.* It seems that this method of prayer is, as far as we can judge, the same which prevailed among the Fathers of the desert; and it is astonishing how many scraps of ancient tradition there are regarding it.[1] Its patristic character is quite the distinguishing feature of the Sulpician method of prayer. It is a piece of the older spirituality of the Church.

The first point, then, is adoration. Here we contemplate the subject of our meditation in Jesus, and worship Him because of it in a befitting way. Hence there are two things to be observed in this first point. Suppose, to take the instance given by Tronson, that we are meditating on humility. In this point we first of all consider Jesus as humble, and in this consideration we include three things: Our Lord's interior dispositions about humility, the words He said and the actions He did. Secondly, we lay at His feet six offerings: adoration, admiration, praise, love, joy and gratitude; sometimes going through all of them, sometimes selecting such as harmonize with the subject of our prayer. This point is extremely important, as it leads us first to contemplate our Blessed Lord as the source of all virtues; secondly, to regard Him as the original and exemplar, of which grace is to make us copies; thirdly, of the two ends of prayer, which Tertullian calls the veneration of God and the petition of man, the first he says is the more perfect; fourthly, St. Gregory Nyssen says that if we look only to our own interests, of the two roads which lead to perfection,

1. I may remark by the way that it is unfortunate that Honoratus à Sancta Maria, who collected the tradition of the Fathers on several supernatural states of prayer, should have taken the wrong side in the great controversy of charity, and so should have disfigured his book, and blunted the effect of his evidence.

prayer and imitation, the first is the shortest, the most efficacious and the most solid. Speaking of the efficacy of adoration as a part of prayer, the Fathers use this comparison. They say we may dye a white cloth scarlet in two ways, first by applying the color to it, and secondly, by steeping it in the dye; and the last is the shortest and makes the color fastest: so to dip our souls in the dye of the Heart of Jesus by love and adoration is a quicker way to imbue them with a virtue than multiplied acts of the virtue itself would be. The reader will see that this doctrine is peculiar, and seems at first sight to differ from the ordinary tone of modern books. This method of adoration is, with slight modifications, applicable to all the six usual subjects of meditation, the attributes and perfections of God, the mysteries and virtues of Jesus, the actions of the Saints, the virtues, the vices, and Christian verities.

The second point is communion, by which we endeavor to participate in what we have been loving and admiring in the first. It contains three things. We have first of all to convince ourselves that the grace we desire to ask is important to us, and we should try to convince ourselves of this chiefly by motives of faith. The second thing is to see how greatly we are wanting in that grace at present and how many opportunities of acquiring it we have wasted. In this temper we must consider the past, the present, and the future. The third and chief thing is the petition itself for the grace in question; and this petition may take four shapes, the types of which are in Scripture. First, it may be simple petition: *petitiones vestrae innotescant apud Deum.* Secondly, it may be obsecration, which is the adding of some motive or adjuration to our demand, as by the merits of Our Lord, or the graces of Our Lady: *in omni obsecratione,* as the Apostle speaks. Thirdly, it may be by thanksgiving, *cum gratiarum actione;* for the Saints tell us that thanksgiving for past graces is the most efficacious petition for new ones. Fourthly, it may be by insinuation, as when the sisters of Lazarus said no more than, Lord, he whom Thou lovest is sick. All these petitions must be accompanied by four conditions: humility, confidence, perseverance and the union of others in our prayer; as Our Lord teaches us to pray for *our,* not *my,* daily bread, and forgive *us*, not *me*, our trespasses. St. Nilus lays great stress on this last particular, and says it is the fashion in which the angels pray.

The third point is the cooperation, in which we make our resolutions. Now three things are required in these resolutions, that they should be particular, that they should be present, that they should be efficacious. They must be particular, because general ones are of very little use except in union with particular ones. They must be present, that is, we must have some application of our resolution present to our minds, as likely to occur that day. They must be efficacious, that is, our subsequent care must be to carry them out with great fidelity, and fully to intend to do so by an explicit intention at the time we make them.

The conclusion of the prayer consists of three things, all of which must be very briefly performed. First we must thank God for the graces He has given us in our prayer, the grace of having endured us in His presence, of having given us the ability to pray, and of all the good thoughts and emotions we have experienced. Secondly we must ask pardon for the faults we have committed in our prayer, negligence, lukewarmness, distraction, inattention and restlessness. Thirdly we must put it all into Our Lady's hands to offer it to God, to supply all defects and to obtain all blessings. Then follows the spiritual nosegay of St. Francis de Sales, which St. Nilus appears to have been the first to suggest to men of prayer.

The Carmelite method, as given by John of Jesus-Mary, forbids any minute composition of place, and recommends only one point of meditation. Its component parts are adoration, oblation, thanksgiving, petition and intercession; but he would not have us take them always in the same order, but take that first which chances to be most congenial to the subject on which we are meditating. On the whole it seems true to say that the contemplative orders hold more to the ancient, or as I have called it the Sulpician method, than to the Ignatian; and all methods seem resolvable into one or other of the two.

These two methods of prayer are both of them most holy, even though they are so different. There is a different spirit in them, and they tend to form different characters. But they cannot be set one against the other. They are both from one Spirit, even the Holy Ghost, and each will find the hearts to which they are sent. Happy is the man who is a faithful disciple of either!

But the class of persons for whom I am writing require something more than these methods of meditation, without their approaching any of what are called the supernatural states of prayer. Many pass beyond meditation, most men slowly, but some rapidly; and when a man's whole life is taken up with God, his studies principally spiritual books, his occupations chiefly religious, he often finds that meditation is no longer the right sort of prayer for him, and that he must practice what ascetical writers call affective prayer. Of this, therefore, I must say something.

The passage from meditation to affective prayer is a crisis in the spiritual life. For we may leave meditation too soon, or we may leave it too late, or we may refuse to leave it at all, even when Our Lord is bidding us go higher up. All these three mistakes are fraught with injury to the soul. By the first we fall into delusions, by the second we lose time, by the third we forfeit grace. Spiritual writers give us the following signs that it is time for us to pass to affective prayer. First, when we are unable to meditate, and feel drawn to affections. Secondly, when, do what we will, we get no fruit from our meditation but wariness and disgust. Thirdly, which I would dwell upon particularly, when we are so thoroughly penetrated with the truths of religion and the maxims of Jesus, that we find it hard to occupy our understanding upon them in prayer, but pass instantaneously and as it were unavoidably into affections of the will. Fourthly, when we have made some progress in the horror of sin, the indifference to amusements, the avoiding of occasions of danger, moderation of speech and mortification of the senses. Then we may begin by little and little to curtail the use of memory and understanding in our prayer, and concentrate ourselves upon the affections of the will; and so by safe degrees we shall pass from meditation to affective prayer.

Courbon thus describes the difference between these two

states of prayer. In the state of meditation we reason upon some subject, or ruminate on a text, or reflect on some truth, or meditate on some mystery, for the purpose of eliciting affections on these subjects. In affective prayer reasonings and reflections have all ceased, and the soul proceeds of its own accord to elicit all the necessary affections. Again, in meditation the soul produces these affections with a certain amount of pain and labor, and has to keep its attention fixed; whereas in affective prayer this operation costs us no trouble, but comes freely and spontaneously. So that affective prayer is superior to meditation in ardor, constancy and continuity.

When we have made the change at the right time and in the right way, the fruits of this new prayer very soon become visible in the soul. The first is a great love of God, breaking forth in acts of the love of preference, complacence and benevolence, and in works of effective love. The next are a desire to do God's will, a burning zeal for His glory, a keen appetite for communion, a hankering after solitude, an avidity to know more about God, a love of speaking of God, an increase of courage, a desire to die, a zeal for souls and a contempt of the world. At the same time this kind of prayer has its own peculiar dangers. We are apt to exhaust ourselves by the vehemence of immoderate affections, to make devotion consist wholly of fervid feelings, to imagine we are feeling what the Saints felt, to believe that everything we do is done by an inspiration, to be too active and precipitate in our good works and to be indiscreet in our zeal. In affective prayer distractions tease us more sensibly than in meditation, because our understanding is less occupied. The subtraction of sweetness is far more sensibly felt; and the world and the devil combine to attack us with greater energy than before. Above all, we are peculiarly liable, to a degree which surprises us, to vanity, anger and want of custody of the senses. Against these, however, we may set the supernatural favors which usually accompany this state of prayer; such as the gift of tears, interior colloquies, touches of the soul, the languor of love, the liquefaction of the soul in God, the wound of love, the glimpses of our own nothingness and the superabundance of spiritual sweetness. But full instruction on these points belongs to a treatise on prayer. Enough has been said of mental prayer for our present purpose. It remains to speak of vocal prayer.

It is one of the marks of false spirituality, as appears from the Condemned Propositions, to make light of vocal prayer. It is the universal custom of the faithful, even if it be not necessary to salvation, as St. Thomas says it is not. St. Augustine seems to hold the contrary opinion, and gives as a reason the model which our Saviour gave us. It is, however, says St. Thomas, of immense utility, and that for three reasons. It awakens interior devotion, and sustains it when awakened. We ought to honor God with all His gifts; and voice is His gift as well as mind. It forms a vent for interior devotion, which increases in vehemence by means of the very vent. In vocal prayer three attentions are requisite, though not always all of them at once, attention to the order and pronunciation of the words, attention to the meaning of the words, and attention to the end of the words which is Him to whom we address them, and that for which we are petitioning.

Speaking in a rough way, there are commonly four kinds of vocal prayer: with a book, without a book, intercessory and ejaculatory. If we pray from a prayerbook it is well to have only one book at a time, and not to change it frequently. We should read with pauses, occasionally closing the book and resting on the thought of God; and we should be careful not to choose a book which is much above our real feelings and present attainments. If we pray without a book, we must be brief and of few words, because of God's majesty; we must scrupulously use words with forethought, and interpose silent intervals in our prayers. In the matter of intercessory prayer, we must be cautious of promising people we will pray for them. We must be wary of perpetual or multiplied novenas. We must never fix a definite length of time for which we will pray for an object, and abandon it then if God has not vouchsafed to hear our prayers. And in our intercession a prominent place must always be given to the Holy Father, and his intentions for the needs of the Church. Ejaculatory prayers should be frequent, but generally speaking not under rule or of obligation. They must be almost incessant in times of temptation, and it is desirable always to have some chosen ones ready.

There are many cautions which are necessary in the use of vocal prayer. We must be careful not to burden ourselves with too many of them, and it is well to begin them always with a mental act of the Divine Presence. When we have given way to distractions, and our attention has been imperceptibly averted from what we are saying, and at last we wake up to a consciousness of it, it very much concerns our peace of mind that we should not say over again what we said with inattention. We must simply stop and make an act of contrition, and so proceed. The opposite conduct gives rise to many scruples, and ends by making vocal prayer burdensome and odious. When slovenly habits have crept over us, we must set matters right by disallowing ourselves in certain liberties which we have taken, and so cure our slovenliness by taking a few steps in the direction of the other extreme. Thus, if we have been in the habit of saying vocal prayers out of doors, or walking about, or in bed, and some perceptible negligence has come of it, it is better for a little while to abstain from doing so, and say them in our own room, or kneeling, or in some slightly penitential way. We must not forget that this blessed right of vocal prayer is not only a frequent source of scruples, but even a most prolific occasion of venial sin; and it is so almost always from want of reverence and forethought. Hence we should never begin with a probable interruption staring us in the face, and we should keep a strict custody over our eyes. It is said of St. Charles Borromeo that he would not say off by heart the more familiar parts of the missal and breviary, because he considered that his keeping his eyes fixed on the book and reading the words so much conduced to devotion.

It is well to meditate occasionally on the dignity of vocal prayers and the communion of saints into which we enter by reciting them, especially in such worldwide devotions as the Rosary and scapular prayers. They who are much addicted to vocal prayer should cultivate a special devotion to the angels before the throne of God, who are ever offering in their sweet thuribles the prayers of the just to His compassionate majesty.

We must remember that, while other means do not always apply to all cases, prayer has not only a fitness but a special fitness for all cases. Some persons, when they have prayed for some virtue or against some vice or temptation for a long while, grow disheartened and leave off. The devil suggests to them that their prayers will not be heard, not for lack of goodness in God, but because they are unworthy to be heard, and that it is true humility in them to think so. But in truth such an abasement of spirit is not humility, but a delusion contrary both to faith and hope; for this theological truth is very much to be remembered, that prayer rests solely on God's goodness, and not at all on our merits. Those who find themselves inapt at mental prayer should cultivate vocal. But if we have taken upon ourselves a burden of much vocal prayer, and find ourselves growing inattentive in spite of ourselves, we must lessen the quantity gradually, compensating for this by a more arduous effort of attention. As a general rule it is best to have only a little vocal prayer, but to persevere in that little with extreme fidelity. St. Theresa says that comfortable postures are best for mental prayer, penitential postures for vocal. Under any circumstances reverential postures are half the battle of vocal prayer. If a man finds vocal prayer an aid to inward recollection, it is a sign he has a vocation to it; but St. Thomas says, if it be a hindrance to inward recollection, he had best abandon what is not of obligation. Finally, those who have for a long time been tepidly neglecting meditation have no better means to refresh themselves, and so get back to mental prayer, than by giving themselves up for a season to habits, perhaps long abandoned, of childlike vocal prayer.

Now a few words on answers to prayer, a subject which teases so many devout souls. St. Bernard says in his Lent sermons that all bad prayers are bad for one of three reasons: either they are timid, or they are tepid, or they are temerarious. We may dismiss therefore these three kinds of prayer as not likely to be answered. Answers to prayer have several characteristics which we ought to bear in mind. For the most part they are long in coming; and the thing asked, when it does come, comes often in another shape; and as often, something else comes instead of it. Answers come quickest when the prayer is secret and undivulged, or when crosses are asked for, so we must be cautious, or when we ask through our Blessed Lady, or as St. Catherine of Bologna tells us, through the Souls in Purgatory, or as St. Theresa tells us, through St. Joseph. It is false spirituality which teaches us not to pray, and to pray perseveringly, for the good of individuals. But our power of impetration depends very much on two things—our having habits of prayer and being in habitual communication with God, and our praying in the pure spirit of simple faith.

We always receive three gifts from God when we pray humbly and earnestly. The first, St. Nilus says, is the gift of prayer itself. "God wishes to bless thee for a longer time while thou art persevering in thy prayer; for what more blessed than to be detained in colloquy with God?" We pretend for awhile not to hear the petitions of those we love, because we so love to hear them asking. So Joseph feigned with his brethren. You say, says St. John Climacus, I have received nothing from God, when all the while you have received one of His greatest gifts, perseverance in prayer. It is often because He so loves prayer that God delays to answer it. The second gift is the increase of our merits by persevering in unanswered prayer. He delays to hear His saints, says St. Gregory, that He may increase their merits. *Eo magis exaudium tur ad meritum, quo citius non exaudiuntur ad votum.* The third gift is that by this perseverance we prepare ourselves to receive the grace with much greater fruit than if it were given us at once. St. Isidore says, God delays to hear your prayer either because you are not in good dispositions to receive what you ask, or that you may be able to receive more excellent gifts which He is desirous of conferring upon you. So, says Gerson, it happens to us as it does sometimes to a beggar, to whom men give a more liberal alms because they have kept him waiting at their door so long. Moreover the relics of our old unconverted lives, not yet burned out of us, cause prayer to operate more slowly than if our penance had been more brisk and vigorous.

Mystical writers give us various signs by which we may know, even at the time, that our prayers have been answered.

We often have an heroic confidence that our prayers have been
answered, without knowing to what we may attribute it; and
when this confidence is coupled with a great love of God,
a contempt of ourselves and an almost irresistible propensity
to break forth into thanksgiving, we may for the most part
assume that our prayer has been answered. Very often this
confidence is preceded by a vehement inspiration to pray for
the object in question, and God, says St. Augustine, would
not thus impel us to pray for a thing He was not about to
grant. Sometimes God sends in addition to these internal marks
an outward sign in the shape of a sorrow or disgrace; such
were the rebuke of Heli to Anna, and of Our Lord to Mary
at the marriage feast in Cana, and of Our Lord to the
Chananaean woman. They were the precursors of answered
prayer. As Job says, he who is mocked by his friend as I
am will call upon God, and He will hear him. Richard of
St. Victor mentions an unusual strength of faith, or depth
of humility, or earnestness of importunity, as inward signs
of answered prayer. But St. Bonaventure fears that in judging
of them we may too readily attribute to the Holy Ghost what
are only the movements of excited nature. Lastly St. Ambrose
gives the following rule. In commenting on the words, "If
two of you shall agree upon earth, concerning anything what-
soever they shall ask, it shall be done for them by My Father,
who is in Heaven: for where there are two or three gathered
together in My Name, there am I in the midst of them," he
says, What are these two or three but the body, the soul and
the Holy Ghost? For when the soul collects all its interior
powers within the sanctuary of its heart, that it may pray to
the Father in secret, and when the body collects its external
senses and unites them to the soul, the Holy Spirit approaches
and breathes into this union quietude and peace, so that the
prayer may be fervent and efficacious; and then it is that Jesus
is present in the midst of the three. O happy union in which
so many combine to supplicate the Eternal Father! What more
could be desired, what more efficacious be proposed? Delight
in the Lord, and He will grant thee thy petitions, says David.
For if it is your joy to please God, it will be His joy to hear
your prayers.

We must be careful however not to fret ourselves overmuch about the answers to our prayers. We should pray in faith and with a deep sense of our own unworthiness, and leave the rest to God. Even in a self-interested point of view no prayer has such a power of impetration as that which comes from a will conformed to the will of God. This was the secret of St. Gertrude's potent intercession.

There is one subject more which demands our attention when we are speaking of vocal prayer. A man who is much given to vocal prayer is in no slight degree in the power of his prayerbook.[1] The choice of favorite devotions is therefore a matter of great importance; and what devotions can we choose so safely as those which are approved by the Church, and those which are indulgenced by the Church. There is a great connection between indulgences and the spiritual life, and the use of indulgenced devotions is almost an infallible test of a good Catholic. St. Alphonsus says that in order to become a saint nothing more is needed than to gain all the indulgences we can; and Bl. Leonard of Port Maurice has something to the same effect. The private and approved revelations of the Saints throw considerable light upon this subject. St. Bridget was raised up in great measure, as she says herself, to propagate the honor of indulgences; and so St. Mary Magdalen de Pazzi saw souls punished in Purgatory for nothing else but a light esteem of them.

In the spiritual life there are what I may call eight beatitudes of indulgences. First, as they have to do with sin, God's justice and the temporal pain of sin, they keep us among thoughts which belong to the purgative way, and which are safest for us, although we are continually and impatiently trying to get out of them. Secondly, they have a peculiarly unworldly effect

---

1. When there are so many excellent manuals of devotion, it may seem invidious to single out one for commendation. Yet without meaning in the least to criticize others, I would venture to call the attention of my readers to a little book, published by Messrs. Burns and Lambert, under the title of *A Few Flowers from the Garden*. Its merits are that it is simple, practical, not overloaded, well selected, suitable to all, contains many indulgenced devotions and has evidently grown up from long personal use. It is not a fanciful or merely literary compilation: and its merits will grow upon those who use it.

upon us. They lead us into the invisible world; they surround us with images of a supernatural character; they fill our minds with a class of ideas, which detach us from worldly things and rebuke earthly pleasures. Thirdly, they keep the doctrine of Purgatory constantly before us, and so force upon us a perpetual exercise of faith, as well as suggest to us motives of holy fear. Fourthly, they are an exercise of charity to the faithful departed, which may easily become heroic, which may be practiced by those who can give no other alms, and which has all the effects upon our own souls that accompany works of mercy. Fifthly, God's glory is very much concerned in them, and that in two ways, in the release of the souls from Purgatory and their earlier admission to His heavenly court, and also in the manifestation of His perfections which indulgences display, such as His infinite purity and detestation of sin, even the slightest, and the exactness of His justice coupled with the ingenuity of His mercy. Sixthly, they honor the satisfactions of Jesus. They are to His satisfactions what the doctrine of all forgiveness of sin is due to Him is to His merits. So to speak, they leave nothing of Him unused; and thus they illustrate the copiousness of His Redemption. They honor likewise the satisfactions of Mary and the Saints, in such a way as still more to honor Him. Seventhly, they deepen our views of sin, and cause us to grow in horror of it. For they constantly keep before us that punishment is due even to forgiven sin, and that that punishment is one of the most intolerable kind, and though it be but temporal, it needs the satisfactions of Jesus to deliver us from it. Eighthly, they keep us in harmony with the spirit of the Church, which is of paramount importance to those who are striving to live interior lives, and are threading their way among the difficulties of asceticism and inward holiness. For to undervalue indulgences is a sign of heresy; and the hatred which heresy has for them is an index of the devil's dislike of them, and that, in its turn, is a measure of their power and of their acceptableness with God. They mix us up with so many peculiarities of the Church, from the jurisdiction of the Holy See to the belief in Purgatory, good works, the Saints and satisfaction, that they almost insure our orthodoxy. And the whole history of the unhappy

errors which have vexed the Church on the subject of the
spiritual life shows us that, to be thoroughly holy, we must
be thoroughly Catholic, and thoroughly Roman Catholic, for
otherwise than Roman we can be neither Catholic nor holy
at all.

Then, as to the indulgenced devotions themselves, there are
these advantages in them. We are sure they are approved by
the Church, because they are more than approved. We know
that numbers of holy souls in the world are using them every
day, and by uniting ourselves with them we enter more deeply
into the communion of saints, and the life of the Church which
is her unity. For the reasons I have already given, we spiritualize our minds and quicken our faith very much by the use
of them. They lead us to pray in a manner and about subjects
which the Church desires; and we attain so many ends at
once when we use them. For by the same act we not only
pray, but we revere the keys of the Church, we honor Jesus,
His Mother and the Saints, we get rid of our own temporal
punishment, or, which is a greater thing, we release the dead
and so glorify God, and as may be seen by looking over the
devotions which the Church has indulgenced, we transfer into
our minds a great amount of touching doctrine which serves
as an aliment for mental prayer and reverential love.

Let us take one instance of this. I cannot conceive a man
being spiritual who does not habitually say the Rosary. It may
be called the queen of indulgenced devotions. First consider
its importance, as a specially Catholic devotion, as so peculiarly
giving us a Catholic turn of mind by keeping Jesus and Mary
perpetually before us, and as a singular help to final perseverance, if we continue the recital of it, as various revelations
show. Next consider its institution by St. Dominic in 1214,
by revelation, for the purpose of combating heresy, and the
success which attended it. Its matter and form are not less
striking. Its matter consists of the *Pater,* and the *Ave* and the
Gloria, whose authors are our Blessed Lord Himself, St.
Gabriel, St. Elizabeth, the Council of Ephesus and the whole
Church, led in the west by St. Damasus. Its form is a complete abridgment of the Gospel, consisting of fifteen Mysteries in decades, expressing the three great phases of the work

of Redemption, joy, sorrow and glory. Its peculiarity is the next attractive feature about it. It unites mental with vocal prayer. It is a devotional compendium of theology. It is an efficacious practice of the presence of God. It is one chief channel of the traditions of the Incarnation among the faithful. It shows the true nature of devotion to our Blessed Lady and is a means of realizing the communion of saints. Its ends are the love of Jesus, reparation to the Sacred Humanity for the outrages of heresy and a continual affectionate thanksgiving to the Most Holy Trinity for the benefit of the Incarnation. It is sanctioned by the Church, by indulgences, by miracles, by the conversion of sinners and by the usage of the Saints. See also how much the method of reciting it involves. We should first make a picture of the Mystery, and always put our Blessed Lady into the picture; for the Rosary is hers. We should couple some duty or virtue with each Mystery, and fix beforehand on some soul in Purgatory to whom to apply the vast indulgences. Meanwhile, we must not strain our minds, or be scrupulous; for to say the Rosary well is quite a thing which requires learning. Remember always, as the *Raccolta* teaches, that the fifteenth Mystery is the Coronation of Mary, and not merely the glory of the Saints. Our beads land us and leave us at the feet of Mary Crowned.

I should not wish to say anything that would seem to limit the devotion of others; but, all things considered, why should we have any vocal prayers which are not indulgenced devotions, now that the Church has indulgenced them in such abundance?

Chapter XVI

TEMPTATIONS

Temptations are the raw material of glory; and the management of them is as great a work as the government of an empire, and requires a vigilance as incessant and as universal. It is a startling thing to look out into the world and study its ways, and then to think that God was made Man and died upon the Cross for its redemption. But it is equally startling to look at the lives of good men and examine their dispositions, and then to put one of the maxims of the Gospel alongside of them. At this very hour thousands of souls are earnestly complaining to God of their temptations, and hundreds of confessionals are filled with whispered and impatient murmurings against the vehemence or the perseverance of them. Yet, St. James says, "My brethren, count it all joy when you shall fall in divers temptations." It is plain, therefore, that we either do not know or do not always bear in mind the true nature and character of temptations. They are nearly as multitudinous as our thoughts, and our only victory over them is through persisting courage, and an indomitable spirit of cheerfulness. The arrows of temptation fall harmless and blunted from a gay heart, which has first of all cast itself so low in its humility that nothing can cast it lower. Be joyous, or, to use Scripture words, "Rejoice, and again I say rejoice," and you will not heed your temptations; neither will they harm you.

But let us obtain a clear idea of the nature of temptations. It seems an obvious thing to say that in the first place they are not sins; yet in nine cases out of ten our unhappiness comes from not discerning this fact. Some defilement seems to come from the touch of a mere temptation; and at the same

time it reveals to us, as nothing else does, our extreme feebleness and constant need of grace—and of very great grace.
We are like men who do not know how sore their bruises
are until they are pressed, and then we exaggerate the evil.
So when temptation presses our fallen and infirm nature, the
tenderness is so sensible and so acute that it gives us at once
the feeling of a wound or a disease. Yet we must be careful
always to distinguish between a sin and a temptation.

Temptations are either in ourselves, or outside of us, or
partly the one and partly the other. Those from within ourselves arise, either from our senses, which are free and undis-
ciplined, or from our passions, which are wild and uncorrected.
Those which are outside assail us, either by delighting us,
as riches, honors, attachments and distractions, or by attacking us as the demons do; and those which partake of the nature of both possess the attractions of both. In one sense,
however, all temptations consist in an alliance between what
is within us, and what is without us. As I have said before,
we must not put too much upon the devil; yet neither on the
other hand must we be without fear of him, or without a
true and scriptural estimate of his awful and malignant office.
He goes about seeking whom he may devour. He is a roaring
lion, when the roar will affright us, and a noiseless serpent
when success is to be ensured by secrecy. He has reduced
the possibilities and probabilities of our destruction to a science
which he applies with the most unrelenting vigor, the most
masterly intelligence, almost unfailing power, and with the
most ubiquitous variety. If it were not for the thought of grace,
its abundance and its sovereignty, we should not dare to contemplate the ways and means of the Satanic kingdom.

Yet nowhere is it a mere fight between man and the devil.
Wherever temptation is, there God is also. There is not one
which His will has not permitted, and there is not a permission which is not an act of love as well. He has given His
whole wisdom to each temptation. He has calculated its effects and often diminishes its power. He has weighed and measured each by the infirmity of each tempted soul. He has
deliberately contemplated the consequences of each, in union
with its circumstances. The minutest feature has not escaped

Him. The most hidden danger has been an element in His judgment. All this while the devil is passive and powerless. He cannot lay a finger on the child until its loving Father has prescribed the exact conditions, and has forewarned the soul by His inspirations, and forearmed it with proportionable succors of grace. Nothing is at random, as if temptations were hurrying here and there, like the bullets in the air of a battle-field. Moreover, each temptation has its own crown prepared for it, if we correspond to grace and are victorious. I do not know any picture of God more affecting, or more fatherly, than the vision of Him which faith gives us in His assiduous solicitudes and paternal occupations while we are being tempted. "Where wert Thou, Lord! while I was being tempted?" cried the Saint of the desert." "Close to you, My son, all the while," was the tender reply. As men feel sorrow to be at times a privilege, because it draws them into the sympathies of their superiors, so is it a joy to be tempted because it occupies God so intensely and so lovingly with our little interests and cares. The highest saint in Heaven can never attain to love God, as He loves a soul struggling with temptations.

Nevertheless, temptation is exquisite suffering, above that of sickness and adversity. There is something loathsome in the breath which it breathes upon us, something horribly fas-cinating in its eye, and paralyzing in its touch. We are faint and sick with the sense of our own corruption and helpless weakness; and the thrilling interests involved in our resisting or succumbing agitate the most inward life of our soul. It is foolish either to deny the suffering or to make light of it. In either case we shall be less able to endure it. It must be in the nearness of God, and in the prompt superfluity of grace, that we must find our cheerfulness and our consolation.

With all his wisdom, the devil is constantly overreaching himself in temptations, not from stupidity, though perhaps God may stupefy him from time to time, but from his ignorance of the invisible amount of grace which has been mercifully sent us. God's love is always so far above either our merits or even our expectations, that neither the tempter nor our-selves can ever come to believe it beforehand. Thus the devil sometimes tempts us too openly, and we are on our guard;

or he sends us the wrong kind of temptation, as one man
sometimes gets a letter intended for another; or he sends the
right temptation at the wrong time; or, as he cannot always
read our thoughts, he puts a wrong interpretation on our outward actions; or he leaves off too soon; or he persists too
long; or he underestimates the effect of penance and our love
of God on the old habits of past sin. So it is that from one
cause or other he is continually overreaching himself. This
is a fact to be dwelt upon. For there are many who would,
if questioned, answer quite correctly about Satan and the limitations of his power, who nevertheless practically in their own
minds entertain a wrong idea of him, and their conduct under
temptation shows the influence which this false view has upon
them. Sometimes they are not nearly so much grieved at their
falls as they ought to be, and sometimes they are panic-stricken
as soon as they feel themselves in his grasp; so that for him
to touch them is to conquer them. I am persuaded that a great
deal of this is from their being possessed, half unconsciously,
with a wrong idea of the devil, who acts upon them as the
dread of ghosts acts upon children, unreasonably yet irresisti-
bly. They look upon him as God's rival, a sort of wicked
god, with godlike attributes all evil, and an omnipotence of
iniquity. They do not remember that he is simply our fellow
creature, and a conquered and blighted creature. We have reason to fear him. Yet we are not panic-stricken with the hourly
companionship of our own corrupt nature. And we have far
more to fear from it than from him.

Great however as are the pain and annoyance which the
soul experiences from temptation, it is very often a gift of
God not to be delivered from them. Sometimes it is even
wise not to pray for deliverance, but only for valor to fight
a good fight. St. Paul three times asked to have his thorn
removed, in imitation doubtless of Our Lord's triple prayer
to have His chalice pass from Him; and the answer which
God vouchsafed was a proof how great a gift the temptation,
or its permission, really was. It has been remarked by an
eminent writer on the interior life, and it may be a great consolation to many to know it, that when the devil attacks our
body it is often a sign that he has been secretly attacking

our soul, and has been foiled. It is also a characteristic of his efforts rather to turn us from virtue than to impel us to vice. This is particularly the case with spiritual people. With them sins of omission make more for him than sins of commission, not only because it is less easy to lead a spiritual man into the former than into the latter, but also because the latter more effectually rouse him to repentance. Lukewarmness is often nothing more than a clogging up of the avenues of the soul with sins of omission, so that the cool and salutary inundations of grace are hindered.

Nevertheless the approaches of the devil need hardly ever take the vigilant by surprise. Whether it be of the spiritual nature of our soul, or of the forewarnings of grace, we have almost always a presentiment of his coming, provided we have a habit of self-recollection. The great thing when we feel that presentiment is not to be perturbed, but to meet him in the calmness of humility. This calmness must never desert us during the whole of the fight, least of all when we feel the delectation which in many cases the temptation will infallibly excite. I say in many cases, because there are whole classes of temptations which would not be temptations at all were it not for the delectation. But the delectation is not consent. We are not the masters of the first indeliberate movements of our own hearts and minds. The enemy may run his hand flourishingly over the keys before we are aware. But there must be a deliberate acceptation and retention of the delectation before it can amount to consent or become a sin.

All men have their temptations, and all men's temptations are multitudinous. But among the various paths by which God conducts chosen souls, one is the way of temptations. These souls then are not in the case of other men. Temptation is their road, and their only road. They pass through crowds of them, and from one crowd into another, each surpassing its predecessor in horror and ugliness. But this is not God's ordinary way, and we are not concerned with legislating for it here. Yet the fact that God can make a way of perfection consist of temptations only, throws considerable light on the nature of temptations generally.

But from the nature let us pass to the times of temptation.

It is to be observed that we may often have seasons of great grace, without being at all aware of it, from the extreme hiddenness of the operations of the Holy Ghost in our souls. But temptation is a much more obvious thing than grace; and it is generally the case that a season of peculiar temptation is also a season of peculiar grace. And this it is a consolation to know. Thus, when St. Stephen's heroic faith was passing through its extremest temptations, he beheld Our Lord, not sitting, but standing, at the right hand of the Father, expressive of the aid He was rendering to His servant in his hour of need. Temptations also vary with the times of the spiritual life to which they belong. The temptations of beginners are not those of proficients, nor those of proficients the temptations of the perfect. If all are terrible, all are in God's hands, and so we may be tranquil and of good cheer. There are also times of temptation, when our own past sin, or our present culpable inadvertence, is the cause of them. We have brought them upon ourselves; and this makes them all the harder for our self-love to bear. Still, even though they are the just and immediate chastisement of our own faults, the patient endurance of them is not the less meritorious; and disquietude forms no part of accepted penance. Times of prayer are also times of peculiar temptation. This was naturally to be expected, inasmuch as there is nothing the devil so much desires to interrupt as our communication with God. Indeed, the access and vehemence of temptations form a part of the supernatural difficulties of prayer. The spiritual life itself, with its times of retreat or of increased recollection, brings us into seasons of peculiar temptation. The world with its outward attractions is removed from us, and the devil, in dread of these epochs of recollection, more than supplies their place with his inward appliances of temptation. There are times also when he teases us with temptations to which he knows beforehand that we shall not yield; yet in which he finds his account because they disquiet us, or dishearten us, or throw us into a general irritability. There are other times in which he tempts us in the grace we have just used to overcome him, and in the strength of which we actually have overcome him. The reason of this is that our success has thrown us off our guard, and we never dream of failing in a virtue which but a moment before has flushed us with the joy of victory. Thus, Our Lord having put His confidence in His Father, the devil first tempted Him by it.

From the times of temptation we pass to its kinds. Some temptations are frequent: and there is a peculiar danger in their frequency. They dissipate us and break up the calm of our recollection. Or they tire us, and at last we sit down and give up the battle out of weariness. Or we get used to them, and lose our wholesome fear of them. These frequent temptations have generally some connection with our ruling passion. Some temptations are durable, and they also have dangers of their own and consolations of their own. Their chief danger is their outliving our powers of perseverance; and their chief consolation is that their very durability is a sign they have not triumphed. The pressure is removed the moment we consent; and consequently the lasting of the burden is a measure of the grace God has given us to resist it. Although Jesus seems fast asleep in the boat, yet that it is not submerged in the dark angry waters is because He is there. There are other temptations which are brief, brief and gentle, or brief and violent. The brief and gentle leave us in doubt whether we have not consented, and so perplex us: the brief and violent stun us for the moment, and leave us in an amazement during which other temptations may come and surprise us. Each virtue has its own attendant temptations, set like spies round about it by the devil. The great object of these is to make us retire from holy enterprise, and reduce us to an unmeritorious inaction. We must meet these as St. Bernard met the devil when he tempted him to vainglory in the middle of a sermon, "I did not begin for you, and so I shall not leave off for you." Temptations which approach us by the senses are proof against all weapons except those of mortification and the Sacraments. Temptations against faith and chastity are two classes apart, and have this peculiarity, that they are never to be directly resisted, but fled from. We must distract ourselves from them instead of striking them. There are other temptations, which are merely feelers to explore our possibilities of sin. The devil sends these out to gain knowledge of us, as he cannot read our hearts;[1] just as a besieging army sends rockets here and there into a city to try for the powder magazines. But among all these kinds of temptations there is no one class which is any sign that our souls are in an evil state. Spiritual writers lay this down as an undoubted fact; and yet how much self-torment there is in the world because silly peevish souls will persist in acting as if its contrary were true. But what are the uses of temptations? So many and so great that I can do no more than indicate a few of them here. They try us, and we are worth nothing if we are not tried. Our trial is the one thing God cares for, and it is the only thing which gives us the least knowledge of ourselves. They disgust us with the world almost as effectually as the sweetnesses which God gives us in prayer. And how hard it is to become thoroughly disgusted with the world: and how very much more we really love the world than we have any idea of! Oh, of what price ought anything to be which helps us to a true and final divorce from this seductive world! They enable us to merit more, that is, they increase God's love of us, and our love of God, and our glory with God hereafter. They punish us for past sins; and we ought to court such punishments eagerly, for five minutes of free-will suffering on earth are worth five years of the tardy cruelties of Purgatory. They purify us for God's presence, which is the very office of Purgatory itself, and anticipate its work and so prevent its fires. They prepare us for spiritual consolations, perhaps they even earn them for us. St. Philip says that God gives us first a dark and then a bright day all through life. Can words tell the joy it is to be consoled by God? Are not souls whom He has touched obliged to hold their tongues, because they have no words to express the happiness it is? And probably without the temptation, the consolation never would have come. Or if it had come, it might have harmed us. The temptation has made us capable of bearing it without loss, and tasting it and not fainting away with its unearthly sweetness. Temptations teach us our own weakness, and so humble us; and could

---

1. Surin says he can; but the consent of theologians is against him; and his phenomena are explicable without denying the admitted maxims of the schools.

our guardian angels do more than this for us, in all the variety of their affectionate ministrations? Dear Prince, more than brother! I say it not in light esteem of his unutterable kindness, who never leaves me a solitary speck in this huge creation of God, and whose services I shall never know till they all meet me at the doom brighter than a thousand suns, and whose love will come to a head rather than to an end when he embraces me in the first moment of the resurrection of the flesh! But he wishes nothing so much as to keep me humble, and temptations help him to do the work. They give us also a greater esteem of grace, and the want of this is daily the cause of more evil in the world than the devil can cause in a whole century. Grace grows by being esteemed. It multiplies itself when it is honored, just as faith merits miracles, while infidelity hinders even Our Lord from working them. They make virtue take deeper root, and so they play their part in the grand grace of final perseverance. How shallow would all spirituality be if it were not for temptations. How shallow good men actually are, who are not much tempted! The Church can never trust them in her hour of need. They are always on the side on which St. Thomas of Canterbury would not have been. Temptations again make us more watchful, and so instead of leading into sin, they hinder shoals of sins. They make us more fervent, and kindle in us such a fire of love as burns away the hay and straw of venial sin, and cauterizes the half-healed wounds which mortal sin has made. A transport of generous love can do a work as great, and the great work as well, as a year's fast on bread and water, with a discipline a day. Lastly, they teach us spiritual science: for what we know of self, of the world, of the demons and of the artifices of divine grace, is chiefly from the phenomena of temptation, and from our defeats quite as much as from our victories.

These are the uses of temptations, and they leave seven permanent blessings behind them. They leave us merit, which is no transient thing. Nay, such is its vitality that when mortal sin has put it to death, penance can bring it to life again. They leave us love, both God's love of us and our love of Him. They leave us humility; and with that all other gifts of God; for the Holy Spirit Himself rests upon the humble, and makes His dwelling in their hearts. They leave us solidity. Our building is so much higher than it was, and its foundations more safely and more permanently settled. They leave us self-knowledge, without which all we do is done in the dark, and the sun never shines upon the soul, and the ground is never clear for the operations of grace. They leave us self-love killed; and has life a fairer task than the burial of its worst and most odious enemy? Its dead body is more to us than the relic of an apostle, and surely that is saying much. They leave us thrown upon God. For no nurse ever put a babe into its father's arms more carefully or more securely than temptations put us into the extended arms of God. And yet we complain—complain of our temptations! Perverse race! It has always been so; from beneath the apple tree in Eden to this hour, we do not know our own happiness, and in our ignorance we pick a special quarrel with it!

Mistakes can be made about temptations as about everything else in the spiritual life; and many have been already implied and explained in what has been said. There are, however, four particular mistakes on which a few words may be of use. The first mistake is that we are apt to think the time spent in combating temptations is time lost. We are all very well and very tranquil, and more or less consciously in the presence of God, at our ordinary occupations; but the time comes for visiting the Blessed Sacrament, and all at once we are assailed with a multiplicity of temptations. We have but a quarter of an hour to be there, and the whole time has gone in doing battle with these miserable temptations; or we rise in the morning, full of the thought of God, and say prayers while we are dressing. We then kneel down and begin our meditation, and a host of temptations forthwith assail us. The hourglass runs down, and what have we done? Nothing but fight, and it seems, too, unsatisfactorily, with these pestering temptations. Now we must remember that we are not to serve God for consolations, or after our own fashion, and according to our own taste; but according to His wisdom and His will. His rewards are not attached to the good works we prescribe to ourselves, but to the combats in which it is His good pleasure to involve us. Time can never be lost which is spent in doing the will of God. On the contrary, all time is lost which is spent otherwise. What is our object? It is either to be glorifying God, or to be perfect, or to reach Heaven. Fighting a temptation is the shortest road to all these three ends.

The second mistake is the misapprehension of temptations by negligent souls. Sometimes they think it a mark of spiritual advancement to be inactive and almost passive under temptations. They apply to themselves advices which belong only to the perfect, or maxims which were intended for the scrupulous. Thus they fall into a pernicious habit of letting dangerous thoughts pass through their minds, without demanding or examining their passports; and this not only weakens their mind, but seems to saturate it with undesirable images and inclinations. Their feeling about sin ceases to be what it was, and their confidence in themselves increases as the probabilities of a fall increase also. The consequence of all this is a state of torpor and of general slovenliness with God, from which if they are roused at all, it is probably by the commission of mortal sin. Lukewarm souls have sometimes been renewed to holiness in this dreadful way, and God has shown them mercy even in the judicial chastisement of this adorable permission. But it is a process, the very thought of which should make us shudder, and which probably never happened to anyone who was negligent because he trusted to repentance willfully delayed, and to the uncertain possibilities of an eventual reconciliation with God. Whoever has familiarized himself with what he knows are temptations, and has domesticated the thought of them in his mind, no matter of what class they may be, has taken a decided step toward that state of tepidity whose logical development is final impenitence.

The third mistake concerns our use of the calms which come between the storms of periodical temptations. Everyone knows by his own experience that he is subject to particular classes, or to one particular class of temptations, which come round in perfect hurricanes, like circular storms with fair and tranquil weather between. We have been going on in our ordinary way. We see no reason for a change, either in ourselves or in external circumstances, when all at once the storm is down

upon us, with the same sort of panic the heathen felt when
it thundered out of a clear sky. We are possessed with the
images of the temptation. Every outward object turns into them.
We hear voices, as we think, and inarticulate sounds shape
themselves into intelligible words. The lines of books run into
the ideas of temptation, and prayers and holy names seem
only fresh food for the beleagured imagination. We are sunk,
overhead, deep down, in temptations, and the masterful current is sweeping in eddies above us. It is not as with Peter
that a Hand was held out as we were in the act of sinking.
We are sunk. Yes! and Jesus is with us in the deep where
we are. Now in the storm we have simply nothing to do but
to hold fast to God with all our might and main. There is
no help for it. We cannot legislate for a hurricane. The real
work of the storm must be done in the preceding calm. It
is a mistake to look upon these calms as a time of rest when
we may give ourselves up to the simple enjoyment of the absence of the temptations, or of the spiritual sweetness with
which these tempests are commonly followed. We must lay
our plans then, and make our resolutions, with a foresight
of what we have to encounter. We must fix on occasions to
avoid, increase our mortifications, and redouble our prayers.
If we have gone down in many a storm, it has been because
we made holidays of our calms. Remember, in the spiritual
life there are recreations; but there are no holidays. That school
breaks up but once, and the home afterwards is eternal.

A fourth mistake is the delusion with which the devil tries
to possess us, that if we give way in some of the circumstances of the temptation, or to the temptation itself short of
sin, we shall weaken it. Our whole mind seems so completely
overlaid with the images of temptation that we think we shall
suffer some permanent moral injury if it lasts, and that anything short of sin is not allowable only, but desirable also,
which will release us from it. It is strange that so gross a
snare should ever succeed; yet it does so in many cases. We
must remember, therefore, that to yield is to weaken ourselves,
not the temptation. We shall get no foothold so strong as our
first; and men often discover to their cost that even a change
of position, without abandoning an attitude of defense, is as

good as a defeat in the time of temptation.

But how are we to overcome temptations? Cheerfulness is the first thing, cheerfulness the second and cheerfulness the third. The devil is chained. He can bark, but he cannot bite, unless we go up to him and let him do so. We must be of good courage. The power of temptation is in the fainting of our own hearts. Confidence in God is another spiritual weapon, the more potent because no one can have confidence in God who has not the completest diffidence of himself. God's cause is ours; for temptation is more really the devil's wrath against God who has punished him, than against us, whom he only envies. Our ruin is important to him only as it is a blow at God's glory. Thus God is bound to us, as it were; as it is for His sake that we are thus persecuted. We may be sure, indeed we know infallibly, that we shall never be tried beyond our strength. Prayer, especially ejaculatory prayer, is another obvious means of victory, together with mortification and the frequenting of the Sacraments, which are all of them wells of supernatural fortitude.

Examination of conscience must help us to detect the weak and vulnerable parts of our nature; and then we must exercise ourselves in acts contrary not only to our peculiar infirmities, but also to our besetting temptations. We must avoid idleness, and crush beginnings. We must not speak of our temptations indiscriminately to persons who have no right to know anything about them, nor even to our spiritual friends. It gives no real relief, and it feeds the ideas. Neither must we be cast down if our director treats our temptations more lightly than we think they deserve. What is the good of speaking to him at all about them, if we are not going to obey his rules and adopt his view and follow his advice?

In times of temptation we must be very careful not to retrench any of our spiritual exercises, a line of conduct for which the evil one may suggest very specious reasons. We have need of all our strength at that moment; and we never know to which of our ordinary exercises God attaches His grace. It would have been better for the Apostles to have struggled through a drowsy, dry, distracted prayer, than to have simply gone to sleep in the Garden of Gethsemane. We must remember also that all our spiritual exercises are less prompt and pleasant when we are under temptations; because we are teased and puzzled by them. Hence nature is more likely to suggest the abridgment or discontinuance of some of them, on the ground of their being useless and spiritless. But although things are established by the mouth of two witnesses, those two must not be the devil and the human spirit. We must also be cautious not to change our purposes at such times. The dust and smoke of the battle hang over us, and darken all things. It is not a time for us to see God's will about changes and vocations. His will just then is that we resist the evil, and therefore that is the single thing for us to do. Nay, we must beware even of any new good which makes its appearance, knocks at the door of our heart, or puts itself ready-made into our hands, at such a season. St. Ignatius long since warned us of a family of temptations which present themselves in the disguise of good. God would not send us the good then, or in that way. His will, once more, is that we should resist the evil. The good will keep, if it be real good; and He will send us peaceable times when we can calmly and deliberately take it upon ourselves.

We must also be upon our guard against very little temptations, or such as we should call little. For things must have comparative magnitudes, even where our souls are concerned. It is no uncommon thing for a man who has resisted great temptations to fall in little ones. This is very intelligible. Wherever there is dignity in an action or a suffering we can the better brace ourselves up to it; for we can draw largely upon nature as well as grace. Self-love likes dignity, and will go through endless pain, as if it were an insensible thing, in order to obtain it. Hence comes the importance of little things in religion. Nature has less to do with them, and so they rivet our union with God more closely. The conversion of souls, works of mercy on a grand scale, visiting prisons, preaching, hearing confessions and even establishing religious institutes, are comparatively easy works when put by the side of exactitude in daily duties, observation of petty rules, minute custody of the senses, kind words and modest exterior which preach the presence of God. We gain more supernatural glory in little things, because more fortitude is required, as they are continuous, uninterrupted and with no dignity about them to spur us on. All the strength we require must be found within. We have no outward place or praise of men to rest our lever on, and furthermore heroism in little things is more a matter of endurance than of action. It is a perpetual constraint.

Moreover, our spirit is more effectually taken captive in little things. Its defeats are more frequent. The very continuity of the actions forms a linked chain, which extends to many things. No attachment is to be merely natural, no word unweighed, no step precipitate, no pleasure enjoyed sensually, no joy to evaporate in dissipation, the heart never to rest on carnal tenderness alone, no action to have its spring in selfwill. We tremble at such seeming impossibilities of perfection—yet it is only the perfection of little things! Then, again, there is something so humbling and secret in little things. Who knows if we count our words, or what feelings we are curbing? God will let us fall in these very respects to hide us more in Himself, and from the eyes of men. We carry the mortification of Jesus about us unseen. It is a slow martyrdom of love. God is the only spectator of our agony. Nay, we ourselves find it hard to realize that we are doing purely for God such a multitude of trivial things; hence we have no room for vainglory, no fallacious support of conscious human rectitude.

But in these little things we not only gain more glory for ourselves, but we give more glory to God. We show more esteem for Him in them; for there must necessarily be more pure motive and sheer faith in little than in great things. Great things by their greatness often hide God; and at the best the esteem in great things is mostly divided between God and the glory of the action, and so the whole work is tainted. Whereas the littleness and vileness of small things, their apparent facility and men's contempt for them, leave the soul face to face with God in the disenchanting twilight of interior mortification. But it is not merely esteem. More actual tribute is paid to God in little things. In great things we have more help given us, and we give God less because we have to labor less. The abundance of grace, the sweetness of it and the animation of spirit from the pursuit of a great object, are three things which lessen our own labor. Yet it is our own toil that is the real tribute to God, just as dry prayers are said to be more meritorious than sweet ones. In great things too we seldom have the liberty of acting as we please. In little ones we have, and we pay that liberty away hour by hour to God as a tribute of fidelity and love.

But esteem and tribute are not all. We sacrifice more to God in little things. We think little of little things, and so we make the sacrifice, not in swelling thoughts of mightiness, but out of a subdued feeling of our own utter nothingness, and of the immensity of our being allowed to make any sacrifice to God at all. We sacrifice also our self-interest, which is not attracted by anything in these ignoble victims; and so we seek God only, and put aside the pursuit of praise and self. We forego also the enjoyment of strenuous manly action; for what manliness, as men count things, is there in regularity, littleness, exactness and obscurity? Yet this is the only road to solid virtue. It was not what we read of in the Saints that made them saints: it was what we do not read of them that enabled them to be what we wonder at while we read. Words cannot tell the abhorrence nature has of the piecemeal captivity of little constraints. And as to little temptations, I can readily conceive a man having the grace to be roasted over a slow fire for our dearest Mother's Immaculate Conception or the Pope's supremacy, who would not have the grace to keep his temper in a theological conversation on either of those points of the Catholic Faith.

One more question remains about temptations. How shall we behave when we ourselves are overcome? There is but one answer, one advice: it is childish: but is there any other? When we fall we must rise again, and go on our way, wishing ourselves, after a Christian fashion, better luck another time.

Chapter XVII

SCRUPLES

A scrupulous man teases God, irritates his neighbor, torments himself and oppresses his director. It would require a whole volume to prove these four infallible propositions; the reader must, therefore, either take them on faith, or make the acquaintance of a scrupulous man. Everyone who is in trouble and disgrace deserves commiseration; but our pity is lessened when the sufferer has no one to blame but himself, and it well-nigh departs altogether when he remains in his suffering of his own obstinate will. Now this is the case with scrupulous persons during all the earlier stages of their complaint, before they become incurable. They are the opprobrium of spiritual physicians, and so intensely difficult is their cure that God has sometimes allowed those who were hereafter to be the guides of souls to pass through a supernatural state of scruples, that they might be the better able to minister to the disease in others. It is a great part of the science of the spiritual life to know a temptation from a sin; and a scruple may almost be defined to be the culpable ignorance of this. Another man may discern that my scruple is not a sin; but if I discerned it for myself, it would not be a scruple; and if I took it on faith when my director told me, I should not be a scrupulous man. This lets us into the secret of the malice of scruples. They are not sins, but they are so full of wrong dispositions that they can become sins at a moment's notice, besides being sources of many sins under the pretext of good. They are little centers of spiritual death spotting the soul, a kind of moral erysipelas.

It is unfortunate that scrupulous persons are always spoken

of with great compassion, far more than they deserve. Hence they elevate their scruples to an interior trial of the soul— which they sometimes are, but very seldom. It is unfortunate also that in common conversation the word scruple is often used in a good sense, as if it were something respectable, and a sort of vague synonym for conscientiousness. It would, therefore, be a great thing if men could get well into their minds this ascetical truth, that there is nothing respectable about a scruple. It has no intellectual worth. It merits no moral esteem. It has not the faintest element of spiritual good in it. It is simply a perversity and a wrongness, deserving of pity certainly, but of the same kind and amount as we have for a man who is going to be hung. Francesca of Pampeluna saw many souls in Purgatory only for scruples; and when this surprised her, Our Lord told her there never was a scruple which was wholly without sin. This was, of course, not meant to apply to supernatural scruples, which we shall consider presently. But scruples are not only bad in themselves. They give rise to countless other mischiefs; and one of the most provoking of them is that men are often deterred from the pursuit of perfection and the constraints of the interior life by the fear of scruples.

A scruple is defined in theology to be a vain fear of sin where there is no reason nor reasonable ground for suspecting sin; and it is sometimes explained in etymology to mean a stone in a man's shoe which makes him walk lame, and wounds him at every step, which is not an inapt figure for expressing its consequences in the spiritual life. We may also compare a scrupulous man to a horse shying at shadows, and so making little progress, backing, disobeying the rein, often endangering the rider and always trying his temper. Moreover, he runs into real sin from startling at the shadow of imaginary sin; and all this is so connected with pride that the tender St. Philip gave no quarter to scrupulous persons who would not pay blind obedience to the rules given them. Thus scruples are quite distinct from delicacy of conscience, which is known by its not only being reasonable, but much more by its being tranquil; neither is a scruple the same thing as laxity, but Gerson thinks that it is almost worse.

The first question for us to consider regards the causes of scruples. These are three: God, the devil, and ourselves, or the human spirit; and to these last the body contributes, as well as the soul.

First, then, scruples may be from God. These are what I have called supernatural scruples. God may permit us to fall into them for various reasons. Sometimes it is to prepare us for the office of directing souls, in which it is important that we should have an experimental knowledge of scruples, so as to guide others safely through them. Sometimes it is as an exterior trial, or what mystics call a purgation of spirit; and their use is one while to wean us from an excessive attachment to spiritual sweetnesses and the extraordinary favors of God, and another while to let us have our Purgatory on earth, and another while to destroy the lingering activity of self-love. He thus cleanses us from our past faults by a most apt, yet extremely severe penance, confirms us in a salutary fear, and humbles us in the very matters wherein humiliation is felt most distressingly. His share in the process is simply the withdrawing of the gratuitous light in which He allowed the soul to walk before. It was under this subtraction that St. Bonaventure would not say Mass and St. Ignatius refused to eat, that Ippolito Galantini was swallowed up in a sea of scruples, that St. Lutgarde said her office so many times over that God sent an angel to forbid her, and that St. Augustine, as he tells us in his *Confessions,* was so teased with scruples about his natural pleasure in eating and drinking.

Secondly, scruples may be from the devil, who is a positive cause of them, which God can never be. St. Lawrence Justinian says: It often happens by the disposition of God that the evil spirits confound the consciences of the weak by doubtfulness and by a host of pricking fears, so that they cannot move their foot through the excess of these terrors of conscience. Nay, their persuasions and importunities can actually bring it to pass that what is a very little sin, or no sin at all, may be turned into a mortal sin. The devil's object is, of course, always real sin; and he knows well that scruples are a sure though a circuitous road to it, and not the less sure for being circuitous.

But thirdly, the greatest fountain of these dishonorable un-worthinesses is in ourselves. It is partly in our soul, and partly in our body. This is the most practical part of our subject, and must be considered at greater length. The causes of scruples from our soul are either intrinsic or extrinsic. The intrinsic are five in number. The first is the want of discernment in temptations, so that a man does not distinguish between temptation and consent. Of this I have spoken in the last chapter. It is difficult to exaggerate its importance, as so many things are vitiated by this unhappy ignorance. The second is a hidden pride, which takes the shape of self-opinionatedness. There are few men who have not some pet opinions to which they cling with an unreasonable tenacity. They may be very humble in other matters. They may even have a certain amount of intellectual humility. But they cannot be made to discern the inordinateness of this tenacity. If it be on a question of theology, ten to one it becomes implicit heresy in a short time. They cannot see the force of any arguments on the other side. They unsuspiciously interpret in their own favor the most plain counter-statements in theologians, whose authority they dare not call in question. From conversations they retire with an exactly opposite impression of the interlocutor's opinion from that which he distinctly meant to convey. Is there any subject on theology which we can never discuss without either sadness or irritability? We may be sure we have got hold of a wrong opinion about it. When this tenacity of judgment fastens upon a question of the spiritual life, it becomes a source of scruples, and a source which is itself poisoned by wrong dispositions. Out of this came Jansenism and Quietism; and in the secret of private and even conventual life it is, as great writers tell us, unceasingly destroying souls. Safe and happy is the man, if such a one there be, and enjoyable the office of his guardian angel, who, outside the limits of the Catholic Faith and the approval of the Church, has an opinion which it would not give him ten minutes' uneasiness to abandon!

The third cause is an excessive fear of God's justice or a distrust of His mercy; for it may take either of these forms. Thus if a man has laid to heart what has been said before of looking on God as a Father, he will escape this snare.

It is not that scruples have any real worship of the Divine Justice, which through an intellectual infirmity leads them to underrate the riches of His mercy. Scruples have nothing to do with God for His own sake. There is no devotional spirit about them, nor even a mistaken one. The disguise may be varied almost infinitely, but it is always self-love which is beneath the veil. It is our fear, not God's honor, which leads us to exaggerate the one attribute and to depreciate the other. The fourth cause is an inordinate anxiety to avoid even the appearance of sin, and to have a full certainty that such and such actions are not sins. We are impatient of the uncertainty in which it has pleased God that we should often walk. We would fain change the assurance of faith for the evidence of sight, or the conviction of reason. God has made faith the light of life. We wish for a light more undeniable and more bright. He who loves God wishes to avoid sin; but to wish to avoid the appearance of sin is by no means an infallible proof of sanctity and love. Short of scandal, the Saints have seen almost a shelter in the semblance of sin. It is sin, and not the appearance of it, which wounds God's honor. So that here again it is self, our own outward reputation or our own inward satisfaction, which we are seeking under the false pretense of God's glory. I cannot repeat it too often, so that we may be inspired with a greater disgust for these plague spots— there is no search after God in scruples. Self is their center, and they revolve round it with odious accuracy and fidelity. The fifth cause is an indiscreet austerity, which shows itself in avoiding the company of others, as if perfection consisted in being morose. There are very few souls which can bear solitude. For the most part it makes them a prey to sin instead of deepening their habits of the presence of God. Hence it was that the old cenobites of the desert were so tardy in allowing the vocation of those who thought themselves called to the hermit's life. With people in the world the same principles are at work in their measure. To shun society and shut ourselves up, as if to keep out of the way of sin, to avoid rash judgments, to do penance and to practice prayer, is a line of conduct which rarely answers. It is beset with temptations, and an atmosphere of delusions is spread all over it.

In spite of the fertility of sin which we find in temerarious criticism, and an ungoverned tongue, and an irritable exacting temper, the majority of men sin less when they are with others than when they are by themselves.

When the causes of scruples are in the soul, but are so in consequence of external circumstances, they come either from the permission of God or the temptation of Satan, both of which we have already considered, or from conversing with scrupulous persons, or reading books of spirituality and moral theology which a prudent director would have prohibited our reading. These two last causes explain themselves, and need not be commented upon.

There remain two more causes, both of which arise from the body rather than the soul. The first is a cold, melancholy and hypochondriacal temperament, and the second is weakness of the head. The scruples which come from a melancholy temperament are, of all, the most difficult to cure. This is especially the case when persons of that disposition are given to immoderate corporal austerities, which seem at once to thicken the gloom of their minds and to strengthen the obstinacy of their self-will. It is very rare indeed that such a person is ever completely cured. Indeed, as we shall see by-and-by, complete cures of this disease are altogether rare. These temperaments have a constitutional aptitude for turning sweets into bitters, and thus the very remedies reinforce the malady. The weakness of head is sometimes natural, and sometimes the result of inordinate study, eager application to prayer, or a foolish abridgment of sleep. It is not easy for a spiritual man to be guilty of either of these three things without sin; so that in this case even the physical causes of scruple we prepare for ourselves, by our own disobedience or the indulgence of self-will. What sight is more provoking, and alas! what more common, than to see a devout man doing a right thing in a wrong way, and maintaining he is right?

The signs of scruples may be inferred from their causes. The first is pertinacity of will and way. It is very rare indeed that a docile man is scrupulous; and when he is so, his scruples are, for the most part, supernatural, and therefore sanctifying. Disobedience is the counterpart of scrupulosity.

Pertinacity is the opposite of the spirit of Jesus.

The second sign is a greedy desire to know our own interior state. This comes to pass when self-love entirely possesses us, as if it were a living demon. We are unable to use the words of Innocent the Third, to "explode the light and rash credulity of our conscience." We must know whether we are in a state of grace. We will not go a step further till we do know. We must be told whether the sin we have confessed be grave or not. We remain dumb till our confessor has told us. God must give us a mathematical certainty in moral questions, or we shall faint. We will give up holiness. We will not try to persevere. "Human reason cannot take in the infinity of particulars," says St. Thomas, "so that our providences must remain uncertain." This is God's will, but it is not ours. A scrupulous man measures nothing by God's will, but everything by his own. What! are we not to know whether what we are doing is certainly pleasing to God? No! says St. Bonaventure; "to know that we have charity is not necessary to salvation; it is the having of it which is so." Thus because we will have more light than God's light, we walk in the darkness, and down the precipice: our first step is in perplexity, our second in cowardice, our third in sadness, and our fourth in irremediable perdition.

The third sign is a frequent change of our opinion for reasons of no moment, together with an inconstancy and perturbation in action. We are not only prone to give way to frivolous fears, but we are fluctuating and unequable in our very fears. We are disquieted and agitated by them, even while we persist in caressing them. If we are asked whether there be sin in such or such an action, we answer that there is not. Yet we are frightened of acting even on the conviction of our own reason, coupled with the admonitions of obedience; as if forsooth our soul were worth so much more than the souls of others.

The fourth sign is what Descuret calls the feeding of ourselves with extravagant reflections on the most trivial circumstances of our actions. It belongs to the perverse genius of scruples to give its attention to what is unimportant, and to withdraw it from that in which the whole gist of the matter

lies. In other words it is an essentially impertinent spirit, in
the etymological sense of the word. It is always busy, but
never at its own business; always at work, but its work is
one of confusion, not of order. It hovers among the flowers,
lights upon them, turns their cups topsy turvy, and empties
them of their crystal dew, but gets honey out of none of them.
Some animals make a noise, not to express their emotions,
but to give vent to their self-importance; and scruples are
like one of these. They are neither of use nor ornament; but
that they can tease is a grateful sign of power.

The fifth sign is a fear of sin even in actions which the
man himself perceives to be undeniably excellent. There is
something amazing in the stupid ingenuity with which the
mind tries to make out a case against good works, and something still more amazing in the power it has of believing in
itself, a belief which is not a whit shaken by the manifest
disbelief of the whole world besides. Occasionally it makes
us suspect that there is truth in what someone said, that all
men were mad, and that what we agree to call madness is
only a question of degree. It is useless to argue with men
in this disposition: our duty is to command them, our temptation is to strike them.

The sixth sign is a habit of bodily attitudes, postures, gestures,
strugglings, half-aloud ejaculations, fidgets, inability to sit still,
which an old Benedictine writer calls simply ridiculous, but
which modern manners would rather deem distressing. I suppose the meaning of this is, after the fashion of Görres' mystical explanations, that the disease of the soul has spread out
and transferred itself into the organization, and has now reached
the feet and finger-ends. This can only be cured as we cure
children who rub their eyes and bite their nails, whether those
practices come of idleness, eagerness, temper, or abstraction.

The seventh sign is a perpetual hankering after our past
confessions, a wish to rake them up and overhaul them, and
see if we cannot find matter for some choice scruple in them.
We do not know what is wrong about them. We even shrink
from specifying, lest the charm should go. But it is a delightful
misery, a wretchedness in which a scrupulous spirit revels.
He fondles it, as an Englishman nurses his beloved melancholy.

We are dying to make a fresh general confession, but not at all inclined to take any great pains to prepare for it, or any vigorous measures against present faults. But it establishes our empire over our director. We triumph over his reluctance; and we go to it infallibly sure of one thing, that what he mistakenly conceives to be our besetting sin, is just the one sin, thank God, which does not beset us. Any one but that. Certainly not that. And all this while we fancy that being in motion is necessarily progress. Alas! we are like the sails of a windmill, always on the move, but only round and round.

But the signs and developments of scruples are somewhat different, according to the causes from which they proceed, and it is very important to notice this phenomenon. For example, when the scruples arise from our own temperament, they are generally the same. They want variety. Pertinacity sticks to the same things, and somber thoughts turn away from change. Thus, we never get out of the identical round which we have paced before, grinding the same clay, to make the same bricks. Our mind is like a staunch Protestant with his twenty-times-answered objection, recurring to it again and again, but carefully abstaining from the slightest allusion to the answer. We have but one note. A parrot speaks plain, but its sphere of conversation is extremely limited. When, however, our scruples proceed from the devil, the case is widely different. Then they are very numerous and extremely variable. They are for the most part very dishonorable to God, and fasten by preference either on His ever-blessed attributes, or on the sweet mystery of the Incarnation, or on the soul-saving Sacraments. They are accompanied by a special darkening of the mind, a sort of eclipse of faith, which is a favorite resort of the evil one. We are numb and cold in prayer, oppressed with an enervating languor, and desire exceedingly to relax our rule of life, at least for awhile. When our scruples are from God, they cease periodically, and cease all at once, just as a porter slips off his burden and rests it on a lamp post. This is an infallible sign of their being from God. It would not happen naturally. The natural deposing of a scrupulous conscience cannot be instantaneous and complete. Another mark of divine scruples is that we go on toward perfection in spite of them, or rather secretly because of them. The more they tease us the more constant we are in our spiritual exercises, the more gentle and forbearing with others, the more obedient to our guides and superiors: and we look to God the more smilingly with all the plenitude of a filial confidence, which is equally clear of servile dread or of presuming familiarity; and there is a look of pain on our faces mingling with the smile.

All scruples which are not supernatural simply turn on two hinges, ignorance and pusillanimity. Let us do away with the first and fortify the second, and these miserable emissaries of evil cannot harm us.

If we cast an eye upon the subjects on which scruples fasten, we shall see still greater reason to turn from them with mingled repugnance and contempt. First of all there is prayer. In an unhealthy state of mind it seems positively to attract scruples to itself. There is no part of it, mental, vocal, or ejaculatory, considerations, affections, or resolutions, which do not seem to be their favorite food, and out of which they do not suck the marrow of the divine life. The Sacraments, especially Confession and Communion, they haunt with a pertinacity only equalled by their versatility. The dry Communion has its own family of scruples; the fervent Communion another. With one man's Confession it is the penance they settle on, with another's the contrition, with another's the narration, with another's the preparation. All is equal to them; for they taint wherever they touch. The keen air which breathes round the heights on which vows are placed does not impede the respiration of scruples. They are little creatures, but robust; and vows are fine game and glorious food for them. Nothing is higher than a vow, and that is not too high for them. Nothing is lower than a fear of bodily discomfort, and that is not too low for them. They are universal insects, and ubiquitous, worse than those that of old teased the African into being a Manichee. Fraternal correction is a perfect luxury to them. It lies in the shade, and there is no strong light upon it, so that it is hard to see the scruple, to be sure of it, and to get a good aim at it. The motives of actions are their favorite hiding places. Temptations are their task.

Imaginary cases are their romps and games. And predestination is to them like the top of a tree on which a bird sits and mocks us on a Sunday, when it knows we have no gun to shoot it with. When a thing is dangerous and yet not dignified, provoking and yet it eludes us, despised yet it disquiets us, absurd and yet we cannot resist being impressed by it, then that thing is like a scruple. We scorn it even while we hate and fear it. Yet we are angry in our hatred, and uneasy in our contempt.

From the subjects let us pass to the effects of scruples. They are three: blindness, indevotion and laxity. If scruples proceed from ignorance, they also increase and deepen it. They so perturb the mind that all spiritual discernment is impossible. They confuse the boundaries of right and wrong. They remove the ancient landmarks between temptation and sin, between delectation and consent. They ravel mortal and venial sin inextricably and indissolubly together. They turn precepts into counsels, and counsels into precepts. They call things by their wrong names, and incur the Prophet's woe of putting bitter for sweet and sweet for bitter. The blind can neither lead the blind, nor walk safely on his own road. The spiritual life is brought to a halt, which must be final unless we can break through the enemy's lines. This is the first effect of scrupulosity; and like the first of Monsieur le Maire's reasons for not firing a salute for Henri Quatre, namely, that he had no cannon, it might supersede the necessity of investigating the other effects, seeing that this first she has brought us to the pass of a dead halt. But as I am writing with an insatiable hatred of scruples, like the wrath with which a man persecutes a hypocrite, I shall proceed. Let them be anathematized in every possible shape, as a heresy in doctrine, a lawlessness in discipline and a corruption in morals.

The second effect then of scruples is indevotion. This is as much as saying that the death of devotion is unfavorable to devotion. But how is it that they kill devotion? Devotion is peace, and they are trouble. Devotion is single-minded, and they are legion. Devotion is docile, and they are disobedience. Devotion worships God, and they worship self. Devotion lives on holy food, and their life is sustained by corrupting the food on which it lives. They prevent the light of prayer from entering our perturbed minds. They interrupt the operations of the Sacraments, and even make them prisoners. They obscure our faith, weaken our hope and relax our charity. They have all the bad effects of temptations without any of the good ones. But listen to the story of the old Cardinal of Vitry, out of Surius. Once upon a time there was a pious Cistercian who was silly enough to resolve to win his way back again to the state of primitive innocence. What he went through, it would be long to tell. Suffice it to say that he could not attain his object, and he felt painfully how far he was falling short. If when he ate there was at all a nice taste in the food, he was miserable. If the least indeliberate ripple of anger came over him, he was distracted. If he fell into a trifling imperfection, he magnified it into a mortal sin, and was crushed. From this excess of scruples he fell into a profound sadness, and from this sadness he tumbled, as all sad men do, down the precipice of despair. All hope of his eternal salvation being now gone, he ceased to frequent the Sacraments; for as St. Bernard says, tribulation had begotten pusillanimity, and pusillanimity perturbation, and perturbation despair, and despair had slain. The monks were brokenhearted. Oh, how fervently they recommended their poor brother to God! They admonished him with sage counsels. They rebuked him with sharp reproofs. But all was in vain. Fortunately a saint was at hand, the Bl. Mary of Oignies, and God permitted her to work a miracle upon this poor son of St. Bernard, else says the cardinal, he would doubtless have been damned. For, he adds, I myself have known a man gash his breast with a knife, because of scruples, and another who for the same reason shot himself through the throat and died. It is scruples which produce what the French physicians call *theomanie,* when they write the devil's side of the lives of the Saints. With so much justice did that grave Dominican, Louis of Blois, say in his magisterial manner, "Excessive fear and inordinate pusillanimity, great sadness and superfluous scruples, unquiet cares and entangled solicitudes—these things let the ascetic avoid."

The third effect of scruples is laxity. Was any man ever

known to be scrupulous in one thing who was not lax in another? The laxest of men are scrupulous men. It is very natural. In the first place, we feel as if we had only a certain amount of conscientiousness, and as we have expended more than was due on one thing, we have all the less left for another. If we have spent it all on one exaggerated duty, then we are without any for the rest of our duties; and so actions slip through, which would quite surprise us if we could get a good view of them, and see them in their true light. A man who has overworked himself is always the most dissipated at recreation. Again, scruples are a tyranny and an oppression; and submission has its reactions. These drive us to seek consolations in worldly pleasures and natural affections, in all that is bright, beautiful and tender round about us; and then it is the old story of Hannibal's soldiers at Capua. Moreover it follows from our blindness that we fight the wrong foe, and then are too tired to fight the right one; but surrender our sword. Not knowing one thing from another, we strain at gnats and swallow camels. If we have got wrong by indiscretion in austerities, now we are more wrong by being over head and ears in comforts. A man who has no spiritual pleasures will compensate himself by the abundance of his bodily enjoyments. And I have found one old writer who says that scruples are a very common punishment for soft and delicate living. And what is all this but laxity? And it is the scruples which the devil causes that mostly set this way.

But it seems as if, historically speaking, laxity, an allowable one, for the Church allowed it, was the first cause of scruples. Rosignoli, in his *Discipline of Christian Perfection,* says that scruples were unknown to the ancient Fathers; and he attributes this to the old canonical penances. Men satisfied for sin much more amply than they do now. The Church Triumphant in joy has so widened that it more than counterbalances the Church Militant in sorrow, and so we live under the regime of indulgences, while our fathers watched and fasted under the reign of canonical penances. The relaxation of discipline, says Rosignoli, had produced a new feature in the Church, namely scruples. He finds no fault. No true son of Ignatius ever blamed the Church. He only mentions it as what he deems a fact. I will say nothing more of this theory than that it is striking and plausible. Gerson, who is the St. Thomas of modern spirituality, is one of the first and greatest methodical writers on scruples. St. Antoninus and St. Laurence Justinian come near to him; and among the quite modern men, Fenelon is by far the sweetest and most admirable scruple-doctor.

Nevertheless there is the thing, if there is not the name, in John Cassian: and something so like it in St. Gregory and St. Augustine, that the portrait can hardly be mistaken; and Innocent III comes still nearer the mark. Some of the temptations in St. John Climacus would in modern phrase certainly be called scruples. At the same time it cannot be doubted that in mediaeval and modern systems of spirituality scruples occupy a much more important place than in the moral and ascetical writings of the Fathers, or the anecdotical chronicles of the Saints of the desert, in the same way that the confession of venial sins and the whole question of confessions of devotion do. The very term confession of devotion, which has quite passed into ascetical terminology, would have sounded strange to ancient ears; though here again I venture to suspect that there was more of the substance of the thing than Gerson seems to allow. However this is not the place for a history of ascetical theology. The devotional instincts and phrases of the Fathers are subjects of intense interest, about which there is sufficient tradition for us to draw some interesting inferences.

The remedies for scruples have been to a great extent implied in what has already been said. But a paragraph may be devoted to their recapitulation. They find their place naturally after the consideration of the causes, signs, subjects and effects of scruples. As the want of light is the chief cause of the disease, prayer is one of its principal remedies. We should meditate on cheering subjects, and cultivate a filial devotion to Our Blessed Lady. We must avoid idleness, and nerve ourselves to bodily mortification. We must not easily change our director, or consult many persons, which is the way with light-minded men and shallow spiritualists; neither must we talk much with scrupulous persons; for the complaint is catching. We must never reflect on our own scruples, but act as we see other good people act, remembering that God is our Father, and the Church a benignant mother. The precepts of God and the Church, says St. Antoninus, were not meant to take away from us all spiritual sweetness, as the excessive interpretations of the scrupulous and timid would make them do; neither did the Church ever intend by her commands to oblige any man to drive himself mad. Therefore no precepts bind in a time or place when the observance of them would be considered absurd by a discreet man. But the boldest thing of all was the practice of St. Ignatius. He made a man who was scrupulous about his office recite it by the sand of an hourglass, and leave unsaid what was not said when the sand ran down. And the patient was cured. We must be careful to avoid the gestures alluded to before, and not think we can drive a wrong thought out of our minds by shaking our heads, twitching our hands, or beating time with our feet. We must also take the mild side in moral questions. Nothing breeds scruples so much as taking up a stricter theory than you can carry out in the details of your practice. The man who adopts a mild theory does it consciously and on a principle. He knows how far he can concede, and where he can concede no longer. The rigorist simply cannot carry out his views, either with others or himself; and then being left without a principle to fall back upon, he retires ever so far, as far as you will push him, into the allowance of things plainly wrong, and if you will, much further. The Commandments of God and the Precepts of the Church, and the reverence of the Sacraments, are in much safer keeping in the hands of a mild theologian than of a stern one: though of course all principles have their extremes and all exaggerations are wrong. But one remedy is as near a specific as anything can be called a specific which does not cure an incurable disease, but restores a man to a passable valetudinarian kind of spiritual existence. And that is blind obedience. The word explains itself. St. Philip says that scruples may make a truce with a man, when once they have beset him, but a peace never. If we have been once scrupulous, and our scruples have not been from God, we shall carry at the least the weakness of them and nervousness of them to the grave, and as Francesca of Pampeluna implies, the relics of them into Purgatory to receive their final cautery. But blind obedience will cure us to all intents and purposes. But how shall we know that we are really obedient? O most scrupulous of questions! But it shall be answered kindly though briefly. By these three signs: When you never say, "Oh, but my director is not a saint," or, "I would obey if I was scrupulous and if this were a scruple, or, I would obey if I could explain myself to my confessor, so that he could really understand my case."

There is quite a consent among theologians that scrupulous persons are allowed certain privileges; and these will come next under consideration. However much there may be of their own fault in what they are now suffering, nevertheless the reality of their suffering entitles them to certain privileges. These privileges however are not rights only; they are obligations also. If they were not so, the invalids for whom they were intended would never dare to use them. The first privilege of scrupulous persons is, that provided they are so instructed by their spiritual guide, it is allowable for them to act even with the fear of sinning while they act. Indeed they are bound to do so; and if they refuse, they willfully commit five separate faults, which approach more or less near to the confines of venial sin, and not seldom overstep it. They presumptuously set up their own opinion against that of their director, which is pride and obstinacy. They refuse him the obedience due to him, and which they have probably promised him. They hinder their own progress in the spiritual life, and so hold themselves back from the perfection to which their state of life, or the grace already conferred upon them, obliges them. In many instances they hurt their bodily health, and increase the weakness of their head: and they cause their common daily duties to be ill-performed, inasmuch as they put away from themselves the means of recovering that light and peace and presence of God which throws the luster of perfection over our ordinary actions.

Their second privilege is that they may be sure they have not committed mortal sin, unless, with full advertence, they can reverently swear that they have done so. The reason of this is founded on the impossibility of the will's changing unconsciously in one moment from excessive fear to relaxation of morals. It is true that scruples lead to laxity; but they neither produce it by an instantaneous change, nor do they introduce it into the subject matter of the scruple itself. The obligation, which is the counterpart of this privilege, is that they should not confess as mortal sins any such dubious actions, nor abstain from their regular Communions on their account. But in order that this privilege should have place, one or more or all of the four following signs should be discerned in the conduct and disposition of the scrupulous person. He should habitually loathe the sin to which he fancies he has consented, so that it may be clear what the normal state of his will is upon the matter. As soon as he catches himself, consciously, delaying on the image of temptation, he should have made some sort of effort and experienced some disquietude. If he has been thrown into an opportunity of committing the sin, and has not done so, we may argue that his will is sound and whole; and if he cannot remember whether he was all the while fully aware of the temptations that were besieging him, he is not to be disquieted, but the doubt is to go in his favor.

The third privilege of scrupulous persons is that they are not bound to examine matters so exactly as others. Their infirmity is the reason of this. They are spiritual invalids, and the life of an invalid is a life of dispensation, by no less an authority than that of God Himself. The probability is they will never have robust health after this, and therefore the slow strength of convalescence should be husbanded. A minute or reiterated examination of conscience or of motives, on the part of a scrupulous man, would be equivalent to the tying and untying of the bandages of a wound, where stillness of the limb and compression of the hurt were just the two things which the surgeon commanded. Neither, as before, are they to be allowed in such fretful examinations without grave cause and the permission of their director. For this privilege, like the rest, must be an obligation in the use.

We certainly care more for our bodies than for our souls. Yet it is only reasonable that what we readily submit to in the case of the one, we should at all events undergo with a good grace in the case of the other. If we have broken our collarbone, or got the cholera, we know that we have a certain course of treatment to go through which nature does not relish; and we do not quarrel with our surgeon or physician if he combines firmness with his gentleness, if he makes us be still when we want to stir, or will not let us have the food we have set our minds upon. So we must make up our mind to let our spiritual physician treat us when we are sick of scruples. Wonderfully difficult as we think our questions of casuistry to be, he will show us no sign of uncertainty or hesitation; so that we shall doubt whether he has weighed it well or heard us rightly. He will give us no reasons for what he advises; for such reasons would only be the seedplots of new scruples. We must be very open with him, though this will cost us not a little. At the same time we must have a real scruple of exaggerating in confession. This is a common fault of scrupulous persons. They think they make sure of an adequate explanation by an exaggerated one, which is not only an error, but an error on the worst side of the two. Much less mischief would come of an undue extenuation.

He will be very gentle to us while we are docile, but short and abrupt when we are pertinacious. He will not let us repeat things confession after confession, though we are yearning to do so. He will make us learn contempt of our own scruples from his contempt of them; and this is as bad as Greek epigrams to a fourth-form boy. He will forbid us to confess scruples, and he will accustom us to go to Communion without absolution, which, with our morbid sensitiveness, is worse than great physical pain. He will stint our allowance of time for the examination of our conscience, and we shall consequently go to it at first with such a nervous precipitation, that before we have finished our act of the presence of God, the time will have run out. He will also force upon us a compulsory promptitude in deciding whether to act or not in any particular case, unless the thing looks like a sin at the very first sight of it. And when we go to him with long faces, because we have made some mistakes in consequence of acting on that principle, he will treat us with hastiness, and our difficulty with contempt. He will never let us know whether he thinks we are mending or not, but will put off our questions with some unmeaning commonplaces. Rest being of all things that of which we feel the greatest need, he will allow us none, but fag us unmercifully with endless and distracting occupations. When we have, as many have, scruples without being habitually scrupulous, that is, when we are over-exact in one matter, and proportionately free and easy in another, he will be severe to us, and will make us look only at our laxity. In these cases we shall try his patience and give him much difficult and tiresome work before he can discharge us from his hospital. We are patients who give more trouble, and less credit, than any others with whom he has to do.

Persons recently converted have scruples about their general confession, either as to its fullness or its sorrow. A spiritual physician will allow them only to reflect generally on their past sins, and very often will prohibit even that. He will never allow them, in a state of scruple, to dwell on particular sins, least of all on circumstances of sins. For sadness is a snare which the devil ordinarily sets at this stage of the spiritual life. When their scruples have passed away, he may possibly allow them to make a quiet general confession, and after that, never let them mention anything else belonging to the past, unless they are either wholly without scruple, or able to swear that they have remembered some sin, which they knew to be both mortal and unconfessed. For the sin has been already indirectly remitted; and we are not bound to the material integrity of past confessions, with so grave an inconvenience as a relapse into scruples. If such persons tell their director that they shall be more at peace if he will allow them to speak, he will still refuse, and will tell them to offer up that inward disquietude as a sacrifice to God. It is a fearful evil to have a convert scrupulous. I fear the chances are against his ever making a thoroughly good Catholic. Scruples fill his veins with the secret poison of self-opinionatedness, just when he has everything to learn and everything to unlearn, and obedience is his sole appointed means of thus changing his whole inner man. Still, it is our comfort to know that the Holy Ghost has reparatory ways and means which evade the definitions

of our poor spiritual science, but whose marvelous healing
operations we are continually witnessing.

But I dare not leave the subject without saying a few words
about reasonable scruples. There are such things. Theology
leaves no doubt upon the matter; and nothing of what I have
said will apply to them. A prudent fear makes a scruple
reasonable, just as a vain fear makes it unreasonable. Thou
hast commanded Thy commandments to be kept most diligently, says the Psalmist. St. Gregory writing to St. Augustine
of Canterbury, and St. Clement V, resolving some doubts in
the Franciscan rule, admit of these scruples and teach that
they are to be respected. For a man is not rightly called scrupulous who fears and loves God to a nicety, as the saying
is—that is, who strives to avoid every venial sin and every
least imperfection. The filial feelings of such men and the
tranquility of their solicitude for perfection show that they
are not scrupulous in the evil sense. There is such a thing
as a wide conscience, and it is wide from the want of reasonable scruples. I only say this to prevent being misunderstood.
It were better always to use the word scruple in a bad sense,
and to call reasonable scruples by their much truer and more
honorable name of conscientiousness.

Let not the imperfect fear, says St. Augustine, only let them
advance. Yet, because I do not let them fear, let them not
on that account love imperfection, or remain in it when they
have found themselves there. Only let them advance as far
as in them lies, and all is well.

God be praised! We have done, done little certainly, but
all we can, for our scrupulous patients. Now let us leave this
close ward, and go out and breathe.

Chapter XVIII

THE OFFICE OF SPIRITUAL DIRECTOR

The present chapter brings us to the most vexed question of the whole spiritual life, the office of a spiritual director. There is no subject about which there is a more harmonious consent up to a certain point, nor one upon which beyond that point there is a greater discrepancy of conflicting opinions. Writers who live in communities and are members of religious houses are prone to exaggerate the director's office, to confound it with that of a religious superior or a novice-master, and to make it unreal to persons living in the world. For when we make a man try to do more than he can, he inevitably ends by doing less, and the fault is ours, not his. On the other hand, if we take vague or lax views of the matter, we run the risk of coming under the censure of the eleventh proposition of the Illuminati and the sixty-sixth of Molinos, propositions unwittingly enunciated, almost in the words condemned by Catholics in common conversation again and again. It is difficult, therefore, to write of this subject with becoming moderation, and yet it is as necessary as it is difficult. The present chapter will contain no theory, but report fairly both sides of the Catholic tradition as it is to be found both in ancient books and modern, inclining perhaps a little to the ancient, because on this point of asceticism as on most others, I find in them an absence of exaggeration which I often desiderate in modern systems. My object will be to prevent any opinion of my own escaping on the subject; or if I fail in this, that it should be only such an expression of opinion as is unavoidable when an author is commenting on those who have gone before him.

The first thing is to be clear, and to be clear we must some-times be guilty of some repetition, which, however, is a less evil than obscurity. I shall divide my subject then as follows. First, I shall speak of the importance of a director; secondly, I shall show what is the meaning of having one; thirdly, the necessity of him; fourthly, the choice of him; fifthly, the change of him; sixthly, the true Catholic idea of our intercourse with him; and seventhly, the suffering he causes us. It is not easy always to decide under what head to arrange particular things, but when we have handled these seven points, we shall cer-tainly leave no important question unconsidered.

I am to speak first of the importance of having a director. The practical and devotional system of the Catholic Church is almost a greater trial of our faith than its doctrinal system. No part of it has been more attacked than this office of a spiritual director, not only by heretics outside the Church, but by ill-read or lukewarm Catholics in it. We may say, there-fore, what we are in the habit of saying of devotion to Our Blessed Lady, that this dead set against it is the measure of the devil's dislike and dread of it. The vital energies of the Church are often laid up very secretly and in unlikely places, and the miserable instincts of heresy may often perform for Catholics the same office that certain dogs are said to do for men hunting for a particular sort of earth nut. Thus, heresy not only gets our truth defined, but it indicates the hidden virtue of each particular truth. It is certainly to take a yoke upon ourselves to have a director. But unless we are prepared for it, it is really useless, not unfrequently worse than useless, to attempt a spiritual or interior life. We may possibly be safe without a director, if we choose to sit down in the dust and ashes of low attainment; but not otherwise. Not only do very good people go wrong for want of a director, and that in external work for the Church as well as in the management of their devotional privacy; but it often seems as if the amount of their goodness only increased the extent and mischief of their error. This comes to pass in two ways. In the one case it is self-love which is always making a man drift impercepti-bly away from high principle, so that, undirected, he is con-tinually settling down to a lower level than the first aspired to, or actually believes himself to be occupying; and these settlements, like those of a new house, are only discovered by the ugly irregular cracks afterwards. In the other case, it is the want of discretion which does the evil. It makes a man afraid that his fervor is going, because his sensible ardor is less; and this runs him first into singularity and then into downright folly. These are the two ways in which devout laymen are often broken to pieces, and cast aside by God as unmanageable and misshapen vessels. They who might have been a St. Edmund, St. Louis, or St. Elzear, turn out to be thorns in the side of the Church, wounding her as far as their littleness can go. This is the reason why so many who live to reform abuses die out of grace. It would not be surprising to know that the Church has actually lost great saints by this mistake. When we look over the multitude of devout souls, what is it that excites our keenest regret? It is the waste of grace, it is the evaporation of high principles, it is the brittleness of noble purposes; and by far the greatest proportion of this is from the want of a spiritual director. Can more be said to show his importance? All the Saints are of one mind: to have a director, to be open and full with him, and to obey him without scruple and without bondage, behold! this is half the battle of the spiritual life!

Secondly, we must consider what the having a director means, what it looks like as an external fact. It gives to the life of a person in the world the similitude of a monastic life, as if they were members of an uncloistered order. For it is impossible he should stop at being a merely spiritual counselor. Prayer and mortification, temptations and the Sacraments, are certainly very difficult matters, and give rise to a multitude of cases of conscience, which it would be neither safe nor easy for us to decide for ourselves. But I doubt whether external conduct and temporal affairs are not more prolific of casuistry, and do not breed a much greater amount of spiritual perplexity. The adjustment of domestic duties requires as much discernment as turning a point in mental prayer. The exactions of society are far more bewildering to see our way through, than the uncertainties of a cloudy vocation. It is a marvel to me that persons should fancy that a director in purely

spiritual things should be a person of higher attainments than
one who is to guide us in spiritualizing worldly things. It
seems to me that this last requires so much more wisdom,
so much more science, so much closer a union with God.
It is generally the case that the proofs of authors who write
good hands are more full of mistakes than the proofs of those
who write bad hands, because the good hands are given to
the boys, the crabbed ones to skillful men. So it may be in
the matter of direction. A priest may be bold to direct a good
nun in a supernatural state of prayer, who if he were humble
and sagacious would tremble to steer a princess to perfection
through the intricacies of town, court and country life.

The spiritual life does not so much consist in a quantity
of devotions, ceremonies, beliefs and peculiar exercises as in
the supernaturalizing of our common life; in a word, it does
not consist so much in certain things as in a manner of doing
all things. Thus every temporal affair, every worldly relationship and every social duty, brings its own case of conscience
along with it, and though men can solve many of these for
themselves at once, and get an increasing facility of solving
others, yet persons in the world see so little ahead of themselves, because of the dust that is round about them, that there
must always remain a number of problems which they must
be content to leave to the solution of others. Nothing then
can be more shallow than the complaints which men make
of spiritual direction as meddling with temporal affairs. Its
very office is to spiritualize these by infusing them into supernatural motives, and helping the blindness or the cowardice
of self-love to bring them all under the obedience of Christ,
and into subjection to the maxims of the Gospel.

No experience can hinder the astonishment which we must
all of us feel at occasional interior revelations of the immense
hold which the world still has upon us, when we have been
serving God for years. Quite irrespectively of sin, worldly
principles possess us. They have shaped our minds, saturated
our affections, warped our will and influenced even the way
in which our senses report external objects. They lie imbedded in our language, and our language tells upon our thoughts,
and our thoughts insinuate motive lightning-like into the very

first steps of our actions. Now spiritual direction, simply regarded as a fact, is a witness against the world, and we commit ourselves to its testimony. It ignores the world's own view of itself in everything, treats its pretensions with contempt, speaks of it as an imposture, and defines it to be merely a vile criminal condemned to be burnt, and the hour of its execution only uncertainly delayed. The world, therefore, finds a voice in such men as Michelet, and expresses its natural resentment with a strength which is amusing. I say, natural resentment, because it must necessarily misunderstand the nature of spiritual direction, and it certainly exaggerates both its influence and its extent. Direction must needs have a look of conspiracy to the world's eye which is peculiarly odious. Yet the view is not wholly incorrect; for what is the Church but a divine conspiracy against the world? Moreover, just as certain words, seemingly innocuous in themselves, drive lunatics into a frenzy, so the interference of an ecclesiastical tie with natural ones exasperates the world in a preternatural way. We Catholics must bear this in mind when the world talks to us of spiritual direction. The interior life is necessarily an unflinching lifelong variance with the world.

Our third consideration must be of the necesssity of a director. This is a most important part of our subject, and I shall attempt to prove it from six different sources: from authority, from common sense, from the nature of the thing, from the peculiarity of the spiritual life, from the genius of the director's office and from the universality of the need.

The argument from authority may be divided into three heads: the practice of the Church, the condemnation of heresy and the drawings of the Holy Ghost acknowledged by orthodox writers on the discernment of spirits.

According to the teaching of the Fathers, the office of spiritual director is shadowed forth in Scripture in the relations of Samuel to Heli, Peter to Cornelius and Ananias to Paul. But without stopping to inquire if the inference is not somewhat wide, let us look at the undoubted practice of the Church. In the Dialogues of St. Gregory, Peter asks if Honoratus had a director. Simeon Metaphrastes says that when Pachomius wished to learn the secrets of a more perfect life, he took Palemon for his director. He also tells us that St. Chrysostom was made spiritual director in his monastery, and the same office was imposed on St. Dorotheus, who was also the special director of St. Dositheus. St. John Damascene was appointed spiritual director to the novices in his Laura. Euthymius told Sabas to take Theoctistus for his director. St. Dorotheus himself had been directed by Seridus, so that the spiritual direction of Dositheus was by that time a formed tradition. John the Prophet was directed by Barsanuphius; and George the Arsilate was the spiritual director of St. John Climacus. Theodore the Studite put himself under the direction of the monk Plato, who had been formed by the direction of Theoctistus, which he thus handed on, as St. Sabas handed on the same tradition in his monastery. St. Romuald was directed by Marinus, and Peter Damian by Leo the Hermit, who he says was not merely his "accomplice" and his friend, but his father, doctor, master and elected lord, who so excelled in the profundity of spiritual counsels that his words were oracles to all who consulted him. St. Antoninus was so famous a spiritual director in his day that he was called the Father of Counsels. John Cantacuzene tells us, and this brings us to the spiritual direction of laymen in the world, that when the emperor Andronicus was near his death, he asked for his director, and when the master of the palace sent a monk whom the emperor did not know, he burst into tears and insisted upon having his own director. The emperor Manuel made Macarius, whom he designates as his spiritual director, one of the executors of his will. When the emperor John went to the Council of Ferrara, he took with him, it is said, his spiritual director Gregory, a cenobite who was afterwards patriarch of Constantinople, as Pontanus mentions in his notes to the history of George Phrantzes, where he shows that these men were not mere confessors but spiritual directors in the strict sense of the word. The modern tradition is too well-known to make instances necessary.

In accordance with the practice of the Church have been her condemnations of those who taught an opposite doctrine. In 1623 the Illuminati taught that there was no need of a spiritual director, but that each soul was to trust to the sacred inspirations of the Holy Ghost, and to follow them at all hazards. This doctrine was condemned by the Spanish Inquisition, whose judgment is applauded by theologians. Molinos held that the Catholic notion of a spiritual director was ludicrous and new *(doctrina risu digna et nova in ecclesia Dei)*, and this proposition was condemned together with the sixty-eighth, in which he dispenses spiritual men from direction as able to guide themselves by their own private spirit.

Madame de Chantal recognized by certain signs that St. Francis de Sales was the man whom God had destined to be her spiritual director; and mystical writers give us certain indications as being assuredly from the Holy Ghost in this matter. One of them is an indefinable attraction which in our best times we never distrust, and which impels us to repose entire confidence in some servant of God, and forms a union of grace between his soul and ours. Another is a peace which spreads all through our soul like a quiet inundation whenever he speaks to us, resolves our doubts, or dissipates our scruples. He seems as it were to magnetize us with a holy joy, which is entirely free from any natural esteem or personal attachment to himself. Another is a certain ardor or vehement desire to be all for God which comes over us when we are with him, or is inspired in us by his words; and another is a certain impression of mingled respect, obedience and docility which makes us see God, and God only, in him and his guidance.

The second argument for the necessity of a director is from common sense. Cases of conscience are continually arising; many of them are very difficult, and these difficulties can only be surmounted by practice, experience, study and authority. The generality of men obviously are without these requisites. That of authority is especially to be dwelt upon. Knots which cannot be untied must be cut; and this authority alone can do. We must consider also the proverbial impossibility of judging in our own cause; and if in addition to this we weigh well the character of self-love, with which unfortunately we have only too intimate an acquaintance, we shall be convinced that the place which a spiritual director occupies in the ascetical system of the Church is nothing more than an expression of her maternal common sense.

The third argument is very like its predecessor; it is from the reason of the thing. The interior life is, as we shall see by and by, full of delusions and dangers. This being so, the analogy of all other arts and sciences would go to prove that we must have a pedagogue, someone to teach us, to keep us in the right way, to prevent our losing time and name in making old discoveries, to hinder our following the fatuous fires which have led others into absurdity or ruin, to show us how to observe, to operate or to experimentalize, to test our results, to correct our processes and to cheer our fatigue. The spiritual life is a daily dying to self and a daily carrying of the Cross; and who has the courage to go on chastising himself all his life long, if he has not someone by his side at once to animate and moderate, prohibit or suspend, his holy cruelty? We have all of us great confidence in ourselves; yet none of us has sufficient self-dependence to enable us to attach much weight to our own consolations of ourselves. No man can console himself. He does not believe in himself with sufficient infallibility. Consolation is a social thing. And can anyone, until he is actually fabricated into a saint, live an unworldly life without consolation? A man is always very wise and right in his own eyes; yet I doubt if the man is to be found who can habitually act without scruple on his own ideas. No man has invariably light to find out when he is wrong, nor patience to wait when he ought to wait, and to refrain himself in trial. Our faculty of deceiving ourselves is uncommonly versatile; and prayer, suffering and action, the three departments of a director, are from their own nature the favorite provinces of self-deceit. To walk alone is impossible; and to wish to walk alone is against humility, and the lack of humility bars all progress, even in merely moral excellence. Moreover experience shows, however little it was to have been expected beforehand, that a man without a director runs at last into mere external practices and a barren formality. For a man only grows interior in proportion as he gains the habit of renouncing his own favorite views, or wills, or ways. Hence, as a question of metaphysics, it must result partly from the nature of man's mind and partly from this subject of the spiritual life to which it is applying itself, that a man who stands alone will have an exceedingly limited range of vision, and will often see objects dim and distorted even within that narrow range. My fourth argument has been almost anticipated in the third. It proposes to show the necessity of a director from the nature of the spiritual life. All animals suffer when they are called upon to live out of their own element. The suffering is brief, because death mercifully interferes. Now the spiritual life is, to a fallen soul, like the life of a fish out of water. First of all it is suffering, and secondly, it cannot be sustained except by supernatural interferences. Life in a battle with eyes blinded with smoke and ears bleeding with the percussion of the artillery, or life in a diving bell with eyes starting, ears ringing and pulses galloping, are pictures of it. Its character is supernatural and can only be administered to by scientific study. Temptations beset it in invisible multitudes, some silent and some clamorous. The delusions that dazzle it are as various and as changeful as the colored flashes from a pigeon's neck. It requires as many consolations as a sick child, and a disburdened spirit is such a necessity to it that it cannot live without it. When we can see in the dark, breathe in a void and grasp the impalpable, then can we manage ourselves in an ascetic life; but not till then. Godinez in his *Praxis of Mystical Theology* says, "Of a thousand souls whom God calls to perfection, scarcely ten respond to the call, and of a hundred whom God calls to contemplation, 99 stop short. Hence I say, many are called but very few are chosen. For besides other great difficulties, almost insuperable by our frail nature, and which surround this business of perfection, one of the chief causes of the failure of so many is to be found in the fewness of spiritual directors to guide our souls, with the pilotage of divine grace, over this unknown sea of the spiritual life."

A fifth argument for the necessity of a director may be drawn from the nature of a director's office. His business is not that of a pioneer. It is rather to go behind, and to watch God going before. He must keep his eye fixed on God, who is in the dimness ahead. He does not lead his penitents. The Holy Ghost leads them. He holds out his hands from behind, as a mother does to her tottering child, to balance his uncertain steps as he sways overmuch, now on one side, now on another. He is not to have a way of his own, to be applied to everyone. This is what a novice master does with his novices. He leads them by an acknowledged tradition, and animates them with the definite fixed spirit of the order, and models them, as a faithful copyist, on their sainted founder. But this is not at all the function of a spiritual director. He only knows that we are in the way which is right for us when he sees God in front. Then he keeps us superstitiously in the Blessed Footprints left behind. He looks after our advance, and when he sees God increasing the distance between Himself and the soul, he spurs on the latter, discreetly and gently, yet firmly and uninterruptedly. He gains as much light from prayer as from his knowledge of character and his personal observation of ourselves. His office is very supernatural, but it is very natural also; and he will not direct us well if he overshadows the natural by the supernatural. It would be a safer mistake if he attributed a light to his natural penetration and sagacity, the divination of his own genius, which was really due to a gratuitous and supernatural discernment of spirits, than if he took that for supernatural which was really natural. It is a perilous thing to make a superstition of direction. Hence a director would rather say supernatural things in a natural way, than emit oracles, observe odd intervals of silence, say pompous obscure words, or talk grandiloquently about God having put things into his mind. To such a one it is almost strange that his guardian angel does not impatiently break silence and say, "All things are God's gifts: go to, simpleton! and help your neighbor to the best of your abilities with a good-humored diligence, and neither make so much of it, nor throw a mystery around it." Yes, above all, let us have no mysteries in direction.

Our director must also look to his own purity of conscience and disinterestedness of conduct, so as to be open to receive supernatural lights and helps when God chooses. He will not talk too much to us, nor care if he be a downright trial to us by his silence. God's past work in each will be the exemplar of his own work for that soul! He will found all he does and all he endeavors in the evidences of God's past grace. How can such an office as this be a mere ornament or accessory? Must it not be at least an integral part of any system, of which it is a part at all?

But sixthly, a necessity must be a very real necessity, if it is universal. Now what class of persons trying to be good does not stand in need of a director? Poor fellows who are trying to extricate themselves out of habits of sin, who have everything to learn, everything to begin, who have no arms and yet the enemy is down upon them, with traitors in their own souls, yet who can scarcely discern the treachery until its fatal consummation by some fresh act of sin, blind and blundering, weak and excited, cowardly and presumptuous, deceitful and disappointing, tiresome and exasperating, yet with a great thick mantle of God's dearest love and glorious converting grace thrown all over them—do they not need a spiritual father? And who is the man who would not be a father to them, and die for their grand immortal souls, if he might, and if Our Lord had not already taken all that luxury for Himself and left us scarce a share?

Are beginners in a perfect life in less need? See what difficult work they have to do, and such utter inexperience in the doing of it. No man can learn a trade without an apprenticeship. And this is such a trade! Discouragement would be the ruin of them, and yet none are so liable to it, and none also have so much which might reasonably discourage them. There they are, among the ruins of themselves. All around them are strewn broken resolutions, vows grown cold, distracted prayers, eccentric scruples, weak-minded enthusiasms, slovenly Sacraments, plans that have suffocated each other for want of room, and all the inexpressible variety of tarnished tawdry thoughts and things and aspirations, scattered about like the finery of a burnt playhouse in the muddy street. And here is the devil marching down upon them, and they must have all in order in a trice, and fight for their lives; for it is no other kind of fight with them just now.

The need of the advanced is hardly less. They are just entering on more supernatural ways. They are crossing the frontiers into a jealous empire. Are their passports in order? Have they nothing contraband in their luggage? They should be advised to travel only with light baggage. How the difficulties multiply! They cannot speak the language, nor catch the manners of the people. They are always in scrapes, and do not know what is wholesome to eat. They give offense, and they take offense, where none was intended on either side. They may get used to it all in time. Meanwhile, their delusions become at once more numerous, more secret, more contradictory and more intricate. The devil displays greater ability than before, and the human spirit has arisen, crowned himself king and commenced an usurpation which, all things considered, bids fair to last. The exercise of humility becomes more needful at every step, and it seems as if nothing but a director could supply a healthy, continuous and refreshing exercise of that invigorating grace.

As to the perfect, I know nothing about them. But I see men as trees walking, and they seem to reel to and fro, as if divine love had intoxicated their human frailty. They seem always at cross purposes with others, and often in plump contradiction to themselves. Occasionally they appear not quite to know which road to take, or what to do. At other times they look stolid and unmeaning, and lifeless as the glistening caverns in the moon. Then again I see the air filled with balloons, and men in them taking every kind of indiscreet liberty. They get out and walk upon the clouds, or put on a pair of wings, and fly through sunset, or shoot up like a rocket, and dissolve in spangles, or balance themselves on a star, or hide themselves in the Milky Way, or sail in opposite directions, as if each soul had a wind at its will. Not unfrequently I see them come down to the earth, in the poorest parachutes, or without them, with appalling velocity; and though I have no notion what their other movements up in the sidereal space may mean, I feel satisfied that this parachute work is extremely dangerous, and unexceptionably wrong. How their director is to reach such people, I cannot tell, but I am sure they need one; and it is not everyone who, like Catherine of Genoa and Claudia of the Angels, has the Holy Ghost for sole director. I suspect some of the parachute souls dreamed He was directing them, and were fatally mistaken.

May I not from these six considerations legitimately infer the necessity of a spiritual director?

Now for the choice of him: this is my fourth point. There are various kinds of directors. One writer divides them into human, spiritual and divine. He calls a human director one who goes according to the spirit of the world and the maxims of human prudence. A soul is very unfortunate when it falls into such keeping as that. A spiritual director he defines to be a man who leads us into mortification and prayer, but has not clear or consistent views of spirituality; so that he sometimes makes mistakes, though God for the most part blesses his purity of intention, and does not allow our souls to suffer loss. A divine director is a wholly supernatural man who lives always in a flood of light and guides us as if he read our hearts and prophesied our future. Then directors have very various gifts. Some have a benediction for beginners, others for the more advanced, others for the perfect. Some are quite wonderful in their management of newly-converted persons. Some have a peculiar aptitude for educated and refined people who make sad blunders with the poor. Some revel in cases of vocation, while others are not at all at home in them. Some have the magnificent grace of making the laboring poor interior, and supernaturalizing poverty and sufferings. Some are expert at scruples, others with interior trials. Some seem inevitably, with the holiest intentions and purest science, to involve their penitents in fancies and delusions, making them sentimental and unreal; while others have the gift of disenchanting the deluded, and of making their penitents at once spiritual, and yet natural common sense persons. Hardly anyone is a good director for all, and not often for one person all his life long. This must be borne in mind, because it has so much to do both with the choice and change of directors.

As to the choice of a director, what has been just said shows that we must be by no means precipitate. It is one of the most serious questions of our life, and the evil of delay is nothing to the mischief of precipitation. It must be the subject of long and fervent prayer, not with the foolish expectation of any miraculous token of God's will at the last, but to get the grace to choose with discernment, in faith, and without human respect. We must ask the special intercession of St. Joseph, the patron of interior souls. Whenever a real attraction to a devout life becomes manifest in our souls, and is more than a transient caprice of fervor, then is the time when God is calling us to choose a director, if we have not already got one. We must look around us, see if we have the inward signs I mentioned earlier on, and then carefully separate all natural feelings from the choice. We must let it be either the deliberate selection of a prayerful and satisfied mind, which I like best, or the result of supernatural attractions, which I like least, because it is less under the control of cool resolve and sober calculation.

It seems singular to couple the change of a director with the choice; yet this must be my fifth point. On the whole, and speaking quite generally, the change of director is an evil. Yet we may err in four ways: either by changing too soon, or by changing at all, or by changing too late, or by never changing. There is nothing more perplexing than the distinguishing the right times from the wrong in this matter. The only thing to be said is that the change of our director is so grave a step and fraught with so many consequences that God hardly ever brings the difficulty to our doors without giving us a more than common light along with it. If we have chosen without deliberation, we may have the less scruple in changing. When we find we do not advance, and are not conscious to ourselves of any abatement in our earnest desire to advance, and we think we perceive some special hindrance in the method of our direction, then we may at least take other advice, and entertain the question of a change. Perhaps it will come to nothing. But while he would be a very indiscreet adviser who should tell us to make light of such a change, I do not know that I am not more afraid of some who represent it as the hugest evil of the spiritual life, the mother of delusions, and tantamount to final perdition. I suspect that so far is it from being desirable that we should stick so scrupulously to our director (I speak diffidently), that when we have lost our liberty and ease with him, he has lost his grace for us; and that without fault on either side. Spiritual direction must be free as air, and fresh as the morning sun. Neither temptation nor scruple, neither mortification nor obedience, must be able to infuse into it one element of bondage. The moment they do, let us break the direction, and take the consequence. For the end of spiritual direction in all stages of the interior and mystical life is one and single and invariable, and it is liberty of spirit. The opposite doctrine does not belong to the wisdom of direction, but to the superstition of direction.

This thought brings me to my sixth point, which is the true Catholic idea of our intercourse with our director. The first characteristic of this intercourse must obviously be openness. Our sins and imperfections, the working of our passions, our inward disorderly inclinations, our temptations and the secret suggestions of evil which haunt us, the style of architecture of our castles in the air, our good works, penances, devotions, lights and inspirations, must all be open to him, not with superstitious minuteness, which degenerates into frivolity, but to such a degree as will enable him to be a fair judge of our interior condition. We must also be obedient as well as open. We have chosen him for his spiritual doctrine, whereby he knows the ways of God, the tempter and the human spirit; for his holiness, whereby he is zealous to advance those whom he directs; for his experience, whereby he gains a readiness in applying principles to practice; and for his aptitude at direction, natural, supernatural, or both combined. Hence we must see God in him: for this is the meaning of obedience. We must submit our judgment to him; for his science is his primary qualification. St. Theresa says our director should be learned and devout, but that if we cannot find both in one man, it is better to have the learning without the devotion, than the devotion without the learning. And of all the Saint's wise words, and they are innumerable, she never uttered one that was more like herself than that.

Unhappily this obedience to our director is a stumbling-block to many of us. I cannot think it would be so, if we had a clear idea of it, or which is the same thing, an unexaggerated idea of it. What shall I say to clear your thoughts without lowering them? In the first place a spiritual director is not a monastic superior. Our obedience to the last must be minute, to the first general. The superior's jurisdiction is universal, the director's only where we invite it, or he asks it and we accord it. The superior commands us unconsulted, the director's commands arise out of our own questions. Nigronius said he never augered well of a man who made his director take the initiative in spiritual direction. The superior turns into precept matters of supererogation; a director must have forgotten himself if he attempts anything of the kind. If we disobey a superior, we sin; it would require very peculiar and unusual circumstances to make disobedience to our director any sin at all.

Now, the wrong use of a right thing is always bad. But the confounding of a spiritual director with a religious superior is fraught with specially pernicious consequences to our souls. If we are living in the world, and aiming at perfection amid the freedom of its distractions and pursuits, our undue subordination to our director is out of keeping with the rest of our life. It is a discord. It is a foreign element, which will cause either corruption or explosion, according to our temperament. It unmans us; and what a host of evils there are in that one word! Moreover, it plays the game of some one or other of the many forms of spiritual idleness, and secretly nourishes our self-love. We like to think we are obedient, and to feel that we are being governed. It is agreeable to us to live in the bustle of a perpetual spiritual administration. We hold endless cabinet councils, and grow pompous and absurd, uneasy, mysterious and conceited. We fancy ourselves great people. We magnify our tiny experiences. At last we grow soft, effeminate, sentimental, feverish and languid. In a great measure it does away with the seriousness of our relations with God, and leads us unawares into a kind of irreverence. We throw things upon our director which we have no power to throw upon anyone but God. We lose the sense of God's immediateness, which is the secret of false spirituality, and ends in moral helplessness.

It is a monstrous thing to say; but it is unhappily no uncommon sight to see a soul made for high things and now gone all astray, simply because a false notion of the kind of obedience due to its director led it to surrender itself indolently to an idea of safety, as if it had transferred its conscience. We cannot get rid of our responsibility. In point of fact, it is physically as well as morally impossible to put our director into the position of a monastic superior, so as to make the famous words of the Saints about blind obedience as true of the one office as the other. Let us ponder the words of St. Theresa. "My directors told me that what was a venial sin was no sin at all, and that what was mortal was only venial. This did me so much mischief that I do not think it superfluous to mention it here as a caution to others. For before God, as I plainly see, I was not excused by this. It is enough that a thing is not good, that we should abstain from it; and I believe that God on account of my sins permitted my directors to be deluded and then to delude me, and then that I should delude many others, by telling them what my directors told me. I was in this blindness for seventeen years." Schram, the Benedictine, quotes the passage, and adds, *"Tremenda, theologia de ignorantiis sepe vincilibus."* Yet it is, as all truth is, theology as salutary as it is tremendous.[1]

Furthermore, as it must be the care of the director to watch and be slow, and thus not to interfere with the work of God in our souls, so also must it be our care not to interfere with that work by exaggerating our relations with our director, and putting upon him what does not belong to the austere simplicity of his office. We must not go to him too often, which is impatience and loss of time. Neither must we seek any extraordinary interview with him without thought and prayer. We must be sure of what we are going to ask, and that it is worth asking, and real, and not an impulse, or a first thought, or a wild idea, or a conclusion we have jumped to in a hurry

---

1. The Saint's words are worthy of notice. "I thought," she says, "that I was not obliged to more than to believe them," (her directors). *Yo pensava che no era obligada a mas de creerlos. (Vida* cap. 5.) This remarkable passage has, as might be expected, attracted considerable notice. It has not only been commented upon by Schram in his *Theologia Mystica;* but also by Arbiol, the Franciscan, in his *Desenganos Misticos,* lib. iii, cap. 9, where he is treating of the delusions of those souls who appear to be far advanced in prayer, and very little advanced in the practice of solid virtues.

and a heat. We must really be serious about these things,
for they touch God. We must not prolong our interviews, nor
say more than is necessary. Indeed our conversations with
him, at least in brevity, pertinence and forethought, should
ever have some analogy with prayer. The penitents who talk
most are the least obedient. "Believe me," said M. Lantages,
superior of the Seminary of Puy, "it is not the long confessions that are the good ones." Neither should we go to our
director merely for consolation; this is greedy and unmanly.
Spiritual direction is meant to elevate people; yet how often
it debases them! This comes of our not remembering that
it, like all things else in the direct service of God, must be
thoroughly reasonable.

It only remains for me to speak of my seventh point, the
sufferings which our director causes us. Our obedience to
him, to be reasonable, must allow itself to be modified by
time, place, person, circumstances, country, proficiency, character, both his and our own, and companions. Yet even thus
it will be a source to us of many sufferings. I need say the
less about them here, because I have enumerated them when
speaking of patience. The mortification of our judgment is
always painful, but it is pre-eminently painful when it concerns devotional tastes. The discomfort of fancying ourselves
misunderstood is not slight. His scanty words are intolerable
to self-love. When he sees we lean too much upon him, he
will draw his arm away, and we shall falter. He will leave
us sometimes to ourselves to teach us to walk, though it may
be at the risk of a sinless fall. He knows we shall never be
brave for God if we have not a certain amount of indepen-
dence of character, even in spiritual matters. He will know
how to combine this with humility. One of his greatest and
most precious secrets is how to keep intact all the rights of
lowliness, without letting it swerve into poor-spiritedness and
a craven spirituality.

We should beware of driving our director into much speaking, either by acting on his human respect or his natural kindness, or wearying him by importunity. There is after all little
to be said where growth is so slow as it is in the spiritual
life. A conversation between an oak and the woodman would

surely soon come to an end, if growth and development, blight, birds, bees and ivy were the only subjects of conversation, and it was not allowed to pass into idle and irrelevant matters. For an oak does not make an inch a month, either of trunk or twig, and it could hardly expect to have its bark brushed and varnished, and picked out with gold. So the soul is not revolutionized every day. Today is yesterday's brother, and tomorrow's also. What is there to be said? All this talking leads to our making new starts in new directions after each palaver. It is taking up devotions and throwing them down again, like a child restless amid his toys. It is heaping practices upon practices, and getting the fruit out of none of them. It is applying remedies, and then applying others before the first have had time to take effect. It is driving God. It is playing rashly with the proverbial delusions of spiritual communications. It is clouding God, and forcing Him up to the surface of the soul, when He is pleased to bury Himself in the depths of it.

It is better to go through the little vexations of our director's slowness and silence than to run the risk of all these mischiefs. And none of these sufferings bring any real feeling of bondage along with them. Bondage is the only thing to dread. All else surely may be borne in so grave a cause. Why ask more of our spiritual than of our bodily physician? The office is analogous, though the subject matter is so different. And then see what blessing we have: safety, victory, inward peace, the merit of obedience and a good man's prayers.

I have seen a geranium brought up from the cellar when the springtime came. It had been a mild winter, and in the warm darkness, it had grown an unwholesome growth! It hung down like a creeper, with lanky whitish-yellow shoots and miserable jaundiced leaves. The growth had been abundant; and it would not be true to say that the abundance was the only good point about it; for it was the worst point of it all. There was but one course. It was cut down, planted out and flowered the latest of its brethren that year, and very poorly after all. Such is the soul that has been over-directed; and the springtime is eternity. Alas! in that matter there comes the cutting down, but there cannot come the planting out.

I never knew or read of anyone who had a director, and then who suffered because he was too little directed. The souls damaged by over-direction would fill a hospital in any decently large town.

I have written with a host of authorities before me: and this I believe to be in the main, the mind of the most approved writers in the Church on this most difficult question. I have sought only one thing, not to swerve from their even-handed moderation.

Chapter XIX

ABIDING SORROW FOR SIN

It is a very troublesome thought that so many persons have lofty and sincere aspirations after high things, and so few reach them; that, as Godinez says, so many are called to perfection, and so few answer to the call; that so many begin ardently and prudently, and yet die leaving their tower unbuilt; that so many, says Arbiol, are conversant with mental prayer, yet never come to perfection. It is a troublesome thought, because it sets us calculating the doctrine of chances about ourselves; and in less selfish moods, calculating the loss of glory to God, and of power to the Church. For every perfect ascetic is a veritable fountain of power in the Church, however hidden, unknown, or mean-looking he may be. There is certainly an analogy between the waste of grace in the spiritual world, and the waste of seeds, and flowers, and fruits in the natural world. Yet there is poor consolation in a barren analogy. It may serve for a book of evidences; but we shall get little light out of it, and less heat. It does not content us. We must pursue our troublesome thought further, until we get some wisdom or warning out of it.

Now the universality of this phenomenon, when reflected on, leads us to suppose that it has some common cause, which is one and the same in everybody. In the spiritual life, a variety of causes will produce a similar effect. But here is a case which holds equally among men of the south and men of the north, among born Catholics and converts, in all countries and in all times, frustrated vocations to perfection. The more we think of it, the more irresistible seems the conclusion that there is one common cause; and if so, how much it imports

259

to discover it! For a long time, I thought it was the want
of perseverance in prayer; but then there were so many instances in which the theory broke down. I must have gone
against the whole tradition of mystical theology, if I main-
tained that mental prayer was at all necessarily connected with
perfection. Nothing grows upon us so much as the wide distinction between the habit of prayer and the gift of prayer.
We may find men who have not missed a meditation for years,
and yet who seem to have no growth about them at all; nor
even any tenderness, which ought to be the infallible product
of persevering prayer, if the prayer is right in other respects.
They are perhaps critical to excess in judging others, or they
are wanton and ungoverned in their loquacity; and month follows month, and year, year; and these unbroken prayers do
not seem to tell upon either of these faults. And can any faults
be named more fatal to piety than criticism and loquacity?
It is as if these men prayed in some way outside their souls,
as if their prayer were an adjunct of their spiritual life, and
not its heart's blood. These inoperative meditations and un-
reforming prayers are very melancholy things. But, having
tried to establish my theory, I found it was out of the question
to attribute these failures to a mere want of perseverance in
prayer.

Then I cast about for another guilty cause; and I took it
into my head that these failures might be owing to a want
of bodily mortification. Why did I not rather suspect the absence of interior mortification? For this reason. Because bodily
mortification seemed so rare that I was afraid interior mortification was put forward as a means of evading bodily mortification. There is something honest, satisfactory and intelligible
about bodily mortification; and I preferred dealing with it.
Moreover, I could not but see that bodily mortification almost
always either brings interior mortification along with it, or
makes a man easily convertible to it. I had more fear lest
the outward should be wanting than the inward. The style
of the times obviously warranted this fear. In truth, I found
that incalculable mischiefs might be put down to this want
of corporal austerity, but that it could not be brought in guilty
of these failures in perfection. First there was the awkward

fact, before observed, that those who made most of the austerities practiced them least. For it is obvious to put innocently impertinent questions to men who preach strong doctrines. I was astonished how little they did who talked so much. This was discouraging at the outset of the inquiry. However, further investigation seemed to show that although there could be no growth without austerity, the growth did not depend upon the austerity. Men mortified themselves and yet seemed to stand still. Much evil was hindered, and much killed. Souls were kept good, who might have fallen away. But they did not seem to shoot ahead. Austerity purified and prepared, and went no further. This was expressed by St. Ephrem, when he quaintly said of his holy friend that the dirt of his body cleansed away the filth of his soul. I must be understood, however, to be speaking of clean macerations. In a word, it appeared that in the soul bodily austerity was medicinal rather than nutritious; and that it sometimes made men irritable, morose and hard-natured, as medicine will do. All honor to it: but it does not secure by itself our growth in holiness.

What was to be the third object of my suspicions? They were awakened by perpetual hints and innuendoes dropped by St. Francis de Sales, which observation seemed more and more to corroborate. I therefore charged with these failures in perfection that form of indiscretion which consists in taking too many things on ourselves, and so acting in an eager, feverish and precipitate manner, which St. Francis calls *empressement*. The circumstances of modern life appeared to beguile men into it more than ever. Its miserable consequences were patent on all sides. It vitiates all it touches, and weakens what is most divine in all our spiritual exercises. It confuses the operations of grace, and turns the fruit of Sacraments on one side. Our duties are all disorderly, untidy and ill-tempered, because they rush pell-mell from morning till night, treading on each other's heels, and turning round to reproach each other. Now let some men be found who have no duties but those which their state of life renders indispensable, whose day is roomy and large, quiet and old-fashioned, everything in its place, and all things clean. They must have but few spiritual exercises, and they must make much of those few, do them slowly and punctiliously, value recollection and have no signs of tepidity. Many such were to be found, but on close inspection growth in holiness was anything but the invariable rule with them. Their slow way of doing things, their roominess, so to call it, was an immense blessing to them, and fraught with many graces. Nevertheless they were for the most part a phenomenon. Unless all the spiritual books in the world have conspired to be wrong, there is no such thing as a dead level in piety, on which people can pace up and down without either advancing or going back, like a comfortable terrace, without a single inequality in it, as if it was laid down and levelled for the purpose of office being said upon it. All theory is positive that there is no such thing. Yet by some means these good men have contrived to make it or to find it. Explain it who will, there they are pacing up and down, thoroughly good, truly edifying, yet on a level, and a low level too. I am not going out of my way to account for it. It overthrew my theory; and with all the good will in the world and out of love for St. Francis de Sales, to give precipitation a bad name I was obliged to return a verdict of not guilty, at least on the charge of causing all these unhappy failures in perfection. But the oftener a man is baffled the more obstinate he grows. Here were three failures, and a determination to try again.

This time I was longer at fault than I had been before. I did not so much cast about for a theory, as watched and waited; and by slow degrees so many facts obtruded themselves upon me that a sort of induction from them was unavoidable. At first it took this technical shape, that all men are anxious to get clear of the Purgative Way of the ascetic life, and enter into the brightness of the Illuminative or the sweetness of the Unitive, and that all failures in perfection, or so nearly all as to satisfy the requirements of a general rule, are owing to this one thing. Nothing ever presented itself to make me doubt the substantial truth of this conclusion. But the Purgative Way is a wide thing, a very comprehensive term. Would experience allow us to narrow it, without making it too narrow to bear the superstructure that was to be built upon it?

The thing was to wait for more facts, so as to have a larger and safer induction. The result was a persuasion, which I venture to record under correction, that the common cause of all failures in perfection is the want of abiding sorrow for sin. Just as all worship breaks down if it is not based on the feelings due from a creature to his Creator, just as all conversions come to nothing which are not conversions from sin, just as all penances come to nought which do not rest on Christ, just as all good works crumble away which do not rest upon our Saviour, so in like manner all holiness has lost its principle of growth if it is separated from abiding sorrow for sin. For the principle of growth is not love only, but forgiven love.

This persuasion was strengthened in me by the gradual observation that the absence of abiding sorrow for sin adequately explained all the separate phenomena that had induced me to accuse and prosecute: first the want of perseverance in prayer, then for the lack of bodily austerities, and last of all, the precipitation of having too much to do. For this abiding sorrow would produce the same continual feelings of our own unworthiness and of our dependence upon God, which would be the fruits of persevering prayer. It would engage us in perpetual warfare with and disesteem of self, and would keep us in the spirit of penance, and that without intermission, which bodily mortification would do excellently but intermittingly. It would give us all the quietness and gentleness with self, the sweetness and forbearance with others, the patience and slowness with God, which we should gain from the absence of precipitation. The salient features, therefore, which had drawn suspicion upon these things were all reunited in this abiding sorrow for sin.

Meditation on the mysteries of Our Blessed Lord, and on Our Lady's life, threw still further light on this supposition. First of all there was this remarkable fact. Jesus was sinless, by His own intrinsic sanctity, the unutterable holiness of His Divine Person. Mary was sinless, by the gift of Jesus and the pre-eminent prevention of His redeeming grace. Yet the characteristic of the lives of both was that they practiced penance in an heroic degree, as if penance might be holy without innocence, but not innocence without penance. The theological ways of accounting for the penance of Jesus and Mary led to more light. It appeared that their life of penance consisted in some measure in an abiding sorrow from first to last. The first moment of conception was the full use and complete energy of reason. But reason dawned upon a wonderful, deep and fixed sorrow. From that instant till the moment of death the sorrow abided with them. It put itself in harmony with every kind of feeling. It adapted itself to all circumstances. It never darkened into gloom. It never melted into light. It lived on the present, and the clear view of the future was part of its present, and it never let go its hold of the past. It was keen and distinct in the soul of Mary, while she magnified God in the exultation of her Divine Maternity. In the ever-blessed soul of Jesus it dwelt amid the fires of the Beatific Vision, and was not consumed. It was a beautiful mystery of perennial sorrow.

The characteristics of this sorrow were that it was lifelong, quiet, supernatural and a fountain of love. These features of it are very much to be weighed and observed. For when we come to look at ourselves, whether it be the rare few who have preserved their baptismal innocence and whose souls are only charged with venial sins, or the great Apostles, unrivalled amidst the Saints, confirmed in grace, and whose grace was superabundant, or the mass of men whose best estate is that of repentant and returning sinners, we shall see that no sorrow is possible to us which shall unite these four characteristics except the abiding sorrow for sin. It is as much lifelong with us as anything can be. It is a prominent part of our first turning to God, and there is no height of holiness in which it will leave us. It is the interior representation of our guardian angel in our souls, and the disposition and demeanor he would fain should be constant and persevering in us. It is quiet. Indeed, it rather tranquilizes a troubled soul than perturbs a contented one. It hushes the noises of the world and rebukes the loquacity of the human spirit. It softens asperities, subdues exaggerations and constrains everything with a sweet and gracious spell which nothing else can equal. It is supernatural. For it has a natural motive to feed upon. It is all from God, and all for God. It is forgiven sin for which we mourn, and not sin which perils self. And this very fact makes it also a fountain of love. We love because much has been forgiven, and we always remember how much it was. We love because the forgiveness has abated fear. We love because we wonder at the compassion that could so visit such unworthiness. We love because the softness of sorrow is akin to the filial confidence of love. Thus abiding sorrow for sin is the only possible parallel in our souls to the mysterious lifelong sorrow of Jesus and Mary; and the fact that sorrow clung to them characteristically in spite of their sinlessness seems to show how much of the secret life of Christian holiness is hidden in its gentle, supernatural melancholy.

Moreover, it was impossible not to perceive that under a variety of names, sorrow, repentance, fear and the like, Scripture speaks of an abiding penance, of fearing always, of fearing forgiven sin, of passing the time of our sojourning in fear, of the sorrow which is unto life. It never contemplates the possibility of the dispositions of repentance ceasing; for the single passage of St. John about love casting out fear is hardly to be understood of this life. So that there seems to be a precept of always sorrowing for sin analogous to the precept of always praying, and subject to the same kind of difficulties in its interpretation. Now what does this abiding sorrow of Scripture mean? Certainly not austerities; for they are occasional and intermitting. Certainly not sadness, which is sorrow with self in it, and where God should be. Certainly not human melancholy, which is either a consequence of sin, or a fruit of idleness, or a disease of a deranged bodily system. Thus Scripture, forming the last link in that chain of proof, which led me to charge failures in perfection on the want of abiding sorrow for sin as their single common cause, a cause uniting in all men with the other causes which affect this or that individual, brings me also into the consideration of my subject. We must first ascertain the nature of this sorrow.

It consists in an abiding sense that we are sinners, without at all bringing up to remembrance definite and particular sins. On the contrary, it would not only avoid such a picturing of sins as a matter of prudence, but it would be quite foreign to its genius to think of it. It is too much occupied with God to do more than to fix its eyes on self with a touching, patient, reproachful look. It consists also in an undoubting and yet an unceasing prayer for pardon. If it were argumentative, it might say that a sin was either forgiven or was not forgiven, that forgiveness was an instantaneous act, whether it were gratuitous or conditional, and that to ask forgiveness for what is forgiven is to approach God with unmeaning words. But David gives it a voice, *amplius lava me,* Wash me more and more, O Lord; and the whole Church throughout the world has adopted his *Miserere,* and is continually upon her knees, crying, *amplius lava me.* Oh, how the soul yearns for that *Amplius!* Theologians tell us that the fires of Purgatory do not amid their other severely benignant offices burn the stains of sin out of our souls; because in truth there are no stains there; the Precious Blood obliterated them in the act of forgiving them. Still there are the fires. So there are the fires of that *Amplius* in the soul. It is a thing to be felt rather than accounted for, to be cherished rather than defined.

It consists also in a dread of forgiven sin, not so much because of Purgatory, though it is far from affecting to be above these mixed and lower motives—poor soul, how should it venture to think itself above anything!—but because of the way in which old habits revive, and the species of old sins haunt the imagination, making it often, to use the forcible words of Scripture, like a cage of unclean birds. It dare not go to sleep with the seemingly dead enemy by its side. Through the cold night, and on the strewn battlefield, it wakes and watches, and in a low voice sings the triumphs of grace, that it may repel the approaches of slumber. It consists also in a growing hatred of sin. This growing hatred is a different thing from the startled horror of our conversion to God, when He tore the mask off its face, and turned the fierce full light of His Spirit upon it, exhibiting its loathsome deformity and preternatural hideousness to our soul that trembled under the idea of His judgments, while our flesh was freezingly pierced with His sharp chastising fears. That hour has passed away. It was a baptism, but He held us in His arms while He baptized us, and we did not perish. But it is an increase of the spirit of Gethsemane in our souls, a communication from that solitary mystery beneath the olive trees, when even Apostles slept. It is the Sacred Heart touching our hearts, and leaving faint stigmata of His own lifelong sorrow upon them.

It consists in a growing sensitiveness of conscience as to what is sin. Ineffably bright as is the sanctity of God and His refulgent glory, to gaze upon it strengthens our soul's eye rather than dazzles it. We see more clearly what is imperfect, unworthy and dishonorable in actions. We discern the complication and mixture of motives more distinctly. And entangled in a confusion of infirmities, a very inevitability of imperfections, where self-love can find no single resting place for the sole of its foot, we grow in a divine sadness, which humility and faith will not allow to be disquietude. With all this, and in the way of consequence, our personal love of our most blessed Lord increases, and love of Him as our actual Saviour from sin. It is our joy to "call His Name, Jesus, because He saveth His people from their sins."

There are two classes of persons trying to serve God: those who do not feel this abiding sorrow for sin, and those who do. Or it would be more accurate to say that the one class has not got it, and does not feel the want of it, and the other either has it, or wants to have it. Various causes hinder men from feeling this want; the most common is tepidity. Lukewarmness is incompatible with this holy sorrow, and cannot co-exist with it. But the characteristic of such men is the absence of spiritual growth, and their perseverance in the ways of devotion doubtful. On the contrary, those who have not this sorrow, but feel the want of it, have this consolation, that the very feeling of the want is a sign of a healthy state, or at least of returning health; though it may be even with them that lukewarmness has brought their necessity safely home to them. Many men are unhappily without it, from their having suddenly or prematurely taken too high a place in the spiritual life, left the purgative way too rapidly, vitiated their palates by mystical books, or undertaken penances too hard for them, and works beyond their existing grace. If we insist upon our souls growing upwards before they have taken root downwards, they are sure to be stunted. Little birds that try to fly before they are fledged fall from the eaves and are hurt or killed, according to the height from which they fall. The love of such men for Our Blessed Lord is cold and poor, and anything like ardor looks to them mere high-flown romance, or a wordy enthusiasm. That the sorrow, however, is not always sensible is no proof that it is not habitual. Yet sensible sorrow, like sensible sweetness, is a great gift, and to be moderately desired and asked of God. Alas! we may often wish to feel as we did when God first turned us to Himself. "Oh, that I was as in former days," says Job. Yet the question is, how far this is possible, and if possible, how far it would be well. The sorrow we must cultivate is of another sort.

The Apostle tells us there are two kinds of sorrow: one of them is sorrow unto death, the other a sorrow unto life. The sorrow unto death is more like self-vexation than genuine sorrow. It is often the consequence of an exaggerated human respect. It is a sorrow for sin which causes fresh sins, by filling us full of irritability both toward others and ourselves. It is without any trust in God, without any realization of grace, and leads to no amendment of life. This is the sorrow unto death in its earlier stages, during which it may occasionally mingle unperceived with the dispositions of excellent and interior persons. Its later stages are the preparations of despair; and its consequence, worked logically out, is final impenitence, and an unfavorable doom.

The sorrow which is unto life is of two kinds. The first is that which works conversion. It is impetuous, outwardly demonstrative, full of self-revenge, greedy of mortification, impatient with too easy forgiveness and eaten up with a desire to suffer which is not as yet really rooted in the soul, an appetite for pain which is more a nervous craving than a gracious hunger after justice, so that it must not be satisfied. This sorrow is naturally transient; for it has an end to accomplish, and then it goes.

The other is the sorrow which we should wish to retain with us always. As I have said, it is lifelong, quiet, supernatural and a fountain of love. Hence it is affectionate, and not reproachful. It knows how to deal gently with self, without dealing indulgently. It is humble, and never downcast at falls.

Strange to say, its fear of Hell is infrequent, faint and intermitting; yet it is never, not for a moment nor even in ecstasy,
without a solemn, reverential fear of God's inscrutable judgments. The celestial raptures of Our Lord's Sacred Humanity
interrupted not for one moment the reverential fear with which
His Body and Soul were penetrated. It is possible for the
fear of Hell to be so strong and so lasting, as to be a spiritual
disease. Moreover, this abiding sorrow is devotional. It inclines to prayer, brings pleasure in prayer, and though a sorrow, is itself a sweetness. It is very confident, and its confidence
rests solely upon God. It lives by the fountains of the Saviour's
Blood, weeps silent tears like one who is continually hearing
good news, and is hopeful.

This affectionate sorrow delivers us from many spiritual
dangers. It throws a tenderness into our whole character, and
makes us deep and pliant. It brings with it the unction of
that special gift of the Holy Ghost which is named "piety."
It hinders our getting into a formal way both of doing our
ordinary actions and of going through our accustomed devotions. The sap subsides in the trees as the cold weather comes,
and the chilly nights quicken its descent. So is the gradual
declension of fervor in our souls. But this sorrow saves us
from it; it is the sap of our spiritual lives, whose character
it is to be perennial, and its foliage evergreen. The leaves
may be cold-crumpled and frostbitten; but the tree is still green.
It also saves us from making light of venial sins, and is always
stopping, even when we know it not, little untruths, teasing
jealousies, wounded conceits and sins of the tongue. For it
is the sorrow which was the Lord's mantle. We are holding
the sacred fringe, and virtue goes out of Him into us, and
the issue of the bleeding soul is stayed.

The fruits which it produces in us are of equal importance
with the dangers from which it preserves us. It makes us
charitable toward the falls of others, and this reacts upon ourselves in the way of an increase of humility. It involves a
continual renewal of our good resolutions, additional reality
and fortitude in our wish to do more for God, and an increasing
power of perseverance, with more stability and less effort.
It blessedly diminishes our taste for the world and its pleasures.

It flings the charm of Heaven around us, and disenchants all
other spells. It leads to a more fruitful, because a more rever-
ent, humble and hungry use of the Sacraments; and no grace
that comes to us is wasted while this sorrow possesses our
souls. It grinds all grist in its mill. There is nothing which
makes our endurance of crosses more patient or more graceful: nothing which gives us so calm and fertile a pertinacity
in works of mercy to others. We are always flooded with inward tenderness, so that there is not an ache or pain in one
of Christ's members which does not awake our sympathy, and
find its account in our sensibility. Devotion to Our Lord's
Passion is meant for the daily bread of Christian thought,
and it keeps fresh and new in this sorrow as in a genial atmosphere. Our perceptions of the invisible world become finer
and keener; we are more liable to be excited by spiritual interests, and more alive to the soul's wants and dangers; and
there is about us a liveliness of thanksgiving, which only shows
the copiousness of the hidden joy in this apparent sorrow.
It is as though the happy resurrection of the flesh were par-
tially anticipated. The coils and drags fall off our soul, and
we have a new facility and promptitude for everything which
has to do with God.

But how are we to get, or if gotten how keep, this dear
and precious sorrow? Need I say that we must make it a subject of special prayer? We must not give way to disgusts with
common devotions, tame books, ordinary practices and com-
monplace direction. We must avoid changing our director
hastily, and prepare carefully and leisurely for Sacraments and
make much of them. We must have a great devotion for the
conversion of sinners, and be very simple in the accusation
of ourselves in the confessional. We must be jealous of anything which hinders our constant growth in personal love of
Jesus. Whatever else stops for awhile, often inculpably, this
love can never stop. There is no end to it. It partakes of God's
infinity. Nothing is above it in kind, nothing co-equal with
it in degree. We must never consciously seek consolation as
a primary object either in sermons, direction, devotion, voluntary bodily inflictions, or spiritual conferences. We must not
seek to be consoled in a sorrow which is our treasure, and

which we are fain should abide with us not only until the day of this world is far spent, but until the new eternal day has veritably dawned. And if we be in the illuminative, or even in the unitive way, never let us part company altogether with meditation on the Four Last Things.

But particularly we must be upon our guard against two foolish mistakes, which betray an ignorance of the first principles of the interior life, and which nevertheless are not uncommon. The first mistake is the putting lightly away of movements of remorse and inward upbraidings, as if they were mere scruples. Directors, in a hurry to get rid of their penitents, or anxious to keep them calm at all costs, often cast them into this delusion. But it is a serious misfortune as well as a grave mistake. It may be some old root of bitterness which is causing the twinge, or some secret reserve with God which has found voice and is upbraiding us. What shall we lose if we leave these things still in us? Or it may be that Our Lord is doing to us something like what we read of various saints, that He is squeezing the last drops of bad blood out of our hearts: and are we to meddle and unclasp the kind firmness of His fingers from the aching place, when if we knew our own good fortune we should see that that ache is worth kingdoms to us? A cloud is always a cloud; but it is wisdom to know when the cloud that is overshadowing us is the Holy Ghost.

The other mistake is thinking it uncatholic to take serious and religious views of things. Converts are very liable to this from the ordinary laws of reaction and recoil. So also are priests, seminarists and religious, as thinking seriousness professional. Levity will not make us happy, and I never read the life of a saint who thought it fine to speak lightly, or who was given to do so. They said little, and what they said was invariably grave. I believe it was their gravity that made them cheerful. There is something undergraduate about this levity. It is partly the conceit, and partly the vulgarity of the spiritual life.

I am confident no vocation to perfection will be frustrated by a soul in which there is this abiding sorrow for sin. It is the quintessence of devotion to the Sacred Heart, and it is there that we must seek it.

Chapter XX

THE RIGHT VIEW OF OUR FAULTS

The sweetest of all the sweet doctrines which St. Francis de Sales was inspired to teach us was that which regarded the right view of our own faults. The consideration of it falls very naturally into this place. On the one hand, we have got clear views of temptations and of scruples, and on the other, a perception of the necessity of an abiding sorrow for sin. That sorrow, as we now understand it, can be no source of scruples, but a right view of our own faults must fall in with and be a part of it. Unfortunately our faults form a great portion of ourselves, and it is plain that the management of them can be no slight affair in the spiritual life, and that our management of them depends very much upon the view we take of them.

Indeed, much of life depends upon taking right views of things. Time is saved. Mistakes are hindered. Sometimes we chance upon a short road to Heaven. Not that the short roads are always the easiest. Strictly speaking, none are short and none are easy; but they may be comparatively so among themselves, and all are full of pleasantness and peace. What do we most abound in? Certainly, in faults. Perhaps a right view of them may be a short road to Heaven. It will, at all events, help us to make a road of what looks like a series of barriers.

If a good person were asked to give an account of himself, it would probably be somewhat after the following fashion:

I am constantly doing things which are wrong in themselves. It is not that I do them on purpose, or with forethought. I hope I do not commit any venial sin deliberately. It is the great object of my life, next to loving God, to avoid that.

Yet neither on the other hand can I say that my falls are altogether surprises. They seem so at the time, but not when I come to look back upon them. The sense of guilt grows upon me in the retrospect, rather than reproaches me at the moment. And, worst of all, I see no visible improvement in myself in this matter. Again, when I do things which are outwardly right, nay, which are generous, and involve some amount of sacrifice, I continually detect some low motive in them. I cannot shake off human respect. Self-love seems inseparable even from my very thoughts, my very sacrifices. It is not as if this happened now and then, but it is going on all day. It runs parallel with the stream of life. I believe I have never done a good work in my life. A spoiled good work is my highest point.

But in prayer I am quite a different person. I seem to have entered another world. I am at my ease and at large. The aspirations of the Saints appear to be mine. Desires of suffering, an appetite for calumny, tremendous penances, ardent resolutions, heroic deeds, all rush upon me at once, and express precisely what I am feeling most strongly in my interior life. Bold words, from which at other times I should have shrunk with reverence, fill my prayers. I plead the right of saints, and urge their petitions, and demean myself as if I were one. And all this before God! I do not mean to be insincere. I feel, or I fancy I feel, what I am saying. Yet when I come back to the level of my daily practice, I feel as if my prayer had been all an hypocrisy from beginning to end. I wish I could think that it were not so. There is no sort of proportion between my prayer and my practice. The first is always running ahead of the last, and so absurdly far ahead!

For when I come to practice, generosity in suffering is just what I cannot realize; and as to mortifications, they are simply to me what punishments are to a child. It would be as surprising to others as it is humiliating to myself, if I were to mention what little things I do for God, and what a laborious effort it takes to do them, and what immense pain it is. How can I complain, and tremble, and put it off, and hunt for a justifiable dispensation, and sink back into comfortable spirituality, as soon as the momentary effort is over. The

revelations I could make of my own pusillanimity, would be
almost incredible. But I was grand at prayer in the morning,
grand as a martyr at the block in front of one of my own
castles in the air.

The upshot of the whole is that I seem to myself to be
getting worse and going back. My sensible fervors have gone,
and I do not see that they have left formed habits behind them.
I wish I could name any one imperfection that I could say
had been effectually weeded out, or any one venial sin, whose
crowded ranks had been thinned, or that I could show anything beyond a scratch here and there on my ruling passion.
All that I can see is that I make as much effort as I used
to do, perhaps more, but apparently with less effect.

Now is a person who gives such an account of himself in
a good way? Let me think. On the whole, Yes. I found my
judgment on two things: the evident desire for perfection with
which he began, and the fact of continued effort with which
he ended. Starting then with these two things, he may reasonably take a consoling view of the rest. But let us speak of
ourselves. Our faults are very numerous and very great: true.
But is there anything to surprise us in them? From our own
knowledge of ourselves and from what we knew of the measure of our grace, are they not what might have been expected?
At times we have thought of our future humbly and prudently,
was it very different from what has actually taken place? The
fact is that neither in the kind nor in the degree of our faults,
is there anything astonishing: and if nothing astonishing, then
nothing discouraging. But this is not going far enough. There
is something astonishing, and the astonishing thing is that our
faults have not been greater. When we weigh ourselves against
our temptations, our estimate of things is very different. How
unlike ourselves we have happily been in many things! This
can be nothing less than the work of grace. Instead of being
peevish because we have been so bad, the wonder is that we
have been so good, and the fear is lest we should be elated
in seeing it.

Common sense also has a word or two to say on the matter.
The faults are committed. They have done their harm, and
gone to God. There is no good in being cast down. There

is much good in not being so. There is no good in being
cast down; for the faults cannot be recalled. We may fidget
about the circumstances, and worry themselves by thinking
how easily the evil might have been avoided. But the fault
itself lost us some of our peace; why should we now lose
more in self-vexation? Discouragement moreover is no part
of penance. It atones for nothing, satisfies for nothing, merits
nothing, impetrates nothing. It does not make us more careful
next time. On the contrary by dejecting us it makes us at
once more open to temptation and less masculine in resisting
it. But on the contrary, there is much good in not being cast
down. We shall be less teased with the imperfection in ourselves, and more occupied with the infidelity to God. To fall
and not be out of spirits with it is not only to keep the courage
we had, but to gain more. It is the humblest course, and on
that account the most acceptable to God. It is the most reasonable, and therefore has the greater blessing.

Sometimes a saint gives us a new thought, which for what
we can see is not to be found in any of the spiritual writers
before him. It is his contribution to the tradition. When he
has said it, it sounds so commonplace that we wonder we
never thought of it for ourselves, like the sayings of all great
minds. Such a thought is that of St. Francis de Sales, the
man of many new thoughts, when he taught us that if in the
spiritual life we often fall without perceiving it, so it must
be true that we as often get up again without perceiving it.
It sounds like a pleasantry; but if a man who has the infelici-
tous habit of disquieting himself about his faults would once
in a way take it for the subject of his hour's meditation, he
would suck from it the very marrow of spiritual wisdom. I
should spoil it, if I enlarged upon it.

We may imagine that we take a sufficiently low view of ourselves, and estimate our attainments, as humility would approve. But any disquietude about our faults which is more than
transient, or a temptation, is a proof to us that we have secretly
been putting a far higher price upon ourselves than we were
warranted in doing. And this turning king's evidence against
us is the only good such disquietude ever does, and that is
as it were in spite of itself. But does not God occasionally

show us fearful things in the depths of our own souls? Sometimes a family with the sunshine of domestic peace and virtue all around it has tenanted an ancient house for years, when lo! the necessity of some repairs leads to the discovery of secret dungeons and horrible places underground, with traces of misery suffered there, and of guilt perpetrated. So it is in our own souls. The access of some unusual temptation, the accidental waking up of some long dormant passion, or a flash of supernatural light from God, illuminate for a moment unexplored cavities and unexpected materials for evil. It may be that the reading or hearing of great crimes may have brought it home to us. But by whatever means we make the discovery, there can be no doubt that we carry about with us immense capabilities of uncommitted sin. Nothing but the merciful turns of a considerate Providence, and the constraining empire of grace, prevent these from being realized in acts. Oh, how we crouch under God's mantle, and hold to His feet, when we first get sight of these things! What an amazing, what a blessed disproportion between the evil we do and the evil we are capable of doing, and seem sometimes on the very verge of doing! If my soul has grown tares, when it was full of seeds of nightshade, how happy ought I to be! And that the tares have not wholly strangled the wheat, what a wonder it is, an operation of grace, the work of the Sacraments! If the heathen emperor thanked God daily for the temptations which He did not allow to approach him, how ought not we to thank Him for the sins we have not committed!

Then, again, have we not times in which, I must express myself so, grace seems to stir up the very dregs of our nature, and throw them into a state of fiery effervescence, by some combination of supernatural chemistry? What devils, what beasts, we look to ourselves! For a moment we feel as if we were polluted by the sins which we might have committed, and though a dream, it is all so lifelike that the horrid impression haunts us for days. We are as heavy as if we had very blood upon our souls. At these moments, and without one atom of vanity or the least fear of complacency, the grateful thought of what we are, the thought which another while vexes and disheartens us, is the pillow of rest to which we turn, to forget in the sense of God's mercies the thought of what we might have been, and yet may be. Strange that our little faults should ever be the chosen place of our repose!

Here is another consoling vision. Compare the drossy mixture which we are of God's grace and the human spirit, with what we should be if, without any touch, or taste, or odor of the devil, God left your human spirit simply to itself. M. Olier could not realize this, but God made him see it by subtracting His succors from him. He showed him what we should be if He were merely to leave us to ourselves. The intense interest of the passages must excuse the length of the quotation.

"This subtraction takes place," says M. Olier, "with regard to sensible grace; for the Divine Goodness does not cease even then to succor us with insensible graces, of a still more efficacious kind. The default of His sensible graces causes strange effects and often prodigious humiliations in the soul. Under the influence of those succors the will and the heart are drawn to God with delight, and something may be observed even in our exterior, the way in which we carry ourselves and the works we do, of an unparalleled sweetness, modesty and equability. When God withdraws these sensible gifts He leaves the soul in its nakedness, and as great lights came from them before, there is nothing left in the soul now but trouble and confusion. Touched with compassion for my state, God mercifully took these gifts away from me, to show me what I really was, and thus tenderly disabuse me of my error. It is really an effect of huge mercy thus to leave us to ourselves, else we should go on esteeming self, and appropriating to ourselves what belongs to God only, until perhaps we might fall into a blindness like that of Lucifer. God thus shows visibly to the soul and depths of its own abjection, and so convinces it of its misery. For this sensible grace, which reined in the corrupt man and held him in check, having now retired, everything is changed both in the interior and exterior. The Holy Spirit then leaves him to feel the amount of his natural unruliness and the corruption of his desires. The bridle is thrown upon the neck of the passions. We feel nothing but anger on the slightest occasions, envy, aversions, sentiments of self-love, until our pride breaks out externally in the fierce and haughty expression of our countenance. Yet very often the soul does not at all contribute to this by any thought or voluntary emotion. It is the natural effect of a rising inundation of pride, now that He is gone who could repress it, and bid it hide itself.

"Thus when the Holy Spirit, who had raised the soul to God for a time, retires, the soul, no longer sustained by the fortitude of this powerful principle, falls in upon itself, and seems by the fall to relapse into an abyss of obscurity, darkness, corruption and confusion, an abyss of passions which, like wild beasts, gnaw and tear themselves. In a word the soul feels as if it had fallen from Heaven to Hell, so appalling is our own reality to ourselves. How much more then to the eye of God, who is purity and sanctity itself. Thus God leaves in the midst of us that fiery furnace, the concupiscence, which, no less than the ashes of Sodom and Gomorrha, advertises us of the judgments of God pronounced against Adam and his posterity. It is a mouth of Hell which we bear about inside ourselves, vomiting a thousand stenches insupportable to God, and which draw down upon our sinful flesh the chastisements of His avenging arm. I am not speaking of the sins which we have committed by our own malice, but only of the humiliation common to all the world. I do not wonder at the Saints arming themselves with holy fury against themselves, and furnished with instruments of penance, cutting their flesh to pieces and making their blood to flow, in the justest of martyrdoms. It was to show men what they ought to suffer in their criminal flesh, that the Son of God vouchsafed to be scourged, and to have His Blood flow, and His bones be dislocated. So when the sensible succors of grace retire, and this subtraction lays our malice bare, we feel it an ease and a relief to be the butt of injuries and outrages, and the object of treatment the most rigorous and the most undeserved.

"See how these subtractions of grace work! First of all they give us a plain and visible knowledge that of ourselves we are nothing but sin. Then comes humility, which makes us love to be treated both by God and men as our sin deserves. God only subtracts these sensible graces to put more excellent ones in their place, like a gardener who roots up one tree to plant a better. But as it is not His will always to accomplish the same operations in all men, He does not prepare them all in the same way. As it is not His intention to take an equally intimate possession of all, He does not so utterly and radically detach some from themselves as He does others. He makes us feel these subtractions and derelictions in proportion to the gifts He intends to confer upon us; and because it is more common to be proud of the gifts of grace than of those of nature, and yet that the former pride is more odious to Him than the latter, this kind Master, careful of our good, makes the gifts of grace rather than those of nature the theater of these subtractions."[1]

So far M. Olier. Oh, a thousand faults that were not mortal sins were far better than this nature, emancipated from the devil, yet without grace, and enjoying its own wretched prerogatives, would be! See what we are at bottom. Why we are saints compared to our real untempted selves, selves uncompounded with grace and God's compassion!

From all these considerations I infer that we ought to be, I do not say thoroughly contented, but fairly happy, if as time goes on we do not add to the kinds of venial sin of which we have to accuse ourselves, nor increase the numbers of those which beset us, nor fall into those with more advertence than before, nor give way more resistingly to surprises of temptation, and still continue to entertain even in our worst times an habitual preference for God. These are five sources of moderate cheerfulness, which, like Cowper's cups of tea, while they cheer, will not inebriate.

But is it safe and wise to give ourselves up to these

---

1. Vie. i. 285. It should be observed that the epithets which M. Olier uses betoken his doctrine on the subject of Original Sin, which appears in a very startling way in his *Catechism of the Interior Life* where, to say the least, he has pushed it to the extremest limits which orthodoxy will allow. Where I have had to use adjectives qualifying our fallen nature and its propensities elsewhere in the book, I have spoken out of the belief that the state of Original Sin is like that of *pura natura*, with the exception that it is a state of privation. As a man's views of Original Sin exercise a great influence on his spiritual life, I have thought it right to take exception to M. Olier's expressions, without intending to say anything disrespectful toward him of whom I have observed elsewhere that of all the uncanonized servants of God whose lives I have read, he most resembles a canonized saint.

considerations? Do we run no risk in thus taking our faults
quietly? Let us then now consider the propriety and spiritual
wisdom of so doing. What is humble is safe, provided it be
true humility. Now, to be indifferent to faults, and to make
no endeavor to improve, would not be humility, but lukewarmness or irreligion. But it is a very different thing to take our
faults quietly, and all the while be doing our very best to
mend, and wishing intensely to be better. Neither is there
any danger of laxity in it, because we are looking to God;
and laxity implies a downward, not an upward eye. It leads
us away from self. Even self-love makes us hate self. So that
all this taking of our faults quietly is in reality based upon
a supernatural principle, which both implies and augments
interior mortification.

Moreover, quietness is absolutely necessary for spiritual
growth under ordinary circumstances. There are sometimes
brief tempests in the interior when we grow, like children
in an illness. But these are eccentric phenomena. It is plain
that quietness must be the prevailing atmosphere of an ascetic.
We must be quiet in order to pray. Mortification must be quiet,
or else it will be merely vehement nature, growing in fury
as it grows in pain. Confidence in God must be quiet. The
very word itself is full of the sound of rest. The receiving
of the Sacraments must be quiet. Noise and hurry would be
simple irreverence. Our love of others must be quiet, else
it will degenerate into earthly tenderness. In a word, there
is hardly a function of the spiritual life which does not require
quietness for its exercise and fulfillment. Yet faults are universal,
daily, in all subject matters, thought, word, deed, look, omission. They cover the whole surface of life incessantly; so that
if we do not take them quietly, we shall never be quiet at
all. This is so absurd a result that it is as good as a demon-
stration that we must take our faults quietly.

The desire of perfection is, as we have already seen, a gift
from God, and a great gift; and a generous and earnest pursuit of virtue is necessary to perfection. Yet we must not be
inordinately attached either to the desire or the pursuit. If
it is God's will to hold us back, we must be content to be
held back. The goodness of a thing is no justification of an

unruly eagerness in acquiring it. The eagerness of the pursuit will more than counterbalance the blessing of the acquisition. Our falls are permitted. Our share in them must be wiped away by cheerful, hopeful sorrow. The rest God will look to, and we must be at peace.

There is also this other disadvantage in the opposite line of conduct. Discouragement necessarily brings with it a greediness for consolation. The more we are disquieted, the more we fly to what will solace and soothe. And this is bringing back self again into everything, besides unnerving us for genuine struggle, and giving us a disrelish for mortification. Consolations from creatures never really help, but very often hinder; and an appetite for them is a bad augury of progress.

But in the spiritual life there is never a permission without a caution, never a relaxation without a saving clause against laxity. So in this case we must be careful to distinguish hopefulness from self-conceit. To be quiet under our faults is not to be free and easy with them; and cheerfulness is a very different thing from vanity. But how to discern between the two? Hope implies a certain amount of doubt, and that again implies fear: so that when we hope in time to advance beyond the circle of particular faults, we have some, but a subordinate, fear that possibly we may not succeed. That fear is plainly self-distrust, and it is subordinate, else it would be discouragement. Conceit has no fear, because it has no doubt, and no hope, because it does not contemplate its success as being in any way uncertain. So that self-distrust is one test by which we can distinguish hopefulness from conceit. A confidence in God more than equalling our distrust of self is another sign. Conceit trusts in itself; and in its reckonings calculates as a right what humility sees to be a grace. A third test is to be found in the gradual growth of the supernatural in our feelings, motives and desires. If we look more to God, if we lean more on Sacraments, if we prefer the divine will to our own spiritual advancement, then we may be sure that our quietness with our faults is hopefulness, and not conceit.

The whole question comes to this. There are two views of growth in grace, the self-improvement view and the will of God view. In these views—for what is more operative than a view—is the root of all the error and of all the wisdom of the matter. If a man puts self-improvement before him as the end of life, almost every step that he takes will be wrong. If he works away at himself, as a sculptor finishes off a statue, he will get more out of proportion, and bring out more black marks and gray blotches, the longer he chisels. Not a motive will be right, not an aim true. If he takes up his particular examen and his rule of life, and his periodical penances, as merely medicinal appliances, if he shuts himself up in a reformatory school of his own, if he models his whole spiritual life upon the complacent theory of self-improvement, his asceticism will be nothing better than a systematizing and a glorifying of self-will. Under such auspices he can never be a spiritual man, and he will hardly be a moral man. Yet how common is this miserable view, even among men living right in the heart of a system so intensely supernatural as that of the Catholic Church.

The will of God view, on the contrary, refers everything but diligence and correspondence to Him. A man follows God's lead, and does not strike out a road for himself. He models himself in his measure and degree on the imitation of Jesus. He seeks to please God, and acts out of love. His inconsistencies neither astonish nor tease him. An imperfection annoys him, not because it mars the symmetry of his character, but because it grieves the Holy Ghost. Sacraments, and scapulars, and beads and medals, relics and rites, all find their places in his system; and the natural and the supernatural form one whole. God is always pleased when a man seeks humbly, and in appointed ways, to please Him. Hence this man is quieted, cheerful and hopeful with his faults. The gaiety of endless success is in his heart. God is his Father. Whereas the self-improvement man either does not succeed in improving himself, or he does so too slowly, or he loses on one side what he gains on the other, or people will persist in being scandalized at his edifying deportment, for with such men edification is the crown of virtue, and if they do not edify, they have failed. Hence he is unquiet, sulky and desponding about his faults. The bitterness of endless piecemeal failure is in his heart.

After death we shall have many revelations. I suspect the hiddenness of our spiritual growth here on earth will give rise to some. How surprised many humble spirits will be at the extraordinary beauty of their souls, when death has disengaged them! So much more is always going on than we in the least suspect!

Chapter XXI

THE IRRELIGIOUS AND THE ELECT

It is the most unconverting thing in the world to tell a man there is nothing in his objection. This is partly the reason of its being easier to convince a man who has a valid objection, than one who has only an invalid one. Not only because we have something definite and intelligible to answer, but also because our candor and fairness in admitting what is real in his objection, softens and wins our opponent's heart. Hence those who will not admit that the Catholic system presents many reasonable difficulties to an external mind, do not only themselves admit a strong argument against its divinity, but will not usually be very fertile of converts, or have much cause to rejoice either in the progress, or perseverance, or thorough Catholicism, of the converts they make.

The same principle is the reason of the present chapter. It is strange that when a man has been so engrossed with interior things, he should be plagued with external difficulties. Yet as he never can get rid of his liability to presumption and discouragement, they each of them find vent in a difficulty which has nothing to do with himself, and is a distraction and an unhappiness to him. It is remarkable how many and what clear-sighted spiritual persons find a real temptation in seeing how wicked the world is, and how good they are in comparison with it, which leads them to presumption, or in the doctrine of the fewness of the elect which casts them into dejection. I cannot say that there is nothing in an objection which teases so many, or nothing reasonable in what men urge, whom I could only call unreasonable by using the word in the usual sense of controversialists, with whom it means a man who is hardy enough to differ from themselves. I shall admit the objections and go into them, and so I hope to blunt them.

The progress of spirituality is the growth of detachment from the world; and there is much that is imperfect and ungraceful on our part in many of the processes. We do not all at once hate the world with a supernatural hatred, when we have ceased to love it. We tremble with our old habitual respect for its judgments, or we regard it with the critical eye of a mere natural aversion. It is when we are in this last stage that the utter badness of the world is a temptation to us to think ourselves saints.

There are, as it were, five visions of the world's wickedness which distress us. For men either harden their hearts, or they pass God over altogether, or they are not converted when they ought to be, or they positively hate God, or they profess to serve Him and are inconsistent, as devotees often are.

The first state is that of impenitence, the state of hardened hearts. Men know that they ought to leave off sin, and refuse to do so—not that they have any conscious hatred of God or any conscious aversion to morality, but because they like sin and are willing to have it with its costs and risks. To a man who is well and high-spirited there is a great deal of natural enjoyment in sin, and to those who are ailing or unhappy there is both repose and consolation in sensuality. The world is also extremely graceful and attractive in its bearing. A man must be already converted before he can see the truth of the harsh judgments we pass upon the world in our pulpits and confessionals; they cannot convert him. Such men wilfully stifle conscience when it speaks, yet there is a blind notion of the duty of repentance left at last, which few can entirely extirpate; and which, if it is allowed to discharge no kindlier office, will at least justify God in the severity of their eternal doom. Christians would do well to remember that all confessions without sorrow, and all relapses into sin, are in reality energetic tendencies to this state of impenitence. There is something in the peculiar malice of a relapse very congenial to final impenitence.

The second phase of the world is indifference. Men pass

God over, and that too without infidels. This is compatible, not only with an external profession of Christianity, but also with an intellectual belief in it. Spiritual men find something irritatingly odious in this state. Indifferent men arrogate to themselves all the candor and moderation in the world. They imagine themselves to be on a height, so that they look up at nothing, but down upon everything. Inside the Church they care very little about doctrines, and wish to stand well with all parties. They have no keen sense of the Church, no susceptibility about the poor, no instinct about the heinousness of sin. They intend to hang on to God by just the necessary duties, and no more. They theologize for themselves and strike out a road to Heaven without love, except that radical love which is in the soul, will, reason, brain, blood, bones and marrow of organized man toward his Creator. All their views and all their interests are steeped in materialism; and in religion they think themselves amazingly prudent in not aiming at too much, or committing themselves to God. They are always ready to dam every zealous work and throw a dash of chill, which is their notion of moderation, into everything. To hear them talk, you would suppose the world was on fire with a romantic love of God, and that our merciful Creator had deputed them to come and play upon the conflagration with cold water, which they do with all the calmness and dignity conceivable. It makes spiritual people seasick to watch these men, and yet they will watch them; they often cannot help watching them, with a kind of fascination.

The third state of the world is unconversion. Men simply do not think of God at all, or they push His grace from them as men repel a shock in the street, without knowing whether it is man or thing they are resisting. They do not wish to make up their minds to be either for or against God, not so much because they are indifferent about it, but because they are deterred by its difficulties. They live as if there were no spiritual world, and no invisible powers. They have all that unsuspiciousness of supernatural things, which is the effect of long self-indulgence, even independent of positive sin. Indeed, they are often outwardly moral; for the characters which shine most in domestic life often belong to this class. When religiousness is obtruded upon them, they rest in vague views of God and profane generalities about His attribute of mercy, or they make the existence of religious differences an excuse for not fairly meeting the question. Good people themselves should remember that all reserves with God, no matter with how much other excellence combined, are so many steps to unconversion.

The fourth state is irreligion. God is an object of positive aversion to many. They are fidgeted by the mention of Him. They rise up in arms when His claims are urged, however modestly. They are vexed with holiness, even where it can cause no practical inconvenience to them. The definition of the Immaculate Conception sours them: so much so, that they cannot sneer. The canonization of a saint provokes them, though how it concerns them it is difficult to see. They have a strong feeling that religion must be put down, and they look to the newspapers to do it. A good word for God they take as a personal affront to themselves, and, if intellectual convictions have moral qualities, they have an ill-tempered disbelief in Hell.

The assertion of the supernatural makes them fretful, and they pronounce very strongly against mortification, as super-stitious and undignified. They are vehement against Church authority, and all ecclesiastical arrangements and jurisdiction are gall to them. Yet they cannot shake off an uneasy and insecure feeling that they are not so infallible as they wish to seem. They feel as if there was an enemy in the rear, who would come up with them someday, as He will do. This per-haps explains the ill-humor which is their prominent charac-teristic. A man who loses his temper because Our Lady has appeared on the steeps of La Salette is evidently not at ease about his own religious convictions; else he would smile, not frown. Everyone likes to be good-humored, and is so, when he can afford to be.

From all these states comes judicial blindness. Men are in a mist, and do not know it: only those who can look upon the mist from without perceive that there is any mist at all. In this blindness they neither see the evil they do, nor the good they might do. They are in darkness as to the real state of their souls, the truths of religion, the character of God and His dispositions toward them. And so they go into eternity, and their eyes are opened, and at last they see.

A melancholy world! No wonder we look to ourselves so good in the middle of it. But to get rid of the temptation we fix our eyes upon the few good men in it, and with the most unsatisfactory result. There is something especially unpleasant in the faults of pious persons. Their inconsistency grates very harshly upon us. They ought to be humble, and they are proud. They should be grave, and they are frivolous. They should be overflowing with mercy, and they are abstracted and unsympathetic. They are peevish, and bear less well than other men either contradiction or interruption. There is an annoying littleness about their faults, which sometimes makes us sigh for the world's great sins. They make sacred things grotesque, and there is a charmed atmosphere of exaggeration round about them. They judge each other, and all walk different roads. Now the sting of the temptation is in this last vision. If we thought ourselves good, when we measured ourselves by the bad people, we are saints by the side of the good. The more we try to do for God the more forcibly all this comes upon us, and times of prayer and penance are its choicest seasons. I admit it is a trial, enough of a trial to be a temptation; and that we had better arm ourselves with some considerations against it.

We must consider, first of all, that men are very different from what they seem, and that our real knowledge of them is very small indeed. Moreover, even when they wish to do the reverse, men put out their bad and draw in their good; although badness is in itself a much more demonstrative thing than goodness. Then what should we have been without grace? And we did not merit it for ourselves at first. It has often failed to move us even when its impulses have been strong and lasting. Had any one of these men ever one such single impulse? Who knows? We cannot apply the doctrine of chance to grace. What would they have been if they had had our grace? It is inconceivable that anyone should have corresponded less faithfully to it than we have done. So far as supernatural things are concerned, look at what an advantageous position we occupy, from our own past experience of God's operations in our souls. Have they anything they can parallel with that? Who knows? And what are they to us? Will not our judgment be solitary? We shall not pass muster in a crowd. We shall each stand alone and apart before the "great white throne" when the books are opened; and as Christ died for each one of us completely as if He had no one else to die for, so we are judged each by himself as if he were the only one to be judged. There is in this temptation, therefore, an unconscious reference to the world as a standard and measure, which shows the imperfection of our state. By our own grace, by our own light, according to our own works, and to our own Master, we shall stand or fall; and by His mercy only shall even His chosen be set up in that day.

We are as ignorant of the future of these men as we are of their past; and this added to our exaggeration of their present, leaves us in a total incapacity of judging. They may be converted; and who knows whether they will not then be great saints? In the fervor of their penance, it will be no hard matter for them to overshoot us, and throw our attainments completely into the shade. They will love more, because more has been forgiven them. We who minister to souls must often have been surprised when bold unblushing sinners, whose very bearing even inspires us with human respect, have fallen into our hands, to see what sweetness of disposition, and childlike character, and attractive moral timidity were covered by that external effrontery of voice, of swagger, of eye and of evil deed. They have as many capabilities of being saints as we have possibilities of being demons. Besides which, if the worst comes to the worst, we surely knew beforehand that the world was God's enemy; for in our baptismal engagements we had pledged ourselves to renounce it. We ought not, therefore, to be surprised at that of which we were not forewarned, but against which we were solemnly forearmed.

As to the criticism of the faults of good people, is not this perhaps rather a sin than only a temptation? We have no business with them. It is not our affair. When the world has become really and genuinely our enemy, we participate in God's right to judge it. But it is not so with His own servants. It is an injury to ourselves, because it takes off our attention

from our own souls. But the main thing to consider is that
we can come to no fair estimate of devout people, or test
their progress in holiness. This is partly for the same reasons
which applied to worldly men, and partly for others peculiar
to themselves. The spiritual life is greatly a matter of exterior
motives and interior combats. Now we can know only the
outside; faults are plainer to see than virtues. One sin does
not make a habit, perhaps not even many. Falls may be surprises, or they may be violences. Old manners often remain
after inward conversion, just as strong scents linger in jars
and bottles. God leads men so differently that there are almost as many diversities in the spiritual life as there are human
faces and features in the world. To know a man's progress
we must know his besetting sin, and we do not know it. It
is not always the amount of grace given which is the index,
but the proportion of correspondence to what is given. Even
the Saints seem paradoxical; and in one word charity means
breadth, and a charity which is not broad is not charity at
all. There is no one in the world who does not excel us in
some one thing; and charity believes in that one thing against
sight, and conjectures more.

So much for the temptation to presumption. I do not say
I have answered it; for I began by allowing it. But I have
fastened a counterweight to it, which ought to make it slide
easily, and not let it jerk us out of our place. I have now
to meet the other temptation to discouragement, which is based
in a continual, ever-present, depressing thought of the number of the elect. I allow the temptation; I do not think anything can exaggerate its misery, and shall only endeavor to
balance it.

We ought to be less inclined to treat this temptation lightly,
because it comes so frequently from physical temperament
or the present state of health, and those who are most affected
by it are the least to blame, either for bringing it on themselves or idly magnifying it when it has come. The same questions which cast a salutary fear into the lukewarm, tease,
bewilder and sadden the good. If the temptation to think ourselves good because the world is bad may be rather a sin
than a temptation, the temptation to despair because the elect

are so few may be called more a suffering than a temptation.

The way in which this temptation comes about seems to be as follows. In most cases the subject is prepared by indisposition, nervousness, bodily ailments, an accumulation of temporal misfortunes or the oppression of some sadness. Then we begin to calculate our own chances of salvation as nearly as it is in our power to do so, which is foolish; but the attraction to do so at times is irresistible. We put the greatness of the reward, and our own demerits, alongside of each other. We measure our actual practice by the requirements of God's law. We stand by the side of the Saints, and see how tall we are. And what is the inevitable consequence of these processes? Do we look as if we were picked out, or elect? Can anyone possibly think so? The occupations of eternity are to a certain extent revealed to us; should we be happy and our tastes suited in them? Then we get darker and darker as we go along. Are we really in any habitual anxiety about the salvation of our souls? Is the spiritual life in any sense a contest with us? If it is, what are we contesting, and with whom?

Then we are snatched away from ourselves, and borne far off, and put down amid uninhabited mountains by a dark sea, whose angry breakers wake eternal echoes. We are in the midst of the everlasting predestination of the Divine Mind. It is the scene of the first act of God toward ourselves. How immense that act, on any view how potent, and how utterly unknown! The freedom of our will is as clearly uninjured by that act as the clouds are unpolluted by the sunbeam. Nevertheless, how awful is the mere fact that the doom we shall eventually work out for ourselves is known already by Him, who has prepared our place for us. Somewhere in creation a lodging is ready, and is empty. It is ours; but where? Above? Below? He must have an impenetrably exterior mind through which this doubt does not often thrill, like a current of electricity. At first sight and first sound, Scripture seems to speak of the fewness of the elect and of the difficulty of salvation, and what we actually observe among men bears this out. How few promise well for Heaven! The freedom of our own will only adds nervousness to the question. God being the Father He is, there would be more security for us in His absolute sovereignty. But He knows best. He has put our souls into our hands, but He has still mercifully kept them in His own. Free will without grace would be demoniacal despair.

Now, not in answer to, but in palliation of, all this, I shall make two observations. The first is this. If we can know nothing about the future, we can at least know a great deal about the present. In spiritual matters God is pleased to instruct His Church by His Saints, and the Church before canonizing them sets her seal upon their writings. Now the Saints mention seven things, which they call the signs of predestination. This means something more than that they are symptoms of our being at present in a state of grace and on the way of holiness. It means that they are to a certain extent prophecies of the future, not infallibly true but supernaturally hopeful. It means that they are the sort of things to be expected in the elect, and not to be expected in others; things essential to the elect, and which through all the centuries of the Church have distinguished the elect. Hence if we find all, many, or a few of them in ourselves, we are legitimately entitled to proportionate consolation. They are: the imitation of Christ, devotion to Our Blessed Lady, works of mercy, love of prayer, self-distrust, the gift of faith and past mercies from God. We must also bear in mind of all these things that it is not the plenary possession of them which counts with God, and so is a sign of predestination, but the earnest desire of them and the sincere endeavor after them. What wonder the theologian Viva should make the number of the saved so large, and the Saint of Geneva almost doubt if any Catholics were lost?

My second observation is this. We are discussing a temptation of the Catholic spiritual life; and we may keep to what is strictly practical. Consequently we are dispensed from touching on the question of the fewness of the elect out of the whole number of mankind. We have nothing to do with curiosity about the future destinies of heathen and of heretics. I do not want to lose my soul by losing my temper with God because He has not told me how He is going to manage His own creation. Their chances will obviously be regulated by the greatness of the boon which the gift of faith is to the soul. To us there can be no trouble in this. The grave opinions of theologians will teach us all we need either know or to surmise, which is very little. Our business is with the doubt whether few Catholics will be saved, and how far we may reverently take comfort from the indications of God's will in His Holy Word, and in the reasons of theology.

First of all we have St. John's *Vidi turbam magnam,* which sounds in our ears at Sext through the octave of All Saints. "I saw a great multitude, which no man could number, of all nations, and tribes, and people, and tongues, standing before the throne, and in sight of the Lamb, clothed with white robes, and palms in their hands." (*Apoc.* 7:9). Secondly, a Spanish theologian says, we may surely with great reverence suppose that it befits the goodness of God that the number of the elect should equal, or surpass, that of the lost. This would carry the benignant interpretation far beyond what the interests of Catholics only would require; and it certainly seems to involve in obscurity certain words of Our Lord which seem very plain. However it is something to know what so holy and enlightened a man as Da Ponte thought. He must have taken into account the multitude of baptized infants. Thirdly, there may be an analogy between the angels and ourselves; and only a third of them fell, as the *Apocalypse* tells us. Neither is it true that the places in Heaven are only the vacancies left by the angels. There is a huge multitude beside. This nearly all theologians teach; and some have said that as many men will be saved as angels, if not more. Of course these are only opinions. But then our temptation is only an opinion also. It is ours against theirs, and ours only so long as it torments us, for we should be glad to get rid of it, if we could. Fourthly, the glory of Our Lord seems to require that the fruit of His Passion should be very multitudinous. The Holy Innocents are a sample of this. Isaias says of His Passion, "If he shall lay down his life for sin, he shall see a long-lived seed, and the will of the Lord shall be prosperous in his hand. Because his soul hath laboured, he shall see and be filled." (*Is.* 53:10-11). Fifthly, the glory and joy of the Blessed themselves seem to require multitude, especially too as they are arranged in different orders and degrees; and multitude is also suitable to the magnificence of place, as Baruch says, "O Israel, how great is the house of God, and how vast is the place of his possession. It is great, and hath no end; it is high and immense." (*Bar.* 3:24). Sixthly, of the two thieves one was saved, and of the twelve Apostles only one fell. These are all bad arguments, taken simply, but collectively they establish a lawful benignant supposition. Seventhly, Our Lord Himself says, "In my Father's house are many mansions," and then as if He foresaw all our trouble, He adds with deep and sweet significancy, "If it were not so, I would have told you." It was these considerations which led St. Francis de Sales and Viva to the belief that by far the greater number of Catholics would be saved.

We read in the life of St. Philip that in the monastery of Santa Marta, a nun named Scholastica Gazzi went to speak to him at the grate and to lay open to him a thought she had never mentioned to anyone else, which was a conviction that she should be damned. As soon as St. Philip saw her, he said to her, "What are you doing, Scholastica, what are you doing? Paradise is yours." "Nay, Father," replied the nun, "I fear the contrary will be the case: I feel as though I should be damned." "No," answered the Saint, "I tell you that Paradise is yours, and I will prove it to you: tell me, for whom did Christ die?" "For sinners," said she. "Well!" said Philip, "and what are you?" "A sinner," replied the Sister. "Then," concluded the Saint, "Paradise is yours, yours because you repent of your sins." This conclusion restored peace to Sister Scholastica's mind. The temptation left her and never troubled her again; but on the contrary, the words "Paradise is yours, yours," seemed always sounding in her ears. Gentle reader! may St. Philip do the same for you and me!

Now, here is no answer to our temptation; but here is another side to it. Let us pray for the gift of holy and discerning fear. Then let us go on joyously, adding grace to grace, and love to love, and doubt not of our eternity. Heaven will come soon. The temptation is to be impatient because it does not come sooner. Yet as God wills. It shall be our act of love to Him that we wait where we are, and for His sake be content to live. Life is a hardship, but not a very grievous one; for it does not hinder our loving God. And short of that, all griefs can be but light.

Chapter XXII

THE TRUE IDEA OF DEVOTION

Devotion is a word which has a great many meanings, and it is unfortunately seldom used in the right one. Sometimes it is used to express a part of itself instead of the whole, sometimes one or other of its accidents, sometimes one of its kinds, sometimes one of its characteristics, and sometimes its effects, as its sweetness, beauty and heroism. But it is useless to appeal to etymology, or to fight about words. The substance is to have a right idea of the thing intended to be conveyed. To point out some of the mistakes of ordinary conversation will be a step toward this.

We say that a person gives too much time to devotion, and not enough to his worldly affairs or works of charity. Here by devotion we obviously mean prayer. We say that a man is too devout; and here by devotion we understand the acts which concern the direct worship of God. When we talk of having had a great deal of devotion at a certain church, or on a certain feast, we mean by the word spiritual sweetness. Or a thing is devout which inspires us with serious feelings, or is in good religious taste. We often use the word for recollection, for much church-going and the like. There is a truth and a meaning in all these expressions, and it is useless to quarrel with them. But they have not unfrequently done harm by making the true idea of devotion less clear. One fact all this shows, that as the word has fastened itself to so many holy practices and clothed itself in so many respectable significations, the thing must be of no inconsiderable importance. Indeed, to the misunderstanding of it much that is unreal, sentimental, fickle and exaggerated in spiritual persons, is to be attributed.

295

In theology, devotion means a particular propension of the soul to God, whereby it devotes itself, commits itself, binds itself over, consecrates itself to the worship and service of God. This it may do by vow, by oath, or by simple sentiment. Thus an author, who once passed under the name of St. Augustine, says that devotion is the action of turning ourselves toward God with a humble and pious affection; humble because of the consciousness of our own weakness, and pious because of our trust in the divine compassion. But St. Thomas more accurately as well as more clearly defines it as the will to do promptly whatever belongs to the service of God, and as Valentia warns us, it is not to be confounded with fervor, no uncommon mistake. St. Francis de Sales defines it to be a kind of charity by which we not only do good, but do it carefully, frequently and promptly. It falls under the virtue of religion. Directly, it is an act of the will, implying indirectly an act of the understanding which excites the will. Its cause is extrinsic, namely, God Himself, acting through intrinsic grace. St. Francis de Sales remarks that, though a kind of love, it is something more than the love of God; and that "something more" is a certain vivacity in doing what the love of God would have us do. Perhaps I may then be permitted to call devotion spiritual agility, which seems to express what St. Thomas and St. Francis say.

Thus it appears that devotion is a very grave, solid, hard-headed, stout-willed, businesslike affair, and not at all the sweet, fervid, heroic, graceful, tender thing it is often taken for. It is well when it has all the qualities these latter epithets imply. But when they are there, they add something to it, and do not express merely its own nature. If it did not sound like a play upon words, I would say that it is desirable we should have a more theological and a less devotional idea of devotion than we commonly have.

Theologians go on to divide devotion into substantial and accidental, and accidental they subdivide again into accidental spiritual, and accidental sensible. Substantial devotion is that intelligent promptitude of the will to serve God, which rests on no attraction of the imagination or sweetness of the affections, but on the principles of the Faith, and fixes the soul

in a solid resolution to serve God, under whatever circumstances. Without this substantial devotion no other is worth
anything, no other is enduring, no other is a reasonable service. Next to the gift of faith we should prize nothing so much
as this substantial devotion. Accidental spiritual devotion is
in reality only a state of substantial devotion, to which God
is mercifully pleased to add His gift of sweetness. A certain
recreation, corroboration, comfort of spirit, flows from Him
into us and rests in our spirit without at all descending to
the sensitive part of our nature. This adds to the agility of
substantial devotion, and gives it more force to overcome
difficulties, and a certain kind of pleasure in overcoming them.
Accidental sensible devotion is a state of substantial devotion,
and also of accidental spiritual devotion, wherein God condescends still further to our infirmities or needs, and lavishes
upon us still more sensibly the caresses of His love, by allowing His sweetness not only to inundate our spirits, but also
to flow down into our sensitive appetites, and sometimes into
our very flesh and blood. Hence it follows that there are two
kinds of dryness and desolation: desolation of spirit, which
consists in the privation of accidental spiritual devotion, and
leaves us in the state of bare substantial devotion; and desolation of sense, which consists in the privation of accidental
sensible devotion, and stays the divine sweetness in the upper
parts of our nature, as Our Blessed Lord cut off the waters
of His divinity from the lower parts of His soul in the Garden
of Gethsemane.

It is thus of great importance to distinguish the effects of
devotion from devotion itself; and St. Thomas helps us to
do this in a very simple and clear manner. The school of
St. Thomas is always speaking of "light" and "understanding"; these are in his teachings what "will" and "affections"
are in the school of Scotus. So here he says that devotion
causes a light in the soul, and that the effects of this light
vary according to the objects on which it falls. If it brings
the beauty of God close to the soul so that it has a certain
enjoyment of Him, the result is joy and gladness. If it shows
God far off, beyond the reach of our nothingness and the
attainment of our weak desires, then it causes the pain, not

altogether painful, of desire and spiritual anxiety. If it shows us our own sinfulness and vileness, the result is a gracious sorrow and holy affliction.

Putting this doctrine of the Angelic Doctor before our eyes, how strange must seem the delusions of those who are perpetually seeking devotion where it is not to be found, and perpetually lamenting the absence of one of its merest accidents and adjuncts, as if the soul had fallen off from God altogether. Many seek it in sweetnesses, which are simply God's gratuitous favors, and which nothing would be less likely to merit than a greediness to have them. Many look for it in freedom from temptations, which may be either a displeased condescension to our slow convalescence from sin, or a withdrawal of the materials of merit because we have been found unworthy of perfection, or an engrossing concentration of the human spirit in some temporary occupation, or a stratagem of Satan for purposes he will hereafter disclose. Some seek it in a multitude of practices, as if a man's strength consisted in the multitude of things he had to do, and not rather that he could do a multitude of things because he was strong: and what if the multitude of things should break his back? Some are so foolish as to seek it in a sensible love of images and pictures, which is like asking matter to have the goodness to make mind spiritual, a thing which a man might not say even of the wonderful Sacraments themselves. This mistake first weakens the head, secondly turns us unreal, and thirdly makes us foolish. Some seek devotion in vehement resolutions. There is little good to be found in vehemence of any kind in the spiritual life. And this amounts to confounding the intention to be virtuous with the actual possession of the virtue itself, to which it is but a help. Some seek it in continually increasing austerities. But it is not the invariable reward even of these. They often make a heart still harder, whose want of tenderness is the true cause of its want of devotion. I distrust all austerities done for a purpose. They should only be the twofold expression of love desiring at once to take vengeance upon self and to imitate her mortified Redeemer. Some seek devotion in sighs and tears, when these sighs and tears themselves must have come out of devotion, and be its outside

accidents, to be themselves worth anything at all. Some place
it in violent contrition. But contrition is a calm, intelligent,
sorrowful purpose, so far as our side goes; its violence and
intensity are the gifts of God. Some even place it in an ability
to echo the hot and fervent words of others, forgetting first
that there is hardly any state of feeling to which we cannot
work ourselves up if we please, and secondly, that there is
no feeling which we cannot deceive ourselves into believing
we feel. Yet what baseless fabrics of radiant devotion often
rest on this treacherous chasm! And lastly some think it consists in discerning what God is actually doing in our souls.
But to see our own devotion is only to know we have got
it, not to cause it. Here are ten delusions which fade away
in the plain light of St. Thomas and his doctrine.

We have already seen in what devotion consists, but how
are we to know it? What are its infallible signs, its invariable
concomitants, if these things are not? It is known by the strong
practical will, which without relying upon itself puts forth
every effort, and does not spare itself. It is known by a promptitude or agility of action which fears no kind of work and
limits itself to no degree, which has no reserves with God,
and does not stipulate for its reward. Perseverance shows it;
for God's favors are meant to be transient, and man's delusions are showy and deceitful, while substantial devotion alone
endures. It shows itself in suffering and self-violence; for though
other things have the spirit to attempt great deeds, devotion
alone can carry them through. It is manifest in the sanctification of our ordinary actions, a grace which has this privilege,
that no delusion can counterfeit it with success. It shows itself
in unselfishness and the renunciation of our own interests,
whereas all its spurious imitations seek self only, under a more
or less palpable disguise. In speaking of its signs, however,
we must remember that substantial devotion is an essentially
inferior thing; and many consequences flow from this one
truth. Moreover it is a habit, and habits do not commonly
become sensible except in acts. It is the doing of the act which
makes substantial devotion apparent, and the sweetness accompanying the doing of it which makes devotion sensible.

What then, it may be asked, are Special Devotions, and

how do they fit in with that has been said of devotion in general? I must repeat somewhat, in order to make this plain. Devotion is a devoting of ourselves to God, a loving promptitude of the will in all that concerns His worship and service, a spiritual agility. It is this which renders all acts of virtue acceptable and meritorious; for it is the hand wherewith grace touches them. It is caused extrinsically by God, intrinsically by meditation; and the effects of it are joy, tenderness, softness of heart and delighted peace. Hence a tender devotion is the characteristic of the Gospel. But as substantial devotion rests on the principles of faith, all forms of heresy lose tenderness, as anyone may see who is acquainted with their history, or has compared the mysticism outside the Church with the mysticism within it. Tenderness in devotion is necessarily orthodox.

Now devotion is a practical acting out of a belief in spiritual things and in an unseen world; and Christianity is a worship not of things, but of Divine Persons, disclosing themselves to us in certain mysteries, which are for the most part mysteries of sorrow and suffering. Thus the Infancy and Passion of Our Lord, the Blessed Eucharist, the dolors of Our Lady, the acts of the Martyrs, are things especially calculated to win and soften. This was the character Our Lord intended to give to His religion; and He made every circumstance of the Incarnation and every feature of the Church contribute to this unexampled and celestial pathos. Every such mystery, circumstance, and feature becomes in its degree the object of a special devotion.

Every man who is a friend of God is in a state of habitual or Sanctifying Grace, in which his friendship with his Creator consists. Upon this habitual grace God is endlessly sending down the impulses of His actual grace, illustrating the understanding, as I believe, in every circumstance of life, and not merely rarely and on great occasions. In addition to these two kinds of grace, every baptized person has infused into his soul seven supernatural gifts of the Holy Ghost. These gifts St. Thomas defines to be certain habits by which a man is enabled promptly to obey the Holy Ghost, and St. Bonaventure, habits disposing a man to follow the instinct of the Holy

Ghost. These gifts lie in the soul as keys of an instrument
on which no one is playing. They are passive, habitual and
form a state, just as Sanctifying Grace does. They are played
upon according to the needs of our spiritual life by what are
called the actual impulses of the Holy Ghost, and which correspond in their subject-matter to actual grace, standing in
the same relation to the habitual gifts as it does to habitual
grace.

Of these gifts, four belong to the intellect: Wisdom, Understanding, Science and Counsel; and three to the will: Fortitude, Piety and Fear. Tender devotion is the fruit of the gift
of Piety, which may be defined to be the divine ray that il-
luminates the mind, and bends the heart to worship God as
our most loving Father, and to help our neighbor as His image.
But tenderness of its own nature *specializes,* that is, it singles
out an object and magnifies it, and for the time excludes other
objects from its loving attention. Thus it always comes to pass
that there is a dash of exaggeration in Special Devotions, which
makes it the more needful that devotion should be orthodox,
and take heed to the analogy of faith. They must be exclusive
in order to be special, and what is exclusive has a tendency
to be exaggerated. It may almost be said that the Incarnation,
which is a galaxy of tender mysteries, involves special devotions in its very idea, and that the gift of piety is the telescope
by which we resolve this galaxy into clusters of constellations
or into single stars. Different devotions are connected with
different virtues, and have special gifts for the attainment of
those most congenial to their own spirit. The Holy Ghost also
leads different souls, either by natural character or supernatural attraction, to different devotions, and gives them various
lights upon them. Thus we have special devotions, and special
saints to further them, to Our Lord's Infancy, His Boyhood,
His Active Life, His Passion, His Wounds, His Cross, His
Risen Life, His Precious Blood, and His Sacred Heart, to
His Mother, His Angels, His Apostles, and the various orders
of His Saints. The unity of our faith hinders the one-sidedness
of our special devotions, and the devotions of all the children
of the Church may be considered as one, full, harmonious,
and for humanity, adequate worship of the most Holy Trinity,

made co-equal to the infinitude of the Divine Majesty, by the worship of the Word made Flesh.

Such is the account to be given of Special Devotions, which are as it were developments of the worship of the Sacred Humanity of the Eternal Word. They are essentially doctrinal devotions, and therefore we should always jealously ascertain that they have had the approval of the Church. But, say some, they change and grow, and this is a difficulty. Certainly; let us see what is to be said in answer to it. I will take the case of devotion to Our Blessed Lady as affording the greatest difficulty, as well as the one for many reasons the most likely to be felt.

It must be admitted then that devotions grow. History is too clear to allow of a case being made out on the other side. If devotion were not grounded on dogma, it would be unreal. We have no business to be devoted to an untrue thing or a fanciful mystery. It would not however follow that because devotions grow, dogma grows. The two propositions are distinct. It is of faith that Our Lord lived a given number of years upon the earth, which were spent in such and such a way. This fact cannot grow out of it. No one can fix a limit to them. It is of course true that each additional definition soon becomes the basis of special devotions; because definition makes the truth plainer and surer to the eye of love, and devotions have a marked partiality for articles of faith. The mind and the heart of the Church, her doctors and her people work and move together; so that devotions almost always represent the turn theology is taking in their day. Sometimes they run ahead of the schools; sometimes the schools run ahead of them. The schools and the people are next found very far apart. The history of the doctrine and devotion of the Immaculate Conception is an illustration of this; while the rise of the devotion to St. Joseph is quite a singular phenomenon in the history of devotions, because it does not seem to have followed this rule.

Now the Church is pre-eminently a soul-saving institution; and doctrine has as much to do with the saving of souls as Sacraments, jurisdiction, discipline, hierarchy and ceremonies, or perhaps even more; and devotions are the application

of doctrine to the souls of the people. We must not lose sight
of the livingness of the Church. If we do, then the growth
of devotions becomes a serious difficulty, and the art of print-
ing would have done as well as a pope. But the Church is
a living soul-saver; and as soul-saving consists, not only in
bidding souls come to her to be saved, but much more in
following them into the wilderness whither they have wandered, the Church is, to a certain extent, dependent upon the
vagaries of the world for her movements. So that variety,
change, adaptation and growth were to be beforehand expected
of her, and are not only not contrary to her unity, but actually
fruits of it. A man is not always in one place because he
is a soldier, but rather because he is a soldier he is succes-
sively in many places serving his country. He follows his
enemy; the Church follows hers, to get back the plundered
souls. The history of Canonical Penances and Indulgences is
an example of this. It also explains the Church's apparent copying of the world, from time to time; though it is always after
a fashion of her own. Her conduct at the time of the Renais-
sance is an illustration of it. This sort of adaptation of the
soul-saving Church to the circumstances in which in every
age she finds herself is effected by the Holy Ghost, who dwells
in her, through the medium of the Popes, the Saints of the
day and the spirit either of old orders who have kept their
fervor, or new ones which He raises up to meet the exigencies
of the times.

The earliest Special Devotion, with a modern look about
it, seems to have been to the holy angels, which fills the acts
of the Martyrs; and St. Gregory's dialogues both represented
the devotions of his day and propagated them to future times,
especially devotion to the souls in Purgatory. Devotions seem
to have become much more numerous when pilgrimages began
to be disused, and to have multiplied proportionately with
the liberality of the Church in granting indulgences. Moreover, as the European mind became more subjective, the reign
of mental prayer was spread; and he must think strangely either
of the copiousness of divine mysteries or of the power of human
contemplation, who should be surprised that eighteen hundred years' meditation on the mystery of the Incarnation has

contributed, and is forever contributing, art and poetry and devotion to the Christian Church.

The whole history of the worship of the Blessed Sacrament is a commentary on this. The same may be said of the Sacred Heart. St. Gertrude asked in vision why there was no special devotion to the Sacred Heart, and St. John answered her that its time was not yet come. It came at last, through Margaret Mary Alacoque and the Visitation. The devotion to the Interior Life of Jesus arose in France, and was part of a reform of the secular clergy. The devotion of the Precious Blood seems to have begun with St. Catherine of Siena, and took a definite shape at Ferrara. That to the Immaculate Heart of Mary was French. That of St. Joseph began among the bachelors of Avignon. That of St. John received a great development in the spirit of St. Sulpice. The Name of Jesus was a Franciscan devotion. The Month of Mary was unknown even to St. Alphonsus Liguori. Yet, when we say that devotions began at such a place or with such a person, we are speaking only of the date of their taking visible shape and consistency. There were always preludes of them in the Fathers and the Saints. This is especially the case with the devotion of the Sacred Heart.

Meanwhile the Church is not taken unawares by any of these things. Rather it is she who gives them out as part of her own life. Thus when the feast of the Eternal Father was asked for in France, Benedict XIV gives at length the reasons why the Church was jealous of this devotion; and the reasons are exclusively doctrinal. The devotion of the Slavery of Mary was condemned also as unsafe in doctrine. The devotion to Our Lady in the Blessed Sacrament, though seemingly countenanced by St. Ignatius, met with the same fate. The difficulties experienced by Juliana of Retinue in the case of the Blessed Sacrament, by the Venerable Margaret Mary in the case of the Sacred Heart, and by St. Bernardino of Siena with his new devotion to the Name of Jesus, show how jealously and sagaciously the Church watches, and curbs, and tests, and ballasts new devotion, or new expressions of an old devotion.

So it is with devotion to Our Blessed Lady. As Scripture says, she was to take root in an honorable people; and taking root is a work of time. Saints have **rooted her,** councils have rooted her, universities have rooted her, monastic orders have rooted her, schools of theology have rooted her, the eventful vicissitudes and personal homage of popes have rooted her. Pius VII at Savona is repeated in Pius IX at Gaeta. As the world got used to the mystery of the Incarnation, it hardened its heart to its tenderness; and this devotion, which is the very spirit of Jesus, breathed over it, like the moist, warm south wind over the garden of spices. The Church has worked it up inextricably into her whole system. God has sanctioned it by revelations, visions and miracles. Even in the weary, thankless, dusty toil of today, we are greeted by Rimini, and refreshed by La Salette. The actual fruits of sanctity in the nineteenth century illuminate the devotion which was the subject of prophecy at the end of the first century in the inspired *Apocalypse*. We cease to envy those who heard Mary proclaimed Mother of God at Ephesus, since we have heard our own Holy Father of today infallibly pronounce her Conceived Immaculate.

But spiritual books often warn us against false devotions. What are these? There are three classes of false devotions: those which are wrong from being too high for the person practicing them, those which are singular and uncommon and those which are too subtle.

Those which are wrong from being too high for the person practicing them come sometimes from the temperament of the person, sometimes from the indiscretion of a director, and sometimes from a strong delusion of the devil. They lead men to force themselves into supernatural states of prayer, and to try to suspend the use of their understanding, and rest passively in God, when they are not called to it by Him. They consist in a wild, unhumble and indiscreet imitation of the Saints. Persons addicted to them disdain common things, affect an interior vocabulary and imitate the grandiloquent language of St. Denys and other mystics. Such persons are not often fond of the writings of St. Theresa. Directors sometimes drive their penitents into these false devotions by too hastily fancying they discern supernatural signs upon them, not sufficiently attending to their advancement in solid virtue, and too readily taking for their full value the descriptions such persons give of their own souls. Such coin must not pass current for a twentieth part of its nominal value.

Other devotions are false by being singular, uncommon, or grotesque. Some souls look with disrelish over a whole host of common devotions, such as the multitude of pious Catholics practice, and with a sort of diseased instinct fasten upon some startling act or word of a saint, which was either really a mistake on his part or a special impulse of the Holy Ghost, and they will proceed to found upon it at once some peculiar and odd devotion of their own. There have been instances of persons whose whole prayers have been to request God to retire from them and keep Himself in His own grandeur, which they founded on St. Peter's words, Depart from me, O Lord! for I am a sinful man. Yet these people ought rather to have been climbing up sycamore trees with Zaccheus, to get a nearer view of Jesus. Devotions founded upon the apocryphal gospels or unrecognized revelations fall under this head; and indeed, everything which is foreign to the common and motherly ways of Holy Church.

Devotions which are false from being too subtle are those which are founded on dubious theological opinions, or on the abstract conceptions of the schools. Such have been certain devotions to the Attributes of God, not very honorable to the Sacred Humanity of Our Lord. They were common among the Quietists; and some may be still found in the works of certain eminent French spiritualists of the school of Bernieres de Louvigny. They generally arise from the activity of the imagination, and often strike us as beautiful at first sight, but without unction in the using. Devotion must be artless, tender, simple, guileless, natural, spontaneous; and how can these things be, when the object of them is obscure, abstract, difficult and subtle? It need hardly be added that all devotions which are false in any of these three ways, are very ruinous to the soul.

But in devotion we have to receive as well as give, to receive more than we give. In truth from first to last it rather seems to be mostly receiving, and little giving. The exercise of devotion finds its chief theater in prayer; and inspirations are God's side of prayer. We must not always be speaking, we must be listening also. We must pause from time to time,

and make all quiet in our hearts, that we may not lose the
heavenly whispers that come floating there. I am not speaking
now of extraordinary mystical colloquies, but of what will
pass in the souls of all recollected men at prayer. As soon,
says St. Gregory, as an inspiration touches our soul, it ele-
vates it above itself, represses the thoughts of temporal things,
and quickens the desire of things eternal, so that it is delighted
with heavenly things only, and weary of earthly; and such
a height of perfection does it communicate to the soul, that
it likens it to the Holy Ghost; for, as Scripture says, What
is born of the Spirit is spirit. These inspirations are the actual
impulses of the Holy Ghost of which I spoke before; and
they may be called the very necessaries of life to those who
are aiming at perfection. They are wanting them nearly all
the day long; for as it is by habitual and actual grace that
we live the life of grace, obeying the Commandments of God
and the precepts of the Church, so it is by the habitual gifts
of the Holy Ghost and His actual impulses and inspirations,
superadded to grace, that we live the lives of perfect men
and of ascetics who are training for perfection. These inspirations are not chance things, or rare, or what are technically
called spiritual favors. We must beware of confounding them
with these. They are our daily bread. They are to perfection,
what grace is to virtue. They flow into us, whether we hear
and feel them or not, in an almost unintermitting stream. Before we gave ourselves up to God without reserve we had
them frequently, more frequently than sinners, who nevertheless have them very often in right of their Baptism; but now
they flow into us in an unintermitting stream. One great mystical theologian calls the gifts of the Holy Ghost the seven
sails of the soul, in which it catches the various breezes of
inspiration, and so navigates the sea of perfection.

The first thing then to be observed about these inspirations
is what St. Thomas tells us, that all the just have a right to
ask for them and to expect them, because of that first infusion
of the Seven Gifts at Baptism, which were communicated to
them simply to make them capable of obeying and quick to
obey these very inspirations; and that we should especially
ask for them when we are attempting the more perfect ways

either of the active or contemplative life. This involves on
our part continual prayer for them, a habit of listening for
them, and an obligation, to be discreetly ascertained, to obey
them. The second important observation to make is that we
ourselves cannot fix the time, place, exercise or occasions
of these inspirations. They depend simply on the will of the
everblessed Giver, the Holy Spirit Himself. "Dost thou know,"
said the Lord to Job, "by what way the light is spread, and
the heat divided upon the earth?" He bloweth where He willeth,
and chooses His own occasions. Thus no vehemence of our
own, no straining of our inward ear, will bring us these inspirations. We must be careful that our listening in prayer does
not become idleness, or degenerate into a quietude to which
we are not called. We must not put out force; that will only
delay the Holy Spirit. We must use patience, and wait; and
patience will accelerate His coming. Nevertheless, which is
the third thing to be observed, there are certain places where
He is wont to come, and therefore where it is wisest to wait.
St. Gregory, in his *Morals*, has given us the whole theology
of inspirations so fully, and with so much system and completeness, that later writers seem to have added nothing to
him. He calls these means of communication which the Holy
Ghost vouchsafes to use, the veins of the whisper of God,
like the veins of water which irrigate the earth, and the veins
which distribute in all our members the blood of life. He
numbers among them prayer, the Word of God, sermons,
spiritual reading, and all the exercises of the contemplative
life. But the richest veins of all are the Sacrifice of the Mass
and the Sacrament of the Altar; and thus the likeliest time
and place for these inspirations to come are indicated to us.

But there are four sources of these inspirations: though indirectly they are of course all from God. The first source
is God Himself, acting directly upon the soul, as in the inspirations of which I have been speaking. The second source
is our guardian angel; the third, conscience; and the fourth,
love. Of the inspirations which come direct from God, I have
already spoken. Scripture speaks of our guardian angel as
a fountain of holy inspirations; and indeed, we could hardly
conceive so inseparable a companion, and so loving and

efficacious a guide as our guardian angel, not frequently communicating his mind to ours, when we are so often made to feel against our wills the impressions of the minds of devils in our almost daily temptations. Thus God says to Moses: Behold, I will send My angel, who shall go before thee, and keep thee in thy journey, and bring thee into the place that I have prepared. Take notice of him, and hear his voice, and do not think him one to be contemned; for he will not forgive when thou hast sinned, and My Name is in him. (*Ex.* 23). So Zacharias says: The angel that spoke in me came again, and he waked me, as a man that is wakened out of his sleep. And I answered and said to the angel that spoke in me, saying, What are these things, my Lord? And the angel that spoke in me answered, and said to me, Knowest thou not what these things are? And I said, No, my lord. And he answered and spoke to me, saying. . .Then presently after the vision changes, and the prophet says, The word of the Lord came to me. (*Zach.* 4). So when Elias fled from Jezabel, the angel of the Lord awoke him as he slept under a juniper, and spoke to him and fed him, and gave him directions to go to Horeb, and when there, not the angel, but God Himself spoke to him. So that the cases of Elias and Zacharias not only established the office of the angel, but also its relation to the direct inspirations of God.

Oh, with what care, says St. Bernard, quoted by Da Ponte, and with what gladness, the angels join themselves to those who sing psalms, assist those who pray, remain with those who meditate, accompany those who contemplate, and preside over those who are occupied in active business! For these supernal powers recognize their future fellow citizens, and therefore, with all solicitude, cooperate with those who are to receive the heavenly inheritance. They rejoice with them, comfort them, guard them, foresee and provide for them, that is for ourselves. Finally, they inspire us to pray, and mortify ourselves, to sing psalms, and to beat our cymbals, for our bodies which we macerate are our cymbals, that God may be pleased with the music of prayer, mingled with the music of mortification. If sleep invades us in these exercises, they arouse us, and say, Arise and hasten, for the active life is a long journey still before you, and the contemplative life still longer, if at least you are to go from virtue to virtue, and see the God of Gods in Sion, who will recreate your spirit, and speak to your heart, and unite you with Himself by the thin, sweet whisper of His inspirations. O lofty angel! adds Da Ponte, whose impulses help me so much to receive these sweet inspirations, assist me always, rouse me from my torpor, animate my confidence, supply my infirmity, so that with thee for my companion, I may promptly walk the ways of mortification and prayer, until I come to the mountain of God, where I may see Him, and enjoy Him in His glory.[1]

The third fountain of inspirations is our own conscience. Its office is to tell us what to pursue, and to warn us what to avoid, and to incline our will as well as illuminate our understanding. Fallen as we are, St. Thomas says that the virtues are natural to us, and in a certain way conformable to the natural propensions of our spirit. The inspirations of conscience call these propensions into play, actively discerning them from under the law of sin, the sting of the flesh, and the buffeting angel of Satan, by which they are overlaid. Its office, says Origen, is to call the house, never to sleep, always to be preaching, and to sit like a pedagogue in the upper chambers of our soul, and give orders. But its inspirations are not only suggestive before action, but when need requires, reproachful afterwards. It is, in fact, the good side of the human spirit, and claims obedience by divine right.

The fourth fountain of inspirations is the stimulus of love. The charity of Christ urgeth us, saith the Apostle. It is of the very nature of love to quicken our perceptions of what the object of our love requires. Its docility is equal to its quickness. An eye can command it without a word, and a smile can sufficiently reward it. It is essentially inventive, full of affectionate wiles, divining unexpressed desires, prophesying the future, and thoroughly alive to every feature of the present. When it sleeps, its heart waketh. So that what with its sensitiveness, and what with its delicacy, and what with its

---

1. *Dux Spiritualis.* Tract 1, cap. xxi., sect. 2. I quote from the Latin translation of Trevinnius, not possessing the Spanish.

contagious nearness to God Himself, it is an independent fountain of inspirations, which, as human, are often marred by indiscretion and extravagance, yet nevertheless, with caution and counsel, are great helps to perfection. All these four kinds of inspiration are, according to their several degrees, entitled to our obedience. They form as it were the rule under which we live, filling the places of superior and subordinate superiors, according to the order and harmony which is in all the works of God, and nowhere more than in the subordinations of the interior life.

As in the matter of devotion it is important to distinguish between inspirations and spiritual favors, one being of the common, the other of the uncommon order, so is it also important to distinguish between tenderness and spiritual sweetness, the former being of the common, the latter of the uncommon order. These distinctions are often overlooked, which leads not only to our having unclear ideas in our own mind, but to our misunderstanding and misapplying spiritual books. Tenderness is the Christian feature of devotion. I am not saying we are not to seek for spiritual sweetness: that is the question for the next chapter to consider; but we must by all means pray for the impulses of the gift of piety, and for our inspirations to play upon that gift, because tenderness is quite an essential in Catholic devotion. We must pray for tenderness as we pray for grace. We must claim it as we claim the spirit of prayer. It belongs to us, not as one of the unusual phenomena of the Saints, but as something without which we can neither pray, confess, nor communicate as we ought to do.

I cannot illustrate my meaning better, nor bring the mind of the Church more forcibly before you, than by speaking of what is called in theology the gift of tears. I am sure most persons will think that, although it is a great and good thing to have this gift, yet it would not come natural to ask for it. But in the collection of collects in the Missal, a set, and those among the most beautiful, are to ask the gift of tears, which is the chosen symbol of tenderness. They are as follows: "Almighty and most merciful God, Who didst draw from the rock a fountain of living water for Thy thirsting people, draw from the hardness of our hearts the tears of compunction, that we may be able to bewail our sins, and through Thy mercy merit their remission. We beseech Thee, O Lord God, propitiously to look upon this oblation, and draw from our eyes the rivers of tears which may extinguish the fury of the fires we have deserved. O Lord God, mercifully pour into our hearts the grace of the Holy Spirit, which may enable us to wash away our sins with the plaintiveness of our tears, and through Thy bounty obtain the fruit of the indulgence we desire." It is our duty, says St. Gregory, in the third book of his *Dialogues,* to implore of our Creator with profoundest plaints the gift of tears; and the *Catechism of the Council of Trent,* speaking of contrition, says that tears ought to be desired and sought for with the greatest care. There can hardly be a doubt then about the mind of the Church.

In accordance therefore with her wish, spiritual theologians have treated systematically of this gift of tears. They have divided tears into four kinds: natural, diabolical, human, and divine. Natural tears are those which proceed from constitution, temperament, age, sex, and the like causes. God, says one writer, has made His tears to rain both upon the just and the unjust, that they may use them or not for the good of their souls. Such tears have no character, either for good or evil; and those who have them not, need not be cast down; for the physical expression, though sweet and helpful, is but the outward manifestation of the inward tenderness. Diabolical tears are caused by the devil acting through our minds on our physical temperament. Such were the tears of Ismahel, the son of Nathanias, of whom Jeremias speaks; and those also of which Ecclesiasticus says, An enemy weepeth with his eyes; but if he find an opportunity, he will not be satisfied with blood. An enemy hath tears in his eyes; and while he pretendeth to help thee, will undermine thy feet. Such also are the tears of hypocrites, who make themselves appear sad to the eyes of men; and mystical theologians remark that heretics have often had a diabolical gift of tears, in order that they may mistake this physical softness of heart for the tenderness of devotion, and so not find out that they have gone astray from the true road of interior piety, and that those whom they delude, women especially, may fancy their leaders are saints, and that where they are, the Church must be also. Human tears are those which flow from the human spirit. Tears at the loss of temporal goods, at the breaking of earthly attachments, or at moving narratives and pathetic incidents, these are all human. Such were the tears of Esau, when, as the Apostle says, he found no place for penance though he sought it with tears, because it was the loss of the temporal benediction, not of the spiritual promises, for which he wept. St. Jerome says that these tears are signified by Micheas, under the names of the wailing of dragon and the mourning of ostriches. It is plain that they are not holy in themselves, and many of them nothing can sanctify, because an evil motive corrupts them. But who would say that the mother's tears for her only son departing to the horrors of the Crimea, or the long, silent streams of the soldier's widow, fructify not in their souls with the fruits of eternal life? Surely, in the good, they are a kind of prayer.

The tears which are from the Holy Spirit, and which we mean properly by the gift of tears, are like those of Tobias, to whom St. Raphael said, When thou didst pray with tears, I offered thy prayer to the Lord; or those of Ezechias, to whom God said, I heard thy prayer, and I saw thy tears; and those of Our Blessed Lord, of whom St. Paul says, that in the days of His Flesh, He offered up prayers and supplications, with a strong cry and tears, and was heard for His reverence. They come from those unutterable plaints with which the Holy Ghost is making intercession in our hearts; and it is their characteristic to clear the mind and not to trouble it, to leave the spirit not perturbed, but delightfully and unspeakably serene. Theologians distinguish five degrees of these tears, which are more or less perfect. The first degree consists of those which we shed over human miseries. Even these may be the gift of the Holy Ghost. Such were the tears of Anna, the mother of Samuel, of Tobias, of Sara the daughter of Raguel, and of Judith. The tears of the second degree flow from the consideration of sin, seen in the light of the divine compassions. Such were the tears that David often shed, such those of Magdalen over her Master's feet, such those of Peter, when he rose from his fall. Tears of the third degree flow from the compassion of Jesus, and the meditation of His Passion. Such were the tears of Mary in her dolors. The tears of the fourth degree arise from the desire of seeing God, and the intolerable burden of His absence. Such were the tears of David, which were his bread day and night, while his soul thirsted for the face of the strong and living God; and the tears that Magdalen wept, when she stood weeping at the sepulchre because Jesus was not there. The tears of the fifth degree come from an ardent love of our neighbor, and a supernatural sorrow for his sins and his calamities. Such were the tears that Samuel shed for Saul, and Our Blessed Lord for Lazarus, and over His beautiful, infatuated and dear Jerusalem.

It appears then that these tears are no slight help to holiness; that while they are gratuitous, they are nevertheless to be impetrated; and that it is the mind of the Church that we should ask for them with persevering earnestness. Still while we are anxious, our anxiety is to be moderate, else it will harm us. Our appetite is not to be inordinate, else it is a symptom of disease. We may take complacency in our tears, yet we must not be attached to them. Neither must we pride ourselves upon them; for they are a gift. Still—what think you, is the mind of the Church about inward tenderness, when, so unlike her usual self, she would have us even pray for its exterior and physical manifestation?

Chapter XXIII

THE RIGHT USE OF SPIRITUAL FAVORS

There is no subject on which the ancient and modern traditions of the spiritual life are more apparently at variance, than concerning the right use of spiritual favors. Ancient books bid us seek after them, pray for them, make much of them; while modern books tell us to shrink from them, to be afraid of them, to be nervously cautious when we have them, and to pray rather to be guided by the common way of faith. There is no real discrepancy in this seeming contradiction. It is the same tradition manifesting itself differently under altered circumstances. But I approach the subject with fear and trembling.

Our first duty is to get a clear view of the question. Spiritual favors belong to what may be called the uncommon order. Nevertheless, there are two classes of them. One class consists of the raptures, ecstasies, visions, locutions, touches, wounds, thirsts, stigmata and transformations which belong to the Saints. The second class includes only two things, spiritual sweetnesses and spiritual consolations, which are the frequent and often daily gifts of the middle-class Christians, that is, those who rise above mere precept, and walk by counsels, without entering into the higher mystical world of the Saints. Now with the first class I have nothing whatever to do. Not a word I shall say will allude to them. It may be true that the ecstatic state is, as some theologians say, the natural state of man; that Adam was created in it, and that Our Lord lived in it; and that the supernatural mystical holiness works its way more or less imperfectly back into it. But nothing of this is applicable to the class of souls to whose interests this treatise is devoted.

I am writing, let me repeat it, for persons living in the world, yet nevertheless aiming at perfection and a disinterested love of God. This must be borne in mind throughout, or else much that is said will inevitably be misunderstood or misapplied. If anyone is so bold as to say that perfection of any kind is impossible to seculars, he must consider the treatise a simple mistake from beginning to end. I have no controversy with him, and shall not stay now to prove a truth, in whose favor I have the whole ascetical tradition of spiritual writers and the indubitable facts of many processes of canonization. Such a controversy would be useless and hopeless. For the sake, however, of those whom such wild, inconsiderate doctrine may trouble—and even hold back from a generous love of God—I will quote from the Bollandists an anecdote of St. Catherine of Genoa, while she was living in a Genoese palace and in the state of marriage. One day Fra Domenico de Ponzo, a Franciscan, hearing Catherine speak in a ravishing manner of divine love, either from a desire to try her or from a wish to induce her to embrace the religious state, began to tell her that in the secular state, and with the tie of marriage, the heart had not liberty to love God, and could not love Him so purely as in the religious state. So long as the Friar contented himself with showing the undoubted superiority of the religious over the secular state, Catherine agreed with him, but when he came to limit the love of God possible in the secular state, she rose from her seat with her countenance all on fire, and her eyes sparkling, and said, "If I believe that the habit which you wear, and which it is not in my power to put on, could add the slightest spark to my love, I would snatch it off your shoulders and tear it to pieces. That your renunciation of everything, and your religious state, may enable you to acquire merits far superior to mine, may be true; I let it pass, and congratulate you on your happiness; but you will never make me believe that I cannot love God as perfectly as you. In fact, my love finds nothing to arrest it, and if it did, it would cease to be pure love." Then turning to God, she cried out, "O my Love! who then shall hinder me from loving Thee as much as I please? For that end I have no need of religious profession. Were I in a camp, in the midst of soldiers, I do not see what obstacle there would be to my love!" She then quitted the room, leaving the company in amazement at her heat and energy; and retiring to her own chamber to give free course to the vehemence of her love, she cried out, "O Love! who then can hinder me from loving Thee? If the world, or the state of marriage, or any other thing could hinder my love, how contemptible it would be! But I know that love overturns all obstacles." God was pleased to reward this outburst by speaking an interior word in her soul, assuring her that no state could hinder the perfection of love, and effacing at once the trouble injected into her mind by the temerarious doctrine of Fra Domenico.[1]

I confine myself therefore to the second division of gifts, and whenever I speak of spiritual favors I shall mean only one or both of two things, either spiritual sweetnesses or spiritual consolations, which, though of the uncommon order and gratuitous, are the ordinary gifts not only of the perfect, but of every soul honestly striving after perfection. It is as if they were merited by our having no reserves with God, and followed as a spiritual consequence from generosity, although from various causes they are often withdrawn or suspended.

Spiritual sweetness and spiritual consolation are in reality

---

1. To persons aiming at perfection in the world, I would recommend a little book published by Pelagaud at Lyons, entitled *Pratique de la Vie Interieure a l'usage des gens du monde:* and also *La Vraie Piété au milieu du Monde,* by M. Huguet, a Marist Father, published also at Lyons, by Girard et Josserand. I should also mention old Water Hilton's *Treatise to a Devout Man of Secular Estate,* though it is not easy to procure. Even in the "Scale of Perfection," addressed to a cloistered nun, he says (pp. 21, 22, London edition of 1659), "Worship in thy heart such as lead active lives in the world, and suffer many tribulations and temptations, which thou, sitting in thy house, feelest not of, and they endure very much labor and care, and take much pains for their own and other men's sustenance; and many of them had rather, if they might, serve God as thou dost, in bodily rest and quietness. And nevertheless they, in the midst of their worldly business, avoid many sins, which thou, if thou wert in their state, shouldst fall into; and they do many good deeds which thou canst not do. There is no doubt but many do thus; but which they be thou knowest not; and therefore it's good for thee to worship them all, and set them all in thy heart above thyself as thy betters, and cast thyself down at their feet." It should be remembered that he who wrote thus was a Carthusian.

two different things, though they may be often spoken of together, because they follow the same laws, while they exhibit different phenomena. Alvarez de Paz warns us to keep the distinction in mind. Spiritual sweetness is a grace from God which produces serenity and tranquility, no matter amid what a tumult of passions and temptations it has entered the soul. We see a difficulty before us at which our infirmity recoils, but sweetness at once smooths it away, levelling the hills and filling up the vales, so that we run, like a railroad, on an easy level. A duty lies at our door for which our character has an insurmountable repugnance; but sweetness surmounts the insurmountable, and the repugnance vanishes. When the soul is hard, it softens it, and when it is docile, it renders it tractable. It lasts longer than consolation. It abides out of prayer, even if it comes in it, and it makes us affable to others, while consolation sometimes leaves us with a temptation to irritability. Consolation, on the other hand, is as it were a honey to the palate of the mind. It infuses delight and pleasure rather than peace and tranquility. It attracts the soul to itself, and then floods it with spiritual sensations of the most exquisite delicacy. It is shorter in its duration than sweetness, but more efficacious. It does a greater work in a less time. It belongs especially to prayer; but it does not usually come until we are weaned from the world, as the manna did not fall in the wilderness till the meal of Egypt was consumed. Thus sweetness draws nearer to tenderness in devotion, though distinct from it, while consolation touches more on those high things on which I have said I shall not enter. Both are divine, but sweetness works in a more human way and is less masterful than consolation. Having thus distinguished the two, I shall henceforth speak of them under the common title of spiritual favors; because, as I said before, while they exhibit different phenomena they follow the same laws, and that is sufficient for my present purpose.[1]

---

1. The same distinction is studiously made by Father Graciano de la Madre de Dios, in the second part of his *Dilucidario del Verdadero Espiritu.* Vol. ii. cap. 74. What we should call sweetness he names *ternuras,* tendernesses, and distinguishes them from *alegria espiritual, jubilo, regozijo,* (mirth) *consolaciones, embriaguez* (inebriation), *hartura* (satiety). The subject is also discussed by Padre Fraz Joseph del Espiritu

I shall now make some observations on the following points: first, the office of these spiritual favors; secondly, the fruits of them; thirdly, the necessity of them shown by their effects; fourthly, the signs of them, fifthly, the delay, denial or suspension of them; sixthly, the way to obtain them; seventhly, the right use of them; and eighthly, the apparent discrepancy between ancient and modern books upon the subject. And as I divide for the sake of clearness, so my division will lead me into occasional repetition.

First, let us speak of the office of these spiritual favors. St. Bonaventure sums them all up in five things. They fill the memory with holy thoughts. They give us a vast intelligence of God. They inspire us efficaciously with conformity to His will. They cause reverence and composition of body and outward demeanor. They lead us to delight in hard work, and, if need be, in suffering for God. Another way of looking at the matter is this. If we consider the nature of devotion and our own nature, we shall see that there are in us three impediments to devotion: the infirmity of the flesh, which caused the disciples to sleep in Gethsemane; sensuality, which was the law St. Paul felt warring in his members against the law of Christ; and the necessary cares of life, which he experienced in bearing the solicitudes of all the churches. Now sweetness and consolations, one with another, remove these

Santo, a Portuguese Carmelite, in his *Cadena Mystica Carmelitana. Colac. Pri. Propuesta i. Respuesta v.* The language of the Spanish mystical writers is for the most part more accurate and expressive than that of others. Thus the Italian term *liquefazione* is much less full and expressive for the particular operation of grace which it describes, than the Spanish *derretimiento*, a rapid thaw. *Saliendo assi de si el alma, y como abriendo los poros para atraer assi el bien amado, esta dilatacion, se llama Derretimiento.* As I am quoting Father Gracian's *Dilucidario,* I may mention, as throwing light on what I have said before of the human spirit, his commentary on those words of Eliu in the book of *Job* (cap. 32), where he speaks of his inward fervor "as new wine which wanteth vent, which bursteth the new vessels." He says that when pious persons, and especially beginners, neglect their studies or the duties of their station for devotional exercises, it is a common thing to say that they are under a delusion of the devil; but in reality, he observes, it is simply the infirmity of the human spirit, which is often inculpable, as it is as yet unused to this "divine inebriation"; and they who are harsh and excessive in their condemnation of it run the risk of frightening men away from the spiritual life.

three impediments; and God will either send them to us without any cooperation of our own, or sometimes to reward preceding efforts or present fervor.

Secondly, the fruits of these spiritual favors rapidly make themselves manifest in the soul. The busy, noisy, populous memory, ever like a seething and seditious city, becomes quiet and loyal and attends to its manufactures, and keeps the feasts of Holy Church with an obedient joy. All trains of thought which concern heavenly things display a copiousness and exuberance which they never had before. Meditations are fluent and abundant. The virtues no longer bring forth their actions in pain and travail, but with facility and abundance, and their offspring are rich, beautiful and heroic. There are provinces of temptations always in discontented and smouldering rebellion. But we have a power over them which is new, and which is growing. We have such a facility in difficulties as almost to change the character of the spiritual life; and a union of body and spirit which is as great a revolution as agreement and peace in a divided household. All these seven blessings are the mutations of the Right Hand of the Most High. Even to beginners, God often vouchsafes to give them, not merely as sugar-plums to children, as some writers have strangely said, but to do a real work in their souls and enable them to drive their way through the supernatural difficulties proper to their state. But proficients should ardently desire them, for they fatten prayer; and the perfect can never do without them, as they can never cease augmenting their virtues and rendering the exercise of them pleasant. What is the deathbed itself but an exercise of virtues, so intense as to compress the growth of ten years into an hour? Nay, even in desolations we need them; for it is an axiom in mystical theology that God both desolates and consoles at one and the same moment, and by one and the same process.

Well, therefore, may Alvarez de Paz say: "They err then who do not magnify this spiritual sweetness, and do not thirst for it in prayer, and are not saddened, if it withdraws. They show that they have never learned by experience its manifold utility. For if they had once tasted it, and seen how by its impulse they rather ran than walked, yea and even flew to perfection, they would indeed have esteemed that to be precious which brings with it so great an increase of virtues and purity. When it has possession of the heart even of a beginner and an imperfect man, it elicits actions which are perfect at all points *(omnibus numeris absolutas)*. And if it hides itself from a man who is advanced in virtue and already perfect, he does not know how to do his ordinary actions without multifarious imperfections during that temporary suspension. It is not the sign of a soft-living man, and an effeminate heart or over-delicate spirit, to sigh after this sweetness; but it is the work of a wise and strong man who, recognizing his inborn infirmity, desires that which will enable him to run to God with more speed and with greater agility, and to do greater and more heroic deeds. He whose judgment is otherwise neither knows himself nor has any ardent desire after perfection, nor comprehends the true and solid riches of this sweetness."[1] (*De Inquisitione Pacis*, ii, 3, 2.).

One of the reasons which have induced some spiritual writers to speak discouragingly of consolations is their laying us open to delusion. This of course expresses an undoubted truth of ascetical theology. Yet I will venture to say that the exaggeration, that common bane of spiritual books, into which some writers have fallen, has done far more harm to the souls of readers by the false and unreasonable suspicions it has created, than even a positive delusion of Satan would have done. Nay, this diabolical prudence, to use a common expression of

---

1. This matter is of such great importance, especially so far as regards the connection between spiritual sweetness and the *solidity* of virtue, that I cannot forbear giving a passage from Da Ponte. It is in his life of Marina d'Escobar, and as he is not there professedly treating of the present matter, the passage shows how completely the view given in the text was part of his mind. He is saying that spiritual favors, crosses, and virtues are the triple cord of the spiritual life, which *Ecclesiastes* says is not easily broken. He gives this reason—*Porque à los favores, y regalos sin las cruces, facilmente suele vençer la soberbia, presuncion, y vanagloria; las cruces, y tormentos, sin alivios de regalos, facilment despenan en impaciencia, tedio, y pusilanymidad de espiritu. Las virtudes ein la mezela de essotras dos cosas nunca son solidas, ni fuertes, ni bien probadas, y assi facilmente las vence la pereza, y tibieza del corazon; pero quando todas tres se juntan, hacen una santidad aventajada, y como inopugnable—Vida Meravillosa*, vol. I. Introd. Sec. IV.

ascetics, is itself a delusion of the enemy, and one of his most fatal and most successful stratagems; and spiritual books are his usual ambuscades. Let us take a case of the worst kind, a case in which the consolations have actually been delusions, and let us learn from the Saints, both by example and doctrine, their heavenly sagacity and enlightened moderation. For our example we may take St. Catherine of Bologna, whose consolations for five years were in great measure delusions, and among them were continual apparitions of Our Blessed Lord, as she believed, but which were in reality fictions of Satan. Yet because of humility and obedience, all turned to her good and to her growth in holiness. Nay, she says she "drew great profit" from her delusions.

But a saint's own example is perhaps less to us than a saint's teaching to souls more like our own. Let us listen then to the great Prophetess of Carmel. St. Theresa is explaining the words of the *Pater Noster,* "Lead us not into temptation." She says that those who arrive at perfection do not pray to be delivered from those temptations which consist in sufferings and combats. On the contrary they desire, and pray for, and delight in such trials, as soldiers wish for war, because they know how great is the profit which they will derive from them. "They are never much afraid of open enemies. . . .What they dread, and ought to dread continually, and beg Our Lord to be delivered from, are traitorous enemies, certain demons who transform themselves into angels of light, and come disguised. These are not found out until they have done great harm to the soul: but they keep sucking the very blood, and destroying the virtues, and we are in the very midst of the temptation without knowing it. It is from them that we must pray the Lord to deliver us." Now after the Saint has thus distinctly pointed out the mischief these transfigured demons may do us, mark what follows. "Observe, that there are many ways in which they do injury, and do not think that it is only by making us believe that the false consolations and delights, which they can produce in us, are from God. *This seems to me the least part of the harm which they can do: nay, rather, it may happen that they thereby cause the soul to advance more rapidly; for with the bait of these consolations it continues*

*more hours in prayer; and not knowing that they come from
the devil, and seeing itself unworthy of such delights, it will
never cease giving thanks to God; it will feel under greater
obligations to serve Him, and it will make more efforts to
dispose itself in order that it may receive still greater favors
from Our Lord, since it believes that they proceed from His
hand.* Always follow after humility. Keep in view that you
are unworthy of these favors, and strive not after them. If
this is done, in my opinion the devil loses in this way many
souls whom he hopes to ruin, and the Lord brings our good
out of the evil which Satan endeavors to do us. For His Majesty looks to our intention, which is to please and serve Him,
when we are with Him in prayer; and the Lord is faithful.
It is right to walk carefully, that there may be no flaw in
humility through some vainglory, and to entreat Our Lord
to deliver you in this peril. Fear not, my daughters, that His
Majesty will allow you to receive many consolations from
anyone but Himself."[1]

So in a like spirit St. Teresa says that it is a false humility
to reject from a fear of vainglory the supernatural gifts and
consolations which God bestows on faithful souls in prayer.
For since we see that they are gifts, and that we in no way
deserve them, they only serve to excite in us an intenser love
of the Giver. "It seems to me," she adds, "impossible according to the constitution of our nature for anyone to have courage for great undertakings, who does not perceive that he
is favored by God. For we are so miserable and so inclined
to things of the earth that we shall be ill able to abhor in
very deed and with great detachment all things here below,
unless we see that we have some pledge from above: since
it is with these gifts that the Lord bestows on us the strength
which we lost by our sins. It will be a hard matter, too, for

---

1. The Saint's words in the passage in italic are as follows: *Este me parece
el menos dano en parte que ellos pueden hacer, antes podrá ser que
con esto hagan caminar mas apriesa, porque cebados de aquel gusto,
están mas horas en la oracion; y como ellos están ignorantes que es
el demonio, y como se ven indignos de aquellos regalos, no acabarán
de dar gracias á Dios: quedaran mas obligados á servirle: esforzarse
han á disponerse, para que les haga mas mercedes el Senor, pensando
son de su mano. (Camino de Perfection.* Cap. xxxviii.).*

us to desire to be held in displeasure and abhorrence by all, as well as to aim at all the other great virtues which the perfect possess, if we have not some pledge of the love which God bears us, and with it a lively faith. For we are by nature so dead that we follow after what we see before us, and hence, these very favors are the means of arousing our faith and of strengthening it. Perhaps, indeed, it is I who am so vile, that am judging of others by myself; and there may be persons who need no more than the truth of the Faith in order to perform works of great perfection, whereas I, as I am so miserable, have had need of everything." (*Vida,* cap. x).

Of course we must not run into the other extreme, and offend against the moderation of the Saints, on the subject of these sweetnesses and consolations. St. John of the Cross makes the best road to the summit, indeed the only one to the topmost peak, of his Carmel, straight and narrow, the way of pure faith and the absence of sensible consolations. But on the other hand, he gives us another road, tortuous but upward, on which he writes the words science, counsel, sweetness, security, glory; and to this he gives the name of the Way of the Imperfect Spirit, with these two mottoes, "Because I took pains to procure these (consolations) I had less than I should have had if I had ascended by the straight path," and, "I went slower, and gained a less elevation, because I did not take the straight path." From this doctrine what other inference can be drawn than that the highest perfection is in the renunciation of these gifts, but that there is also a perfection which seeks them, and a perfection too by which the tops of Carmel may be scaled? It will be well indeed for most of us if we can mount to perfection at all, even by the less perfect road. But the following passage of St. Theresa will put both sides of the question before us at once, and with a clearness which precludes the necessity of comment.

"It is most worthy of note, and I say it because I know it by experience, that the soul which begins to travel along this way of mental prayer with determination, and can bring itself not to care much or to be much elated or cast down, because these delights and tendernesses are wanting, or because the Lord bestows them, has already accomplished a great part of the journey. There is no fear of such a one turning back, however much he may stumble, because the building is being begun on a firm foundation. For the love of God consists not in having tears, or in these delights and tendernesses, which we desire for the most part on account of the consolation which we receive from them, but in serving Him with justice and strength of mind, and humility. The other seems to me more like receiving and giving nothing ourselves. For poor women, such as me, weak and without strength, there appears to me a suitableness in my being led (as God is now doing with me) by consolations; in order that I may be able to support certain labors which it has pleased His Majesty that I should have: but for the servants of God, men of weight, learning and understanding, whom I see make so much ado because God does not give them devotion, it disgusts me to hear of it. I do not say that they should not accept it, if God gives it them, and esteem it highly, since in that case His Majesty sees that it is suitable: but when they have it not, they should not distress themselves: and they should understand that it is not necessary, inasmuch as His Majesty does not give it, and they should be masters of themselves. Let them believe that it is a fault: I have proved it and seen it. Let them believe that it is an imperfection, and that they are not walking with liberty of spirit, but that they will find themselves weak in what they undertake.

"I do not say this so much for beginners, though I lay such stress upon it, since it is of the greatest importance for them to begin with this liberty and determination: but I say it for others, and they are many, who have begun and never could succeed in finishing: and the reason of this, I believe to be in a great measure that they have not embraced the Cross from the beginning. They are ever in affliction because it seems to them that they are doing nothing; when the understanding ceases to operate, they cannot endure it: and yet perchance this is the very time when the will is growing stout, and acquiring strength, though they perceive it not." (*Vida* c. xi).

Thirdly, emboldened by the doctrine of Alvarez de Paz, I will go on to say that some measure of these spiritual favors is necessary, and that the necessity may be shown by their effects. Can we do without fervor, which it is their special office to produce? Are not copious and tender affections something more than a help to us in prayer? Do we not actually measure our growth in holiness by our facility in the exercise of virtues? Shall we persevere in mortifying ourselves, if we do not at last come to love mortifications? We are full often in absolute need of something more than their own light to be thrown on the truths of faith. Even to preserve reverence, mysteries must sometimes be compelled by pressure to give out the savory taste and the recreating odor they contain. Worldliness is a wide thing with an obstinate life, and it sometimes bursts out even in a devout soul like a devouring conflagration. Nothing can extinguish it but an abundance of spiritual sweetness. A drunken man dares what a sober man will not dare, from a leap out hunting to higher things. So in the spiritual life we have many a leap to take in the darkness of faith, which we never should take were we not inebriated with divine love and the wine of spiritual consolations. Discretion is indispensable to the spiritual life; but the delicacies of it are never found apart from the serenity of spiritual sweetness. This is the reason St. Ignatius tells us never to decide on anything in times of dryness and desolation. Now look at these nine wants. Are they not absolute wants to the spiritual man? And what are their satisfactions but the nine effects of spiritual favors?

If you please, we may look at it in Da Ponte's way. He says that when we give ourselves up to God and aim at perfection, we labor under two necessities. Observe, he calls them necessities. The first is perseverance in prayer, and the second is perseverance in mortification; and he adds that it is quite hopeless for us to dream of persevering in either of them without spiritual favors. According to his doctrine, God shows us this by the very seasons which He usually selects as the times of His visitations, which are times of prayer, times of mortification, times of sorrow, times of dryness and times of distraction. But hear two of the great Fathers of the Church. St. Gregory says, I will go to the mountain of myrrh and the hill of frankincense. What is the mountain of myrrh, but lofty and solid mortification? And what is the hill of frankincense, but great humility and prayer? It is then that the Spouse comes to this mountain and hill, when He familiarly visits those whom He sees striving to mount on high by the mortification of their vices and distractions, and to smell sweetly of pure and lowly prayer. And what comes of this visitation except that the just, like trees of myrrh and frankincense planted on this mountain and hill, distill their precious liqueurs in greater abundance and excellence, while they exercise higher and more fervent affections of mortification and prayer? This is what the soul herself felt when she said, Come, O south wind, blow through my garden, and let the romantical spices thereof flow, that is, the odoriferous dew of the tears which flow from our eyes. By this the soul signified that the visitation of the Holy Ghost, which is represented by the moist and warm south wind, was *necessary (necessaria)* to soften the heart that it might bring forth abundantly the tender affections of devotion, the eye sweet tears, and the hands fervent works. For that visitation is nothing else than the choicest myrrh which drops from the hands of the Spouse. (*St. Gregory in loc.*)

St. Bernard, that saint in whom antiquity so suddenly puts on a modern look, thus describes the unfortunate predicament in which the heart is placed from which these spiritual favors have been withdrawn. "From this proceeds the barrenness of soul and the lack of devotion which I feel. Hence it is that my heart is dried up, and my soul like a land without water. I cannot shed tears. I can find no savor in the *Psalms.* I have no pleasure in reading good books. Prayer does not recreate me. The door is not opened to meditation. I am lazy in work, sleep at my vigils, prone to anger, obstinate in my dislikes, free in my tongue, and unrefrained in my appetite. Alas for me! for the Lord visits the mountains which are round about me, but He comes not near to me. Am I then one of the hills over which the Spouse leaps so as not to touch it? For I see one man singular in his gift of abstinence, and another admirable for his patience. One has ecstasies in contemplation, another penetrates Heaven by the importunity of his intercessions. Others excel in various virtues, as mountains that the Lord visits, and on which the Spouse of holy souls leaps and exults. But I miserable, who feel none of these things, what am I but one of those mountains of Gelboe from which, for my sins, the Lord has turned aside, when He compassionately visited the others? Wherefore, my soul, you ought to tremble, when you feel the grace of this divine visitation taken from you. In that failing, you will fail, and whatever good you have will fail with you." It seems then to be the doctrine of the Saints that these spiritual favors, I speak of consolations and sweetnesses, are not ornaments and crowns, but are to be numbered among the necessary vital forces of the spiritual life.

Fourthly, we have to consider the signs of these spiritual favors. Some are premonitory warnings of God's coming, and some are tokens of His actual presence in the soul; and it is of no little consequence to be acquainted with both of these classes of symptoms. The premonitory warnings of God's coming are five in number. Sometimes, without any cause of which we can take cognizance, an instinct awakes in our soul to expect God, an impulse to get ready for His coming. It causes no inward perturbance, though it is a surprise; neither does it throw us into any confusion, though its first effect is to deepen our reverential fear. At other times we feel, without anything either in our inward dispositions or external occupations to account for it, interior admonitions to sanctify ourselves, to make acts of contrition, to go to Confession, or suddenly to turn our attention with considerable vivacity upon some particular venial sins. We feel and act as if we were on the eve of some great feast. Or again we feel wrapped in a delightful peace. The peace may have been sudden, as in a schoolroom when the master's step is heard, or it may have deepened gradually till it became sensible. Or like sudden appetites which come on us, we all at once are aware of an unusual hunger after justice and holiness, as if there was some void in our soul which we were aching to fill. Or again we are sensibly possessed with an intense and very humble, but also very efficacious, desire to be more pure, in order to win God down to us; for we know that pure souls are His magnets and attract Him. This last is considered to be in most cases quite the immediate precursor of Our Lord. He comes swiftly then, as to Mary the moment her beautiful

Fiat was pronounced. He comes to exhort, to teach, to console, to reprove, yet to reprove so lovingly that a divine reproof is a thousand times sweeter than earth's best consolation.

There are also five signs of God's actual presence in the soul, for the purpose of dispensing His spiritual favors. The first is a sudden breadth of mind, as if walls had been thrown down and we saw far away over immense and various landscapes, all lying with the most gorgeous golden sunshine upon them. The second is an outbreak of torrents of thoughts and affections, as if at once the windows of Heaven had been opened and the fountains of the great deep broken up as at the Deluge. The third is a clear apprehension of heavenly things, as if we saw exactly how the heavenly court is arranged, and what are the external occupations of the blessed, and as if we too were put in momentary possession of their feelings about earth and the things of earth. The fourth is a feeling as if devotion were feeding us with substantial food, so solid does it seem to be, and such conscious vigor and strength is it pouring into every faculty of our soul, and perhaps even into the tired limbs of our body. The fifth is a fastidious contempt of the world, which makes us turn with sick hearts and weary eyes from every manifestation and development of it. It is like learning the treachery and meanness of a friend. From that moment fresh attachment seems an impossibility. Any one or more of these signs is a token to us of a divine visitation.

It should be observed also that the manner of God's entry into the soul is twofold. Sometimes He arrives in the upper part of the soul, and thence, like dew, He insinuates His sweetness gradually all through us, even to our bodies. At other times He arrives in the lowest depths of our soul, and breaks upward like a crystal bubbling fountain, which fast inundates us till we overflow. The first method seems to concentrate us in Him, the second to make us spread ourselves out in love and works of mercy toward others. The last is more the method of sweetness, the first the method of consolation, were it not that God comes as He wills, and will not be bound by systems.

Fifthly, we have to consider, still following in the track of the old spiritual masters, the reasons we may reverently venture to find for God's denying, delaying, or suspending these spiritual favors. St. Gregory says that it is lest we should think these gifts come from our own nature, were our own inheritance, or were due to us by any title of justice. We cannot be kept in too complete a dependence upon God, and the occasional subtraction of the divine favors admirably affect this. At other times He does it to increase our appreciation of His favors, to make us desire them more spiritually, and to long for His return more fervently, treating us, says St. John Climacus, as a mother does her sucking child. Another reason is that we may humble ourselves and lay His absence to the charge of our own sins, to our ingratitude, our negligence, our want of humility, and especially our want of reverence in our way of receiving Him when He comes: or it may be to caution us against vanity and too great a complacency in ourselves, as if His favors were attestations of our sanctity, instead of excesses of His mercy. Sometimes the weakness of our bodily constitution makes it necessary for Him to withdraw His favors for awhile, lest our health should give way under the application to divine things which they cause in us, or we should lose our sleep and appetite, and so be unable to go through the duties of our office or station in life. Sometimes He foresees that we shall be so allured by the sensible sweetness of His favors if He continues them, that we shall be guilty of an indiscreet excess, as children make themselves sick by eating sweets; and so a reaction would come over us; and a spiritual languor, nausea and unprofitable idleness would take possession of us. Sometimes He suspends His favors because we begin to have a repugnance to our external work and the assistance of our neighbor, and to perform our obligations in a very perfunctory way, because we affect the sweetness and solitude of this divine intercourse. For while it lasts, it mostly abstracts the soul from other things, and altogether possesses it.

At other times He withdraws to give us the opportunity of exercising true and solid virtues by turning His previous visitations to account. For solid virtues are found in God only, not in His sweetnesses and consolations. So that if the sweetness lasted we should not know ourselves as we ought to do, and we might mistake for our own activity what was in reality the energy of His sweetness. Again, He delights to see us laboring on without the succors of His sensible favors, because it is an image to Him of His own ever-blessed Passion, and because it is then we are winning the brightest crowns for ourselves. Furthermore, He would have us expert in the spiritual life and proved with a diversity of trials, that we may know how to bend over the oar in a calm, as well as shake out our sails to the wind in a breeze. Sometimes He would advance us all at once in heroic humility, or give us our Purgatory here for some infidelity, or burn and eat away certain spots of sin, by some most grievous dereliction, such as Job had when he cried out, "Thou wilt take me as a lioness, and returning Thou tormentest me wonderfully." Sometimes He sees in us that common fault, a want of esteem of grace, and He comes and goes, that by a comparison of our two states we may measure at once our own imbecility and the efficacy of grace. Into the deeper mysteries of dryness and desolation I need not enter. They would not be practical to those for whom I write.

Generally speaking the abundance of divine favors depends on our proficiency in the spiritual life. Gerson, in his *Mountain of Contemplation,* remarks that there are three seasons of favors, which resemble three seasons of the year. The state of beginners is the winter, when the sun is hidden from us by clouds and fogs, and the cold is great, and the rain frequent, though the sun sometimes shines and the days are occasionally smiling. For in their beginnings they have to sustain great obscurities, the relics of their past lives, and the contradiction of still unmortified passions; yet God sometimes visits them and shows them His glad and beneficent countenance. So far was that great master of mystical theology from thinking spiritual sweetness merely a bait for children in holiness. Those who have made some progress in prayer live in a kind of early spring. They have a greater variety. On one day the sky is clear and serene, the next it is cloudy and rainy. Yet the sun often makes his appearance. So the Sun of justice frequently visits the proficients, and indulges them, and gives them sensible tokens of His presence, and leaves with them the odoriferous flowers of fervent desires. Nevertheless He withdraws Himself from them, so that a little while they see Him, and again a little while and they do not see Him; in order that this variety may increase their hunger and appetite for Him, and make them prepare themselves so as to retain Him longer when He visits them. The perfect live in summer, when the rays of the sun are more ardent, and fewer clouds pass over His face; yet there are occasional storms, thunder and hail and tremendous rains, such as winter does not know. Thus the perfect enjoy a more stable and durable quiet, and God's visitations of them are much more frequent. Yet occasionally He tries them with more awful inward conflicts and penal desolations, so as to advance them in humility. Yet in the midst of these tempests He sends upon them scattered rays of light, so that the nights seem almost to be days because of the frequency of the divine lightnings.

Sixthly, we have to consider the way to obtain these favors. The teaching of all the old spiritual books is that we are to besiege God for them, like the importunate widow in the Gospel. If we are to know, says one, how we are to desire them, let us look how the old Patriarchs desired Christ. They must be our model. As they yearned for Him in the flesh, so must we yearn for Him in these favors; for it is truly Himself we seek when we seek them. *Sicut antiqui patres!* It is hard to have before us an example of more intense desire. To be humble when they come, and grateful as well as humble, is the way to win them back again with increased riches, and more exuberant sweetness. When Our Lord sees that we are solicitous to retain Him, and will not let Him go, as Jacob held the angel fast till morning light, He indulges us, and if He quits us then, He soon returns again. If we are anxious forthwith to turn the sweetness of His favors into solid virtues, increased mortification, redoubled prayer and practical holiness, we have insured His speedy returns and His more frequent visitation. There are two cases also in which it pleases Him and makes Him love to haunt us, if we say, *Fuge, Dilecte mi,* Fly, my Beloved. One is when discretion tells us that exuberant devotion is becoming injurious to our health, and encroaching on our work; and the other is when obedience and duty call us off from the secret caresses of His love. We must learn, as St. Philip said, to leave Christ for Christ. Moreover if we would enjoy to the uttermost the frequency of these divine favors, we must beware of an inordinate and irregular greediness for them, and of any complacency or return upon self in them. Louis of Blois mentions the case of a pious person who was punished with a dryness of fifteen years because of one vain complacency in her spiritual favors. We must also cautiously avoid all culpable distractions at prayer; for God only fills empty souls, says St. Bernard, quoting the miracle of Eliseus and the oil (*Kgs.* 4:4). When the vessels were full, she said to her son, "Bring me yet a vessel." And he answered, "I have no more." And the oil stood.

Seventhly, we have to consider the right use of these spiritual favors. After what has been said, a few words will dismiss this part of our subject. We have seen that we must value them and pray for them, and yet not be greedy of them. We must desire them, not for their own sakes, but for their divine effects and solid virtues. We must commute sweetness into additional practice, and consolation into increased strength, as fast as they come. We must receive them with the profoundest humility, and with a growing fervor. They must become the marrow of our mortifications, and be abundantly and unsparingly poured out in kindness to others, and in zeal for souls, and in ministries to the poor. We must with a holy superstition keep them secret, as the secret of a king. As soon as they are known they will evanesce. This is their way. When God means us to let any of them be known, He will give us such a light that we cannot mistake Him and such an impulse that we cannot resist Him. Perhaps this will not be once in our whole life. Then also we must have the art of forgetting them and remembering them at the right times. This must be according as presumption and discouragement, those two sleepless deflecting powers of the spiritual creation, try to disturb the equilibrium of our soul. Finally they must make us languish after God; for what do they show us, with their Heaven upon earth, so much as this, that it is not really Heaven that is sweet, but the God of Heaven?

Eighthly, we have to consider the discrepancy between ancient and modern books on the subject of these favors. What has been already said shows that these gifts have a dangerous side, and that caution and moderation are required in the using of them. Barring certain exaggerations, I do not think any really contradictory propositions could be drawn from the two classes of writers on the subject. The genius of the ancients led them to put forward the beauty and desirableness, nay, the necessity, of these favors; while the spirit of the moderns led them to dwell on the dangers of an immoderate appetite for them and the perils of an incautious use. It is the very aim of a spiritual writer to speak to those of his own day. He is without meaning if he does not. Now I suppose that modern writers found the world very much more effeminate than it was in the days of Gerson, Richard of St. Victor, Tauler, Ruysbroke, Hugh of St. Victor, St. Bonaventure, and Louis of Blois, to say nothing of St. John Climacus, St. Nilus, Cassian and St. Gregory. This want of mortification would at once make the appetite for spiritual sweetness more immoderate and the use of it less cautious. The greater subjective turn of the human mind, and possibly the weakened nerves of the race, have rendered delusions much more common than they were, or possibly, as the times of Antichrist draw nearer, Satan's chain may be lengthened; or we may take the view that they were more common when the modern spiritual school was forming than they are now, when the Jesuit writers have so flooded with scientific light every nook of ascetical theology. Moreover the number of new saints, and the publication of their lives, make the knowledge of these favors more common, and people more readily fancy they are in spiritual states analogous to those they read of in the lives of the Saints. Possibly humility is less flourishing in the world than it was, though it never can have flourished much. Moreover, heresies abound in false sweetnesses, and are multiplied on the matters which concern the ascetic life. Jansenism had not only a system of false dogma, but one also of diabolical spiritualism; and Quietism had almost frightened men away from an act of pure love, especially when they found all Quietism out of favor with the Holy See, even in Fenelon's extremest mitigations of the heresy. I venture to make these conjectures in defense of the modern writers, especially as they are more attainable by most readers, and are safer in that their writers had the advantage of many definitions of the Church which their predecessors had not; and I am anxious to show that the tradition of the spiritual life in the Church has always been substantially one and the same. I may therefore be permitted to add (which I do, speaking under correction), that I cannot help thinking that in the grand French ascetics of the seventeenth century there is an extremely faint reflection of Quietism, which appears here and there in their systems, like wayward summer lightning, especially when they speak of the abnegation of self, of the discernment between God and His favors, of the blessings of aridity, of what they call the nudity of faith, and other homogeneous subjects. Not that there is not a holy truth in all these things; but I cannot disabuse myself of the prejudice, if it be a prejudice, that there is a little exaggeration in their way of putting them forward, and that that exaggeration is in the direction of Quietism. As Alvarez de Paz says, no one should be heard on the subject of spiritual sweetness whom God has not led by them.

In the life of St. Jane Frances de Chantal we read as follows. (Vol. ii. p. 25. *Oratorian Edition*). While she was in one of the largest cities in France, a religious, a person of great virtue, desired to speak with her respecting her soul, which she readily allowed. These two great servants of Our Lord, discovering to each other in all simplicity the paths by which Our Lord had led them, the religious said to our Mother that she was occasionally so tired interiorly as to be reduced to great weakness and extreme languor; so that she was obliged to be contented with knowing that God is God, without daring to call him *her* God, or even thinking that He was *her* God. Our saint's reply was as follows: I shall leave that point to you, my dear Mother, and I shall never practice this abnegation. However tormented and beaten down my soul has been, it has never been so low that I could not say, My God, Thou art my God and the God of my heart. For if the Faith teaches me that He is my God, the Baptism which I have received makes me realize that of a truth He is *my* God. The religious immediately replied, that it seemed to her that in saying that word, *my* God, we had not arrived at a perfect spirit of abnegation. To this our Mother replied that our feeling of abandonment could never equal that of the Son of God, and that in the greatest of His trials, He had said, My God! My God! Why hast Thou forsaken Me? adding, I have often said to Our Lord, when most severely tried, that if it was His pleasure that I should dwell in Hell, provided it could be done without my offending Him, and that my eternal torment should be to His eternal glory, I should be satisfied, but that for all that He should be always my God. The religious thanked our Mother for the light which she had imparted to her, declaring that she was well fitted to be her mistress in divine love, that she would never forget her maxims, and that there was no more delicate matter in the spiritual life than the knowing how to follow the example which the Father has set us in His Son Our Lord. The Saint very often recurred to this conversation, it made so strong an impression on her.

What, then, is the result of our inquiry on this most delicate subject of spiritual favors? Briefly, it comes to this. They are from God, and they are signs of love. He knows best the times and seasons, the ways and the means of sending them; and as He always sends them for good and never for a snare, this consideration of His knowledge of us should enable us to abate any exaggerations of fear or caution we may have about them. The idea of their being merely sweetmeats to allure children is as false in theology as it is surely intolerable as a question of taste and reverence, and contradicted by all experience, as the Saints are the persons who abound most in these very favors. Neither are they to be considered as one of God's many ways of leading souls. Some He leads by an abundance of them. Others by fewer. But none either by absolutely few, or by none. We must therefore make them the subject of earnest prayer.

By them we attain an experimental knowledge of God, which, while it requires to be corrected by theology, is greater than any that theology can teach us. They give us power over nature and against evil. They subject to us the human spirit and the demons. They give us a facility in fulfilling our vocations. They intensify our love, fortify us in temptation, give us confidence in God, enlarge our gift of faith, and make us the comforters of our brethren. May we not say with the people of Capharnaum, "Lord! give us always this bread"? Or, with truth in every word, make the prayer of the poor Samaritan woman our own, "Sir, give me this water, that I may not thirst, nor come hither to draw?" (*John* 6:34, 4:15).

Chapter XXIV

DISTRACTIONS AND THEIR REMEDIES

It is usually said that prayer has four enemies: distractions, scruples, dryness and desolation. Scruples have already been treated of; and for the class of persons I am addressing, enough has been said of dryness and desolation when we considered the denial, delay or suspension of divine favors. It remains now to say something on the subject of distractions, which the soul in the progress of the spiritual life finds one of its most obstinate and most tiresome impediments: tiresome, because it takes the smoothness, sweetness and facility out of all devotion, and obstinate, inasmuch as it appears to acknowledge the power of no specifics, but to be irritated and worsened by the very application of remedies. For there is nothing which looks so much like our own fault as distractions, and I fully believe that no impediment of the spiritual life is more often without any fault at all. In most cases it is an unavoidable mortification, and the fault it leads to is not want of attention at prayer, but want of patience at having our prayer teased, embittered and dishonored.

Distractions are said more particularly to infest beginners; and they contain two things, the wandering or removal of the mind from the subject of prayer, and the occupation of the imagination by impertinent and irrelevant ideas. Hence it comes to pass, from their very definition, and while they greatly injure vocal prayer, they do not spoil it altogether; whereas mental prayer is destroyed by them; for in mental prayer we pray while we are attending, and no longer; no matter, say St. Isidore and Alvarez de Pas, how long we may remain upon our knees. Even when they are quite inculpable, St. Thomas teaches us that they deprive us of "spiritual reflection of the mind," which comes from prayer. They are like the gnats on a summer evening, which tease with their shrillness more often than they pierce with their bites. We strike them and they yield; but it is in vain; the pliant cohorts form again still more closely serried ranks and pipe on a higher note than they did before. Where we go, they go; and it is only the thin air of the high hills of mortification or the coming on of the grateful deep night of contemplation which can effectually draw off from us these irritating tenants of the twilight.

We must then begin our inquiry into this subject by laying to heart the doctrine of the Abbot Moses in Cassian, namely, that it is impossible for us to be altogether free from distractions, useless to attempt it, and foolish to be dejected, because we have not accomplished that impossibility. Conscious and deliberate acquiescence in and retention of distractions are of course our own affair; for it is in our power to withhold them; but the indeliberate occupation of our minds by them it is not in our power to prevent. Nothing can hinder, says the Abbot, bitter thoughts from disturbing us, wrong thoughts from staining us, and vain thoughts from disquieting and fatiguing us. The first sort of distractions he calls sand, the second pitch, and the third straw. The author of the treatise on the love of God, among the spurious works of St. Bernard, seems to countenance the doctrine already laid down, that they accompany us to the mountain of contemplation, and leave us there; for he compares them to Abraham's young men, while he likens his body to the ass, and his reason to Isaac, and he says, "You cares, you anxieties, you toils, you pains, you slaveries, all you distractions, stay you here with the ass, the body: I and the boy will go with speed as far as yonder, and after we have worshipped, will return to you. Thus there is a sort of parallel between distractions and venial sins. We cannot avoid them at all; but let us take them in detail, and we can avoid them one by one. Thus, to anyone who has made up his mind entirely to cure himself of distractions, I would say, "You will never succeed." You are aiming at a state which is only transient, even with the Saints, and belongs to contemplation. Your strife will increase your malady;

and your want of success will plunge you in self-vexation and pusillanimity. Every reason I gave you to be quiet with your faults tells with greater force in the case of distractions; for they are much more inevitable than faults. A complete and final cure is out of the question.

So well-aware is the tempter that distractions are one of the unavoidable infirmities of our nature, and at the same time one of the most vexing and annoying to the human spirit, that he often tries to delude spiritual persons into taking the diminution of their distractions as the test of their progress in the spiritual life. He gains many objects by this one stratagem. He calls off their attention from real faults, especially those of the tongue and misuse of time, and from the means of advancement, where their attention would be profitably employed; and he fixes their eyes, and aims, and desires, on an object, as hopeless as the unprofitable labors which are put among the punishments of the heathen hell. Forever to be rolling a stone up an impossible hill, and forever to be filling at the fountain the vessel that leaks, this is what these poor souls have condemned themselves to do; and as they have taken it as the measure of their progress, through what anxieties, and strainings, and forced marches, and discouragements, and swamps of sadness, will not the Will of the Wisp lead them! To resolve to be altogether quit of your distractions is to keep and to pay a standing army of them; and in the end they will be the sovereign, not you. Despots have slaughtered Janissaries whom they could not disband, and have broken the stone turbans off their graves. You will have no such success with your distractions.

When we proceed to examine the sources from which distractions come, we must bear in mind the definition of them and the two processes which it implies, the removal of the mind from the subject of prayer, and the occupation of the imagination by irrelevant ideas and images. With this definition for our guide we shall discover that this great Nile of distractions has five fountains: disordered health, the action of the Holy Spirit, the devil, inculpable self and culpable self.

By disordered health I do not so much mean actual illness, when in all probability ejaculatory acts of love, of patience, and of conformity will form the whole of the sufferer's prayers, with a constant quiet eye on his crucifix, or some other emblem of the Passion. I rather mean the valetudinarian state which is now so very common, with its distinguishing bodily feebleness and daily tendency to slight headache, especially when, as is often the case, the feeling of fatigue is greatest at first rising in the morning. With many persons this is so distressing that they are quite unable to make a morning meditation. In these cases, bodily strength is wanting to keep off or to banish distractions. The greater the effort made, the greater will the vehemence of the distractions be, and the result of a violent effort will be an inability to pray at all. Such persons must be quiet and tranquil, and try to keep God's presence lovingly before them with gentleness and without scruple. It will seem to themselves that they do not pray at all, and that their attempts are so many constellations of venial sins. But this is really very far from being the case. They must take the annoyance as they would any other consequence of ill-health, and learn humility as its endurance. If they are quiet, they will have a spot within where there is peace, even while distractions are raging without; but if they make vehement and ill-advised efforts, they will only surrender to the distractions that inward sanctuary also.

The action of the Holy Spirit is another fountain of distractions. Just as persons in the higher stages of the spiritual life are supernaturally tried and purified by desolations and aridities, so those who are passing through the earlier stages, and along the more ordinary paths of perfection, are sometimes put into a crucible of distractions, in order to ground them in more solid devotion, to burn away the remains of sin, and to subdue the vivacity of self-love. It is not easy for a man to know when the distractions he is suffering from are supernatural. Perhaps the knowledge would interfere with their efficacy. Still it is a consolation to know that there are cases in which distractions are a divine trial; and that one probable sign of their being so is when we are unable to attribute their unusual inroad, or its perseverance, to any other cause or to any fault of our own. There is also another class of supernatural distractions, which must be noticed. These infest us when the Holy Spirit is calling us to a different subject of prayer, or to a higher state of prayer, and we are unconsciously or consciously misunderstanding and resisting the vocation. He will let us have no rest until we obey Him, and He sends us these distractions to harass us into obedience.

Thirdly, distractions may come from the devil, and in a very great number of cases do so. It is obvious that devotion is fatal to his kingdom in the soul, and consequently must always be one of his main objects of attack. His distractions may be known, first by their torrent-like abundance, secondly by the vivid pictures which accompany them, thirdly by their disquieting the soul in a peculiar and disproportionate manner, fourthly by their disconnection with the ordinary engrossing actions of our state of life, fifthly—and in this respect they are the opposite of diabolical scruples—by their want of variety, and their always returning to the charge in the same shape, and sixthly, by their being of such a nature, as if dwelt upon will easily become sin. Reguera, in his *Mystical Theology,* tells us not to pursue distractions at all, but to treat them as a man does barking dogs as he passes through a street. This advice applies with peculiar force to those distractions whose origin we have reason to believe is diabolical.

Inculpable self is the fourth source of distractions, or rather contains within itself four distinct springs of them. The first is the imagination, which is much more strongly developed in some persons than others, and much more susceptible of images presented to it. Thus there are instances of men unable to make what is called the composition of place in meditation, that is, the picture of the mystery, because the vividness of the picture so excites their imagination that it is a source of distractions to them all through their hour of prayer. The ruling passion is another of these springs. All ideas and objects connected with it seem to participate both in its domineering spirit and its tenacity. They are always seen as it were through a magnifying medium, and lay so strong a hold upon the mind that it is difficult to shake them off; and when, as in the act of prayer, other external objects are shaken off by the ordinary efforts we naturally make at that time, those which are connected with the ruling passion only seem to have the field more comparatively to themselves, and to subject the mind to a more rigorous tyranny.

The third spring is what has been called the *"ingenium vagum,"* the genius of dissipation, the turn of mind which makes a man diffuse himself over many objects, and turn away with repugnance from interior things. It is just the opposite of concentration. It has no fixity, no steadiness. It is a constitutional flaw in the mind, analogous to irresoluteness in the will. It loves novelty and change, and show, and sound, and hurry, and many things to do, and the luxury of complaining it has many things to do. Like all constitutional faults, it is full of the possibilities of moral evil, still it is itself constitutional, and so inculpable. In speaking of the human spirit I quoted Scaramelli to show that there was a profoundly melancholy temperament which could nail itself so undistractedly to an object as to be mistaken for a supernatural gift of contemplation. The *ingenium vagum* is just the very opposite to this; and as the former is without merit, so is the latter without blame. The fourth spring is the unskillfulness of our spiritual director. Directors who drag their penitents rather than follow them to keep them in the way are necessarily the cause of habitual distractions, because the souls of their penitents are always in an unreal and forced state, and are not developing in the way of the Holy Spirit. Hence they are feverish, panic-stricken, obstinate, now querulous, now fantastic, one while dumb, another while loquacious, and a few years hence would have given up the pursuit of perfection altogether. The prayers of such persons are composed of two-thirds distractions and one-third petulant complaint of the distractions to God. Other directors have a pet method prayer, and will insist on all their penitents praying as they do. None are to pray lower. Perfection, say they, requires such or such a degree of prayer. None are to pray higher. It would be delusion. Such a director looks down upon his flock as on a lower level than himself on the mountain. He is piping up above. It does not strike him that he is ever to look up, sometimes with dazzled eyes and aching neck, at penitents above him. All above him are stragglers. He sends his dog for them, and they come precipitately down at the peril of their lives. Others take Scaramelli and such books and pass their penitents through twelve or fifteen degrees of prayer in succession, like the stages of an operation, a manufacture, or a medical cure. They can tell as well where they are in prayer as they can show by a map how far they are on their road to a given place. The consequence, to the poor penitents, of all this narrowness and pedantry is their being devoured by wolves the whole time of prayer. To be in a state of prayer in which God does not will us to be is a kind of spiritual dislocation. We shall be easy in no posture, and recollection is impossible. These four springs together make up the source of inculpable self.

The fourth and last fountain of distractions is culpable self. All distractions, from whatever source, are culpable, if we clearly perceive them and deliberately entertain them. They become culpable in the same way as temptations become sins, by advertence and consent. But beyond this, there is a class of distractions arising immediately from ourselves, and which are always culpable. They have two springs, the body and the mind. The body culpably causes them, when we practice no sort of mortification, and foresee that the result of that neglect will be distractions. Irreverent postures in prayer, and continual changes of position, and all want of outward modesty and propriety also give rise to distractions which are culpable. The remedy for these is of course as obvious as their cause. Then the mind is another prolific spring of several classes of distractions for which we have no one to blame but ourselves. We have debauched our own minds. We have disarmed our spirit and left it a helpless prey to those merciless distractions.

Among our many faults there are seven especially, which not only indirectly, but directly, play into the hands of distractions. The first is a carelessness about very minute sins, which, like the dead flies in the apothecaries' ointment, may be indefinitely small, and yet corrupt the purity of intention of all we do. They dissipate the mind, induce one or other of the forms of spiritual idleness, involve supernatural objects in a sort of fog and weaken grace at every turn. The second fault is tepidity, of which I shall have to speak in the following chapter. The third is curiosity, and especially a thirst for news, whether it be of the great world, the camp and the court far off or details of what our neighbors are saying, doing and suffering, or an inordinate love of writing and receiving letters, or the puerile magnifications and idolatries of domestic life and love. All these must be paid for, to the uttermost farthing, by these inexorable distractions. Shylock will not stick to his bond more pertinaciously than they. The fourth fault is going to prayer without due preparation. We walk in and out of the presence of God, without doing reverence or homage or observing any of the ceremonial of His august celestial court. There is no one perhaps with whom we are more rude than with the Incomprehensible God; and we are never really familiar with those to whom we are rude. Hence come distractions, which can breathe any air but that of holy familiarity with God. A fifth fault is our want of custody of the senses, not merely in the time of prayer but out of it. Distractions being an infirmity of our nature, we cannot purchase, I will not say immunity, but a sufficiently ample jurisdiction over them, without a sacrifice on our own part. We cannot enjoy to the full our unshackled liberty of looking where we will and listening to what we will, even far short of sin, and not take the consequences which follow by the mere operation of the natural laws of mind. The manner as well as the amount of custody of the senses is different in each case; but without some manner and some amount we shall always be powerless over distractions. Our sixth fault is our neglecting to practice ejaculatory prayers. They are, so to speak, the heavenly side of distractions, thoughts of God which distract us from the world and interfere with the quiet possession which the world has taken of our souls. Ejaculations are our doing for God what distractions do against Him. They have a speciality to evict distractions. There is no better practice for bringing them under our control. Our seventh and last fault is our taking no pains to watch from what object it is that the thickest swarms of our distractions arise, and then mortifying ourselves in those very things. Obvious as this duty is, it is one very commonly neglected. Men look at distractions as unscientific people look at a phenomenon. It tells them nothing. It leads to nothing. They do not ask

whence it comes nor whither it goes. It is simply a phenomenon. So here are these distractions. No matter whence they
come; the question is what we are to do with them. Certainly;
but it is just to find out this last, that we must know the first.
If our imagination is fairly sinking at prayer in a sea of distractions, it is very well to work at the pumps, but it is something more to find out the leak. Attention to these seven faults
will in time produce something like subordination in our distractions; and we shall never get much beyond this, until our
whole state is higher and more supernatural. It is one of the
essential and incurable defects of the state of proficiency, as
compared with the state of the already perfect; just as there
are essential and incurable defects in beginners which gradually disappear in proficients. Anything that helps to purity of
intention helps also to the subjugation of distractions.

But the great thing to be borne in mind is that the time
of prayer is not the time for the true combat with distractions.
If we delay till then, even our very victories will be melancholy; for they will be won only by the loss of our prayer.
How many persons complain of their distractions, and even
look forward with a sort of dread to the time of prayer because of the mental suffering it will bring with it; and yet
how few make it the business of their lives, out of prayer,
to hinder the recurrence of these same distractions! I have
already said, and I will repeat it, that when a man is not
seriously directing his life out of prayer against the sources
of distractions, prayer must necessarily be the most distracted
of times. For we empty the heart of many things, and distractions gush in to fill up the void. We shall never get rid of
distractions or get a decent mastery over them by fighting
against distractions, but by fighting against something else,
against the source or cause of the distractions; and our fight
must cover the whole breadth of our daily life.

There are two practices of interior spirituality which excellently accomplish this end; and they occupy the entire ground
of life. One of them is the having a rule of life; and the other
devoting our undivided attention to the perfecting of our ordinary actions. With regard to the rule of life, it is so completely a question for consideration in each particular case

that I shall not enter into it at any length. It gives sanctity in the world a kind of shadowy likeness of sanctity in a convent, which acts sometimes well, sometimes ill. With some persons the captivity and bondage of it rapidly advance them in holiness. With others its arrangements only minister to delusion and self-love. In the case of some it meets their faults, and strangles them with a sort of slowly twisting bowstring. In the case of others, it ruins their delicacy of conscience; their attention is called off from real faults and even crying imperfections, and is so fixed on obedience to the details of their rules that their conscience comes soon to feel keenly the one, which is of little consequence, and be callous to the other, in which even questions of sin are often concerned. People will confess with real sorrow a breach of their time-paper, who forget even to mention that they spoke sharply to their servant, or discussed the character of an absent neighbor. Of all the appliances of the spiritual life there are none which can with less wisdom and safety be indiscriminately applied. Upon the whole, fewer can wear the yoke than not; or at least as many get injury as get benefit from this form of spirituality. Only, where it succeeds, it succeeds admirably. But in the case of persons living in the world, I believe rules have stunted more souls than they have advanced.

But there are none to whom Our Lady's devotion, her shape of the spiritual life, cannot be applied with abundant blessings: I mean the attempt to do perfectly our ordinary actions. This is the most excellent of practices, and walks in a clear air which delusions seldom can obscure; and our power over our distractions grows in proportion to our perseverance and our skill in this exercise.

Methods for this practice abound in our most approved spiritual writers. I will select one out of many, because of its simplicity, clearness and spirituality. There are then two things to be regarded in every one of our ordinary actions: the exterior and the interior. The exterior is to it what the body is to the soul, as necessary and yet also as subordinate. Where outward discipline is wanting, interior perfection cannot be observed, says William of Paris. The religion of our exterior, says St. Bonaventure, excites the affection of our interior. The perfection of the exterior of our actions is attained by the presence of three virtues: fidelity, punctuality and modesty. Fidelity enables us to admit nothing, punctuality to procrastinate nothing, and modesty to do all things with gracefulness and edification.

For the interior of our actions three things also are required: to do all for God, in the presence of God, and in the sight of Jesus.

To do our actions for God is to refer them to Him by an act of intention. Many actions are done for a bad intention, such as the desire of praise; and then the act is vitiated. Many also are done with merely human intentions, as for the pleasure of a thing, and then there is not merit. And alas! multitudes of actions of multitudes of men are done with no intention at all; and custom, precipitation and negligence devour what might have been the pure food of God's greater glory. Oh, what teeming years of human life are wasted through this unthinking absence of all intention; and we thought ourselves so good because after all we were not so bad; and now tears of blood will not weep them back again! When we are doing a great thing for God, we must momentarily collect ourselves before acting, and try to touch lightly with our intention the beginning, middle and end of each considerable action, and not throw away, as fish too small for the table, the little actions of the day.

Now I have said certain things here which will immediately turn to scruples in some minds, if I do not meet them by giving some signs which, without an absurd over-exactness of self-inspection, will enable us to know whether on the whole we are doing our works for God. Here is one sign: We are really working for God. If we could say yes, did anyone suddenly ask us if what we are doing is for God? Another is, if we are not uneasily anxious about the judgment men will pass upon our actions. A third is, if we are not wholly indifferent, but quite tranquil about success. A fourth is, if we take as much pains in private with what we are doing as in public before witnesses. A fifth is, if we are not jealous either of associating others with our works, or of their equal or greater success.

We do our works in the presence of God, which is the second

grace the perfection of our ordinary actions requires, when we practice the presence of God while we do them. There are six ways of practicing the presence of God which are given in books, and from which souls should select those which are most suited to them, but not try to practice more than one. The first is to try to realize God as He is in Heaven. The second, to regard ourselves in Him as in His immensity. The third, to look at each creature as if it were a sacrament having God hidden under it. The fourth is to think of Him and see Him by pure faith. The fifth, to look at Him as in ourselves, rather than outside of us, though He is both. And the sixth is to gravitate toward Him by an habitual, loving mindfulness of heart, a kind of instinct which is no uncommon growth of prayer, and comes sooner than would be expected, when men strive to serve God out of the single motive of holy love.

The third requisite for the perfection of our ordinary actions is that we should do them in the sight of Jesus, that is, to use the words of the missal, by Christ, with Christ and in Christ. To do our actions by Christ is to do them in dependence upon Him, as He did everything in dependence on His Father and by the movements of His Spirit. To do our actions with Christ is to practice the same virtues as Our Lord, to clothe ourselves with the same dispositions and to act from the same intentions, all according to the measure of the lowliness of our possibilities. To do our actions in Christ is to unite ours with His, and to offer them to God along with His, so that for the sake of His they may be accepted on high.

This is a good old-fashioned French method of perfecting our ordinary actions, and not so hard as at first sight it seems to be. To try and combat our distractions when the time of prayer has come is like speaking reason to a seditious multitude. What I have said is not perhaps satisfactory. It is hard to be told that we cannot shake off altogether a yoke so degrading and so wearisome. But will facts warrant me in promising more? No man short of a real contemplative will ever reign like a despot over his vast hordes of distractions. He is a happy man, and has done much, who has set up a constitutional monarchy among them.

Chapter XXV

LUKEWARMNESS

Bellecio in his treatise on solid virtue puts lukewarmness almost at the very commencement. This has always seemed to me an inconvenient arrangement. Lukewarmness is in no sense a beginning. We may begin by being cold, but not by being lukewarm. For lukewarmness implies that a great deal has gone before, that a height has been climbed, and that from cowardice, human respect or weariness, we have come down from it. Like certain phenomena in geology, it is at once an evidence of a former state of things, and of the catastrophe which overthrew it. He who was never fervent can never be lukewarm. Cold he may be, and low, and mean, and ungenerous, and a poltroon, but not lukewarm.

I prefer therefore to consider lukewarmness in this place, because the knowledge we have now gained of the various appliances of the spiritual life will enable us the better to understand its true nature; and also because all the component parts of the spiritual life being also, when spoiled, the component parts of lukewarmness, this is the natural place it occupies. In fact, all that has gone before of struggle, fatigue and rest, with their helps, hindrances, phenomena and developments, issues simply in one of two states, lukewarmness or fervor. Either we are lukewarm, or we are fervent. These are the ends of our whole voyage as proficients: either we run on the sandbanks and go to pieces at the very base of the lighthouse, or we hit the mouth of the harbor and lie snugly in its deep water with the mountains of God embracing us on either side. The rudder of the spiritual life, the little-seeming power which governs the whole ship, is discretion. This turns us off from the treacherous shoal, keeps us in the deep midway channel, and steers us fairly into port. Hence my last three chapters will naturally be occupied with the consideration of lukewarmness, fervor and discretion.

There is nothing in the spiritual life which arrests our attention so forcibly as lukewarmness, because of the unusual language in which it has pleased God to express His ineffable disgust with it, and the startling doctrine which accompanies the declaration of His loathing, that coldness is less offensive to Him than tepidity. Who is it then with whom God is so exceedingly displeased, that He is sick of His own redeemed creature? We tremble at the answer. It is the man who is patient when he has nothing to suffer, who is gentle while he is uncontradicted, who is humble when men leave his honor untouched, who wishes to be a saint without the trouble of it, who seeks to acquire virtues without mortification, who is willing to do many things, but not to take the Kingdom of Heaven by violence. Alas! here are verified the dread words of the Prince of the Apostles. The time is that judgment should begin at the house of God. And if first at us, what shall be the end of those who believe not the Gospel of God? And if the just man shall scarcely be saved, where shall the wicked and the sinner appear? (*1 Ptr.* 4:17).

The diseases and evils of the body are, as might be expected, seeing they are the immediate outflowings of sin, in a great degree typical of the miseries and misfortunes of the soul. If we seek the correlative of lukewarmness, we shall find it in blindness. It is a blindness which does not know even its own self, and does not suspect that it is blind, or that other men see better than itself. It is a judicial blindness, because it once saw better itself, and now does not remember either what it saw, or that it ever saw at all. It is usual to consider that this blindness is owing principally to three causes, the frequency of venial sins, habitual dissipation of mind and the ruling passion. The frequency of venial sins is like travelling in the wilderness, where the bright air is imperceptibly filled with fine sand. Habitual dissipation of mind is like reading in the sunshine, and living in a light too strong for our eyes. The ruling passion is an external violence which menaces us

and makes us shut our eyes, and have them always shut, that
we may not see what it would fain hide, and so when we
open them after long being used to darkness, it is the very
light itself which blinds us.

The immediate results of this blindness are three also. In
the first place conscience becomes untrue. The body does
not move firmly and in a straight line in the dark. So the
conscience also must see in order to keep its balance. But
if we falsify the oracle, and still believe it, what is the consequence but error and corruption everywhere? If the light that
is in us be darkness, says Our Lord, how great is that darkness! So first there comes a false conscience. But in proportion as conscience becomes dark, and so cold, and finally
numb, in the same proportion the bad instincts of the human
spirit, like owls at night, get more far-sighted, animated and
vivacious. These instincts lead us with uncommon tact to avoid
anything which will restore animation to the conscience. For
their purpose it had best remain under chloroform for life.
Thus they make us shrink from anything like vigorous spiritual
direction. We suspect we shall be awakened, and driven, and
made too good. Discretion, that is, the discretion of the blind
conscience, tells us this shrinking is wisdom and sagacity.
We must, it says, be moderate in everything, but of all things
amazingly moderate in the love of God. So in hearing sermons, reading books, cultivating acquaintances, patronizing
works of mercy, it draws back from everything that is likely
to come too near or hit too hard. It is the old story of the
earthen jug and the brazen jar, as they went down the stream
together. Here is the second result of this blindness, which
renders the cure still less likely. Indeed it is a characteristic
of tepidity that everything we do while we are in that state
has a tendency to confirm us as incurable. Out of the two
preceding results flows a third, which is a profane use of the
Sacraments. To go to Holy Communion when we are physically drowsy, yawning and half asleep, or to make our general
confession half stupefied with laudanum would be fair types
of the way in which we morally use the Sacraments. Thus
frequent or even daily Communion seems to have only a negative effect upon us. We do not know how bad it might be

without it; and that is all. Weekly confession gives us no additional power over our commonest imperfections. Matters look as if they had come to a standstill, if there were any such phase of the spiritual life. But no! we are blind men, whose faces have been turned unwittingly. We are retracing our steps; and the only wonder is that the easier task of going down hill does not by its contrast make us suspicious of some mistake. Alas! we are asleep as well as blind. The finest things we do now are no better than feats of somnambulism.

It is plain from this description that what is of the greatest practical utility in this matter of lukewarmness is a thorough acquaintance with the symptoms by which the insidious disease allows itself to be detected. These are seven in number; and according as we perceive that we unite them in ourselves, either in number or degree, so we have reason painfully to doubt whether our spiritual eyesight is not failing. The first mark is a great facility in omitting our exercises of piety, which is the exact contradictory of fervor. Everyone has his routine of pious exercises; and there are few days in which they do not entail upon us some little inconveniences. Perhaps it is one of their special uses to do this, especially if habitual distractions are going to make the exercise itself of small value. Now these little inconveniences suggest dispensations, or at least delays, which we see confusedly will turn out dispensations at the last. Clearly there are cases in which conflicting duties or the needs of charity will interfere, and it will be more perfect to give way to them than to read or meditate. But most often the inconveniences concern only ourselves. We have the power to dispense ourselves; and we grant these dispensations either rarely and with reluctance, or often and with facility. If the latter be the case, behold the first mark of tepidity! I do not say that by itself it proves everything; but it proves much. At all events, wherever there is lukewarmness, there also is this symptom. But we are not only easy in omitting exercises of piety, we are negligent in those which we do perform. We care more about the fact of going through them, than the manner or the spirit of it. Thus our prayers rise to Heaven with an equipage of venial sins in attendance upon them, and the angels are reluctant witnesses of our

Confessions and Communions. This is a second symptom.
Here is a third. The soul feels not altogether right with God.
It does not exactly know what is wrong; but it is sure all
is not right. It casts about to see. It quarrels with everything
it does, and questions each of them, and yet the mischief eludes
it. It is angry with its Confessions; yet it is not easy to settle
how to amend them. Something always seems unexpressed,
something left behind which ought to have come out and does
not. What is it? Then the Communions are overhauled in a
similar way, the examens of conscience tortured, meditations
reprimanded, spiritual books cashiered, together with a determination to reform everything. General orders are issued from
self's headquarters, in which strong things are said ambigu-
ously. Everyone feels he is aimed at. Blame lies everywhere.
Yet all to no purpose. At last when we have given the matter
up, we suddenly come upon the offending thing, just as we
look for a lost article till we are hot and tired, and then all
at once see it lying in open day in a spot we have searched
four or five times before. Now when we have this feeling
of not being altogether right with God, and yet will not
vigorously face the inquiry and make the disturbance I have
described, and buckle to the triple task of discovery, punishment, and reformation, it is a symptom of our being lukewarm.

A fourth symptom of lukewarmness is an habitual acting
without any intention at all, good, bad or indifferent, of which
I spoke in the preceding chapter. A fifth is a carelessness
about forming habits of virtue. This is the opposite of the
inordinate appetite for self-improvement already considered;
the truth lying here, as it mostly does in spiritual matters,
in a mean. A sixth symptom is a contempt of little things
and of daily opportunities. This is a necessary part of our
blindness. We can only despise little things because we do
not discern the capabilities of glorifying God, and advancing
our own spiritual interest, which they contain. The seventh
and last symptom is a thinking rather of the good we have
done than of the good we have left undone, resting on the
past rather than striving for the future, loving to look at people below us rather than people above us. Our own ease and
self-complacency find their account in this attitude of the soul.

This is the way in which tepidity attacks the inmates of convents. When religious become lukewarm, they like to measure themselves with the poor citizens of the world, rather than with the grand saints of their own order. They are ever calculating the sacrifices they have made, and fondly realizing to themselves the glory of their self-devotion. When these signs are observed, superiors recognize in them the alarming symptoms of tepidity. It all lies in one word. Such religious do what St. Paul said he did not do. They count themselves to have apprehended. "Brethren, I do not count myself to have apprehended. But one thing I do; forgetting the things that are behind, and stretching forth myself to those that are before, I pursue toward the mark, for the prize of the supernal vocation of God in Christ Jesus. Let us, therefore, as many as are perfect, be thus minded." (*Phil.* 3:13).

From these fatal marks let us pass to consider the extraordinary hatred which God has of this state. "These things saith the Amen, the faithful and true witness, who is the beginning of the creation of God. I know thy works, that thou art neither cold nor hot. I would thou wert cold or hot. But because thou art lukewarm, and neither cold nor hot, I will begin to vomit thee out of my mouth." (*Apoc.* 3:14, 15, 16). This passage is without any parallel in Scripture. God not only prefers coldness, but He rejects tepidity. It turns Him sick who is eternal love. The charity of the Heart of Jesus, our only home, cannot retain us. His disgust is too strong for Him to resist it; and He rejects us with an unconquerable nausea which even redeeming love cannot temper or allay. It is a most awful figure, and one which, but for His own word, we should not dare to have mentioned in the same breath with His adorable majesty. How much He must have meant to teach us by the singularity of that terrific language! Now God is infinitely just, therefore His hatred of this state cannot be too great. It is not in His majesty to exaggerate. But He is also infinitely forbearing, so that His punishment must be, if anything, short of its horrible deserts. What then must its real horror be?

But why does He hate it so? Let us venture to search for reasons. Because it is a quiet intentional appreciation of other things over God. It cheapens God, and parts with Him second-hand. Meanwhile, as it is not open wickedness, but is even an open profession and exterior practice of His service, it pretends friendship, and takes rank in the world as one of God's friends; and hence it involves the twofold guilt of treachery and hypocrisy. It thus has a peculiar ability to wound God's glory by the scandal it gives. It has God's honor in its power, and treats it shamefully and cruelly. It profanes grace by the indifference with which it misuses it. It takes it as a right, and misapplies it, as a dishonest man spends money on purposes for which it was not trusted to him. It is taking a liberty with the majesty of God's exceeding goodness, which is a terrible thing to do. It were better to play with His thunderbolts, than to make sport with His compassions. And all this is done with knowledge, the double knowledge of God and of evil. What wonder that it turns God's whole being, and sours even the sweetness of the Sacred Heart!

A few words on its remedies, and the hateful subject may be dismissed. Its cure is immensely difficult; St. Bernard would make us almost despair of its being curable at all. Only, we made up our minds at the beginning to hold this all through, that nothing is incurable, though many things in the spiritual life are nearly so; and neither doctor, nor father, nor saint, but only the Pope, shall drive us from this doctrine. St. Bernard therefore will be satisfied if we say that its cure is immensely difficult, because all the Saints have said so, because the evil is unsuspected, because even the good is mixed with evil, because men do not realize the possible forfeiture of grace to keep precepts when they have been playing fast and loose with counsels, and because, as St. Theresa teaches, for some souls perfection is accidentally necessary even for their salvation!

How absurd it seems to mention the feeble remedies! The first is to quicken faith by meditation on eternal truths, so as to possess our minds habitually with their overwhelming importance and their exacting purity. The second is, not having so many things to do. It is no use. The times are busy. But we cannot save our souls if we have so many things to do. But the remedy? Good soul! there are some knots in life which cannot be untied; the thing is to cut them, and leave the consequences to help themselves. If you have more duties to do than you can do well, you must boldly neglect some of them. Only have faith, and God will spirit the consequences away, so that you will see nothing more of them. The third remedy is the practice of silence, not in any offensive or singular way, but proportionably to our state of life. The fourth is to persevere in our spiritual exercises in spite of dryness and distractions; and the fifth, which is nearer a specific than any of the others, is a habit of mortification, not interior, but exterior. The interior will look out for itself when its time comes. Just now I want the flesh to suffer. If you turn away from this I give you up. It is the quinine for your ague. Alas! alas! what does all this come to but the admission that the only sure remedy for lukewarmness is never to be lukewarm, an oracle worthy of the pompous physician of the old comedy? Yet does it not in reality say a great deal?

I fear this evil of lukewarmness is very common, and that at this moment it is gnawing the life out of many souls who suspect not its presence there. It is a great grace, a prophecy of a miraculous cure, to find out that we are lukewarm; but we are lost if we do not act with vigor, the moment we make this frightening discovery. It is like going to sleep in the snow, almost a pleasant tingling feeling at the first, and then—lost forever.

Chapter XXVI

FERVOR

Fervor is the state of the Saints on earth, and in one sense of the blessed in Heaven; and in its degree, it ought to be the normal state of all who are aiming at perfection. It is at once the growth of holiness, and the strength by which holiness grows. Every chapter hitherto has tended to this, and to avoid recapitulation, I shall confine myself now to conveying a clear idea of genuine fervor. This seems what is most wanted. How few could define fervor if they were asked!

Fervor, considered as a state, is a similitude to God. It is equable like God. It is moderate like God. It is hidden like God, only escaping to view by its own irrepressible excellence. It is silent like God. Praise is in no way its food, neither is it desirable for it. It thinks long before acting, as God condescends to seem as if He also did. It is unanxious about results, which is one of the marvels of God. And it is fiery like God, consuming obstacles, and its very power causing it to make no noise. We must meditate separately on each of these clauses, if we would gain a clear notion of fervor.

Fervor acts in the practical spiritual life, as might be expected from the above description. It has no fits and starts. It is never run away with by a new idea. It never boils over, and puts the fire out, that is, it never quenches the Holy Spirit by indiscretion. It is not eager for heroic opportunities, though it expatiates magnificently on them when it has them. It is a stable vital force in the soul, thrusting its way with uniform power and noiseless pressure. Common trivial things persevered in and animated by an unremitting attention, these are its delight, and the infallible proofs both of its presence and its power. As a graceful person walks or stoops or stands grace-fully, and whatever he does is done with a grace, so pure charity is the gracefulness of fervor. It is punctual as it were spontaneously and by nature. It omits nothing, anticipates noth-ing, defers nothing. When time is lost, it can make it up with-out precipitation, and without compressing, or elbowing, or dislodging other duties. Its conduct is a sort of mirror, upon whose faultless crystal, eternity and Heaven and the likeness of God are forever unbrokenly imaged, beautiful to see, com-monplace as the commonest daily life, and yet enchanting as a fairy tale, and heroic as the old apostolic days. Its smile is sweet and serene, like an angel's. It can be angry, but beau-tifully, divinely, attractively. But it cannot frown; it is so flooded with inward peace it has lost the power. It cannot brood sadly or gloomily; for its nature is as that of the undulations of light. It is sweet to the taste as well as bright to the eye, and it makes music as it undulates, and it smells of the flowers of Eden. It is as if the savor of the Fall had never passed upon it, as the odor of the fire passed not on the garments of the Three Children. It is the only thing in the world that is in perfect keeping and proportion; for it bears a proportion in its conduct to the claims of God upon the soul. This is what makes its beauty austere. It is one of the antiques, an antique of the Christian deserts, of the old monasteries, of the palaces whose kings wore sackcloth beneath their ermine. We could adore it, it is so beautiful and godlike; were it not that it says to us with the angel in the *Apocalypse,* "See thou do it not; for I am thy fellow-servant, and of thy brethren who have the testimony of Jesus." (*Apoc.* 19:10).

What are the fruits of this fervor? Eye has not seen, nor ear heard, nor heart of man conceived. The variegated splen-dors of Heaven, the riches of the treasures at God's Right Hand, those are the golden fruits of its eternal autumn. It does no more than bloom here; but its blossoms are more healing than the fruits of other things. An infusion of their leaves is the wine, the medicine and the nutriment of the soul. First of all they give us courage, a courage to go even beyond nature, and to keep up the fight when by the laws of our being we should have yielded. So that we may resemble our dearest Lord, who supported Himself supernaturally to suffer, and made Himself live by miracle in order to love and suffer more, and drank many a cup of various bitterness to the dregs, when those that had gone before would naturally have brought about His death. Fervor gives us a self-distrust because of the deep knowledge it conveys to us of the nature of divine grace, and of ourselves. Mortification, which is a mountain of toil to the cold and lukewarm, is to fervor a relief and a necessity. It is the ordinary safety valve by which it allows its fires to escape, which otherwise would shrivel what they ought only to mature. When St. Francis de Sales came to die, his last lesson—the crowning part of his long, deep, fiery, beautiful wisdom—was ask nothing and refuse nothing. This is a short, perhaps inspired, definition of fervor. It is the "holy indifference" of St. Ignatius become domesticated as a permanent majestic habit of the soul. It has no choice; it takes things as God sends them. This is the most enviable part of its loveliness. Yet strange to say, by a secret of its own, it knows how to combine with this almost passive tranquility the two apparently contradictory excellencies of being immediate and unintermitting. It is swift as lightning. It darts on its duties, like the rapid noiseless hawk, and is down, and up again poised in air, so that our eyes doubt if in truth we saw its descent and its rising again. And it holds on its course like the smooth earth turning day and night on its unseen axle. Thus immediately and untiredly it works at present duties; and thus immediately and untiredly it loses no time between duties. I believe it sees God, and is always copying, within its sublime possibilities, the gracious mysteries of the Divine Nature.

Are there any rocks upon which fervor can make shipwreck? No! it would cease to be fervor before it could run on a rock; for it would see visible rocks, and it would divine sunken rocks, and would never neglect its chart. But there is a false fervor which is always running on rocks, and we may know it by the rocks it runs upon. It is a history of shipwrecks from first to last. There is a fervor which looks fine, and seemingly sails well, but when it has caught the wind full in its sails, it begins judging others both in thought and word,

imputing motives and criticizing the navigation of its neighbors. In a moment you hear the dull sound of the strike. With
what a momentum she went upon the rocks! And now the
harmless summer sea, whose fault the disaster could in no
wise be accounted, is covered with the shivered timbers of
a broken and lost spiritual life. There is another fervor, like
that of the Pharisee's prayer, which consists more in the contempt of others than in a loving hatred of ourselves. This contempt is a very common habit of mind in these days, and
nothing can be more incompatible with spirituality. There is
a third fervor, which is the intoxication of a weak head and
a vain will with one or more spiritual ideas, and the result
of which is a little crude practice of mortification with a very
abundant spirit of reforming things, persons, places, domestic
circles and institutes. A fourth fervor is the singularity of a
very active but one-sided and self-sufficient mind. And a fifth
is the mere life of changeableness, with its prolific plans, su-
perficial rapidity, and loudness of brief and brittle purposes.
These are sometimes called the rocks on which fervor strikes
and makes shipwreck of itself. But it is surely more true to
say that they are counterfeit fervors, which have nothing in
common with the austere and beautiful thing which we are
considering. Yet genuine fervor has most unjustly to bear the
burden of their mis-doings. Hence the scandal which these
indiscreet fervors give, which would be no scandals if they
were known to be what they really are. They assume principles which do not belong to them. They wear borrowed clothes
and call themselves by other persons' names; and then by
their vagaries fatigue all good people in their neighborhood.
It is these false fervors which bring piety into dis-esteem,
as well by their obtrusiveness, as by their inconsistencies and
inequalities. With them everything is exaggerated: doctrine,
practice, ritual and mortification. They are ruled by the spirit
of publicity. They deal in broad principles and round asser-
tions. They like to differ from all around them, while agree-
ing is tame and uninteresting. They present to people an image
of God without His beauty; and what can be more terrible
than this, which is the opposite of all He has ever been pleased
to do Himself? Counterfeit fervors, unlike most other

counterfeits, copy nothing in their original but its fires. In all other things they are in even verbal contradiction to it. And yet how sad to think that true fervor, all in celestial armor clad, grave, tranquil, majestic, serene, establishing everywhere the royalties of God in the human soul, should have to bear the burden of the wild and puerile furies of half-converted, half-cleansed, and not so good as half-humbled souls!

I said I would confine myself to conveying a clear idea of genuine fervor. If I have also given a picture of these caricatures of fervor, it is to make the true idea clearer. I have now three observations to make, to which some importance is to be attached.

First, it is a common idea that fervor is part of our training, part of our novitiate, something by the help of which we get out of certain difficulties; and when we have done with it, it passes in its turn. Everyone has it, or ought to have it, as children should have the measles, and it goes from one to another doing its work, with more or less success. This I think is a not uncommon idea of fervor. We must take this then as our first fixed point about the doctrine of fervor, that it is not a transient thing which does a work and passes off; but that it is a permanent state; nay, that its whole essence is in its permanence, and that it has the fewest alternations of any state which is known to human fragility and inconstancy.

Secondly, fervor is a tried state, and therefore not to be confounded with the effervescence of conversion. This last is essentially transient. It comes with a commission, and goes when it is executed. Nevertheless, we must not think lightly of this effervescence, or, as it is sometimes called, our first fervors. They came to us from God, and were freighted with a hundred benedictions. They were young, perhaps, and their zeal was indiscreet, and their taste questionable, and their conceit unquestionable. But amid it all there was a sweet power of God, which neither reverence nor gratitude will permit us now to despise. What God has once touched is sanctified. Never let us speak lightly, or think lightly, of what God once made a channel of grace, even if it were in our darkest days. Oh, how many of us may have cause to look wistfully back even to the rawness of those beginnings, and to pine for a purity of intention and a simplicity of affectionate goodwill which now perhaps is far from us, and nothing better come in its stead! Those first fervors do not come twice. If we have not used them, we have abused them. If they have gone and left their work undone, nothing will do it now. We must be the worse for the want of their work to the last day of life. It is as if an angel had come to us, and had gone, and left no blessing because we were not humble enough to ask one. But we may come to have genuine fervor without having had them. It is like the sweetness which the maturity of sorrow gives to the Christian soul compared with the sweetness of sunny generous youth. It has come out of trial. It has learned secrets. It has washed its robes in the Blood of the Lamb.

Thirdly, by some perversity of mind, men will always picture fervor to themselves as something which is about to cool down. It were truer to deem of it as ever on the increase. For it is the characteristic of fervor to be always augmenting, and to increase with very visible yet still tranquil rapidity toward death, just as a stone seeking its center grows rapid and impetuous as it nears it. We may prophesy death sometimes by the way fervor sucks us in and overwhelms us with divine love. O that we may feel it so, as body weakens, as ailments multiply, as sorrows bend our backs, and pains increase; so that we may pass out of the world, not cold, not lukewarm, not seeming to hang on to God by threads of grace or a timely Sacrament, but all in a glow of spiritual health and love, a sweet Purgatory which will carry us clear over that painful one which lies beyond the grave, and is so tedious and so slow in its sacred operations!

Chapter XXVII

DISCRETION

A postscript on the rudder of our spiritual ship, and my work is done. There is a well-known story that at a conference of monks in the old times, when different holy men had said which virtue they thought the highest, and for what reasons, the great St. Anthony decided in favor of discretion, because it moderated all the other virtues. St. Joseph is the most perfect model of this virtue, and all spiritual writers agree that it would not be easy to exaggerate its excellence. It may briefly be defined to be persevering love.

It is too often the case that a thing is best described by a description of its opposite; and in this instance I must partly illustrate discretion by examples of indiscretion, if not mainly so. First, therefore, I shall speak of doing too much, secondly of doing too little, and thirdly, of the manner of what we do.

First of doing too much. I do not mean too much for God, but too much for our grace to bear, or our courage to sustain. Nothing can be too much, for nothing can be enough, for God. But our grace is limited. God calls each one to a certain height and no higher; and although we can never know to what height we shall reach before we die, yet still at each step grace is dealt out to us by measure, and we must be careful not to run beyond our present grace. Grace does not do away with either our weakness or our cowardice. We must not give way to them, but we must take them into our calculations, and not only allow for them but give them liberal allowance. Mortification is a matter in which an honest will may be carried away by mere natural motives and may do too much; and this applies equally both to interior and exterior mortification. Discretion bids us keep in mind that mortification is always a means and never an end. It tells us that discontinued mortifications are the very bane of spirituality. No man undertakes to do a thing for God, and lays it aside because he finds perseverance in it too much for him, without his soul being seriously damaged by it. He has taken up a disadvantageous position. This is not a reason for not trying, but it is a reason for trying soberly, discreetly and with deliberation. Discretion will have mortification free from the slightest blemish of singularity. It will have charity to others lord paramount of all self-denials and austerities. It gives the relative duties of our states, that eighth sacrament as I have called them, precedence over them; and when mortification wears out our good temper and makes us short and snappish, discretion would have us after a little trial lose our penance rather than our temper.

In our prayers and spiritual exercises discretion will have us moderate and tranquil, and all things in **due keeping** with our state of life. It allows of no eagerness or **anxiety**. It condemns all inordinate pursuits, even though the acquisition of virtue be the object of them, and it equally prohibits all greediness of spiritual favors. It takes out of our hands books which are too high for us, as scrupulous and disturbing. It watches over a vocation as if it were its enemy; for to commit ourselves to a way of life in which we cannot persevere, is like doing something which will make us bedridden all our days. And when discretion has taught us all this, it adds that everything combines to show that we must either take council in the spiritual life, or give devotion up altogether, and sit down acquiescing in low ways and little things.

The second kind of indiscretion consists in doing too little—too little for God, and too little for the grace He has given us. Men sometimes make up their minds that they have gone as far as they intend to go in the spiritual life, that they have got up to a certain level and do not intend to mount higher. They forget that God is the master, not themselves; and that their business is to follow the lead of grace, whithersoever it may take them. Besides, there is no such thing as a level in the spiritual life. All is ascent or descent, advance or retreat.

Whatever is not the first, is assuredly the last. The question is not what we will do, but what God will do. What indiscretion can be greater than to disobey God or to dictate to Him? Yet worldly people do not like to be told this. They delight in the admonitions of discretion, when they go toward curbing those who do too much, and they willingly make themselves missioners of the Order of St. Anthony to preach his favorite virtue. But they chafe when the same principles are applied to doing too little. Christian art represents St. Anthony as *followed* by a pig: the figure is instructive, though inelegant. The indiscretion of being inconsiderately generous with God is patent enough to them. The indiscretion of being disobediently mean and close with Him is neither so obvious to them, nor so readily acknowledged. For, in their vocabulary, discretion means easiness and indevotion, a habit of surrendering God when the world finds His service inconvenient to itself. Such men habitually turn a deaf ear to inspirations, suspect higher calls, and yet purposely will not face them or examine them, lest haply they should be found to be from God.

The indiscretion of all this is manifold from the very statement of it. It angers God not only by its ungenerosity, but by its irreverence; and it may even endanger salvation by causing Him to withdraw from us succors which happen in our case to be necessary to our perseverance, but which He is in nowise bound to give. Another form of this indiscretion is our modelling our conduct on safe principles, in which we persevere even when we have perceived that they are not the best principles, and when we have felt that God is distinctly pressing us to a higher line of conduct. In this case the principles, however safe in the abstract, cease to be safe for us. They become rash, heady and self-willed, and often partake of the repugnant character of lukewarmness. Thus in our social intercourse we sometimes humor matters, not for charity's sake but for peace, and we allow God to be slightly a sufferer in some encounter with the world. Our high principles have capitulated, leaving Him as a hostage in the hands of His enemies. This soon comes to lead us a step further. We slide imperceptibly, so imperceptibly that we should be shocked if we were accused of it, into making our own ease and the good opinion of men our rule, instead of the will of God and the maxims of the Gospel. Downward descents are tempting, and this step leads us lower still. We judge, interfere, and are vexed with others who are more devout than ourselves. This is sinking through lukewarmness, and out of it, below it. Cold people are mostly indiscreet. They cannot see that hesitation is not discretion. Only conceive hesitating with God! As if He were taking us the wrong road! Oh, what so imprudent as this prudence, what so indiscreet as this discretion!

All this is a want of caution, of moderation and of considerate, foreseeing, calculating discretion. And this for three conclusive reasons. We gain nothing by it. We inevitably lose much, and we run the risk of losing everything. Sometimes how rash it is to be so unsafely safe! And how fatal is that moderation which leaves us short of the spot where God is waiting for us!

Thirdly, I must say a few words of the share discretion claims in the method of our actions. Generally speaking, discretion may be resolved into obedience, the not worshipping our own lights nor following our own wills. A very eminent spiritual writer simply speaks of the two virtues as if they were one, or of discretion as if it were but a function of obedience. Speaking however in detail, discretion of manner consists in five things which I will state as briefly as possible, in order that they may be the more readily impressed upon the memory.

Discretion acts slowly and after prayer, doubts impulses, and takes counsel.

Discretion does little, one thing at a time, calculates its own strength, perseveres in its little, is on the lookout to add, and prognosticates nothing.

Discretion does its work very carefully, attends to the circumstances of its actions, and never pulls them to pieces again when it has once made them up.

Discretion gently forces itself to its work, and insists on an interior spirit, pure motives, and the practice of God's presence.

Discretion does all its work for God supremely, as a man's

chief work and indeed only great work, appreciates its importance, estimates its difficulty, and is not hopeful but sure of
its results.

What is not discretion then, but the most temerarious indiscretion, is to be afraid of God and of holiness, to wish
to stand well with the world, to be in a visible mean, that
is a mean everyone can see and praise, between extremes,
to fear committing ourselves with God, to be frightened of
enthusiasm when we know that we are really not at all drawn
to it, as a rule rather to give God a little less than His due
than a little more, for safety's sake. Now look at the beautiful
contradiction of all this in St. Joseph's life, so tried and check-
ered with gravest doubts, and dreams, and changes, as if he
were set to be the sport of all the unlikelihoods of grace and
of all the perplexing unearthly ways of God: and how quiet,
how docile, how all for God, how interior, how never looking
before light and grace given, how childlike and prompt the
moment it came! And what was the end of it all? Like St.
John, but before him, he lies at last on the Sacred Heart of
Jesus, and discretion dies of love!

Kind Reader! I can say no more to help you in your growth
in holiness. May God give you grace now you have finished
the book to forget all that may be theory of mine, and to
remember only the wisdom and the practice of His Saints!
And in charity breathe one aspiration to the inexhaustible compassion of the Most High, that he who has ventured to preach
to others may not himself be cast away.

THE END

TAN·BOOKS

TAN Books was founded in 1967 to preserve the spiritual, intellectual and liturgical traditions of the Catholic Church. At a critical moment in history TAN kept alive the great classics of the Faith and drew many to the Church. In 2008 TAN was acquired by Saint Benedict Press. Today TAN continues its mission to a new generation of readers.

From its earliest days TAN has published a range of booklets that teach and defend the Faith. Through partnerships with organizations, apostolates, and mission-minded individuals, well over 10 million TAN booklets have been distributed.

More recently, TAN has expanded its publishing with the launch of Catholic calendars and daily planners—as well as Bibles, fiction, and multimedia products through its sister imprints Catholic Courses (CatholicCourses.com) and Saint Benedict Press (SaintBenedictPress.com).

Today TAN publishes over 500 titles in the areas of theology, prayer, devotions, doctrine, Church history, and the lives of the saints. TAN books are published in multiple languages and found throughout the world in schools, parishes, bookstores and homes.

For a free catalog, visit us online at
TANBooks.com

Or call us toll-free at
(800) 437-5876

Spread the Faith with . . .

TAN·BOOKS

A Division of Saint Benedict Press, LLC

TAN books are powerful tools for evangelization. They lift the mind to God and change lives. Millions of readers have found in TAN books and booklets an effective way to teach and defend the Faith, soften hearts, and grow in prayer and holiness of life.

Throughout history the faithful have distributed Catholic literature and sacramentals to save souls. St. Francis de Sales passed out his own pamphlets to win back those who had abandoned the Faith. Countless others have distributed the Miraculous Medal to prompt conversions and inspire deeper devotion to God. Our customers use TAN books in that same spirit.

If you have been helped by this or another TAN title, share it with others. Become a TAN Missionary and share our life changing books and booklets with your family, friends and community. We'll help by providing special discounts for books and booklets purchased in quantity for purposes of evangelization. Write or call us for additional details.

TAN Books
Attn: TAN Missionaries Department
PO Box 410487
Charlotte, NC 28241

Toll-free (800) 437-5876
missionaries@TANBooks.com